AFRICA AND THE WORLD TRADING SYSTEM

VOLUME I: SELECTED ISSUES OF THE DOHA AGENDA

EDITED BY

T. ADEMOLA OYEJIDE

&

WILLIAM LYAKURWA

A PUBLICATION OF

THE AFRICAN ECONOMIC RESEARCH CONSORTIUM

Africa World Press, Inc.

P.O. Box 1892
Trenton, NJ 08607

P.O. Box 48
Asmara, ERITREA

Africa World Press, Inc.

P.O. Box 1892
Trenton, NJ 08607

P.O. Box 48
Asmara, ERITREA

First Printing 2005

Book Cover: Roger Dormann
Book Design: Raphael Freeman, Jerusalem Typesetting

Cataloging-in-Publication Data is available from the Library of Congress.

ISBN: 1-59221-132-1 (cloth)
ISBN: 1-59221-133-X (paper)

Contents

Chapter one

Introduction and Overview

William Lyakurwa, AERC

THE WORLD TRADING SYSTEM consists basically of a set of national laws, bilateral agreements and internationally negotiated plurilateral and multilateral arrangements that together govern the conduct of cross-border exchange of goods and services. This system provides an international legal framework in the context of which countries voluntarily and multilaterally limit the restrictions to such exchanges. With the completion of the Uruguay Round (UR) of multilateral trade negotiations, what is in essence a new global trading system has been established together with a new institution, the World Trade Organization (WTO), to manage it. The emergence of the WTO as the preeminent institution on the trade and trade-related aspects of global policymaking makes it of critical importance for Africa as the region embarks on dramatic change in its development strategy and enters the phase of closer integration into the world economy.

Africa's economic policy landscape has been undergoing a marked (although incomplete) transformation over the last decade or so. The rather strong commitment to import substitution strategies of the 1960s and 1970s is gradually giving way to more outward-oriented development strategies. This transformation is by no means linear. The degree of trade liberalization varies widely across Africa and there have been sharp policy reversals in a number of countries. But the general trend is clear and reflects several factors including perceptions of the failure of import substitution strategies in Africa and other regions, the apparent success of more outward-oriented strategies particularly in Asia, and the increased leverage in Africa of multilateral development agencies (such as the World Bank and the International Monetary Fund), as well as the major bilateral donors, all of which condition financial assistance on greater liberalization of recipient countries' trade and payments regimes.

In spite of specific cases of policy reversal, the emerging outward-oriented policy stance in African countries has been accompanied in many cases by substantial unilateral trade liberalization. These changes should ultimately lead Africa towards the search for more secure foreign markets that are also relatively free of trade barriers, without which an outward-orientation strategy could be futile.

Africa has not performed well in trade terms in the recent past. While world trade increased markedly during the 1990s, and the share of developing countries in total world trade has increased significantly, Africa's trade virtually stagnated. Given the general recognition that Africa's economic recovery requires a significant boosting of its trade, both through recapturing lost market shares and by seizing emerging new opportunities, the region's place and prospects in the global trading system clearly assume an increasing significance for policy.

African countries have, traditionally, not been active or assertive participants in the various multilateral trade negotiations that have defined the rules and procedures of the global trading system. This suggests that Africa has not paid adequate attention to the external developments that affect its trade and trade prospects. Whatever may be its motivating factors, this passive posture could be counterproductive in the light of recent strategic changes and ongoing policy reorientation in the region.

The research project titled Africa and the World Trading System was initiated by the African Economic Research Consortium (AERC) against this background. It intended to identify and examine the critical analytical and policy issues involved in Africa's economic links with the rest of the world, particularly in the context of the emerging global trading system. The project had two distinct but closely inter-related component parts. The first part consisted of research that was analytical and/or empirical in nature but region-wide in scope and focus. This component was also designed to provide the framework for the selection of the menu of issues that was subsequently explored in greater detail, using the country case study approach, in the project's second component. The papers generated in the first component of the project are presented in this volume, while the country case studies are contained in Volume II.

The ten framework papers that are presented as chapters 2–11 in this volume cover a range of issues that can be broadly categorized into four. These include questions related to the post-Uruguay Round (UR) access conditions facing African exports, particularly in their major markets and the extent to which the systemic reforms and rule changes embedded in the "new" issues introduced into the multilateral trade agenda have affected or are likely to affect African countries. The other two broad categories of issues are the implications of the UR agreements for the development strategy that may be pursued by African countries, and questions about the extent and effectiveness of African participation in the WTO process. An overview of the analysis and findings of the ten framework papers in each of the four broad categories of issues is offered below.

1. Market Access

Analysis of market access conditions that African exports face following the implementation of UR agreements constitutes the core of the papers by Stephen Yeo (Chapter 2) and Richard Blackhurst and William Lyakurwa (Chapter 3), as well as Ademola Oyejide's paper on agriculture (Chapter 4) and Colin McCarthy's analysis of mining, manufacturing, and services (Chapter 5).

Yeo shows that the UR led to significant reductions in the tariffs levied by the industrial and many of the developing countries. In particular, the (trade-weighted) average rate of tariffs levied by the industrial countries fell by about 40%, although the reductions were smaller for goods imported from developing countries (30%) than for goods imported from the developed countries (45%). In addition, the average tariff reductions for imports from the countries of sub-Saharan Africa (SSA) were lower than those for other low-income countries. With specific reference to tariffs facing African agricultural exports in the markets of the developed countries, Oyejide suggests that while these were reduced by 32%–48%, the reductions are unlikely to have a substantial impact on African agricultural export volume because they apply to existing tariff rates that are already quite low.

In addition, African agricultural exports are likely to be constrained by tariff peaks, such as those characterizing the food products and processed foods that are imported from developing countries into the markets of the developed countries. According to Blackhurst and Lyakurwa, even after the full implementation of the UR agreements, about 10% of the tariff universe of the Quad countries (United States, European Union, Canada and Japan) will continue to exceed the level of 12% ad valorem. In particular, peak tariffs are prominent in such sectors as the major agricultural staple products; fruit, vegetables and fish products; and the processed food industry. Thus, tariff peaks affecting products of current and potential export interest to African countries are common in virtually all markets; they extend beyond agricultural products and include textiles and clothing, footwear, and leather and travel goods; as well as automotive and other transport and high technology goods, such as consumer electronics and watches.

Three other problem areas are identified in the framework papers that focus on market access. First, Oyejide argues that tariff escalation constitutes a problem for many African countries seeking to diversify their exports through agricultural processing. More generally, Yeo concludes that while the UR agreements led to a reduction in the extent of tariff escalation, they did not eliminate the problem. It is shown, in addition, that tariff escalation actually increased for some products of importance to African countries. A good example of this anomaly is the import of cocoa into the EU markets, whose tariff escalation "wedge" rose from 7.1 before to 8.0 percentage points after the UR.

Second, African countries will suffer loss of exports as a result of the erosion of their trade preferences emanating from the tariff reductions achieved by the UR negotiations. As McCarthy argues, while the effect of the erosion of African preferential margins may not be large on average, it could be quite significant for some countries. Yeo suggests that substantial losses might be incurred by Côte d'Ivoire, Kenya and Mauritius. McCarthy focuses on the case of Lesotho, to which export-oriented foreign investment in clothing and textiles has been attracted partly to circumvent the quotas on Taiwan's textile and clothing exports and partly to enjoy the added benefit of exporting from an ACP (Africa–Caribbean–Pacific) preference receiving country. McCarthy argues, in this context, that for African countries with duty-free access to the EU (via the Lomé Convention), the phasing out of the

Multi-Fibre Agreement (MFA) could be "bad news" since it will introduce competition from other non-ACP developing country producers with more efficient industrial sectors.

Third, the UR agreement on agriculture poses its own peculiar problems for many African countries. Oyejide discusses two of these in Chapter 4. One relates to the increasing food import bill that food-deficit low-income African countries could face as a result of the liberalization of agriculture and reduction of export subsidies in the developed countries. The other is the likely displacement of African producers (benefiting from Lomé commodity protocols) in the EU market by agricultural producers from the Temperate Zone countries. Particularly vulnerable to this risk are countries such as Mauritius and Swaziland (with respect to sugar) and Botswana and Namibia (with respect to meat).

But market access problems may not necessarily be of significant importance for many African countries. The paper by Blackhurst and Lyakurwa and that of McCarthy downplay market access as the binding constraint to the expansion of African exports. They argue that inadequate domestic supply response, not the level of market access abroad, is the prime explanation for Africa's poor export performance. However, the Blackhurst–Lyakurwa paper suggests that further reductions and bindings of tariffs would not hurt African exports, particularly if these changes translate into a substantial reduction of tariff peaks and an elimination of tariff escalation.

2. Systemic Reform, Rule Changes and "New" Issues

The UR negotiations led to significant systemic reforms of the world trading system, some changes in its basic rules and the introduction of several "new" issues. The post-UR multilateral trade agenda continues to reflect a widening of the range of "new" issues that the WTO is under increasing pressure to take on board.

The argument presented in Yeo's paper is that African and other developing countries stand to benefit substantially from the systemic reform of the world trading system because they strengthen its rule-based nature and thus offer more protection for small and poor countries that can exercise little economic or political power. But a key element of the systemic reforms is the adoption, in the UR, of the "single undertaking" principle, which has, in effect, placed all WTO members under virtually the same set of rights and obligations. Patrick Low (in Chapter 7) suggests that along with the widening of the scope of the world trading system, this has considerably strained the absorptive and compliance capacity of many African countries.

An analysis of the implications of the systemic reforms and rule changes for African countries is offered by Ademola Oyejide in his paper on "special and differential treatment" (Chapter 6). According to this paper, special and differential treatment (SDT) consists of a set of rights and privileges that endow the developing and least developed countries with a unique status in the world trading system. This has three basic elements. One grants the developing and least developed countries more favourable access, through trade preferences, to the markets of the developed countries. The second gives them substantial policy discretion in their own domestic markets, which, in effect, permits them to maintain tariff and non-tariff barriers against imports. The third element grants them exemption from certain disciplines of the world trading system. Oyejide argues that in the post-UR era, SDT for developing countries has been reduced essentially to extended transition periods at the end of which all WTO member countries must comply with the same basic set of obligations. In his view, the rationale for establishing SDT remains unchanged as far as many African countries are concerned. Hence, if the systemic reforms and rule changes brought about by the UR limit their access to trade preferences and restrain their discretion for the disciplined use of appropriate trade and industrial policies for infant industry protection, export promotion and revenue-raising, they would, in fact, have a negative impact on many African countries. In other words, while Yeo's paper (Chapter 2) concludes that the systemic changes are likely to have a positive impact even though the timing and size of this impact may be uncertain, Oyejide's conclusion is that those systemic changes that undercut the key SDT provisions may have a negative impact on African countries.

Patrick Low's paper identifies additional areas where the systemic reforms of the global trading system and the associated rule changes may create difficulties for many African countries. He notes, in particular, that WTO disciplines in the areas of trade-related investment measures (TRIMS) and subsidies have become more stringent. Furthermore, he argues that the net long-term cost problems associated with the agreement on intellectual property protection (TRIPS) are likely to be acute in many African countries with limited technological development, where technology transfer and knowledge diffusion are constrained, and where local innovation has yet to take off.

3. African Development Strategy in the WTO Framework

Three papers address various dimensions of the question whether, and if so, the extent to which the emerging world trading system will affect the type of development strategy that African countries can adopt. The papers more or less take as given the need for a new development strategy, broader than economic adjustment, that would enable African countries to achieve the deep, sustained and equitable growth they consider necessary for addressing the region's widespread poverty problem.

The paper by Ibrahim Elbadawi and Gerry Helleinier (Chapter 9) notes the lack of universal agreement on the appropriate development for all the varied countries of Africa. It claims, however, that as far as trade policy issues are concerned, there is indeed a remarkable consensus on the need for significantly improved export performance and sufficient incentives and other support to induce increased and sustained investment in export-oriented activities. In their paper (Chapter 8), Charles Jebuni and Samuel Wangwe are much less reticent about an appropriate development strategy. They see an emerging consensus on an African development strategy whose key attributes consist of a market-friendly policy environment in which the private sector acts as an engine of growth that is export-led and where the policy environment reflects sustainable country-specific trade liberalization.

The Jebuni–Wangwe paper finds the WTO framework broadly consistent with this development strategy since it increases both market access and security of markets for African exports and is thus broadly supportive of an export-led growth strategy. Elbadawi and Helleiner generally share this view. They regard the WTO's principal contribution to Africa's development prospects as the achievement of a greater degree of market access for African exports abroad rather than its possible impact on African trade policy. But they also pinpoint several areas where the WTO framework may have profound implications for African industrialization and development strategies and policies. They argue, in particular, that the new trading regime has reduced the scope for using some measures that were integral parts of the East Asian development strategy. Thus, the more generalized protection regime against which the targeted policies in East Asia were implemented appears to be no longer possible, while the related infant industry protection and export subsidies and promotion policies may no longer be permissible.

Both papers broadly agree on at least three key points. First, the move towards a more liberal import regime will take some time and reflect country-specific sustainability considerations. Second, successful outward-orientation in African countries may require active supply-side measures, including strategic and selective interventions in support of investment in export activities and by local firms. Third, and to accommodate the first two prescriptions, WTO disciplines should be applied more flexibly to African countries to permit them to construct their own pragmatic development strategies and to build the capacity for sustained economic growth.

The paper by Paul Collier and Jan Gunning (Chapter 10) explores ways of making African trade policy more rational, sustainable and credible. The paper cites previous evidence showing that in spite of extensive trade reforms, trade policy reversals have undermined the confidence of private investors. Hence, the trade policy reforms have failed to generate appropriate response in terms of improved investment, export performance and overall economic growth. Could the WTO framework provide a policy commitment arrangement that would endow African trade policy with enhanced credibility? The Collier–Gunning paper says "No" to this question because the ties that bind African countries under the WTO rules are much too loose to make their trade policy credible. Thus, rather than relying on the WTO framework to provide this all-important policy commitment mechanism, the paper advocates the use of North–South (or more specifically Africa–EU) reciprocity to achieve lock-in of African trade policy reform. In this context, revoking Africa's valuable access to the EU market would be a credible threat against the reversal of trade policy reform in Africa. As an additional "sweetener", Collier and Gunning suggest that the EU should also offer to African countries protection from anti-dumping actions by the EU in the context of the proposed reciprocal arrangement.

4. African Participation in the WTO Process

Papers by Blackhurst and Lyakurwa (Chapter 3) and by John Ohiorhenuan (Chapter 11) address the question of African participation in the WTO process. As discussed above, the WTO framework is likely to have profound implications for African development strategies and policies. Hence, the extent and effectiveness of African participation in the WTO process should be of significant policy interest.

The Blackhurst–Lyakurwa paper identifies two levels of participation: through a country's resident delegates in Geneva and through the support staff based in the country's capital. Its assessment is that at both levels, Africa's participation in the WTO process has been considerably less than desirable. Noting that active participation in the WTO's day-to-day work requires an adequate staff resident in Geneva, the paper finds that in the late 1990s, as many as 50% of WTO members from sub-Saharan Africa had no resident representative in Geneva. Among the one-half that did, the vast majority had very small staffs who covered not only WTO activities but also those of other international organizations based in Geneva. On the home front, participation was also found to be less than satisfactory, partly because of staff inadequacies and lack of effective inter-ministerial coordination.

Ohiorhenuan's paper offers four additional reasons to explain Africa's lack of active and effective participation in the WTO process. First, African countries and their delegations appear to be constrained by an inadequate understanding of the complexity of the issues discussed and negotiated in the WTO process. Second, many African countries do not have access to in-depth analysis of the implications of various issues and proposals for their national interests. Third, these countries have weak institutional capacities in their public and private sectors as well as civil society, to stay on top of the negotiations that constitute a key component of the WTO process. Finally, the WTO process itself remains insufficiently transparent to the extent that the most important decisions are often made by the larger and more powerful countries with little or no input from the poorer and smaller members.

In the light of these constraints, both papers suggest various ways to enhance African participation. Beginning with what African countries can do for themselves, these include establishing and expanding their permanent representation in Geneva; creating or enhancing inter-ministerial and public–private sector consultative mechanisms on WTO matters; and pooling resources via joint activities and even representation among groups of like-minded African countries. In addition to these, it is suggested that the WTO can and should assist in enhancing the participation of African countries by carrying out their trade policy reviews more frequently (than the mandatory once in six years), increasing the budget for technical assistance, and bringing WTO services closer to the African countries through the establishment of regional offices in Africa.

Chapter two

Trade Policy in Sub-Saharan Africa: Lessons from the Uruguay Round Experience

by Stephen Yeo
Centre for Economic Policy Research[1]

---

1. Introduction

The Uruguay Round transformed the world trading system, through a series of far-reaching measures that:

- Bound tariffs on almost all manufactured products and reduced tariffs to very low levels.
- Brought agricultural trade under multilateral disciplines for the first time, "tariffied" the non-tariff barriers in agriculture, bound the resulting tariffs and reduced the levels of these tariffs, and reduced or eliminated export and production subsidies in agriculture.
- Eliminated quantitative restrictions such as voluntary export restraints (VERS) and the Multi-Fibre Arrangement (MFA).
- Created the World Trade Organization (WTO) and strengthened its monitoring and dispute settlement procedures.

- Reformed the system of safeguards, anti-dumping and countervailing duties.
- Extended multilateral disciplines to trade in services through the General Agreement on Trade in Services (GATS).
- Imposed multilateral disciplines on a number of trade-related investment measures (TRIMS).
- Obliged WTO members to observe common minimum standards for the protection of intellectual property rights through the TRIPS agreement.

African countries participated more actively in the Uruguay Round than in previous negotiations. Yet their participation appeared to have achieved very little. Most quantitative estimates of the Round's impact suggest that the countries of sub-Saharan Africa were little affected. Other measures agreed to in the Round may benefit the continent in the longer term, but there seems little evidence that the Round has had a significant impact on Africa.

Africa is likely to gain slightly from tariff cuts and the elimination of non-tariff barriers on manufactures trade but will find itself slightly worse off as a result of cuts to developed countries' subsidies to their agricultural exports, which tends to increase world food prices. Africa is likely to lose a little from the reform on textiles and clothing trade. These effects are small, however: they typically represent shifts of less than 1% in output or trade flows, small changes relative to the uncertainty inherent in the model simulations themselves.

The effects of the Round that we can quantify seem to be negative, but small in magnitude. The systemic changes are likely to have a positive impact, but one whose timing and size are uncertain. On balance then, Africa seems little better or worse off as a result of the Round, even though it participated more actively in the negotiations than in previous Rounds. We consider, and discard a number of possible explanations: each has an element of truth, but is ultimately unconvincing. The remaining explanation is more convincing, but also somewhat dispiriting. African countries achieved relatively little in the Round because they failed to liberalize their own trade policies, and they failed to do so because neither their own policy communities nor their publics were convinced that liberal trade policies were the right policies. Until this attitude changes, Africa is unlikely to adopt, much less sustain, liberal trade policies. We then consider the implications of this line of thought, and conclude that we should pay more attention to the design of trade policy institutions in Africa. Institutional design can make it more or less easy to pursue liberal trade policies: some arrangements for running trade policy play into the hands of protectionists, while others enable politicians to resist the appeals of special interests. There are arguments that responsibility for trade policy should not be given to "sectoral" ministries or even, in Africa, to ministries of finance. Instead, it should be entrusted to an agency with limited but clear mandate: to oversee the nation's trade policy in as open and transparent a manner as possible. One of the agency's most important tasks would be to measure the costs to trade of existing and proposed trade policies, and to ensure that these costs are made known to the public and to policy makers. Creating such an institution would clearly be politically difficult. It might be possible, however, to take a first step in this direction if African countries were to request and participate in trade policy reviews on a more frequent basis. This would increase the transparency and credibility of their policies. Even this may prove unwelcome to governments brought up on a steady diet of protectionism. In this event it would be useful to proceed on an unofficial basis by carrying out "shadow" trade policy reviews: unofficial examinations of a country's trade policies that aim to highlight clearly the impact and true economic costs of these policies.

2. The Uruguay Round: Outcome and Impact

This surveys the quantitative estimates of the Round's impact based on simulations and projections of a variety of partial and general equilibrium models. These estimates suggest that while the Round will have a significant impact on global trade and economic welfare, its effect on sub-Saharan Africa is likely to be much smaller, and if anything, negative. Other arguments and evidence point in the other direction, suggesting that Africa, along with other developing countries, stands to benefit substantially from the Round's "systemic" changes to the world trading system, which strengthen the rule-based nature of the system and potentially, at least, offer more protection for small countries with little economic or political power.

Things we can quantify...

A number of attempts were made to measure the global impact of the Round, both during the negotiations and following the conclusion of the Agreement. These attempts involved the use of both partial equilibrium models (for particular sectors) and computable general equilibrium (CGE) models that attempted to measure the overall impact of the Round, taking into account its full general equilibrium effects. These exercises are certainly interesting and informative, and attracted widespread press commentary at the time. But it is worth bearing in mind that they take into account only a subset of the measures agreed to in the Round, namely those that could be directly measured on a simple numeric scale: changes in tariff rates, measures such as the "tariffication" of non-tariff barriers in agriculture and reductions in these tariffs, the elimination of voluntary export restraints (VERS) and the Multi-Fibre Arrangement (MFA), and reductions in agricultural and other subsidies. For some other aspects of the agreement, such as the new rules governing trade in services, we lack not only a suitable conceptual framework but also much of the relevant data necessary to measure the effect of the rules. And for some of the other measures, such as the introduction of the single undertaking or the strengthening of the disputes procedure, it is not easy to imagine how one might estimate the impact on trade flows, output or welfare. So the most important aspects of the Agreement are not necessarily those that lend themselves to quantitative modelling, as Blackhurst et al. (1995) observe.

Overall impact of the Round

General equilibrium assessments of the impact of the Round were carried out by a number of modelling teams, based at the GATT Secretariat (Francois et al., 1994, 1995), the World Bank (Hertel et al., 1995), the OEOD Development Centre (Goldin et al., 1993; Goldin and van der Mensbrugghe, 1995) and elsewhere (Harrison et al., 1995, 1997). These modelling exercises yielded an often bewildering variety of results. Francois et al. (1996), Harrison et al. (1997) and Martin and Winters (1995b) provide useful summaries and comparisons of the models and the simulation results. They note that the differences in estimated impact of the Round can be attributed to a variety of factors:

- Whether the simulation used the actual outcome of the Round or predictions of the outcome made during the negotiations: the latter tended to overestimate the liberalization that took place in the Round and so produced higher estimates of welfare gains.
- Whether the impacts of the Round were measured in percentage or in absolute terms (and if so, in which year's magnitudes).
- Whether the model is "static", taking the capital stock as fixed; or "dynamic", allowing the capital stock to expand in response to changes in relative prices that resulted from the Round: dynamic models (not surprisingly) produced much larger estimates of the gains from the Round.
- The degree of sectoral and regional disaggregation and detail present in the model: models with less regional detail, for example, tend to produce smaller estimates of gains from the Round, because they "smooth out" the differences across regions that are the source of gains from trade; models that emphasize a particular sector often do so at the expense of important features of other sectors.[2]
- The structure of the model, in particular assumptions concerning supply elasticities and elasticities of substitution, and the magnitude of returns to scale.[3]

Once the first three factors are controlled for, the simulations are easier to compare and to understand, since the remaining differences can be attributed to the assumptions concerning the last two factors. The most interesting simulations are those using OGE models, based on the actual changes agreed in the Round (Francois et al., 1995; Harrison et al., 1997; Hertel et al... 1995). These are summarized in Table 2.1.

The results in the first three rows of the table are the most directly comparable, since they are all based on simulations of the impact of the Round on the 1992 world economy. The "steady state" in these simulations represents the equilibrium in which the capital stock has adjusted in response to the changes in relative prices and outputs brought about by the Round.

The simulations assuming increasing returns to scale and allowing for

Table 2.1: Estimated impact of the Uruguay Round on global welfare

	Harrison, Rutherford and Tarr		Francois, McDonald and Nordstrom		Hertel, Martin, Yanagisha and Dimaranan	
	Billion dollars	GDP (%)	Billion dollars	GOP (%)	Billion dollars	GOP (%)
CRTS static	93	0.4	40	0.2	–	–
IRTS static	96	0.4	99	0.4	–	–
IRTS steady state	171	0.7	193	0.6	–	–
CRTS static 2005 projection	162	0.7	–	–	258	1.0

CRTS and IRTS refer to constant and increasing returns to scale. [Source: Harrison et al. (1997:1424, Table 6).]

the adjustment of the capital stock (row 3) produce broadly similar global welfare gains – $171 versus $193 billion. The simulations assuming constant returns to scale (row 1) produce apparently conflicting results, but Harrison et al. (1997) argue that in moving from the model with increasing to that with constant returns to scale, Francois et al. (1995) inadvertently introduced lower demand elasticities as well, and this, not surprisingly, produces a much smaller impact. The results in row 4 also seem to differ from each other significantly and also from the results in the first three rows. Row 4 represents simulations in which the welfare impact in the steady state is projected forward to the year 2005, when the Round is to be implemented fully. Since the world economy is much larger in 2005, the absolute gains are larger, while the percentage gains are similar to those in row 3. The $258 billion figure obtained by Hertel et al. (1995) is higher than the comparable figure of $162 billion obtained by Harrison et al. (1997), but they attribute the difference to the assumption by Hertel et al. (1997) of higher demand elasticities and how binding the MFA would have been in 2005 had it still been in force.

Focusing on the results for the 1992 economy, we see that estimates for the increase in global welfare range from $170 to $193 billion, or 0.7 to 0.8% of world GDP.

The distribution of this gain across regions and especially the impact on sub-Saharan Africa are also of interest. Given the broad agreement among the models on the global impact of the Round, Table 2.2 presents the disaggregated effects for only one of the models (Harrison et al., 1997)

Table 2.2: Estimated impact of the Uruguay Round on national and regional welfare

	Agriculture	MFA	Manufacturing	Complete UR	Complete UR (% GDP)
Australia	0.9	0.1	2.3	3.3	1.3
New Zealand	0.5	0.0	0.9	1.4	4.4
Canada	0.2	1.0	1.3	2.6	0.6
United States	3.2	9.2	13.7	26.7	0.6
Japan	16.8	-0.5	6.2	22.7	0.7
Korea	5.2	-0.4	2.7	0.5	2.8
EU	26.4	7.6	14.9	0.9	0.9
Indonesia	0.3	0.9	1.4	2.6	2.4
Malaysia	2.2	0.3	2.6	5.0	10.2
Philippines	1.2	0.2	1.1	2.4	4.8
Singapore	0.5	-0.2	0.4	0.7	1.9
Thailand	1.4	0.8	10.3	12.6	12.1
China	-0.8	1.7	1.2	2.0	0.5
Hong Kong	0.6	-1.5	-0.2	-1.1	-1.3
Taiwan	0.0	-0.3	1.3	1.1	0.7
Argentina	0.7	0.1	1.6	2.3	1.1
Brazil	0.1	0.1	4.0	4.3	1.3

	Agriculture	MFA	Manufacturing	Complete UR	Complete UR (% GDP)
Mexico	0.7	0.2	1.4	2.3	0.7
Latin America	2.0	0.3	3.2	4.7	1.9
Sub-Saharan Africa	-0.5	-0.1	0.2	-0.7	-0.5
Middle East and North Africa	0.1	0.2	1.9	1.5	0.3
Eastern Europe and FSU	-0.0	-0.3	2.3	1.2	0.2
South Asia	0.2	1.9	5.3	6.7	2.3
Other European countries	1.6	-0.8	7.0	8.8	0.9
Developing countries (total)	13.9	3.4	40.5	55.2	1.4
Industrial countries (total)	49.8	16.9	46.3	115.4	0.8

Notes: The results presented above refer only to the steady state of their irts model. Figures are in $ billion for 1992. Note that the results for the us given in Table 5 of Harrison et al. (1997) are incorrect. The correct figures can be found in Table 13, p. 239 of Harrison et al. (1995) and are given in the table above. [Source: Adapted from Harrison et. al. (199:1421, Table 5).]

It is worth pausing at this point to examine the intuition behind these results. We can think of the changes in output and welfare as driven by:

- *Efficiency gains:* As you reduce your tariffs and eliminate non-tariff barriers (such as those in textiles and clothing and in agriculture) your consumers are able to purchase goods at a lower cost, while your firms can take advantage of abundant factors of production and economies of scale to produce goods more efficiently.

- *Terms of trade effects:* As your trading partners reduce their levels of protection, the demand for your exports rises, and your terms of trade improve.
- *The impact of abolishing the MFA:* As MFA quotas are eliminated, demand in the industrial countries rises and production relocates from countries that happen to have quotas to countries that have a genuine comparative advantage in producing textiles and clothing.

The largest absolute gains from the Round accrue to the European Union, the United States and Japan – $49.9, $26.7 and $22.7 billion. It is important to clearly understand the source of these large gains. The EU, the US and Japan are better off in these simulations, not because the Uruguay Round enables them to conquer global export markets, but because they stop doing economically crazy things. The EU is $26.4 billion better off merely because it scales back its Common Agriculture Policy, which keeps European food prices at levels far in excess of world levels and subsidizes exports of the food produced in Europe in response to these high prices. The United States gains $22.9 billion from eliminating its quotas on textiles and clothing and reducing its tariffs on manufactured goods. Japan gains $16.8 billion because it lowers its tariffs on imported food.

The largest gains in percentage terms accrue to the East Asian countries – Korea, Malaysia, Philippines and Thailand. They too benefit from liberalizing their imports of agricultural and manufactured goods. The abolition of the MFA quotas allows them to expand their exports of textiles and clothing as well.

Table 2 reveals that sub-Saharan Africa is worse off as a result of the Uruguay Round's measures on agriculture, the MFA and manufactured exports. It suffers a net welfare loss of $0.7 billion, 0.5% of its GDP. Given the logic of the model, and given the policies pursued by Sub-Saharan Africa (which are described below) the reasons for this loss are easy to understand:

- Sub-Saharan Africa did not engage in any liberalization of its agriculture sector and so its consumers and its farmers find themselves a little better or worse off. On the other hand, Africa is slightly worse off through a "terms of trade" effect – the rise in the price of its food imports, as world food prices rise following the cuts in subsidized food exports from the EU and elsewhere.

- Sub-Saharan Africa is slightly worse off as a result of the elimination of the MFA, as efficient producers of textiles and clothing who were formerly constrained by quotas no longer need to sell their products at lower prices in developing country markets, since they are now able to shift their exports to the newly open markets in the industrial countries where they can obtain higher prices (Martin and Winters, 1995b).
- These results show sub-Saharan Africa to be slightly better off as a result of the tariff reductions on manufactured goods. This result holds whether one measures welfare in terms of output or real wages. Similar results can also be found in Francois et al. (1995: tables 15 and 16, pp. 157–8). This is a slightly surprising result in light of the concerns expressed during the negotiations about the effects of "preference erosion" on the exports of developing countries (discussed in detail below).

Are these results for sub-Saharan Africa robust across models? Yes and no. Hertel et al. (1995) obtain a similar result – a fall of 0.51% in income as a result of the Round. The simulations by Goldin and van der Mensbrugghe (1995) show falls in real income of 0.4% for South Africa, 0.1% for Nigeria and between 0.2 and 0.3% for the rest of Africa. Francois et al. (1995) obtain more cheerful results for Africa (as well as for most other regions of the world), with increases in real income of between 1.1 and 1.4%.[4]

We can get a sense of whether the differences across models are significant by looking at the results of the "sensitivity analysis" carried out by Harrison et al. (1995: Table 11, p. 234). This involves perturbing the values of key parameters in the model, such as the elasticity of primary factor substitution and of domestic demand. These elasticities are independently and simultaneously perturbed from their benchmark values using random numbers drawn from a *t* or uniform distribution and the model is solved for each set of perturbations. This process is repeated and the values of the solved endogenous variables (in this case the UR impacts) are tabulated as a distribution, for which a mean and standard deviation can be calculated.[5]

This distribution gives some indication of the sensitivity of the results to variations in the model's parameter values (but not, of course, to uncertainty concerning the structure of the model itself).

The procedure yields, for the global welfare gains discussed above, a standard deviation of $3 billion for an estimated gain of $171 billion. For sub-Saharan Africa the sensitivity analysis is only available for the absolute, not the percentage welfare gain. For a mean welfare gain of -$0.35 billion, the mean square error is $0.05 with a minimum of -$0.46 billion and a maximum of -$0.21 billion.[6] The differences between the results of Harrison et al. (1997) and those obtained by Goldin and van der Mensbrugghe and by Hertel et al. do not appear large by this measure. The positive result obtained by Francois et al. does, however, seem a long way from these results.

On balance, then, most of the CGE simulations of the impact of the Round suggest that sub-Saharan Africa will suffer small income losses as a result of the reforms to agriculture and elimination of the MFA, a small gain as a result of reductions in manufactured goods tariffs and a small net fall in income overall. The biggest gainers from the Round in these simulations are the countries that liberalized their own trade policies, such at the EU and the United States. This is confirmed in the detailed analysis presented below, which shows that Africa took on relatively few obligations in the Round, removed very few of its own distortionary trade policies and, as a result, realized few benefits from the Round.

Tariffs

Reductions in tariff rates: The Round led to significant reductions in the tariffs levied by the industrial and many of the developing countries. In addition, the industrial countries bound almost all of their tariffs, and the proportion of bound tariff lines for developing countries rose as well. The (trade-weighted) average rate of tariffs levied by industrial countries on manufactured goods fell by 40%, from 6.3% to 3.8%, as a result of the Round. The reductions were larger for goods imported from other industrial countries (45%) than from developing countries (30%). The average rate of tariffs levied by the developing countries fell too, by 28% and 29% (Martin and Winters, 1995b: p. 9).

Bindings: In addition to these reduced rates, there was an important increase in the number of "bound" tariff lines, and in the proportion of trade represented by these tariff lines (see Table 2.3). For the industrial countries, the number of developed country imports subject to bindings rose from 94 to 99%, and bound zero duties rose from 20 to 44%. Developing countries – but not sub-Saharan Africa – were also active in this respect, binding 61% their tariffs during the Round.

Table 2.3: Uruguay Round bindings

	% of tariff lines		% of imports under bound rates					
	Pre-UR	Post-UR	Pre-UR	Post-UR	Already bound free	Bindings with reductions	Bindings without reductions	No offer
Total	43	83	68	67	–	–	–	–
Industrial economies	78	99	94	99	18	64	3	16
Developing economies	21	73	13	61	1	32	26	42
Transition economies	73	98	74	96	12	76	1	10

Source: Blackhurst et al. (1995: Table 2) and WTO (1997).

Reductions in rates tend to attract the most attention in discussions of tariff reform, but bindings are important too. They represent a commitment by the country not to increase a tariff above the bound rate. In many cases, as we will see below, the Uruguay Round resulted in bindings that exceeded the actual rates of protection in force before the Round. Such bindings clearly do not lead to a reduction in the actual tariff rate. Are they nevertheless useful? Francois and Martin (1995, 1997) have argued that they are: even bindings that exceed the applied rate increase the transparency of policy and reduce uncertainty for firms seeking to enter a market. Francois and Martin argue that trade policy, like other policy regimes, is subject to uncertainty and variability, and they attempt to model the benefits of rules-based commitments in the presence of stochastically varying protection, using the notion of the expected cost of protection. They estimate the effect of tariff bindings on imports of wheat, sugar and beef, commodities where bindings have been typically set at levels substantially higher than the average rates of protection, and find that the introduction of bindings will yield substantial reductions in the expected cost of protection.

Tariff escalation: Developing countries have long sought to reduce the escalation of industrial country tariffs. Escalation occurs when higher tariff rates are applied to "more processed goods. This raises the level of effective protection in the industrial country, favouring the import of raw materials and discouraging imports of processed goods. Developing countries dislike escalation because it discourages the development of processing industries. Economic theory suggests that it may be undesirable as well: uniform tax rates are in general preferable from an efficiency point of view.

Escalation is usually measured by the wedge between the tax rates applied to raw and finished products. The evidence presented in Harrold (1995: tables 13 and 14) and in Table 2.4 suggests that the developing countries did succeed in their goal of reducing escalation, but did not manage to eliminate it entirely. Before the Round, for example, the tariff rate rose 6.5 percentage points for tropical industrial products; after the Round this fell to 2.4, a decrease of 4.1 percentage points. The pattern for other goods is similar.

Harrold (1995: 30) notes, however, that this did not hold for some other goods of importance to sub-Saharan Africa, such as imports of cocoa into the EU. The tariff on cocoa beans fell from 2.1 to 0.0, but on chocolate from 9.2 to 8.0, causing the wedge to rise from 7.1 to 8.0 percentage points.

Cocoa is a significant export for West African countries, who might be expected to object to an increase in escalation. In fact this might be considered as something of a defeat for one of the few initiatives that the African countries seem to have taken in the Round. Oyejide (1990: 433) describes a proposal by five African countries to the negotiating group on tropical products, which called for immediate binding; duty free entry for raw tropical products; the harmonization of tariffs on processed and semi-processed products at the *lowest current rate in developed countries* (in order to reduce tariff escalation); and the elimination of internal excise taxes and quotas. The EU response was to offer a progressive reduction of tariffs and QRs on tropical products, and of taxes on tropical beverages. The EU was willing to cut tariffs on chocolate by 25–100% to levels of 9–12%. The

Table 2.4: The impact of the Uruguay Round on tariff escalation

Product group	Import value units	Percent	Pre-UR	Reduction (absolute)	Reduction (%)
All industrial products					
Raw materials	36,665	22	2.1	1.1	52
Semi-manufactures	36,464	21	5.3	2.4	45
Finished products	96,534	57	9.1	27.0	30
Tropical industrial products					
Raw materials	5.1	35	0.1	0.1	100
Semi-manufactures	4.3	30	6.3	2.9	46
Finished products	4.9	34	6.6	4.2	64
Natural resource based products					
Raw materials	14.6	44	3.1	1.1	35
Semi-manufactures	13.3	40	3.5	1.5	43
Finished products	5.5	17	7.9	2.0	25

Source: GATT Secretariat MTN/gng/w/122 and Blackhurst et al. (1995: Table 4). The data are in billions of US dollars.

Round in fact achieved a slightly better outcome of 8.0%, but this actually resulted in greater tariff escalation. Oyejide also notes that the problem of high internal excise taxes on cocoa exacerbated the escalation.

Tariff peaks: The Uruguay Round reductions were not uniform across commodities, in contrast to the attempt to harmonize rates in the Tokyo

Round. To some extent this was disadvantageous to developing countries. Tariffs were cut by over 60% on wood, pulp and paper, furniture and metals. Wood and wood products in particular are important for some countries in West Africa. Tariffs on some goods, such as fish and fish products, leather, textiles, and clothing, footwear, and travel goods were cut by less than 40% and typically remain at higher levels (usually 12–18%). Fish and fish products are important for certain sub-Sahara African countries, and textiles and clothing for developing countries as a whole. As a result, the average tariff rate applied to exports of all developing countries fell by only 37%, less than the average for all rates (although this does not take into account the effects of eliminating the MFA quotas, which should more than offset this effect).

"Concessions received" by Africa:[8] The discussion of tariff peaks suggests that sub-Saharan African countries may have emerged from the Round with relatively modest reductions in the tariffs facing their exports; this is confirmed in Table 2.5, drawn from Wang and Winters (1997). The average tariff reduction for sub-Saharan African countries was 0.4 percentage points for industrial goods, versus 1.1 points for other low-income developing countries. In part this reflects the fact that received fewer new bindings on its goods than did other developing countries (20% versus 40%). But as Wang and Winters (1997) note, this could be viewed as the other countries catching up: sub-Saharan Africa began the round with a much higher proportion of its exports in bound categories (86.7 versus 76.4%). And in some respects, this is the story of Uruguay Round tariff cuts for Africa. It began the Round facing lower tariffs than did other developing countries (3.2 versus 7.4%). Africa was still ahead after the Round (2.2% versus 5.9%) but the difference had narrowed. Harold (1995) notes the concessions received by sub-Saharan African countries (Table 2.6).

The debate on preference erosion: Many sub-Saharan African countries benefit from the Generalized System of Preferences (GSP) or the Lomé Convention, which entitles them to receive lower rates of tariff on their exports to the industrial countries and the EU, respectively. Under the GSP, individual industrial countries can provide, at their discretion, preferential treatment for imports of specified goods from developing countries. Preferences under the GSP have some disadvantages. Their coverage is limited and

Table 2.5: MFN tariff reductions for sub-Saharan Africa and other low-income developing countries

	% exports bound	UR increase	% exports affected	Tariff reduction	Post-UR bound rate	Post-UR applied
Sub-Saharan Africa						
Agriculture excluding fish	80.8	19.2	4.1	0.7	18.6	14.9
Fish and fish products	79.0	20.5	51.2	2.5	7.7	6.6
Industrial goods	86.7	8.9	18.5	0.4	3.2	2.2
Merchandise trade	78.4	13.5	29.7	1.4	4.1	2.7
Other low-income developing countries						
Agriculture excluding fish	59.9	39.8	99.0	1.0	28.5	15.9
Fish and fish products	68.2	25.9	51.8	1.7	4.4	3.7
Industrial goods	76.4	14.2	39.5	1.1	7.4	5.9
Merchandise trade	70.5	18.3	36.0	1.1	8.9	5.8

Source: Wang and Winters (1997, Table 1).

typically does not extend to "sensitive products". They are also uncertain in the sense that they can be withdrawn unilaterally by the industrial country. Lomé cannot be withdrawn unilaterally by the EU and so is more valuable to its beneficiaries. It allows tariff and quota free access for manufactured products, freedom from MFA quotas, tariff reductions for CAP agricultural goods, and tariff- and NTB-free access for other agricultural goods not covered by the CAP.

As the average tariff rate on manufactures has been reduced in the Tokyo and Uruguay Rounds, the beneficiaries of GSP and Lomé have expressed concern that their preference margins – the difference between the preferential rates they enjoy and the average MFN tariff faced by their competitors – has fallen steadily. This concern has a sound arithmetical basis: in a world of zero MFN tariffs, preference margins cannot exceed zero.

Table 2.6: Tariff concessions received by selected sub-Saharan African countries

Country	Exports to OECD	Industry share in exports	Average tariff pre-UR	Average tariff post-UR	Reduction (%)
Benin	44	25.2	3.8	0.7	82
Botswana	230	86.8	11.1	9.4	15
Burkina Faso	98	40.5	3.2	1.1	66
Burundi	154	31.4	8.0	6.9	14
Cameroon	1,660	44.5	4.7	3.4	28
CAR	101	61.5	5.1	3.7	27
Congo	646	93.6	4.7	2.1	55
Côte d'Ivoire	2,200	30.7	5.9	7.6	15
Gabon	1,470	98.5	4.0	0.8	88
The Gambia	97	27.4	12.3	9.6	22
Ghana	821	60.1	5.5	4.3	22
Kenya	762	20.1	9.3	7.6	18
Lesotho	44	91.7	10.9	9.1	17
Madagascar	283	33.8	13.8	11.1	20
Mali	85	22.3	3.3	1.2	64
Mauritania	411	99.3	6.7	3.9	42
Mauritius	902	64.9	57.5	55.8	3
Namibia	43	96.3	2.8	0.8	71
Niger	300	98.6	2.8	0.1	96
Nigeria	8,810	42.2	1.7	0.6	69
Senegal	472	67.1	10.9	7.4	32
Sierra Leone	201	86.7	4.8	2.1	53
Swaziland	228	35.4	71.3	67.5	5
Tanzania UR	300	28.6	11.6	9.9	15
Togo	198	60.8	4.0	2.2	48

Source: Harrold (1995:23, Table 10).

Table 2.7: Tariff reductions on African exports to the EU, US and Japan

	Value unit	Average tariff pre-UR	Average tariff post-UR	Reduction (%)
European Union				
Industrial products	3,711	1.4	0.8	43
Wood, pulp, paper and furniture	216	0.3	0.2	33
Textiles and clothing	333	2.2	1.8	22
Leather, rubber, footwear and travel goods	118	0.9	0.7	22
Metals	1,578	0.1	0.0	100
Chemicals and photographic supplies	341	4.9	0.6	88
Mineral products, precious stones and metals	779	0.0	0.0	0
Fish and fish products	156	15.3	11.0	30
Japan				
Industrial products	867	5.6	3.1	45
Textiles and clothing	62	0.3	0.0	100
Leather, rubber, footwear and travel goods	17	0.2	0.0	100
Metals	474	5.4	2.5	54
Fish and fish products	275	8.2	5.6	32
United States				
Industrial products	592	1.2	1.1	8
Textiles and clothing	27	16.1	14.5	10
Leather, rubber, footwear and travel goods	18	1.9	1.3	32
Metals	278	0.6	0.6	0
Mineral products, precious stones and metals	171	0.1	0.0	100

Source: Harrold (1995: Table 9, p. 23).

The developing countries viewed the erosion of these margins as a burden imposed on them by the Uruguay Round Agreement. To what extent were these margins eroded, and what impact is this likely to have on their export performance? And could the developing countries, and sub-Saharan Africa in particular, have taken action during the Round to prevent the erosion of these preferences?

Harrold (1995) argues that the worries of the developing countries about preference erosion were exaggerated. Even before the Round, most of their exports (with the exception of textiles, clothing and footwear in the US) entered the industrial countries duty free, with no quotas or ceilings. EU tariffs facing sub-Saharan African countries were low indeed, and only Uganda faced an average tariff exceeding 0.5%.

Preference margins were also small, even before the Round: for goods entering the EU, for example, 23 of 31 sub-Saharan African countries enjoyed average preference margins of less than 3%, and for three countries the average margin was between 1 and 2 percentage points. Exports to the US faced somewhat higher tariffs (because textiles and clothing are excluded from the GSP) but lower preference margins (Harrold, 1995, Table 11, p.27). Yates (1994) reports somewhat larger margins, ranging from 0.9 to 4.4 percentage points.

Since many sub-Saharan African goods entered the EU and US tariff free, the Uruguay Round tariff cuts could not do anything but reduce sub-Saharan African preference margins. Calculations by Amjadi et al. (1996) indicate that as a result of the Round the average sub-Saharan African preference margin fell from 4.3 to 2.5 percentage points. This 1.8 percentage point drop is slightly less than the 2.5 point fall in the tariff rate on manufactures in the Round.

Does a margin of 2.5 or even 4.3 percentage points give African exporters a significant competitive advantage? This is not likely, especially if one takes into account the administrative costs entailed by rules of origin, which define the circumstances under which a particular product is eligible for favourable tariff treatment. Herin (1986) and Baldwin (1994: 33–4) discuss the experience of rules of origin in the EU-EFTA free trade agreement. There, the costs of complying with rules of origin were such that exporters preferred to pay the MFN tariff on almost 20% of EU-EFTA trade rather than comply with the rules of origin. So it seems doubtful that margins of only one or two percentage points give sub-Saharan African exporters a significant edge over their competitors.

Nevertheless, these preferences do convey some advantage, however slight. What impact is their erosion in the Round likely to have on sub-Saharan African exports? Harrold (1995) reports partial equilibrium calculations of the impact of the Uruguay Round tariff reductions on exports from the least developed African countries. Exports decrease by 0.1% or $7.5 million overall, with a fall in the EU, which is partially offset by increased textiles and clothing exports to the US market. Partial equilibrium projections by the ODI also suggest a negative impact, but of a somewhat larger magnitude.

UNCTAD (1996) estimates that for the larger group of sub-Saharan African countries (for which trade flows are of course larger), the erosion of preferences will lead to a loss of less than 0.3% of 1992 exports. The Harrison et al. CGE model reported in Table 2.1 above is more optimistic: it predicts that the Uruguay Round reduction in manufactures tariffs would have a small positive impact in sub-Saharan African countries (though this is the effect on welfare, not exports).

Harrold (1995) also calculates the change in exports following the complete removal of MFN tariffs on the exports of the least developed African countries, i.e. a complete disappearance of preferences. This results in a 1% or $67 million fall in total exports, with a fall in the EU market being offset by a $17 million gain in the US market. Yates (1994) finds a similar pattern, but a somewhat larger effect for all sub-Saharan African countries. There is a loss of $250 million from the complete liberalization of MFN tariffs in the EU. The biggest losers are Côte d'Ivoire, Mauritius and Kenya. For the top 30 sub-Saharan African exporters the losses represent 2% of exports. Liberalization by Japan causes trade losses of $14.3, while in the US, exports rise by $89 million. The overall effect is a fall of approximately 1.5%.

"Commitments made" by Africa: The concessions received by sub-Saharan African countries represent only one side of the Uruguay Round "bargain". The market access concessions they offer to other countries are equally, if not more, important. Sorsa (1995) argues that these commitments represent a lost opportunity: "sub-Saharan countries have not used the Round to support domestic efforts at trade policy reform. The Round provided an opportunity for countries to go beyond their unilateral liberalization efforts in exchange for multilateral concessions, or to bind their domestic reforms to an international framework". Harrold (1995: 33), who provides more detailed evidence on this issue, reaches a similar conclusion: "for most sub-Saharan African countries, the commitments under the UR will not represent any meaningful liberalization". Those sub-Saharan African countries that bound their tariffs did so at rates far higher than existing levels of protection.

Table 2.8 reveals that sub-Saharan African tariff levels remain high even after the Round, and are high even when compared to other developing countries. Wang and Winters (1997: 5) note that actual tariff rates average 26% in sub-Saharan Africa versus 17%, and total charges on imports average 33%, versus 26% in other developing countries.

Columns 4–7 of Table 2.8 show clearly that many of the sub-Saharan African countries that chose to bind their rates of manufactures tariffs did so at very high levels – usually in excess of 100% and far above current levels of protection. As discussed above, bindings can in principle reduce uncertainty and add credibility to trade policy, but with the exception of the Southern African Customs Union (SACU) countries and (possibly) Ghana, the levels chosen by most sub-Saharan African countries are unlikely to achieve even this modest objective. This contrasts sharply with the policies of other regions. In Latin America, for example, Chile offered to bind 100% of its tariff lines as early as the Tokyo Round, and Costa Rica, El Salvador, Mexico and Venezuela bound 100% their lines when they joined the GATT during the period 1986–91. Following the Uruguay Round, 100% of Latin America's tariffs are now bound.

NON-TARIFF BARRIERS (NTBS)

The Uruguay Round Agreement calls for the elimination of many of the most important non-tariff barriers to trade. In addition to the tariffication of agricultural NTBS (discussed in below), these measures include the phasing out (over a ten-year period) of the quotas imposed under the Multi-Fibre Arrangement (MFA), and the elimination of all "voluntary" export restraints (VERS) within a four-year period. The MFA quotas will be phased out in favour of tariffs gradually, with 49% taking place after ten years (i.e. in 2005).

NTBS were largely applied by the industrial countries to certain exports from developing countries, principally food, iron and steel, petroleum,

Table 2.8: Commitments by sub-Saharan African countries

	Agriculture	Industry				
Country	Average bound rate in UR	Average applied rate	% of tariff lines bound pre-UR	% of tariff lines bound in UR	Average bound rate in UR	Average applied rate
Benin	80	–	29	1.4	69	–
Burkina Faso	150	–	29	1.2	150	–
Cameroon	310	–	0	0.1	177	–
Congo	30	–	0	3.2	15	–
Côte d'Ivoire	215	–	29	0.4	257	–
Gabon	260	–	?	1.3	206	–
Ghana	98	22	0	1.1	33	16
Kenya	100	44	0	1.6	54	35
Madagascar	280	1	?	11.1	280	–
Mali	110	–	29	1.3	45	–
Mauritania	54	–	29	2.8	110	–
Mauritius	135	–	0	1.6	82	–
Namibia	40	–	31	68.0	17	22
Niger	132	–	29	2.4	180	34
Nigeria	230	47	0.1	7.0	128	36
Senegal	180	44	29	2.4	180	34
South Africa	40	7	31	68.0	17	22
Swaziland	40	–	0	31.0	17	22
Tanzania	240	–	0	0.1	240	–
Uganda	80	–	0	2.7	50	–
Zambia	124	–	?	4.0	42	–
Zimbabwe	161	24	8	0.8	66	31

Source: Adapted from Harrold (1995, Table 15, p. 35). For Senegal and Zimbabwe, WTO (1997) gives a figure of 40% for the percentage of bound tariff lines and textiles and clothing. The elimination of these NTBs is likely to have an important impact on the developing countries, largely because of the elimination of the MFA. The impact on Africa is, however, less clear. Before the Round, 10.8% of sub-Saharan African exports were subject to NTBs, versus 9.7% for industrial countries and 16.6% for all developing countries (Harrold, (1995). The figure for sub-Saharan Africa will fall to 3.3% when the Uruguay Round measures are completed.

Table 2.9 shows the impact across sub-Saharan African countries of the removal of NTBs. The table suggests – and both Harrold (1995) and Amadji and Yeats (1995) confirm – that the impact of removing these NTBs is likely to vary sharply from country to country, largely as a consequence of the MFA.

The elimination of the MFA means that developing country exporters will lose the "quota rents" they currently enjoy because of the higher prices induced by the quotas in industrial country markets. Africa is likely to face higher prices for textiles and clothing, since exporters who were formerly quota-constrained will no longer need to dispose of surplus production in developed countries, but can instead sell in industrial country markets. And as the NTBs are eliminated, production will shift to the most efficient producers. Harrold argues that this will lead to strong export growth in, for example, Mauritius, 61.6% of whose products (mainly textiles and clothing) currently face NTBs. Amjadi and Yeats (1995) are more sceptical, noting that African producers of textiles and clothing, as well as footwear and ferrous metals, will face more severe competition from Asian producers once NTBs are lifted, and it is unclear whether sub-Saharan African producers will be able to compete successfully.

Agriculture

The Round achieved a significant breakthrough by bringing trade in agricultural products within the GATT for the first time. Even though little or no liberalization in agricultural products was actually achieved in the Round, the conversion of NTBs into tariff equivalents, the binding of virtually all agricultural tariffs and the reductions in subsidies marked a significant step towards rule-based trade in agricultural products. Tariffication of existing NTBs also established a basis for negotiations over tariff reductions in the future.

Table 2.9: Share of goods exports to OECD affected by non-tariff barriers

	Pre-UR	Post-UR
Angola	4.7	4.7
Benin	1.3	0.3
Burkina Faso	12.3	0.0
Burundi	0.1	0.0
Cameroon	20.8	19.7
Cape Verde	39.5	0.0
CAR	0.1	0.1
Chad	0.1	0.1
Comoros	0.6	0.6
Congo	38.5	38.0
Côte d'Ivoire	14.1	1.5
Djibouti	5.2	5.2
Equatorial Guinea	0.1	0.1
Ethiopia	1.8	1.2
Gabon	15.8	15.8
Gambia	0.5	0.3
Ghana	0.4	0.2
Guinea	0.3	0.1
Guinea Bissau	1.6	0.1
Kenya	3.5	0.3
Liberia	0.0	0.0
Madagascar	7.6	2.9
Malawi	29.6	3.7
Mali	0.4	0.2
Mauritania	1.3	1.0
Mauritius	61.6	2.2
Mozambique	10.3	0.6
Niger	0.2	0.1

	Pre-UR	Post-UR
Nigeria	14.4	14.4
Reunion	83.0	0.0
Rwanda	1.1	0.2
Sao Tome & Principe	17.2	2.7
Senegal	19.1	0.0
Seychelles	91.4	84.7
Sierra Leone	0.1	0.0
Somalia	9.0	0.0
South Africa	13.0	3.7
Sudan	12.4	4.1
Tanzania	3.8	0.5
Togo	0.5	0.1
Uganda	0.0	0.0
Zaire	0.0	0.0
Zambia	0.7	0.0
Zimbabwe	20.3	8.0
SSA	13.1	8.0

Source: Harrold (1995: Table 18, p. 40–1).

The agreement stipulated that all NTBS were to be converted to their tariff equivalents and bound at agreed maximum rates. These tariffs were then to be reduced by 36% over six years by the industrial countries, and 24% by developing countries over ten years (the least developed countries were exempt). In principle such tariffication marks a step toward liberalization, but in practice, the procedures allowed under the Agreement – "dirty bindings" – in many cases resulted in higher levels of protection than existed before the Round.

These "dirty bindings" are documented by Hathaway and Ingco (1995) and Ingco (1995, 1996). Several aspects of the procedure led to high levels of tariff equivalents. First, the tariffs were based on the choice of 1986–98 as a base period. During these years world prices were very low and so the difference between the world price and protected or internal prices was very high. The result, according to Ingco (1995), was that the average level of agricultural tariffs – even after the Uruguay Round reductions – exceeded the average level of protection over the period 1982–93.

Developing countries were allowed even more latitude in setting the tariff equivalents: they could adopt "ceiling bindings", bound tariffs set at levels unrelated to (and well above) previous levels of protection. As a result, many countries in Africa (and South Asia as well) simply declared a uniform pattern of 100%, 150% or 200% bound tariffs on agricultural goods, even though in most cases the previous actual rates of protection were less than 50%. This can be seen clearly in Table 2.8, which gives data for the 22 countries that had submitted offers by late 1994.[9] The bound rates for wheat and sugar cane were 100%, while the actual rates of protection before the Round were 10% and 44%, respectively (Martin and Winters, 1995b). It is worth noting, though, that Africa is not unique in this respect: the bound rates in Table 8, though high, are in many cases of the same magnitude as those adopted by other developing countries and lower in some cases than those of the EU (Martin and Winters, 1995b: 18).[10]

The Round introduced export subsidy disciplines, which prohibit the introduction of new export subsidies and require that industrial countries reduce subsidies on each commodity by 36% in nominal terms over six years and the volume of subsidized exports by 21%. Developing countries were obliged to reduce their subsidies by two-thirds of these amounts over ten years, while the poorest countries were exempted from the reductions. Nevertheless, as Martin and Winters note, many support programmes are exempt (particularly in developing countries), and support for individual commodities can even increase.

What impact are these agricultural reforms likely to have on sub-Saharan Africa? Most observers during the Round and subsequently identified an increase in world food prices as the most important factor. The industrial countries – in particular the EU – are obliged by the Agreement to reduce the level of subsidized agricultural exports by 21% overall. Since the EU in particular can no longer dispose of its surplus production on world markets at subsidized rates, prices would tend to rise. Concern over the prospect of rising food prices was in large part responsible for the adoption of the "Decision on Measures Concerning the Possible Negative Effects of the Reform Programme on Least-Developed and Net Food-Importing Countries".

Initial estimates made during the Round predicted increases of 5–8% in the price of temperate crops, but these proved exaggerated, in part because they were based on overoptimistic views of the liberalization the Round would ultimately achieve, and because they ignored substitution away from more expensive foods by consumers (Harrold, 1995: 18). Nevertheless, it seems likely that the Round would lead to some increase in "temperate" food prices.

The terms of trade effect on sub-Saharan Africa will then depend on whether Africa is a net food importer or exporter. As Harrold (1995) notes, Nigeria is large net importer and South Africa a large net exporter. Overall sub-Saharan Africa is a net food exporter. Some sub-Saharan African countries are, of course, net importers, most as a result of wars and other disturbances. For these countries Harrold calculates a food deficit of $2 billion. This represents 3% of total imports, so a rough calculation suggests that even a 5% rise in food prices would lead to a 0.15% increase in the import bill. Similar calculations by the ODI (1994) focused on the impact of changes in the prices of temperate crops, where sub-Saharan African countries have a net deficit of $1.5 billion. The ODI projections suggested that a 5% price increase would increase the net deficit by £100 million: this would represent less than 1% of the total sub-Saharan African import bill. These rough, partial equilibrium projections are consistent with the more elaborate CGE simulations by Harrison et al. (as discussed), which suggest that the Round's agricultural reforms would lead to a fall of 0.5% of GDP in sub-Saharan Africa. It seems reasonable to conclude, therefore, that the terms of trade effect of the Round is likely to be negative but small.

And things we can't

So far we have focused almost exclusively on changes in tariffs and non-tariff barriers to trade – the aspects of the Round whose impact can be most easily quantified. There are, however, strong reasons to believe that it is the other aspects of the Uruguay Round Agreement that will have the most important long-run effect on the world trading system – and on the countries of sub-Saharan Africa.

"SYSTEMIC" CHANGES

Perhaps the most fundamental change brought about by the Round is the shift towards a more rule-based, and so more transparent and predictable, world trading system.

First, and most obviously, the Agreement led to the establishment of the WTO, which is responsible for administering the multilateral agreements (the GATT, GATS and TRIPS). In the earlier rounds many of the rules and disciplines were optional – most developing countries were not obliged to sign up to everything and most chose not to adopt many of the rules. The Uruguay Round marked a significant departure from this approach. It constituted a "single undertaking" and almost all the rules and disciplines agreed to in the Round apply to all members of the WTO. Developing countries no longer have the option of "opting out" – they are instead granted longer transitional periods before they must implement WTO rules and disciplines. Some aspects of "special and differential treatment" remain, however. Developing countries are, for example, allowed to adopt new subsidy programmes for agricultural exports, provided these are part of national development plans, and the least developed countries are exempt from the subsidy rules. But other important measures, such as the rules concerning the protection of intellectual property (TRIPS) are binding on all WTO members. Developing countries have, for example, a longer period in which to introduce system

The world trading system is thus more rule-based as a result of the Round: there are more rules and (with a few exceptions) they apply to all members. But systems of rules require monitoring and enforcement, and the Round strengthened these as well.

Enforcement through the dispute resolution mechanism is much stronger as a result of the Round. GATT enforcement procedures were easily delayed or blocked by the parties to the dispute, either at the stage where a panel was established to investigate the dispute or when the panel issued its report. Under the GATT, a consensus was needed to establish a panel or accept its report: now a consensus is needed in order to stop the proceedings from advancing at any stage of the dispute settlement procedures. In addition, stricter time limits on the operation of dispute panels are likely to reduce delays and obstruction by the parties to the dispute.

The strengthening of the dispute settlement procedure is likely to favour the developing countries: they have recourse to the "rule of law" as a partial substitute for their lack of political and economic muscle in trade disputes. It is true, as Oyejide (1990) remarks, that these countries are likely to lack "familiarity with and knowledge of the legal intricacies of the mechanism, and ... the resources and skills needed to initiate, prosecute or defend cases in pursuance of their interests". But in addition to training courses provided by the WTO, they are entitled to the "good offices" of the WTO Director-General in mediating disputes outside the formal dispute settlement mechanism.

As Martin and Winters (1995b: 2) note, the WTO's system of trade policy reviews can potentially play an important role in making national trade policies more transparent and clarifying the true costs of trade barriers. The largest trading nations are subject to review by the WTO every two years, the next largest every four years, this group and other members (including the majority of developing countries) every six years, with longer intervals for the least developed countries.

It is understandable that the largest countries are reviewed most often, but on the other hand, the least liberal trade regimes – those most in need of review – are often to be found in the developing world. So, far from being a burden to be avoided at all costs, the developing countries should welcome the reviews and request them more often, as a way of creating greater incentives to liberalize their trade regimes, to lessen the probability that reforms will be reversed and so add credibility to their trade policies. We return to this theme below.

Services (GATS)

The Uruguay Round brought about another fundamental change in the world trading system, by extending to international trade in services the multilateral disciplines the GATT had established for goods trade.

The GATS rules differ sharply from the GATT regulations on tariffs. Trade in goods has traditionally been regulated by taxes (tariffs) or relatively straightforward quantitative restrictions. For services, taxes and tariffs have played a less important role than direct regulation or control over rights of establishment. As a result, attempts to create international rules for trade in services inevitably involve issues of domestic regulation and rules concerning inward investment

Countries that wish to participate in the GATS must first decide whether a particular service will be subject to the GATS (the "positive list" approach) – a service is not regulated by the GATS unless the country specifically decides it should be. Even though a service has been added to a country's positive list, it may still be subject to national controls, which may operate through restrictions on market access, limitations on national treatment of suppliers or (temporary) derogations from MFN treatment among suppliers (these have been used in particular by the US) as a bargaining lever in the services negotiations. These controls may operate at national, sectoral or service level, and registered restrictions can be bound or unbound.

Measuring GATS commitments is not a simple matter. Counting the number of sectors on a country's positive list is not enlightening, since a sector may be listed but subject to a large number of national controls. It is relatively simple to judge how much protection is achieved by a given tariff or quota, but much harder to measure, for example, how much protectiveness is created by measures for regulating the banking system.

Nevertheless, it is clear that the developing countries made far fewer GATS commitments than did the industrial countries (Martin and Winters, 1995b: 21–2). The industrial countries listed 47% of their service sectors, versus 16% for the developing countries. A country may add a service sector to its positive list, but may still maintain exceptions: restrictions on market access, limitations on national treatment of suppliers or (temporary) derogations from MFN treatment among suppliers. The industrial countries listed 27% of their service sectors without such exceptions versus only 7% for developing countries. Four developing countries listed only one (out of 155) service sector, and five listed only two.

Hoekman (1995a: 349) concludes that GATS "... continues the GATT tradition of putting very little pressure on small and poor developing countries to fully participate, as these have little to offer in the multilateral mercantilistic game of 'give and take'".

Ironically, as Hoekman also notes, it is the developing countries that may have the greatest need to liberalize their services sectors. Services are not only a consumer good, but also an input into production. Liberalization of services benefits not only consumers, who receive better quality services, but also firms, which have access to less expensive or better quality inputs and so are more competitive internationally.

Amjadi and Yeats (1995) provide evidence that freight rates on African exports are considerably higher than those on similar goods shipped from outside the region. These high transport costs have placed African exporters at a competitive disadvantage, reduced exports, and discouraged investment and the location of export-oriented industries in the region. They attribute these high costs not only to governments' failure to maintain and upgrade the transportation infrastructure, but also to government policies (such as the cargo reservation system) that shelter the transportation sector from competition. Mohieldin (1997) finds similar evidence for Egypt, where the government has sheltered key producer services, such as insurance, telecommunications, ports and transport, from foreign (or domestic) competition, usually through state monopolies. The result is also high costs and less competitive exporters.

The approach adopted in GATS presents some problems for governments trying to enter into or to lock in liberalization. Access commitments, for example, are sector specific and so negotiations will inevitably be sector specific as well, driven by interests in that sector. This will encourage sectoral reciprocity and limit the possibilities for cross-sector trade-offs, that were an important feature of the GATT rounds. The GATS, or rather the forces that gave rise to the GATS, pose even more serious long-run challenges for the developing countries, since it extends the disciplines of the international trading system into areas that have previously been considered the exclusive province of national governments. Governments of developing countries, which have, for example, barely begun to consider how they might construct a regulatory regime for their banking system, may find their task much more difficult if they wish at the same time to open up these sectors to foreign competition.

Intellectual property (TRIPS)

The Uruguay Round also extended multilateral disciplines to the protection of intellectual property through the TRIPS agreement. Members of the WTO must accept, for example, the Berne and Paris Conventions on copyright and industrial property. They must also establish acceptable national systems for the registration and enforcement of intellectual property rights. Developing countries can take advantage of longer transitional periods before they must comply with these new rules.

There is little dispute that the enforcement of intellectual property rights is an essential element of a rules-based trading system. Such a system benefits the developing as well as the industrial countries, but there seems little doubt that the TRIPS Agreement places a significant burden on developing countries, despite the extended transitional periods available to developing countries. The Agreement requires substantial changes to their legislation and enforcement regulations, in return for what are in practice very small gains.

Trade related investment measures (TRIMS)

The negotiations over the Agreement on Trade-related Investment Measures (TRIMS) proved particularly controversial, particularly among the developing countries. The Agreement bans restrictions on investments that impose quantitative restrictions or that violate the national treatment rule. Examples include requirements for local content and trade balancing.

The developing countries argued at the start of the Round that policies concerning investment did not fall within the scope of the GATT. The industrial countries, led by the United States, argued that policies that distorted capital flows could also distort trade. The TRIMS Agreement represented a compromise, in which investment measures directly affecting trade were declared to be within the scope of the GATT, and some were prohibited, with provision for a further review within five years.

Suspending market access

The Uruguay Round marked an important change in the treatment of safeguards like anti-dumping and countervailing duties. Countries were encouraged to use safeguards instead of anti-dumping measures. Safeguards were made more user friendly: they could be applied on a discriminatory, not an MFN, basis and the exporting countries no longer had a right to compensation. At the same time an attempt was made to specify more objective and transparent criteria for establishing that dumping has taken place, in the hope that this would make it less easy to prove dumping.

During the 1970s and 1980s these measures were typically applied by the industrial countries to exporters from developing countries. Measures that limit the scope for contingent protection were therefore in the interests of developing countries. More recently, however, developing countries begun to use these provisions as well.

3. The Uruguay Round: Processes and Lessons

African participation in the negotiating process

In previous Rounds, the sub-Saharan African countries acted mainly through the G77 group of developing countries. They participated more actively in the Uruguay Round than in earlier rounds, as Oyejide (1990) notes but this increased participation seemed to achieve little. Why did the Uruguay Round make so little difference to sub-Saharan Africa?

The strategy adopted by the developing countries in the 1960s and 1970s involved the promotion of industrialization through import substitution and highly protective trade regimes; little involvement in the GATT or the multilateral negotiations except through the G77 group of developing countries; and requests for the granting of access to industrial country markets through systems of preferential tariffs, granted on a non-reciprocal basis. By the onset the Uruguay Round this strategy had reached a dead end, for a variety of reasons. African countries faced the disappearance of their preferential access to industrial country markets, as the average level of MFN tariffs fell close to zero. The largest gainers in the Round were those countries who liberalized their own trade policies, but the sub-Saharan African countries found it difficult or impossible to engage in any liberalization themselves. And as Wang and Winters (1997) note, the cuts in industrial country tariffs occurred in sectors of less importance to them.

Why did sub-Saharan Africa achieve so little in the Round? There are a variety of possible explanations: "There was nowhere to go but down". A key objective of the sub-Saharan African countries was the preservation of tariff preferences, but this was impossible in a world where MFN tariffs were close to zero and still falling. Tariff preferences were bound to be eroded and African countries could do nothing to prevent this. But on the other hand, these tariff concessions were only one side of the negotiations: more important were the gains they might have achieved if they had liberalized their own economies.

"The multilateral system was rigged against us." This is a commonly held belief, particularly within African governments, but it does not withstand careful scrutiny. Before the Round, the sub-Saharan African countries already received significantly better treatment than any other group of developing countries. And the systemic changes introduced in the Round, which tend to make the world trading system more rule-based, are beneficial to smaller countries with less economic or political power. So the Round strengthened, not weakened, aspects of the system that benefited sub-Saharan African countries.

"Sub-Saharan African countries were overwhelmed by the complexity of the negotiations." This argument suggests that they suffered because they lacked negotiating experience and expertise in economic policy analysis and in international trade law. This is a more convincing argument. Many developing countries experience great difficulty ensuring that they are properly represented at the WTO, as Oyejide (1990) notes. In this respect it is worth noting that one group of sub-Saharan African countries that did engage in some liberalization was the SACU countries, who arguably suffered less than other sub-Saharan African countries from a lack of negotiating, legal and economic expertise.

"African countries failed to unite and act in a coordinated fashion." This argument attributes the lack of success in the Round to the failure of developing countries in general, and African countries in particular, to coordinate their negotiating strategies. There is some truth in this argument as well. The coalition of developing countries who were members of the G77 displayed less unity during the Uruguay Round than in previous rounds. In particular some of the large developing countries such as Brazil and India changed their position on the services negotiations during the Round, and ended up with a more positive attitude than the least developed countries. But greater African unity during the negotiations may not have improved the outcome for sub-Saharan Africa. Wang and Winters (1997), in their analysis of the potential for active African participation in future trade negotiations, analyse the status and bargaining position of the sub-Saharan African countries acting individually and as a group, and find that acting as a group, the sub-Saharan African countries had little more clout than when acting individually.

Nevertheless, it may be advantageous for sub-Saharan African countries to cooperate with each other for the purposes of information gathering and policy analysis at the WTO, since this may help address some of the difficulties they face because of the scarcity of skilled economists, lawyers and negotiators. Such joint action may, however, prove difficult to set up and it may also be difficult to monitor the quality of such joint services.

"They were distracted by other policy pressures." Here the argument is essentially that sub-Saharan African countries were too busy dealing with the difficulties of structural adjustment programmes. This is consistent with the observation that the SACU countries did succeed in liberalizing, but is not entirely convincing. Even if the South African government had no structural adjustment programme to occupy its attentions, it clearly had other policy preoccupations during the period 1986–93! Yet it was able to play an active role in the Round and achieve significant domestic liberalization.

This argument also ignores an important fact: sub-Saharan African countries undergoing structural adjustment programmes typically attempted to liberalize their trade regimes, but seldom chose to bind their tariffs, even though under the Uruguay Round rules they would receive negotiating credit for having done so (and a number of Latin American countries did receive such credit).

So each of these explanations has an element of truth, but each is less than convincing. One explanation remains. It is more convincing, but also somewhat dispiriting: African countries achieved relatively little in the Round because they pursued the wrong strategy. They focused on obtaining concessions from the industrial countries and they failed to liberalize their own trade policies.

This was not accidental. African countries failed to liberalize domestically because neither their own policy communities nor their publics were convinced that liberal trade policies were the right policies. Sub-Saharan African countries did not take advantage of the opportunities to liberalize that the Round presented because they did not want to liberalize. There was little support among the policy making elite or among the population as a whole for measures to liberalize trade because the benefits of liberalization to consumers were very diffuse and widely spread. Exporters (or potential exporters) might be expected to have a stronger incentive to support freer trade, but they lacked either the political influence or the "export optimism" required to lobby strongly for lower tariffs. Why? The answer may be "export pessimism": Several decades of steady decline in the market shares of African countries in industrial country markets may have convinced firms that success in exporting manufactures was very unlikely – and here tariff escalation may also play a role – making it less attractive to export more processed goods.

Lessons from the Round

If this diagnosis is correct, what is the correct prescription for African trade policy?

Some of the problems described above may right themselves: Export pessimism, for example, may be dispelled by more success in exporting. The recent buoyant export growth in some sub-Saharan African countries may help convince firms that they can be even more successful in exporting if they, and their economies, become more competitive, that one way of increasing competitiveness is through more liberal trade policies and more competitive service sectors.

Some initiatives have considerable political appeal, but are unlikely to deliver economic benefits:

- *Fighting to preserve or enhance GSP or Lomé tariff preferences:* These are already small and confer little or no competitive advantage, especially when one takes into account the administrative costs involved in exporting under preferential schemes (which typically involve compliance with complex rules of origin). In the future, preferences will be even less important than they are today – there are no tariff preferences to be had in a world of zero tariffs.
- *Fighting to increase Africa's influence within the WTO's decision making structure:* Oyejide (1990: 439) describes a proposal by African countries to create an ombudsman for developing countries. This is a worthwhile idea, but seems unlikely to be adopted, since there is already a provision for the Director-General to assist the least developed countries by mediating in trade disputes. Oyejide (1997) proposes a rather stronger measure – the creation of regional "executive directors" in the WTO. As in the Fund, these would be chosen by groups of member countries to represent the interests of these countries in decisions taken by the WTO. Such a measure would certainly increase the power of African countries,

> but would be difficult to implement, given the organization's formal structure. Unlike the Fund, the WTO has no capital or shareholders: it is governed by a Ministerial Conference, which meets every two years, and by a General Council comprising the entire membership, which oversees the Dispute Resolution Procedure. There is nothing in this structure that is equivalent to the Fund's executive directors, nor does it seem likely that the WTO's industrial country members would agree to the creation of such positions.

There may, however, be some scope for African countries to tackle the scarcity of policy and legal analysts and experienced negotiators. One obvious route is to step up existing efforts by the WTO (and others) to train developing country representatives. Another useful initiative might be for African countries to be represented jointly in WTO meetings. Such representatives need not negotiate jointly on behalf of the countries they represent, but could attend as observers and ensure that the countries were properly briefed on the meetings. This would ensure that the countries' representatives were alerted to important issues as soon as they arose and were fully briefed on the discussions that took place, even if they could not be present themselves. It might also be feasible for the countries to jointly commission policy analyses on areas of common interest, which would also help ensure that issues of importance were pursued in a timely manner. Such joint appointments would obviously be politically sensitive, and also raise problems in monitoring, but might go some way toward addressing the scarcity of skilled personnel available to sub-Saharan African countries.

The most important initiatives, however, must be taken at the domestic level, not in Geneva. Here it is worth considering proposals by Hoekman (1995b) and Winters (1995b), who advocate the creation of agencies whose sole statutory task is to monitor a country's trade policy.

Winters (1995b) notes that in a democracy, the voters must be free to choose the policies they desire, even if these policies are unwise when assessed by some objective criterion. He makes the important point that "the most important element of a sensible trade policy – by which I mean a liberal one – must be convincing a substantial body of electors that maintaining open borders represents the best general prescription" (Winters 1995a: 19).

He then goes on to discuss the issue of designing trade policy institutions, and discusses in some detail the historical experience of running trade policy in democracies, and in particular where responsibility for trade policy should be assigned.

The forces of protection tend to be better organized and more vocal than those who argue for a liberal trade policy. This is typically the case because of the asymmetry between the gainers and losers from trade policy. The small number of producers who are hurt by imports each face high costs, while the more numerous consumers each receive only a small benefit. If the objective is to adopt and sustain liberal trade policies, trade policy institutions should be designed to offset this asymmetry and make it harder rather than easier for special interests to secure protection for their industries.

Responsibility for trade policy can be assigned to the legislature, the executive or the bureaucracy. Each has advantages and disadvantages, but Winters argues that within the executive, day to day responsibility for trade policy should not be assigned to sectoral ministries but instead be given to ministries with a broader responsibility for the whole economy, such as the ministry of finance or the prime minister's office. In the African context, however, the finance ministry may prove a bad choice: taxes on trade form an important source of government revenues, and so the ministry may be unsympathetic to low tariffs because of their effect on the budget deficit.

Hoekman (1995b) argues along similar lines, but advocates instead that responsibility for trade policy be assigned to an executive agency reporting to the head of the executive branch of the government. This agency should have as its sole responsibility the scrutiny of trade policy. It should also have as part of its mandate the responsibility for gathering data and carrying out analyses that make the costs of particular trade policies clear and transparent, and of ensuring that this information is readily available to the public during discussions of trade policy.

Winters (1995b: 33) suggests that this agency also be legally obliged to prepare – and make public – estimates of the costs and benefits of each existing and proposed trade policy measure, using the checklists prepared by the OECD (1986) and the GATT (1985).

Is this proposal politically realistic in the African context? Perhaps not: countries that have displayed no signs of enthusiasm for liberalizing their trade policies on a long-term basis may not be any more excited by a proposal to establish an agency whose sole statutory function is to advocate policies they dislike. Any country willing to establish such an agency may have little or no need for it (at least in the short run). Pressure from the international financial agencies might induce countries to establish such agencies, which then carry out their mandate more or less effectively for a longer or shorter period of time. But in the end, they risk being rendered impotent by political and bureaucratic hostility.

It may therefore be useful to consider a more modest initial step toward the creation of such an official body. The goal is to provide an incentive for a developing country to first create such an institution, and then ensure it has sufficient resources to carry out its mandate to scrutinize trade policies. The first step would be to persuade African governments to request WTO Trade Policy Reviews (TPRS) on a more frequent basis than the six-year intervals. This might require additional funding, since the WTO may not have the resources to finance additional TPRS. They do, however, have funding from member governments to encourage the integration of the developing countries into the world trading system. It might be possible to use these funds to finance a cooperative effort between academic researchers and government departments, in which the researchers would work with government officials to collect and prepare data on that country's trade and trade policies (possibly using the TPR structure and format). One aim would be to assemble the data in a form suitable for inclusion in the integrated database (IDB); the other would be to build local expertise in collecting trade data and analysing the impact of trade policies.

This might represent the first step in encouraging public debate on trade policy in sub-Saharan Africa and building a constituency in favour of adopting – and sustaining – open and liberal trade policies in these countries.

Notes

1 Centre for Economic Policy Research, 90–90 Goswell Road, London EC1V 7DB: syeo@cepr.org

2 The simulations of the RUNS model by Goldin and van der Mensbrugghe (1995) focused on agriculture, to some extent at the expense of important features of other sectors, such as the impact of the MFA in the manufacturing sector. As a result, their simulations suggested that agriculture would generate a very large proportion of the gains from the Round.

3 Although Harrison et al. (1997: 1420) argue that comparisons between simulations assuming constant versus increasing returns to scale.

4 See Francois at al. (1996) for more detailed cross-model comparisons of the simulation results.

5 For more details, see Harrison et al. (1997: 236–7 and Table 11) and Harrison and Vinod (1992).

6 The welfare gain of −0.35 is taken from Harrison et al. (1995) and differs from the figure of −0.5 in Table 2, which is drawn from Harrison et al. (1997), who did not report the results of the sensitivity analysis for their revised results.

7 Petroleum products, which are important for a number of West Africa countries, were not considered during the Round, and so remain unbound, although the current tariff rates are very low. See Blackhurst et al. (1995).

8 Information on the concessions received and commitments in the Uruguay Round is in principle available in the GATT/WTO Integrated Data Base (IDB). The IDB contains data on commitments made on all tariff lines, both before and after the Round and on imports by origin on a tariff line basis, at a six digit HS level. Many of these data can be found in Finger et al. (1996). They can also be downloaded from the World Bank website at http/www.worldbank.org/htm/iecit/urdata.html). Unfortunately, the IDB contains relatively few data on developing countries. Of the 94 developing country participants in the Uruguay Round, only 26 are represented in the IDB. For Africa, the IDB contains data on only four countries: Tunisia, Senegal, South Africa and Zimbabwe. As a result, the IDB is useful for calculations involving the concessions received by the African countries, since they export mainly to the industrial countries, whose imports are captured in the IDB. The IDB is less useful as a source of information on the commitments made by sub-Saharan African.

9 Note that these are commitments. Sub-Saharan African countries were given the option of deferring their bindings until the year 2000.

10 It is also worth recalling the argument of Francois and Martin that bindings, even at high rates, can nevertheless reduce the average expected level of protection.

References

Amjadi, A. and A. Yeats. 1995. "Nontariff barriers Africa faces: What did the Uruguay Round accomplish, and what remains to be done?" *Working Paper No. 1439.* Washington D.C.: The World Bank.

Amjadi, A., U. Reincke and A. Yeats. 1996. "Did external barriers cause the marginalization of sub-Saharan Africa in world trade?" *Working Paper No. 1559.* Washington D.C.: The World Bank.

Amjadi, A., U. Reincke and A. Yeats. 1997. *Did Domestic Policies Marginalize Africa in International Trade?* Washington D.C.: The World Bank.

Baldwin, R.E. 1994. *Towards an Integrated Europe.* London: Centre for Economic Policy Research.

Blackhurst, R., A. Enders and J. Francois. 1995. "The Uruguay Round and market access: Opportunities and challenges for developing countries", in W. Martin and L.A. Winters, eds., *The Uruguay Round and Developing Countries*, Discussion Paper no. 307. Washington D.C.: The World Bank.

Croome, J. 1995. Reshaping the World Trading System: A History of the Uruguay Round. Geneva: World Trading Organization.

ECA. 1995a. "Africa's participation in future multilateral trade negotiations within the framework of the World Trade Organization: Summary of the conference of African Ministers Responsible for Trade, Regional Cooperation, Integration and Tourism, First Session Addis Ababa, 15 December 1995". ET 7–13 February E/ECA/TRADE/95/13. Addis Ababa: Economic Commission for Africa.

ECA. 1995b. "Note on the Follow Up on Resolution 783 (XXIX) Regarding the Implementation of the Uruguay Round Agreements: Summary of the conference of African ministers responsible for trade, regional cooperation, integration and tourism, First Session Addis Ababa, Technical Committee Of Experts 21 December 1995". ET 7–13 February E/ECA/CMT/1/1/2. Addis Ababa: Economic Commission For Africa.

Finger, J.M., M. Ingco and U. Reincke. 1996. The Uruguay Round: Statistics on Tariff Concessions Given and Received. Washington, D.C.: World Bank. The data in the volume can be downloaded from http://www.worldbank.org/html/iecit/urdata html

Francois J.F. and W. Martin. 1995. "Multilateral trade rules and the expected cost of protection". *CEPR Discussion Paper no. 1214*. London: Centre for Economic Policy Research.

Francois J.F. and W. Martin. 1997. "Bindings and rules as trade liberalization" In K. Maskus, P.M. Hooper, E.E. Leamer and J.D. Richardson, eds., *Quiet Pioneering: Robert M. Stern and his International Economic Legacy*, eds., University of Michigan Press.

Francois J.F., B. McDonald and H. Nordström. 1994. "The Uruguay Round: A global general equilibrium assessment". *CEPR Discussion Paper No. 1067*. London: Centre for Economic Policy Research.

Francois J.F., B. McDonald and H. Nordström. 1995. "Assessing the Uruguay Round". In W. Martin and L.A. Winters, eds., *The Uruguay Round and Developing Countries*. Discussion Paper no. 307 Washington D.C.: The World Bank.

Francois J.F., B. McDonald and H. Nordström. 1996. "A user's guide to Uruguay Round assessments", CEPR *Discussion Paper no. 1410.* London: Centre for Economic Policy Research.

GATT. 1985. *Trade Policies for a Better Future – Proposals for Action.* Geneva: General Agreement on Tariffs and Trade.

Goldin, I., D. Knudsen and D. van der Mensbrugghe. 1993. "Trade liberalization: Global economic implications". Paris: OECD, and Washington, D.C.: The World Bank.

Goldin I. and D. van der Mensbrugghe. 1995. "The Uruguay Round: an assessment of economywide and agricultural reforms". In W. Martin and L.A. Winters, eds., *The Uruguay Round and Developing Countries.* Discussion Paper no. 307. Washington, D.C.: The World Bank.

Harrold, P. 1995. "The impact of the Uruguay Round on Africa". *Discussion Paper no. 311.* Washington, D.C.: The World Bank.

Harrison, G.W., T.F. Rutherford and D.G. Tarr. 1995. "Quantifying the Uruguay Round". In W. Martin and L.A. Winters, eds., *The Uruguay Round and Developing Countries.* Discussion Paper no. 307. Washington, D.C.: The World Bank.

Harrison, G.W., T.F. Rutherford and D.G. Tarr. 1997. "Quantifying the Uruguay Round". *Economic Journal,* 107 (September): 1405–1430. (A revised version of Harrison, Rutherford and Tarr 1995).

Harrison, G.W. and H.D. Vinod. 1992. "The sensitivity analysis of applied general equilibrium models: Completely randomized factorial sampling design." Review of Economics and Statistics, 74 (May): 357–362.

Hathaway, D. and M. Ingco. 1995. "Agricultural liberalization and the Uruguay Round." In W. Martin and L.A. Winters, eds., *The Uruguay Round and Developing Countries.* Discussion Paper no. 307. Washington, D.C.: The World Bank.

Herin, J. 1986. "Rules of origin and differences between tariff levels in EFTA and the EU." *Occasional Paper no. 13.* Geneva: EFTA.

Hertel, T, W. Martin, K. Yanagisha and B. Dimaranan. 1995. "Liberalizing manufactures trade in a changing world economy." In W. Martin and L.A. Winters, eds., *The Uruguay Round and Developing Countries,* Discussion Paper no. 307. Washington, D.C.: The World Bank.

Hoekman, B. 1995a. "Assessing the General Agreement on trade in services." In W. Martin and L.A. Winters, eds., *The Uruguay Round and Develop-*

ing Countries, Discussion Paper no. 307. Washington, D.C.: The World Bank.

Hoekman, B. 1995b. "Trade laws and institutions: good practices and the World Trade Organization." *Discussion Paper no. 282*. Washington, D.C.: The World Bank.

Ingco, M. 1995. "Agriculture liberalization in the Uruguay Round: one step forward, one step back?" *Working Paper no. 1500*. Washington, D.C.: The World Bank.

Ingco, M. 1996. "Tariffication in the Uruguay Round: how much liberalization?" *World Economy* (July) 425–66.

Martin, W and L.A. Winters. eds. 1995a. *The Uruguay Round and the Developing Economies*. Discussion Paper no. 307. Washington, D.C.: The World Bank.

Martin, W and Winters. L.A. 1995b. The Uruguay Round: Widening and Deepening the World Trading System. Washington, D.C.: The World Bank.

Martin, W and Winters, L.A. eds., 1996. *The Uruguay Round and the Developing Economies*, Cambridge: Cambridge University Press (a revised version of Martin and Winters (1995a)

Mohieldin, M. 1997. "The Egypt-EU Partnership Agreement and liberalization of services." In A. Galal and B. Hoekman, eds., *Regional Partners in Global Markets: Limits and Possibilities of the Euro-Med Agreements*. London: CEPR and ECES.

Page, S. and M. Davenport. 1994. *World Trade Reform: Do Developing Countries Gain or Lose*? London: Overseas Development Institute.

ODI. 1994. "The impact of the GATT-Uruguay Round on ACP states: report for the ACP Secretariat". London: Overseas Development Institute.

ODI. 1995. "Developing countries in the WTO." *Briefing No. 3 (1995)*, Overseas Development Institute, May.

OECD. 1986. *International Trade and the Consumer*. Paris: Organization for Economic Cooperation and Development.

Oyejide, T.A. 1990. "The participation of developing countries in the Uruguay Round: an African perspective." *The World Economy*, vol. 13, no. 3: 427–444

Oyejide, T.A. 1997. "Trade policy and regional integration in the development context: Emerging patterns, issues and lessons for sub-Saharan

Africa." Paper prepared for the Plenary Session of the May 1997 Workshop of the African Economic Research Consortium, Nairobi.

Sorsa, P. 1995. "The Burden of sub-Saharan African own commitments in the Uruguay Round – Myth or reality?" *Working Paper* WP/95/48-EA. Washington, D.C.: International Monetary Fund.

Tylers, R. and R. Falvey. 1989. "Border price changes and domestic welfare in the presence of subsidized exports." *Oxford Economic Papers*, vol. 41: 434–51.

UNCTAD. 1996. *Developing Countries and the Uruguay Round*. Geneva: United Nations Conference on Trade and Development.

Wang, Z.K. and L.A. Winters. 1997. "Africa's Role in multilateral trade negotiations." *Policy Research Working Paper no. 1846*. The World Bank, November. (Revised version of a paper presented at the Plenary Session of the May 1997 AERC Research Workshop in Nairobi)

Winters, L.A. 1995a. "Who should run trade policy in Eastern Europe and how?" In L.A. Winters, ed., *Foundations of an Open Economy: Trade Laws and Institutions for Eastern Europe*, chapter 2, pp. 19–37. London: Centre for Economic Policy Research.

Winters, L.A. ed. 1995b. *Foundations of an Open Economy: Trade Laws and Institutions for Eastern Europe*. London: Centre for Economic Policy Research.

WTO. 1997. *The WTO and Developing Countries – An Interactive Guide*. http://www.wto.orglwto/download/wtodc.exe. Geneva: World Trade Organization.

Yates, A. 1994. "What are OECD trade preferences worth to sub-Saharan Africa?." *Working Paper 1254*. Washington, D.C.: The World Bank.

Chapter three

Markets and Market Access for African Exports: Past, Present and Future Directions

by Richard Blackhurst and William Lyakurwa

Acknowledgements

The authors would like to thank those who made helpful suggestions on an earlier draft presented at the October 1997 meeting in Accra, as well as Ulla Kask who provided excellent assistance with many of the statistics.

1. African Traditional and Non-Traditional Exports

A 1997 report to the UN Secretary General indicates that economic growth in Africa slowed to 3% from 4.4% in 1996 (UN, 1997). Declines in agricultural production and exports, as well as in oil prices, contributed to the slower growth. Given the significance of agriculture, low output also adversely affected income, consumption and the growth in the processing sectors. In some countries, political instability or civil strife negatively affected economic growth in 1997. Growth in Africa could slow even more if export growth is held back by the currency crisis and economic slowdown in East Asia, which has become the fastest-growing trading partner for some sub-Saharan African (SSA) countries.

In recent years, unlike the period of the mid 1980s, sub-Saharan African countries' exports have begun to show some signs of recovery. This may be attributed partly to the structural adjustment and trade liberalization measures adopted since the early 1980s. For example, Africa's exports grew by 12% in 1995 in value terms, a considerable improvement compared with the 3% of the previous year and the preceding three years of negative growth in value. However, Africa's export growth continued to lag behind world trade in both value and volume terms. Yeats and Ng (1996) in a study of 30 products exported by sub-Saharan African countries over the periods 1962–64 and 1991–93 have shown that while world trade in all non-fuel goods increased at a compound rate of 11.8%, the corresponding growth rate for 30 African products was more than six and half percentage points lower. Based on the available statistics, countries with growth in exports exceeding 20% included Angola, Central African Republic, Kenya, Reunion, Tanzania and Togo (WTO, 1996).

As can be observed in Appendix Table A1, merchandise exports for a number of sub-Saharan African countries experienced fluctuations over the period 1984 to 1995. Except for the period between 1991 and 1995, the trend for the majority of sub-Saharan African countries has generally been upwards.

Notable exceptions are Democratic Republic of Congo (DRC – ex-Zaire), where earnings declined from $2.5 billion in 1988 to $1.6 billion in 1995; Nigeria, where earnings dropped from $1.6 billion in 1990 to $1.1 billion in 1995; and South Africa, where earnings fell from $2.4 billion in 1990 to $1.9 billion in 1995.

The countries that experienced the highest rate of growth in export earnings in the late 1980s and early 1990s are those that suffered the worst decline in earnings in the late 1970s and early 1980s. These countries include Ghana, where earnings increased from $808 million in 1989 to $1.4 billion in 1995; Madagascar, where earnings increased from $314 million in 1990 to $639 million in 1995; and Tanzania, where earnings increased from $290 million in 1986 to $639 million in 1995 (Figure 3.1).

Agricultural raw material exports experienced much higher degrees of fluctuation in export earnings than did mineral and oil exports. Figure 3.2 shows that the shares of sub-Saharan African countries in world exports generally declined in all categories of resource-based exports for the period 1970–95. As a percentage of total world exports, sub-Saharan Africa's share dropped from 0.8% in 1970 to about 0.3% in 1995 (Figure 3.3).

Figure 3.1: Merchandise exports of selected countries, 1980–1995 (000's US dollars)

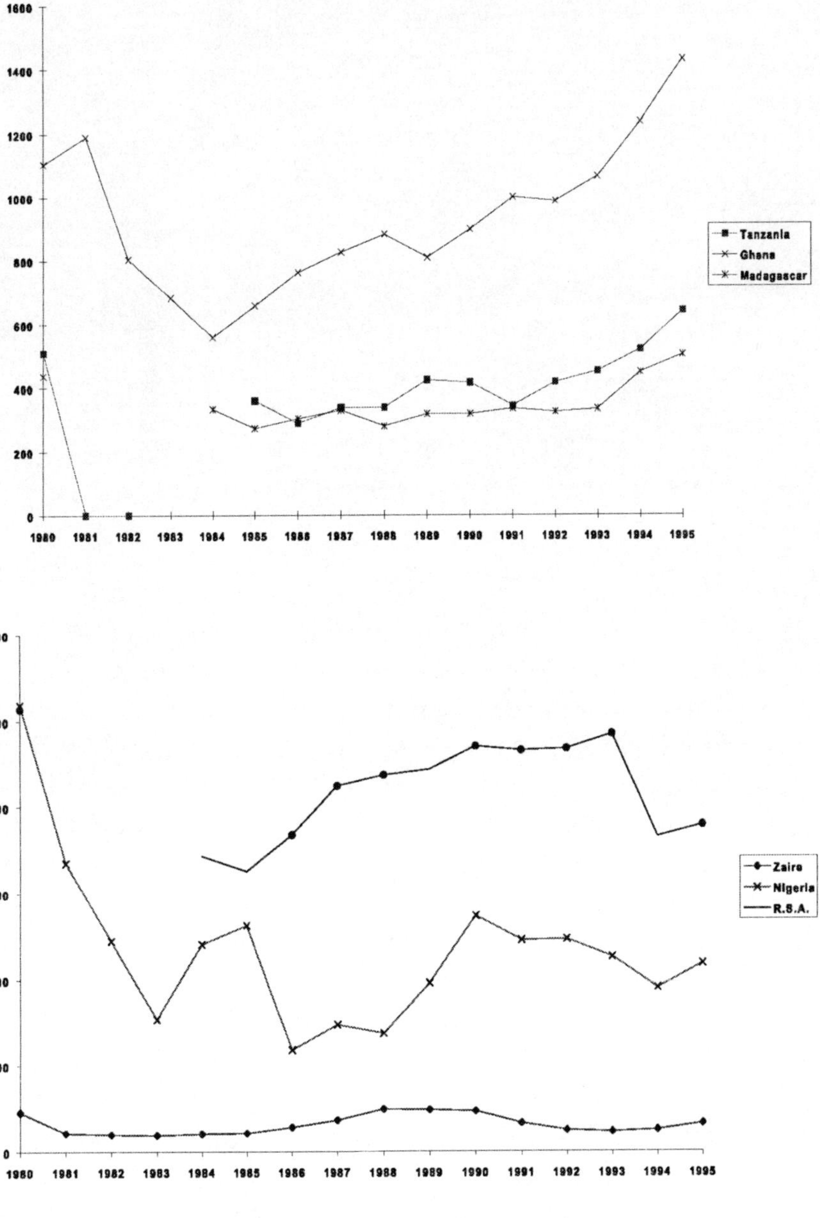

Source: Appendix Table 3A1.

Figure 3.2: Shares of sub-Saharan African countries in world exports of primary commodities, 1970–1995 (percentages)

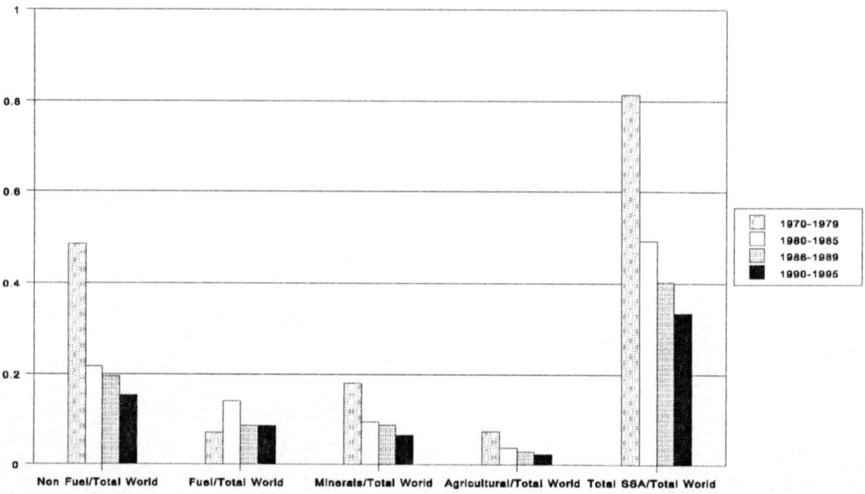

Source: Appendix Table 3A2.

Table 3.1 indicates that most sub-Saharan African countries are essentially primary commodity exporters, where the share of primary commodity exports as a proportion of total merchandise exports has remained high – above 70% in most countries except Mauritius and Zimbabwe. However, Kenya and Seychelles experienced significant improvements in export diversification, with the share of primary commodity exports in total merchandise exports declining from 94% in 1980 to 71% in 1993 for Kenya and from 97% to 71% for Seychelles. Countries where the share of primary commodities in total exports remained low in 1993 include Botswana (13%), Lesotho (14%) and Swaziland (43%).

Not only do most sub-Saharan African countries depend on primary commodity exports, but export earnings are also highly concentrated in a few primary products. Table 3.2 shows, for example, that some countries depend on three commodities for as much as 90% of their total merchandise exports, and for most of the countries the figure is above 50%. Countries with very high export concentration include Angola, Uganda, Seychelles, Nigeria, Zambia and Gabon. All except Uganda are mineral and oil export-

Table 3.1: Share of primary commodities in all merchandise trade values

Region (country or area)	Exports of primary commodities as a percent of total exports: (A) Excluding fuels				(B) Including fuels			
	1975	1980	1990	1993	1975	1980	1990	1993
CENTRAL AFRICA								
Cameroon	89.2	63.3	44.6	44.9	89.5	92.6	95.6	86.1
Cent. African Rep	83.5	84.5	68.2	46.3	83.6	84.5	68.2	46.3
Gabon	15.4	18.9	26.4	24.8	94.9	99.2	99.0	99.0
Zaire	98.0	60.5	83.6	66.5	99.0	72.8	99.0	99.0
EASTERN AFRICA								
Ethiopia	83.6	92.3	85.7	95.6	86.6	99.7	91.7	96.5
Kenya	53.0	58.6	72.9	59.5	69.7	93.8	85.9	70.9
Mozambique	82.2	75.1	84.0	91.8	93.4	80.0	85.1	93.4
Uganda	99.0	98.2	99.0	99.0	99.0	99.0	99.0	99.0
Tanzania	79.4	85.4	73.7	77.4	84.4	90.2	73.9	77.9
SOUTHERN AFRICA								
Angola	31.7	10.0	0.3	0.5	96.0	88.7	92.9	76.2
Botswana	64.0	37.5	14.5	13.1	64.0	37.5	14.5	13.1
Lesotho	77.7	27.5	22.1	14.0	77.7	27.5	22.1	14.0
Malawi	88.2	86.0	91.6	88.1	88.3	86.2	91.6	88.1
Swaziland	80.0	79.0	83.3	43.2	80.0	79.0	83.3	43.2
Zimbabwe	71.7	51.9	57.3	63.3	73.1	53.2	58.0	63.7
WESTERN AFRICA								
Côte d'Ivoire	82.0	84.1	64.3	76.9	87.6	86.3	78.2	98.1
Ghana	86.0	87.6	93.6	73.6	88.5	87.9	97.7	80.0
Nigeria	6.3	2.0	2.3	2.5	99.0	95.5	95.7	89.3
Senegal	82.7	65.7	68.7	37.3	89.7	84.5	81.7	48.3
ISLAND STATES								
Madagascar	87.3	91.3	78.1	82.3	95.9	97.1	78.6	82.7
Mauritius	87.6	71.4	33.2	31.4	87.6	71.4	34.6	31.4
Seychelles	33.1	23.9	24.6	32.0	99.0	96.9	68.2	71.1

Source: UNCTAD Commodity Yearbook 1995, United Nations.

Table 3.2: Share of three leading commodities in total exports

	Export dependence on three leading commodities		Dependence on three non-oil commodities		Three leading commodities in 1990–92
	avg 75–77	avg 90–92	avg 75–77	avg 90–92	
CENTRAL AFRICA					
Cameroon	69.1	81.0	69.1	25.8	Fuels – woods – coffee
C. African Rep.	69.9	55.7	69.9	55.7	Wood non coniferous – live animals – cotton
Gabon	91.0	99.0	15.3	19.2	Fuels – manganese ore – wood
Zaire	83.5	81.5	81.6	59.5	Copper – fuels – coffee
EASTERN AFRICA					
Ethiopia	70.5	79.0	70.5	78.0	Coffee – hides & skins – fuels
Kenya	60.5	56.0	44.9	45.6	Tea – coffee – fuels
Mozambique	48.0	58.1	46.3	58.1	Fishery commodities – nuts – cotton
Uganda	97.9	81.5	97.9	81.5	Coffee – cotton – sesame seeds
Tanzania	52.5	43.5	52.5	43.5	Cotton – coffee – tea
SOUTHERN AFRICA					
Angola	99.0	94.5	24.9	0.3	Fuels – fishery commodities – coffee
Botswana	61.9	10.4	61.9	10.4	Nickel intermediate products – bovine meat fresh – copper ore
Lesotho	48.3	11.1	48.3	11.1	Wool – cereals preparations – wheat & wheat flour
Malawi	78.2	88.8	78.2	88.8	Tobacco – tea – sugar

	Export dependence on three leading commodities		Dependence on three non-oil commodities		Three leading commodities in 1990–92
	avg 75–77	avg 90–92	avg 75–77	avg 90–92	
Swaziland	47.2	33.3	47.2	33.3	Sugar – fuels – fishery commodities
Zambia	93.2	99.0	93.2	99.0	Copper metal – sugar – groundnuts
Zimbabwe	25.2	53.0	25.2	53.0	Tobacco – nickel refined – cotton
WESTERN AFRICA					
Côte d'Ivoire	75.7	55.0	75.7	48.1	Cocoa & products – fuels – wood
Ghana	83.1	67.4	83.1	67.4	Cocoa & products – aluminum – wood
Nigeria	97.5	99.0	4.9	1.8	Fuels – cocoa & products – natural rubber
Senegal	59.5	49.3	59.5	43.8	Fishery commodities – fuels – groundnut oil
ISLAND STATES					
Madagascar	59.5	43.4	59.5	43.4	Vanilla – fishery commodities – coffee
Mauritius	79.6	32.3	79.6	31.2	Sugar – fuels – fishery commodities
Seychelles	99.0	78.6	30.4	30.6	Fuels – fishery commodities – copra

Source: UNCTAD Commodity Yearbook, United Nations (1995).

ers. African countries' exports are also concentrated in a few markets, mainly the European Union, North America and Japan. As stressed below, this has implications for efforts to increase both product and market diversification.

Yeats and Ng (1996) have shown that for a combined total of 30 African export products, covering the period 1962–64 and 1991–93 Africa's market share declined by over 11 percentage points (from 20.8% to 9.7%), which implies annual trade losses for the region of just under $11 billion – equivalent to the total development assistance of $10.9 billion in 1991. Which countries or groups of countries were gaining market shares as sub-Saharan Africa's share was declining? Primarily the OECD countries. In addition, market shares for middle income Asia rose by over 4 percentage points, while those for non-OECD Europe and central Asia increased by almost the same amount. Latin America's trade shares, in contrast, declined but by only about one-third as much as the decline in Africa's share. The key point to note is that no other country group has experienced a loss of market share – erosion of competitive position – that comes close to matching that of Africa.

Over the decade of the 1980s, for example, there were rapid declines in the share of world exports for both Ghana and Zambia. Ghana's merchandise export earnings declined from $1.1 billion in 1980 to $560 million in 1984, recovered to $890 million by 1990 and have continued on an upward trend since 1990, primarily because of structural adjustment and trade liberalization measures under way since the early 1980s. Zambia, on the other hand, saw its merchandise export earnings drop from $1.46 billion in 1980 to $550 million in 1985 because of a very sharp drop in world copper prices (the main export product). The trend, though fluctuating, has been reversed since 1987. Rates of growth of GDP and per capita GNP have declined sharply in both countries. Is this purely a case of lack of market access, of a terms of trade shock, of domestic supply constraints or a combination of all three factors? We return to this question below.

Sekkat and Varoudakis (1998) and Elbadawi (1998) have shown that the evolution of the share of manufacturing in total exports has remained extremely low in most sub-Saharan African countries, although some countries have made considerable progress. The most remarkable examples are Côte d'Ivoire and Mali in the Franc Zone, and Ghana, Madagascar and Tanzania (during the 1990s) in the non Franc Zone, each of which achieved a steady increase in the export share of manufacturing (Figure 3.3; see also Appendix Table 3A3).

Mauritius has been particularly successful in promoting manufactured exports, mainly through a reliance on export processing zones (EPZ). Starting in the 1970s, with a share of manufactures in exports below that of Kenya, and with a share of manufacturing value added in GDP lower than Senegal's, manufactured exports in the first half of the 1990s reached more than two-thirds of Mauritius' total exports (Elbadawi, 1998). As for the relative importance of non-traditional exports as an indicator of export diversification, the sub-Saharan African countries still lag behind the fast growing economies of East Asia, but are comparable to Latin America. For sub-Saharan Africa, the share of non-traditional exports in GDP in 1994/95 was 3.8% compared with 9.2% for East Asia and 3.6% for Latin America. The best performers have been South Africa (5.7%), Tanzania (8.8%) and Zimbabwe (7.1%) (Figure 3.1; also Appendix Table 3A1).

A broad overview of historical trends is very helpful in "setting the scene" and putting the analysis in perspective – in other words, for explaining why the issues being examined are important. The next stage in developing policy relevant analysis is to move to a more detailed and disaggregated examination of the current situation.

Leading current exports from 20 African countries

One of the principal themes of this paper it that the analysis of a country's traditional and non-traditional exports and export markets must be done at a *highly* disaggregated level. This is true because – for most purposes – data on market access barriers are meaningful only at a highly disaggregated level. Granted, for general trade policy discussions it is useful to know, for example, that the European Union's average tariff on fish and fish products is far above the average for all EU goods. But no country or firm actually exports "fish and fish products". They export one or more very narrowly defined categories that vary by type of fish and degree of processing and, similarly, the tariffs and non-tariff barriers they encounter can vary enormously within what appears to the non-specialist to be a more or less homogeneous product category. (One of the main reasons why national tariff nomenclature is so highly disaggregated – often 15,000 to 20,000 separate items – is the desire of governments to give special protection to certain firms producing particular narrowly defined products.)

BASIC DATA

The most disaggregated internationally comparable trade data are six-digit Harmonized System (HS) data taken from the UN COMTRADE database (HS trade data are better than SITC trade data because trade barrier data are available in HS). At the time of writing, the latest year for which com-

Figure 3.3: Share of manufacturing exports in total exports

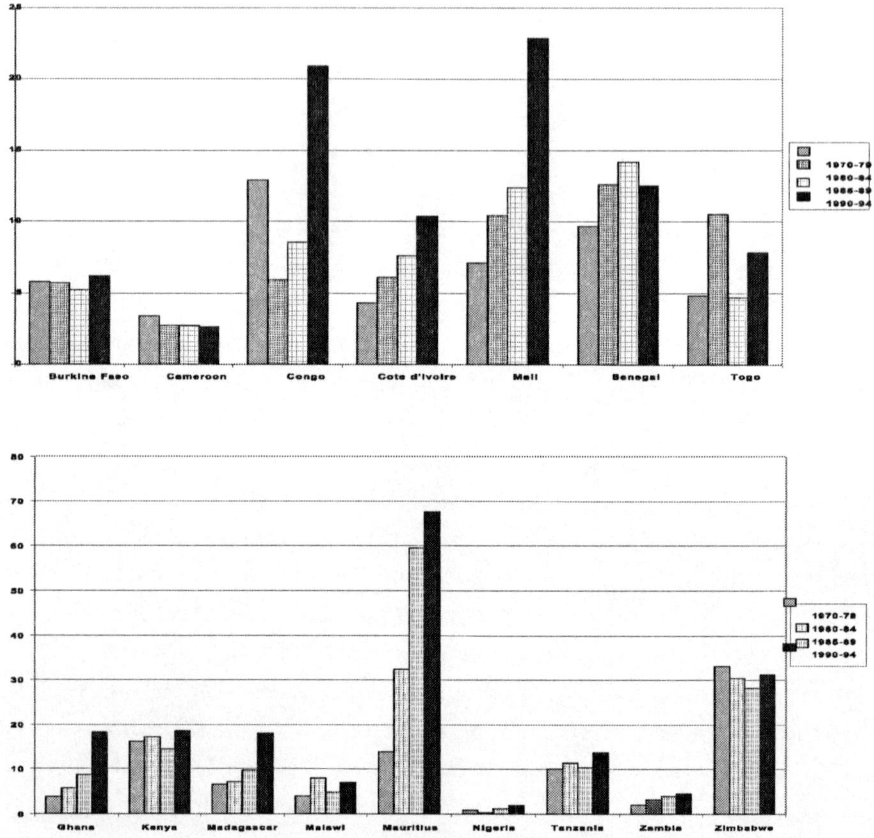

Source: Appendix Table 3A3.

plete data were available was 1995. Our analysis is based on data for the 20 sub-Saharan African countries listed in Table 3.3 (actually 19 countries plus SACU). This is a reasonable cross section of countries: 9 of the 20 are classified by the UN as least developed countries (LDCs) and 2 – Ethiopia and the Seychelles – are not yet members.

Our "export" data are actually partner import data from an aggregate of 23 major importing countries that in 1995 purchased well over 90% of world exports of goods and services. The reason for choosing this particular group of partner countries is that it is the one used in the 1997 WTO study from which we take much of our data on trade barriers confronting Africa's

Table 3.3: The 20 exporters in our sample: Merchandise "exports" in 1995 to 23 countries

Total (millions $)	Country[a]	Leading six-digit categories[b]	Six-digit categories in excess of $1 million
17,976	SACU	33	787
12,129	Nigeria	2	66
3,155	Côte d'Ivoire	9	90
2,611	Gabon	4	20
1,619	Cameroon	9	42
1,490	Congo, D.R.	5	40
1,477	Mauritius	25	100
1,459	Zimbabwe	26	125
1,340	Ghana	11	58
1,181	Kenya	20	71
875	*Zambia*	3	27
563	*Madagascar*	15	55
563	*Tanzania*	30	55
525	*Uganda*	2	15
395	*Ethiopia*	4	24
381	Senegal	14	35
362	*Malawi*	4	27
225	*Mozambique*	8	22
139	Central African Rep.	6	7
44	Seychelles	7	5

[a] Italics indicate a country the UN classifies as a least developed country.

[b] Six-digit HS categories that account for 3% or more of total merchandise "exports" to the 23 country aggregate, except in cases in which the "3% and above categories" do not account for at least 75% of total merchandise "exports" to the aggregate. In which case the largest categories accounting for less than 3% were added in descending order until the 75% figure was reached.

Source: UN COMTRADE.

exports (the 23 countries, which are listed in Appendix Table 3A4, include all of the OECD countries except Mexico, plus Poland and 13 of the larger traders among the developing countries; it also includes SACU, one of our 20 African exporters).[1]

CURRENT LEADING EXPORTS

The first step was to identify the leading six-digit export product groups for each of our 20 countries (see the note to Table 3.3 for the definition of "leading export"). For the 20 countries as a whole, there are a total of 136 leading exports.[2]

If there were a complete overlap of product groups among the 20 countries' leading exports, there would be a total of 33 six-digit product groups (the number for SACU), whereas if there were zero overlap there would be 237 different leading exports (the sum of the figures in column 3). Our figure of 136 leading exports lies almost exactly half way between those two extremes. *The substantial diversity of export structures among the 20 countries is evident from the fact that two-thirds (91) of the 136 leading exports appear on only one of the 20 lists of leading exports.*

CURRENT EXPORT DIVERSIFICATION

"Export diversity" is not only a relative concept, but also a subjective one. One criterion might be based on the presumption that the number of leading six-digit export groups should be positively related to the level of total exports (in other words, that larger traders are expected to have more diversified export structures). If SACU is excluded, the mean and median values of the figures in column three of Table 3.3 are 10.7 and 9, respectively (with SACU they are 11.8 and 8.5, respectively). By this criterion, Côte d'Ivoire, Cameroon and Ghana are the "typical" countries *among the 20 in our sample.* Four countries exhibit well above average *relative* export diversity – Tanzania, Zimbabwe, Mauritius and Senegal. (Considering the difference in the size of total exports, it could be said that SACU's exports are much less diversified than the exports of these four countries.) At the other end of the spectrum, six countries exhibit well below average export diversity – Nigeria, Gabon, DRC, Zambia, Uganda and Ethiopia.

The picture changes, but not dramatically, if the criterion is the number of six-digit product groups for which exports exceed $1 million (again we might expect a positive correlation with the size of total exports). If SACU is excluded, the mean value of the figures in column four of Table 3.3 is 46.5 (83.6 with SACU) and the median is 55. Nigeria moves much closer to the norm for the 20 countries, Côte d'Ivoire improves, Zimbabwe and Mauritius continue to exhibit well above average export diversity, and SACU achieves an export diversity much more in line with the total value of its merchandise exports. The typical countries among our 20 by this criterion are Cameroon, Madagascar, Tanzania and Ghana.

At the two-digit level, the HS classification covering the entire range of goods is divided into 21 broad "sections" (product groups). Yet another measure of export diversity (not shown in Table 3.3) is how many of those 21 broad product groups are represented in each country's list of leading six-digit exports – in other words, to what extent do a county's leading six-digit export categories range across the expanse of those 21 broad product groups? Once again, Nigeria and SACU define the two extremes (1 and 11, respectively). But there is a narrowing of the variation among the countries. For example, by this measure the merchandise exports of Senegal and Mozambique are as diversified as those of Mauritius and Kenya (7 out of 21 sections represented) and only marginally less so than those of Tanzania (8) and Zimbabwe (9).

PER CAPITA EXPORTS AND INCOME

Table 3.4 provides figures on per capita exports of goods *and services*, based on the countries' own statistics for exports to *all destinations*, and purchasing-power-parity-based per capita income estimates for the 20 African countries. The export figures vary enormously, from an estimated $9 per person in Mozambique to $3,743 for the Seychelles, with a median value of $98. While the three countries with the highest per capita exports – the Seychelles, Gabon and Mauritius – have the three smallest populations among the 20 countries, it is also the case that South Africa (SACU) has the fourth highest exports per capita and the fourth largest population among the 20 countries.

Service exports, presumably mainly earnings from tourism in most instances, are exceptionally important for the Seychelles (four times larger than exports of goods), and play an important role in a number of the other countries. Estimates of the share of services in total exports of goods and

Table 3.4: Per capita trade and GNP (US dollars)

Country	1995 exports of goods and services[a]	1996 PPP-based GNP	Country	1995 exports of goods and services	1996 PPP-based GNP
Seychelles	3,734	–	Nigeria	96	870
Gabon	2,647	6,300	Ghana	88	1,790
Mauritius	2,101	9,000	Central Afr. Rep	57	1,430
SACU[b]	760	7,450	Malawi	45	690
Côte d'Ivoire	314	1,580	Tanzania	39	–
Zimbabwe	217	2,200	Madagascar	38	900
Cameroon	177	1,760	Congo, D.R.	32[c]	790
Senegal	138	1,650	Uganda	23[c]	1,030
Zambia	128	860	Ethiopia	13	500
Kenya	99	1,130	Mozambique	9[c]	500

[a] Based on each country's own export data, except for the DRC, for which the import figure of the 23-country aggregate was used. Services data are for 1995 except that in five instances it was necessary to use 1994 data, in two instances 1993 data and in one instance 1991 data.

[b] South Africa only.

[c] Exports of goods (merchandise) only.

PPP – purchasing power parity

Sources: UN COMTRADE, TWO Annual Report 1997; UN World Population, 1996; World Bank World Development Indicators, 1998.

services range from 32% to 46% for (in ascending order) Kenya, Mauritius, Madagascar, Ethiopia and Tanzania.

A comparison of the per capita export and income estimates in Table 3.4 – where the countries are ranked in descending order of exports – confirms the generally positive relationship of the two series. Using the 20 countries as the point of comparison, Zambia's per capita exports are larger than would be expected from its per capita income, while Ghana, the Central

African Republic and – especially – Uganda have lower levels of exports per capita than would be expected.

THE MOST IMPORTANT EXPORTS

As our intention is to present reasonably detailed data on trade barriers facing Africa's key exports, 136 products is an unwieldy number. Using a dual "size/frequency" criterion, we have narrowed the list of current leading exports to the "most important exports" for our group of 20 countries.

Appendix Table 2A6 lists those current leading exports that meet either of two criteria: Part A lists the 25 most important on the basis of export value for the aggregate of the 20 countries, while Part B lists the 25 that appear most frequently on the 20 countries' individual lists of leading exports (products with the same frequency were ranked in descending order of the value of exports).[3]

The 17 six-digit products that appear on *both* the value and frequency lists – our definition of the most important – are shown in Table 3.5. There are no surprises in the table. All of the products are either agricultural (including timber) or mineral based, and range from unprocessed to partially processed. Noticeable differences between the two rankings include cotton (fifteenth in terms of aggregate value, but second in terms of the frequency with which it is a leading export), tuna (sixteenth in value versus fifth in frequency) and tea (twenty-fourth in value versus sixth in frequency).

Potentially important non-traditional exports

Postwar experience suggests that (for most countries) a heavy reliance on exports of primary commodities significantly reduces the contribution trade can make to economic development. Thus when analysts are working with countries whose current exports are very heavily concentrated in a relatively small number of primary products, and whose export performance over the past decade or so has been conspicuously disappointing, it is not surprising that there is a great deal of interest in exploring the potential for developing "non-traditional exports". When the exports of a country or group of countries are very heavily concentrated on certain foreign markets – as most of Africa's exports are on the EU market – it is also worthwhile to explore the options for expanding traditional exports to non-traditional foreign markets.

Table 3.5: The most important merchandise exports of our group of 20 African countries

090111 (2nd, 12)	Coffee, not roasted not decaffeinated	440722 (19th, 4)	Lumber, okoume, obech, sapelli, sipo, acajou, makore, etc.
090240 (24th, 5)	Tea, black (fermented or partly) in P kgs>3 kg	520100 (15th, 7)	Cotton, not carded or combed
160414 (16th, 6)	Tuna, skipjack, bonito, prepared/perserved Not mince	710210 (11th, 3)	Diamonds, unsorted
170111 (10th, 6)	Raw sugar cane	710231 (9th, 6)	Diamond (jewellery) unworked or simply awn, cleaved
180100 (4th, 4)	Cocoa beans, whole or broken, raw or roasted	720239 (9th, 6)	Diamonds (jewellery) worked, but not mounted or set
240120 (13th, 3)	Tobacco, unmfg'dstemmed or stripped	720241 (8th, 2)	Ferro-chromium >4% carbon
270900 (1st, 4)	Petroleum oils, oils from bituminous minerals, crude	740311 (12th, 3)	Copper cathodes and sections of cathodes unwrounght
440334 (17th, 3)	Logs: okoume, obeche, sapelli, sipo, acajou d'Afrique, etc.	810510 (22nd, 3)	Cobalt, unwrought, matte, waste or scrap, powders
440399	Logs, non-coniferous, nes		

Notes: See text for definition of "most important." The figures in parentheses indicate, respectively, the ranking of each product among all 136 products in terms of value, and the number of times each product appears on the list of leading products of each of the 20 counties. For example, the first product – 090111 – ranks second out of 136 in terms of the total value of exports of the 20 countries, and it appears on the list of leading exports of 12 of our 20 countries.

Source: Compiled by authors.

Exploring the prospects for, and the policies needed to promote, non-traditional exports is an unusually challenging topic. Because of space and time limitations, the treatment in this paper is limited to a few general observations related to domestic conditions that create a favourable "climate" for export diversification. Work on non-traditional exports that goes beyond an in-depth analysis of such conditions – that is, that moves on to an examination of the prospects of specific products – inevitably involves a large element of attempting to "pick winners". It may be too strong to say that experience has completely discredited such efforts, but there certainly is no empirical basis for claiming that this is a promising route to developing internationally competitive exports.

A wider project on Growth, External Sector and the Role of Non-Traditional Exports in sub-Saharan Africa (headed by Gerry Helleiner) has already produced material that is very useful in getting started on this topic.[4] Among the insights in Helleiner (1997) are:

- Sub-Saharan Africa's endowments of relatively abundant natural resources and relatively scarce human skills appear to offer little hope of developing significant manufacturing for export in the near future, except in some unskilled labour intensive primary processing activities. (p. 4)
- Sub-Saharan Africa's best strategic course is almost certainly consciously to build upon its primary production base; in most cases, this means smallholder agriculture. (p. 7)
- Trade theory and policy have unduly dominated development discussion. In actual fact, trade typically *follows* developments in publicly provided infrastructure, other malleable endowments and prior *private investment decisions.* To the degree that private investments are influenced by governments at all, they are usually, in large part, the product of other (non-trade) kinds of policies. (p. 6, emphasis in the original)
- *Generalized* encouragement of exports, particularly via "sound" exchange rate management, meets with widespread approval in Africa today. On the other hand, more *directed* and *selective* policies to meet expansion objectives are more controversial. Further, the building of appropriate *capabilities* and *institutions,*

where action is much more difficult to quantify, may be as critical to success as incentive structures (which seem to have proven insufficient in recent African experience). (p. 8, emphasis in the original)[5]

- The credibility, basically the predictability, of African governments' own trade (and other) policies is fundamental to their effects. If private decision makers do not think the new incentive structures or institutions are likely to be sustained they will not respond in the expected development-oriented way. Sustainability (stability) of policies is therefore likely to be far more important than technocratic "perfection" – not only in trade matters but in general. (pp. 8–9)
- Africans can usefully draw on others' related experiences, particularly in low income (or recently low income) Asia. The advantage of the African "latecomer" lies not only in the possibility of technological "catch-up" but also in the possibility of learning from others' experiences, positive and negative, with alternative patterns, processes of change and policies. (p. 9)

These various points cover much of the territory transversed by the growing literature on meeting the pressing need to improve the supply-side response throughout sub-Saharan Africa.

In the effort to expand and diversify African exports, the transport sector is an important example of a priority area for reform. Data presented in Yeats (1997) demonstrate conclusively that unnecessarily high transport costs put African exports at an important cost disadvantage vis-a-vis exports from competitors.[6] Moreover, he adds, "The structure of African transport costs also seems to have an important adverse impact on the types of goods exported ..." often working "... against local processing of domestically produced commodities" (p. 19). He continues, "Evidence suggests that the anticompetitive cargo reservation policies adopted by most African governments have had a major adverse influence on freight costs. So, the answer is clearly deregulation." (p. 19, footnote omitted)

DON'T NEGLECT TRADITIONAL EXPORTS

There is absolutely no doubt that for trade to be a strong stimulus to development and growth in Africa, the composition of exports needs to shift towards more processed goods, including manufactures. At the same time, the discussion of transport costs calls attention to the more general point that Africa's poor export performance cannot be blamed entirely on the product composition of current exports. It would be unfortunate if an excessive concern with promoting non-traditional exports were to lead to a neglect of the potential to expand traditional exports – especially in those cases where governments pursue activist interventions in the market, *since there is no way for government policies to favour one industry without disadvantaging other industries.*

The option of promoting traditional exports in non-traditional markets – which for most African countries means everywhere outside the EU – has already been mentioned. Two other considerations argue against neglecting traditional exports. First, in the case of traditional markets, the necessary export/marketing chains are already well established. Second, because sub-Saharan Africa is a very small supplier in the world market for most of its exports, the *excess* elasticity of demand for *its exports* (as distinct from the elasticity of demand for each of those exports from all sources) can be quite high.[7]

A 1996 World Bank study argues along similar lines, calling into question the conventional wisdom that "commodity dependence" is always bad for economic growth.[8] The authors conclude (Yabuki and Akiyama, 1996: 40):

> Problems often associated with commodity-dependence do not arise because of commodity-dependence per-se and … can be alleviated through appropriate policies. … In other words, … countries can be both commodity dependent and have high export and income growth.
>
> An examination of the components of successful commodity sectors in various countries strongly suggests that it is the initiatives and innovative actions of the private sector that make these commodity sectors dynamic and vibrant. Such successful cases are found in the coffee sector in Uganda, the gold mines in Ghana, and the cut-flower industry in Colombia. Transfers of foreign capital and technology that have played important roles

in developing new commodity and processing industries in a number of countries are best achieved when the private sector takes the initiative.

... important roles for governments to play ... include eliminating price controls and state monopolies, promoting research and development, developing infrastructure in transportation and communication, enticing foreign capital and technology transfers, and establishing a legal system for the use of innovative financial instruments.

DO WTO RULES RESTRICT EFFORTS TO IMPROVE THE SUPPLY-SIDE RESPONSE?

A reasonably complete answer to this question would involve first preparing an inventory of policies that have been advocated as solutions to supply-side rigidities, and then systematically going through the WTO rules and disciplines at a detailed level to see which of those policies are covered by the rules and disciplines, and – for those that are covered – what the rules and disciplines permit or do not permit. Even then, however, there would remain a number of uncertainties. This is because there are "grey" areas surrounding nearly all the rules and disciplines that can only be definitively clarified by decisions of WTO dispute settlement panels and the Appellate Body.[9]

Such an answer would also distinguish between the eight WTO members among our 20 countries that are least developed countries and the ten that are not, since the LDCs are allowed more latitude in certain circumstances. (The two non-members, Ethiopia and the Seychelles, are of course not bound by WTO rules, but the fact that the Seychelles is in the process of acceding to the WTO is no doubt nudging the trade regime in the direction of WTO conformity.) Because they are developing countries, the ten that are not LDCs also get some additional latitude vis-a-vis the obligations of the developed countries, but much less than that available to the LDCs.

In the latter part of 1998 the WTO Secretariat published a *Guide to the Uruguay Round Agreements* (the official report, *The Results of the Uruguay Round of Multilateral Negotiations: The Legal Texts*, is an exceptionally reader unfriendly publication, partly because of the rhetoric but mostly because of its organization). In addition to explaining the results of the Uruguay Round in a straightforward and easy to understand way, the new *Guide* contains a

24-page synopsis of provisions concerning developing countries and LDCs that greatly facilitates the identification of special provisions for these two groups of countries.

On a general level, the special treatment for LDCs is most evident in the Marrakesh Decision on Measures in Favour of Least-Developed Countries. As the *Guide* notes (pp. 226–27), the substance of the Decision includes the following:

- While complying with the general rules set out in the Uruguay Round agreements and related accords, LDCs will only be required to apply individual commitments, obligations and concessions that are consistent with their individual development, financial and trade needs, or their institutional capabilities. [Para. 1]
- The rules and transitional provisions resulting from the Round should be applied in a flexible and supportive manner to LDC members. This includes any determinations and authorizations that might be made by WTO councils and committees in different situations involving LDCs (such as extensions of transition periods, time-limited exemptions, etc.). [Para 2(iii)]

These general points are in addition to instances in which LDCs are explicitly subject to fewer obligations or easier rules. To take just one example, and again quoting from the *Guide* (p. 230), under the Agreement on Agriculture, "LDCs are not required to undertake reduction commitments in agricultural market access, domestic support or export subsidies [Article 15.2]." Under that same agreement, developing countries other than LDCs "do not have the commitment to reduce certain domestic support measures which are an integral part of their development programs (investment subsidies which are generally available to agriculture and agricultural input subsidies generally available to low-income or resource-poor producers [Article 6.2]." Part Five of the new *Guide* details numerous other special provisions, including those in the Agreement on Subsidies and Countervailing Duties.

For those who believe that the textbook infant industry argument finds meaningful support in the real world experience of developing countries during the past two or three decades, and that such protection has a role in overcoming domestic supply constraints, it will be comforting to know that the WTO rules allow a country (that is already a WTO member) to have any level of protection it desires, subject to three easy-to-meet conditions: it must be tariff protection (no quantitative restrictions, except in well-defined special circumstances), it must be applied on an MFN basis (regional integration agreements being a permitted exception), and it must not involve raising a bound tariff above the bound level. Moreover, should the first or third condition prove too burdensome, the country would have recourse to the seldom-used GATT Article XVIII:C.

Analysts with an interventionist bent, and who are confident (1) that governments in sub-Saharan Africa have the necessary design and implementation capabilities to intervene effectively in the economy at a fairly disaggregated level *and* (2) that interventionist programmes will not be captured and distorted by special interest groups, view this combination of fewer WTO obligations and eased rules for developing countries – especially for LDCs – as providing an important degree of "flexibility" in the search for policies to improve the domestic supply response. Other analysts, skeptical that either of these conditions holds anywhere – least of all today in sub-Saharan Africa – and concerned about the stability (predictability) of African trade regimes, and the associated problem of creating policy credibility vis-a-vis foreign and domestic investors, view this added "room for maneuver" in the use of trade-related policies as a serious disservice to the WTO's developing country members.

2. Market Access Barriers Facing African Exports

Market access for their exports does *not* rank high on the list of problems currently confronting sub-Saharan African countries. In the last decade or two, for example, exports from many developing countries in Asia and Latin America, with less favourable access to the EU market (they do not receive Lomé preferences), have out-performed Africa's exports to the EU by a wide margin. Inadequate domestic supply response, not the level of market access abroad, is the explanation of Africa's poor export performance.

It is also the case, however, that a new round of multilateral trade negotiations under the WTO is expected to be launched in late 1999. Agriculture and services will be on the agenda for certain, but there are a number of other candidates for the agenda as well – including further tariff cuts and bindings on industrial products, state trading, government procurement, competition policies, investment policies, and reform of the rules governing free trade areas and customs unions. The upcoming round of negotiations may well determine the level and pattern of protection in WTO countries for the next 15 to 20 years – that is, the pattern and level of protection in the period when Africa's efforts to improve its domestic supply response, *if successful*, will begin to pay off in enhanced export competitiveness.

Thus, while the focus of efforts must be on improving the domestic supply response, African governments cannot afford to neglect the preparations, already under way for the new round. They need to be active in Geneva and in the capitals of important trading partners – potential as well as current – lobbying to get topics of interest to them on the agenda.

Preparing for the new round involves two distinct categories of policy analysis and planning for African governments: one is concerned with foreign obstacles to Africa's exports and the prospects for negotiating reductions in or elimination of those barriers; the other involves each African government deciding which of its own import barriers it would be willing to reduce and by how much. This section of our paper is intended to be an input into the first category of analysis and planning for the new round. The final section of the paper includes some material that is relevant to the second category of Africa's preparations for the new round.

Selecting import markets and barriers to be examined

As was noted above, our analysis of Africa's exports focuses on the 23 major importing countries (counting the EU member states as one) used by the WTO Secretariat in preparing data on trade barriers for the October 1997 meeting on LDC trade issues. For two of the products (diamond jewellery worked but not mounted, and ferro-chromium > 4% carbon) information was available for only a small number of importing countries.

Those tables – a sample of which is provided in Appendix Table 3A4 – provide information generally for each of the importing countries, on (1) five types of tariffs (the post-Uruguay Round bound MFN tariff, the applied MFN tariff, the GSP/GSTP tariff, the tariff applicable to imports from LDCs and "other" non-MFN tariffs); (2) quantitative restrictions;[10] and (3) other duties and charges. Even a cursory look at the tables makes it clear why work on market access barriers at a highly disaggregated level (the only level that really matters for most purposes) is so challenging. Not only is it difficult and time consuming to compile the information, but much of it risks being out of date within a short time (the bound MFN rate is the only import barrier for which it is possible to be reasonably confident that it will not change until the next multilateral negotiation). It is also evident from the tables that the six-digit HS level is not sufficiently disaggregated for a number of products (for example, when the figure in the "MFN tariff" column shows a range – say 0–10 – it means that different rates are applied within the six-digit category).

It is not easy to summarize the information in the 17 tables covering our products. In terms of buying power and/or population, the major actual or potential markets among the 23 importing countries are the EU, the United States, Japan, China and India. An impressionistic summary of the information in the tables for the 17 products suggests the following overview:

- *European Union:* With the exception of South Africa, each of our 20 African countries receives Lomé preferences (and South Africa is negotiating a free trade agreement with the EU). For 12 of the 15 products for which we have EU data, these preferences are non-operative because the post-Uruguay Round bound rate is zero (the three exceptions are prepared or preserved tuna/skipjack/bonito, raw cane sugar, and tobacco). The Sugar Protocol provides important benefits to certain of our 20 African exporters.
- *United States:* Nine of the 15 products for which we have data have post-UR bound MFN tariffs of zero. Among the other six products, one has a 1% tariff, two have GSP rates of zero and four have a zero duty for imports from LDCs. The only barriers of any consequence appear to be those applied on imports of raw sugar and prepared or preserved tuna/skipjack/bonito from the non-LDC countries among our 20 African exporters.
- *Japan:* Nine of the 16 products for which we have information have post-UR bound rates of zero. Of the seven with non-zero rates, five have a zero duty on imports from LDCs, three have a GSP rate of zero, and two have a GSP rate below the MFN rate. Judging from the tables, the most important barrier facing the 16 products appears to be the 6.4% GSP rate on prepared or

preserved tuna/skipjack/bonito (versus an MFN rate of 9.6% and a rate of zero for imports from LDCs).

- *China:* Because China is not (yet) a WTO member, the tariff data refer to 1997 applied rates only, which means that the rates today or one year from now may be quite different from those in the tables (tariff concessions are an important part of the negotiations on China's accession to the WTO). Tariffs are high on six products – ranging from 20% for cocoa beans to 70% for black tea (in between are coffee, tuna/etc., sugar and tobacco); tariffs on the remaining nine products range from 1½% to 9%, with a (simple) average of about 4%. The tables contain no Chinese non-tariff barriers on these 15 products (licensing, where is exists, is automatic).
- *India:* The trade regime for the 15 products for which we have data is very restrictive. Tariffs on four products are unbound (tuna/etc., petroleum, unsorted diamonds and copper cathodes); six have bound tariffs of 100% or 150%, and four have bound tariffs of 25% or 40%. Applied 1997 tariffs on cotton and the two non-tropical woods are zero, on coffee and black tea they are 10%, and on the remaining ten products they range from 25% to 40%. There is a "special tax" of 5% on all 15 products, and 7 of the products are subject to import licensing.

For the 15 or 16 important exports for which we have data, two broad generalizations can be drawn from this brief survey:

- With the exception of tuna/skipjack/bonito, and in some instances sugar, access to the markets of the main industrial countries is virtually unrestricted.
- Access to the Chinese and Indian markets (and to a number of other developing country markets, no doubt including those of our 20 African exporting countries themselves), in contrast, remains highly restricted for many of Africa's important exports.

Other markets and other products

This brief synopsis covers the important exports to five foreign markets.

What about other markets and other products – not only non-traditional exports, but also the other 119 products on our 20 countries' lists of leading exports?

There is no way to broaden the discussion without moving to very general descriptions based on broad averages and generalizations – that is, to a level of discussion of trade barriers whose value we have questioned more than once already in this paper. However, there is at least one useful role that moderately disaggregated data on trade barriers can fulfil. Coupled with knowledge of the country's current and expected future export interests, such data can guide analysts to those parts of trading partners' trade regimes that warrant closer examination in the course of preparing a list of the country's goals in a new round of trade negotiations. As we noted above, there is an urgent need for African governments to begin this kind of work in preparation for the round of WTO negotiations that will be launched in late 1999.

The study (WTO, 1997) from which Appendix Table 3A4 was taken focused on exports from LDCS – more specifically, on the leading 112 six-digit HS LDC exports (9 of our 20 African exporters are LDCS). The data revealed that about 70% of LDC merchandise exports enter industrial country markets duty free, either under tariff lines that have bound MFN zero tariffs (about 30%) or as a result of GSP or special LDC preference schemes. It adds, however, "... the picture varies from one developed country market to another. Certain [markets] offer preferences on an extensive range of products ... [While some] others offer practically no tariff line that is entirely free of tariffs or specific duties" (p. 4). On the issue of tariff escalation, the study concluded, "Tariff escalation will decline significantly following full implementation of Uruguay Round commitments, but it will still persist to some extent for many product chains" (p. 5).[11]

A recent joint UNCTAD/WTO study (UNCTAD, 1997) focused on post-Uruguay Round tariff peaks, defined as rates above 12%, in the EU, the United States, Japan, Canada, Brazil, China, Korea and Malaysia. It includes ad valorem estimates of specific and combined rates, which is particularly important because so much of the tariffication in agriculture in the Uruguay Round involved the use of (inherently opaque) specific duties. Among the points in the study are:

- About 10% of the tariff universe of the Quad countries will continue to exceed the level of 12% ad valorem after full implementation of the Round. This rate refers to effectively applied tariffs for imports from developing countries. All presently applied tariff suspensions, as well as general GSP concessions as applied in favour of developing countries in 1996/97, were subtracted. Developing countries apply rates above 12% ad valorem more frequently than the Quad countries but have fewer extremely high rates. (pp. 3–4)
- The problem of peak tariffs occurs in six sectors: (1) major agricultural staple food products; (2) fruit, vegetables, fish, etc. (3) the food industry; (4) textiles and clothing; (5) footwear, leather and travel goods; and (6) the automotive sector and a few other transport and high technology goods such as consumer electronics and watches (p. 4) (These are the sectors in which the tariff reductions by the industrial countries in the Uruguay Round were below the average reduction for all products.[12])
- ... in the agricultural sector ... quite a number of peak tariffs remain applicable to LDCs in all major markets. ... [In the United States] peak tariffs on exports above the [preferential] tariff quotas remain applicable to LDCs. ... [In Japan] ... LDCs continue to face peak MFN rates for beef and other meat products, sugar and sugar products, various fruits and fruit juices, etc. The EU applies extensive preferences to agricultural imports from ... [ACP] countries. But high tariffs, including MFN peak rates, remain in effect for a number of major food products, in particular for imports beyond limited preferential tariff quotas or past trade levels. ... Many other agricultural and processed agricultural products obtain only a partial reduction of MFN duties. ... Consequently, even many preferential ACP rates remain at peak levels. (p. 8)

Summary of market access barriers facing African exports

Certain broad guidelines, which can be used to give direction to the detailed analyses and preparations of African governments for the upcoming WTO round, emerge from this brief review of evidence on barriers to Africa's exports:

- Among the 17 currently important merchandise exports, tariffs (and other barriers) remain a problem for tuna/skipjack/bonito and sugar in the markets of the major industrial countries.
- All or nearly all of the 17 products face high tariffs and other barriers in the markets of developing countries.
- Options for expanding traditional and new *primary commodity exports*, to traditional and new markets (including other developing countries), should not be neglected.
- Recalling the earlier discussion of *non-traditional exports*, it seems very likely that for at least the next two or three decades the comparative advantage of countries in sub-Saharan Africa will lie mostly in the products of smallholder agriculture and manufactures whose production is intensive in unskilled labour.
- Tariff peaks affecting products of current or potential export interest to African countries – including major food products, vegetables, fruit, fish, textiles, clothing, footwear, leather and travel goods – are common in virtually all countries.

An obvious and important conclusion is that tariffs – the traditional trade policy tool that risks being neglected these days as new and more "glamorous" topics come onto the WTO's agenda – matter very much for Africa's exports. It is critically important to African countries that further reductions and bindings of industrial tariffs are added to the agenda of the upcoming WTO round (agricultural tariffs are already on the agenda).

3. African Participation in the WTO

The issue of the participation of sub-Saharan African countries in the WTO can be divided into (1) participation in the routine day-to-day activities, defined to include not only activities in Geneva, but also implementation of new Uruguay Round commitments at home; and (2) participation in the preparations for the new round of multilateral negotiations scheduled to be launched on the eve of the new century. Although there is not, as will be seen, a clean and neat separation between the two, it is a useful distinction for an initial discussion.[13]

First, however, a point of central importance to both categories of participation. The GATT and now the WTO are what is often called "member driven" organizations. Relative to the IMF and the World Bank, the member countries play a *much* more active role in the full range of WTO activities. The counterpoint to this is that relative to the secretariats of the IMF and World Bank, the WTO Secretariat has *very* limited authority and influence over what takes place in the WTO (budgetary considerations do *not* explain the fact that the WTO Secretariat has only one-fifth the staff of the IMF and one-thirteenth the staff of the World Bank).

Because the participation of member countries is so central to virtually everything that takes place in the WTO, a lack of active participation in WTO work by resident delegates and their backup staff in the national capital can be much more costly to a country than would be the case with a similar level of neglect vis-a-vis other international economic organizations. *There is no one to represent the trading interests of sub-Saharan African countries in the WTO except those countries themselves.*

It is a very welcome development, therefore, that the four decades of mutual benign neglect between the sub-Saharan African countries and the GATT/WTO has come to an end. But a great deal more needs to be done by these countries before it can be said that they are adequately representing their vital trading interests in the international organization that sets the rules governing trade in goods and services, settles trade disputes, and periodically organizes multilateral negotiations to reduce barriers to trade.

Participation in day-to-day activities

Active participation in the WTO's day-to-day work requires an adequate size staff resident in Geneva. Here, two sobering sets of statistics may be noted. A survey based on data for June 1997 revealed that one-half of the WTO members from sub-Saharan Africa – 18 out of 36 – had no resident representative in Geneva to cover *any* of the Geneva-based international organizations (altogether, 34 members or one-quarter of the WTO membership had no resident delegate in Geneva). To the extent these 18 African countries are represented in WTO activities, it is by staff that must come from embassies elsewhere in Europe or from national capitals. Among the one-half that does have one or more permanent representatives in Geneva, the vast majority have very small staffs that are required to cover not only WTO activities, but also those of other international organizations (UNCTAD, ILO, ITU and so forth). In contrast, for all WTO members with resident representatives in Geneva, the average number of professionals who work *more or less full-time on WTO matters* is just under five.

The other statistics concern the number of meetings each week in the WTO building. All WTO councils, committees and working groups are open to all members. There are 4 councils, 18 committees, the Trade Policy Review Body, working groups on investment, competition and government procurement, 28 accession working parties, "heads of delegations" meetings, and meetings of various ad hoc and negotiating groups. Allowing for vacation periods, and *not* counting the informal meetings that took place outside the WTO building, there was an average of 46 meetings a week of all kinds in 1996, of which nearly 16 per week – more than three per day – were important enough to have interpreters present. With this level of activity, adequate coverage of work going on at the WTO is a challenge for even the large delegations.

Moreover, it is important to keep in mind that it is not just the staff resident in Geneva that matters, but also the size of the support staff in the capital. This is especially true now that WTO activities cover issues that (1) are *much* more technical than the traditional fare of tariffs and quotas (they include financial services, telecommunications, sanitary and phytosanitary standards, protection of intellectual property, environmental policies and trade, investment policies, competition policies, and so forth), and (2) involve several ministries besides the trade ministry, and thus require effective inter-ministry coordination in capitals.

All but the very largest delegations cope with this situation by focusing on those WTO activities that they judge to be the most relevant to their current trading interests, and "free riding" on the work of other delegations for the rest. This clearly is the most that any of the countries in sub-Saharan Africa can hope for. Modest as it is, only South Africa appears to be anywhere near even this "second best" solution.

An option the WTO Secretariat has tried to promote without success is to have groups of developing countries – for example, from the same region or regional integration agreement – cooperate by dividing up responsibility for covering the different WTO meetings each week (the Nordic countries are probably the only group that ever managed to do this for any length of time). Granted that such cooperation is perhaps unlikely in a major trade negotiation because of a diversity of negotiating strategies and goals, it is *not* easy to understand why it is so difficult when it comes to the WTO's mostly routine day-to-day work, where intuition suggests there would be a broad range of common interests among many countries in sub-Saharan Africa. (The nature of the obstacles to such cooperation among these countries, options for overcoming the obstacles, and the pay-off from doing so, would be a very interesting and timely research project.)

To take just one current example, consider the Committee on Rules of Origin. This is an important topic for the countries in sub-Saharan Africa, yet (with the partial exception of Nigeria) their input into the Committee's work has been minimal and not at all coordinated among the group. This is despite the fact that the technical complexity of the topic makes it a perfect candidate for cooperation among a group of countries with limited technical and negotiating resources, not to speak of limited political leverage when each is working alone.

Through its technical assistance activities, the WTO Secretariat helps the lower-income WTO members to cope not only with the level and complexity of the WTO's day-to-day work, but also with the challenges of implementing their Uruguay Round commitments. The problem is that the amount of resources available for capacity building and other forms of technical assistance – money plus WTO Secretariat staff who are both experienced in the complexities of issues on the WTO's agenda *and* available to work on technical assistance activities – is grossly inadequate.

One relatively objective way of backing up this assertion is to compare the increase in the number of countries needing technical assistance with the increase in resources for supplying the technical assistance.[14] Between the launching of the Uruguay Round in September 1986 and April 1997, the membership of the GATT/WTO increased from 85 to 131, an increase of 46 members or 54%. All of the new members – except the EU, Liechtenstein, and four East European countries – are developing countries, including eight LDCs. In addition to the 40 new developing country members, there are 28 countries in various stages of acceding to the WTO, virtually all of which need technical assistance during their accession and will continue to need technical assistance after they become members.

Of the 85 members in 1986, approximately 55 were developing countries. Now there are about 95 developing countries in the WTO – an increase of 72%. If we include the 28 countries in the accession process, since 1986 the number of countries that, in principle, would benefit from WTO technical assistance activities has increased from 55 to 123, or by 124%.

What happened to the technical assistance budget between 1986 and 1997 (excluding special off-budget, one-off grants by individual member countries)? There was an 84% increase in the nominal budget (unadjusted for inflation), and a 47% increase in the number of staff in the Technical Cooperation and Training Division.[15]

This is not the whole story, however. Over that 11-year period there was a very major increase in the scope of the WTO's activities and responsibilities, and thus an increase in the overall budget and staff of the WTO Secretariat. *That increase in the scope and complexity of activities, by itself, increases the need for technical assistance, independent of any increase in the number of countries needing technical assistance.* Perhaps a more telling comparison, therefore, is between the shares of the GATT/WTO budget and staff accounted for by the Technical Cooperation and Training Division in 1986 and in 1997. In 1986, the Division spent 4.7% of the GATT budget and had 5.1% of the staff; in 1997, the respective figures were 4% and 5.5%.

One interpretation of these figures is that although the budget and staff of the Division, by remaining more or less constant as proportions of the overall Secretariat budget and staff, have kept pace with the expanding scope and complexity of the WTO's activities, there has been no increase at all in resources in response to the big increase – 72%, or 124% if we count acceding countries – in the number of countries needing technical assistance.

The off-budget support from individual WTO members is an attempt to fill the resulting gap. But it is insufficient, not only in terms of the amounts of money involved, but even more importantly because it does not result in any increase in the number of professional staff permanently employed by the WTO Secretariat. This is a critical consideration because the nature of WTO activities is such that, in most instances, meaningful technical assistance can only be provided by people with a reasonable amount of experience working at the WTO Secretariat.

A substantial increase in regular budget funds for technical assistance, including additional professional staff, would allow the WTO not only to expand its existing technical assistance activities, but also to introduce new ones. A leading example of a very useful new activity is the proposal that the WTO open regional offices devoted primarily to technical assistance activities – for example, four in English-speaking Africa, two in French-speaking Africa, four in the former Soviet Union, and three or four each in Asia and Latin America (currently the WTO has no staff outside Geneva). An even more ambitious proposal – not strictly speaking technical assistance, but nonetheless designed to enhance developing country participation in the WTO's work – is to provide funds to every WTO member, from the regular WTO Secretariat budget, for three delegates resident in Geneva and working full-time on WTO matters.[16] *If either of these proposals – especially the latter – sounds far-fetched, consider the fact that if the WTO Secretariat budget were doubled, there would still be 11 international economic organizations with larger budgets* (Blackhurst, 1998).

The 36 WTO members from sub-Saharan Africa represent more than one-quarter of the WTO membership, and the total number of members with an equally strong interest in expanded technical cooperation activities (out of a total developing country membership of about 95) must be at least double that number. Coupled with the fact that WTO members attach great importance to making decisions on the basis of consensus – including decisions on the agenda of the upcoming round – these numbers suggest that a cooperative effort, led by the sub-Saharan African countries, might just be successful in obtaining a major increase in the WTO's technical assistance budget. True, most of the additional money would come from the major developed countries (budget shares are based on shares of world trade). But it would be entirely appropriate for the African group to point out – as part of the argument in favour of such an increase in resources for technical assistance – that it is precisely the large traders who are so fond of describing the WTO as "member driven", and that this is a unique opportunity to demonstrate that their commitment is to a truly "member driven organization" rather than to a "large trader driven organization".

Participation in preparations for the upcoming round

Another area of WTO activity where the participation of sub-Saharan African countries is severely restrained by shortages of money and experienced professionals is the planning and preparation for the new round of multilateral negotiations that will be launched in late 1999. As with participation in the WTO's routine activities, and implementation of Uruguay Round commitments, technical assistance from the WTO Secretariat can be helpful to countries having difficulties identifying what should be their goals in the new round and in participating in preparations for the round. Unfortunately, however, the same severe limitations on Secretariat resources and staff also apply. Countries that want to pursue their trading interests in the new round must do it themselves.

At Marrakesh it was agreed that agriculture (including agricultural tariffs) and services would be on the agenda. Discussions are already under way to determine what other topics, if any, will be added to the agenda. The governments of sub-Saharan African countries should be playing an active role in these discussions, and it should be a collective effort since individually they are too small to have much of an impact. But this presupposes having not only the resources to lobby aggressively, but also the resources to decide (in advance) exactly what to lobby for.

RECONSIDER TARIFFS

It was argued above that because tariffs remain a serious obstacle to many of Africa's current and potential exports, it is important that African governments lobby actively to get industrial tariffs on the agenda. A closely related consideration, not mentioned above, is the proliferation of free trade areas and customs unions around the world. It is very much in Africa's interest to minimize the extent to which those regional groupings discriminate against Africa's exports, and the best way to do that is through extensive MFN reductions in tariffs (the principal motivation behind the Kennedy Round in the mid 1970s was the desire of third countries to minimize the discrimination against their exports in the markets of the original six members of the European Economic Community).

The opportunity to negotiate reductions in foreign tariffs on Africa's exports is not the only reason why it is important to have industrial tariffs on the agenda of the new round. Equally or even more important is the opportunity it will provide for further liberalization of African trade regimes, in a reciprocity setting in which they can "get something in exchange from their trading partners" for liberalizing actions that would be worth doing unilaterally if there were no new round.

South Africa's tariff regime is characterized by moderately high tariffs and a high proportion of bindings (98% of lines). The tariff regimes of virtually all other sub-Saharan African countries are characterized by high applied tariffs and *very* small percentages of lines bound (and where tariffs are bound, they are often bound at very high rates). It was very unfortunate that these countries failed to use the Uruguay Round tariff negotiations to substantially reduce levels of protection and increase levels of bindings. (This is the principal reason why all estimates of gains from the Uruguay Round show very small gains – in some instances even losses – for sub-Saharan Africa. It is also an important reason why intra-African trade flows remain so small.) Provided that industrial tariffs are on the agenda, the new round will be an early opportunity to correct that mistake.

It is important to keep the argument for lower tariffs in sub-Saharan Africa in perspective. It does not have to be an argument for free trade, nor an argument against the use of infant industry protection or against import substitution. A tariff regime in which 100% of the lines are bound at rates no higher that 30% ad valorem, and with applied rates averaging one-half the bound rates – in other words, a tariff regime not unlike many in Latin America – would offer plenty of scope for infant industry protection and import substitution. *Such a tariff regime would also be a major improvement over nearly all current trade regimes in sub-Saharan Africa.*[17] Once such a tariff regime has been in place for a while, the debate over further liberalization could move on to the pros and cons of free trade, infant industry protection and import substitution.

The 100% level of tariff bindings – even when this includes ceiling bindings[18] – is important for the increased predictability it brings to the trade regime. This is no small consideration in sub-Saharan Africa, where policy credibility at home and abroad is one of the greatest challenges faced by governments that are serious about economic reform and anxious to attract domestic and foreign investment.

Imagine two sub-Saharan African countries that have just announced economic liberalization programmes and whose political regimes, economies and policies are identical in all respects, except one: country A has applied tariffs of 15%, 100% of which are bound at 30%, while country B has applied tariffs of 15%, none of which are bound in its WTO schedule. If your pension fund was committed to investing in one of the two countries, which one would you recommend?

WHAT ELSE BESIDES TARIFFS?

As noted earlier, other candidates for the agenda of the upcoming WTO round include state trading, government procurement, rules for foreign investment, competition policy, and reform of the rules governing free trade areas and customs unions. Again the shortage of experienced analysts and negotiators means the governments in sub-Saharan Africa cannot cover all or even most of these issues. One issue they may want to involve themselves in, if rules on foreign investment make it onto the agenda, is the use of financial incentives (such as tax holidays and subsidized infrastructure) to attract foreign direct investment. More specifically, since there is no way the countries in sub-Saharan Africa can match the funds spent by the OECD countries and the higher income developing countries to attract FDI, it is very much in their interest that new WTO rules on FDI include very strict limitations – if not a prohibition – on the use of such financial incentives.

Appendix Table 3.A1: Merchandise exports to the world (millions of US dollars, 1980–1995)

Country/Region	1980	1981	1982	1983	1984	1985	1986	1987	1988	1989	1990	1991	1992	1993	1994	1995
CENTRAL AFRICA																
Cameroon	1,418	1,610	1,637	1,317	1,289	1,409	1,603	1,729	1,670	1,837	1,906	2,159	1,937	1,651	1,432	1,662
CAR	147				85	92	66	129	134	148	151	126	116	132	151	173
Gabon	2,531				2,012	1,952	1,271	1,286	1,196	1,629	2,490	2,230	2,257	2,326	2,365	2,643
Zaire	2,269	1,079	986	956	1,023	1,071	1,399	1,813	2,460	2,417	2,326	1,649	1,246	1,144	1,256	1,632
EASTERN AFRICA																
Ethiopia	459	701	727	798	417	334	464	391	381	444	366	276	154	222	281	454
Kenya	1,363							907	1,014	922	993	1,052	1,008	1,099	1,482	1,875
Mozambique	281				96	77	79	97	103	105	126	162	139	132	164	174
Tanzania	508					359	290	337	338	423	415	342	416	450	519	639
Uganda	319	300	292	275	385	387	436	384	298	282	210	176	172	157	254	595
SOUTHERN AFRICA																
Angola					2,053	2,224	1,319	2,322	2,520	3,014	3,884	3,449	3,833	2,900	3,002	3,519
Botswana	545				674	744	714	1,592	1,478	1,820	1,753	1,903	1,725	1,725	1,880	1,848
Lesotho	58				29	23	26	30	64	66	60	58	105	95	136	168
Malawi	281				309	249	245	279	294	269	412	476	397	321	373	410
Swaziland	368				237	176	267	424	466	494	554	580	608	626	827	781
Zambia	1,457	789	748	498	661	547	704	873	1,155	1,410	1,264	1,085	1,111	949	1,067	1,190
Zimbabwe	281				1,148	1,109	1,301	1,455	1,668	1,692	1,726	1,785	1,530	1,610	1,947	2,216
WESTERN AFRICA																
Côte d'Ivoire	3,013	2,266	1,623	1,404	1,309	1,413	1,621	3,091	2,664	2,697	3,003	2,705	2,945	2,519	2,869	3,870
Ghana	1,104	1,189	803	683	558	658	763	825	881	808	897	998	986	1,064	1,236	1,431
Nigeria	25,956	16,758	12,215	7,707	12,020	13,113	5,899	7,383	6,875	9,812	13,670	12,264	12,307	11,297	9,534	10,916
Senegal	422	928	959	924	534	554	620	671	679	758	894	803	828	707	794	969
ISLAND STATES																
Madagascar	437				333	274	304	329	280	318	318	334	324	332	447	502
Mauritius	434				373	435	675	892	1,001	995	1,201	1,213	1,303	1,299	1,344	1,539
Seychelles	6							8	17	15	28	19	20	22	27	22
DEVELOPED AFRICA																
RSA	25,698				17,163	16,293	18,385	21,219	21,871	22,191	23,549	23,306	23,413	24,261	18,296	18,976

Sources: unctad Commodity Yearbook 1995, United Nations

African Development Indicators 1997, World Bank

Appendix Table 3.A2: Sub-Saharan African exports by category as a ratio to total world exports

	Non-fuel/ total world (%)	Fuel/ total world (%)	Miner-als/total world (%)	Agricultural/ total world (%)	Total SSA/ total world (%)
1970–1979	0.485	0.073	0.181	0.076	0.814
1980–1985	0.217	0.141	0.096	0.039	0.493
Growth (%)	(123.40)	48.100	(87.3)	(94.00)	(65.10)
1986–1989	0.195	0.088	0.090	0.030	0.403
Growth (%)	(11.40)	(60.20)	(7.70)	(28.10)	(22.50)
1990–1995	0.154	0.088	0.067	0.025	0.333
Growth (%)	(26.90)	0.000	(34.50)	(23.40)	(21.10)

Source: UNCTAD (1995).

Appendix Table 3.A3: Average share of manufactured exports in total exports

	Country	1970–79	1980–84	1985–89	1990–94
CFA	Burkina Faso	5.81	5.73	5.22	6.22
	Cameroon	3.45	2.75	2.76	2.64
	Congo	12.94	5.97	8.58	20.89
	Côte d'Ivoire	4.35	6.11	7.63	10.43
	Mali	7.14	10.45	12.39	22.84
	Senegal	9.69	12.63	14.19	12.52
	Togo	4.85	10.53	4.67	7.86
Non CFA	Ghana	3.87	5.65	8.77	18.24
	Kenya	16.15	17.17	14.49	18.57
	Madagascar	6.54	7.14	9.62	18.04
	Malawi	4.02	7.98	4.86	7.01
	Mauritius	13.83	32.36	59.46	67.61
	Nigeria	0.92	0.42	1.27	2.00
	Tanzania	10.18	11.39	10.41	13.74
	Zambia	2.16	3.23	3.99	4.47
	Zimbabwe	33.08	30.42	28.19	31.29

Source: Sekkat and Varoudakis (1998).

Appendix Table 3.A4: HS 090111 coffee (not roasted or decaffeinated)

Market	Tariffs* MFN bound**	Applied	GSP/ GSTP	LDC	Other	Other duties and charges	Quantitative restrictions
Australia	1	0	0	0	@1		
Brazil	35	10	0	0		Charges***	
Canada	0	0	0	0			
Chile	25	11	0	0		Air cargo and dispatching tax, 5.3–7%	
China	N/A	40	0	0			Automatic license
Chinese Taipei	N/A	5	0	0			Permitted with license
Egypt	10	5	0	0	@2		
EU	0	2.5	0	0	@3		Tariff quotas
Hong Kong, China	0	0	0	0			
India	100	10	0	0	@4	special tax 5%	Non-automatic license, import licensing
Indonesia	40–50	0–30	0	0			
Japan	0	0	0	0			
Korea	54	3	0	0			
Malaysia	sp	0	0	0			Import authorization
Morocco	34	25	MOP 50%	0	@5	Charges****	
Norway	0	0	0	0			
Poland	15	10	0	0			
Singapore	10	0	0	0			Authorization
South African CU	119	0	0	0	@6		
Switzerland	sp	sp	sp	sp			Automatic license
Thailand	90, sp	40	0	0	@7		
Turkey	50	13	0	0			
USA	0	0	0	0			

@1 – Forum Island (LDCs) receiving duty-free preference: Kiribati, Solomon Islands, Tuvalu, Vanuatu and Samoa

@2 – Niger receives preferences under a bilateral trade agreement.

@3 – E.C. Lomè rates to all LDCs, except Afghanistan, Bangladesh, Bhutan, Cambodia, Laos, Maldives, Mayanmar, Nepal and Yemen; GSP suspended for Myanmar.

@4 – SAPTA members that are LDCs receiving margin of preference: Bangladesh, Bhutan, Maldives and Nepal.

@5 – Guinea, Mauritania and Sudan receive preferences under bilateral trade agreements.

@6 – Malawi and Mozambique receive duty free preference. Lesotho receives duty free as a parts of SACU.

@7 – Laos receives 20% preference rate under a bilateral trade agreement.

Source: Compiled by authors.

Appendix Table 3.A5: The 136 leading exports

Commodity Code	Product description	Number of times it appears in our 20 tables	Total value, aggregate of our 20 countries (US$000)
10600	Animals, live, except farm animals	1	12,948
20130	Bovine cuts, boneless, fresh or chilled	1	43,288
20230	Bovine cuts, boneless, frozen	2	28,623
30269	Fish, fresh or chilled, whole	1	26,763
30342	Tunas (yellowfin), frozen, whole	1	4,708
30343	Skipjack, stripe-bellied bonito, frozen, whole	1	9,557
30379	Fish, frozen, whole	1	6,155
30410	Fish fillet or meat, fresh or chilled, not liver, roe	3	20,009
30420	Fish fillets, frozen	4	176,139
30559	Dried fish other than cod, not smoked	1	777
30613	Shrimps and prawns, frozen	5	195,164

Commodity Code	Product description	Number of times it appears in our 20 tables	Total value, aggregate of our 20 countries (US$000)
30749	Cuttle fish, squid, frozen, fried, salted or in brine	1	17,644
30759	Octopus, frozen, dried, salted or in brine	1	7,978
60310	Cut flowers and flower buds for bouquets, etc., fresh	3	158,529
70810	Peas, shelled or unshelled, fresh or chilled	2	17,780
70820	Beans, shelled or unshelled, fresh or chilled	2	49,187
70990	Vegetables, fresh or chilled	1	16,456
71310	Peas dried, shelled	1	4,552
71333	Kidney beans and white pea beans, dried shelled	1	4,164
80130	Cashew nuts, fresh or dried	2	105,204
80290	Nuts, edible, fresh or dried,	1	7,089
80300	Bananas, including plantains, fresh or dried	2	269,577
80430	Pineapples, fresh or dried	1	105,833
80440	Avocados, fresh or dried	1	15,656
80510	Oranges, fresh or dried	1	166,448
80610	Grapes, fresh	1	156,193
80810	Apples, fresh	1	164,128
81090	Fruits, fresh	1	48,494
90111	Coffee, not roasted, not decaffeinated	12	1,816,993
90240	Tea, black (fermented or partly) in packages > 3 kg	5	289,396
90420	Capsicum or pimiento, dried, crushed or ground	1	10,522
90500	Vanilla beans	1	70,966
90610	Cinnamon and cinnamon-tree flowers whole	1	816
90700	Cloves (whole fruit, cloves and stems)	2	18,776
00590	Maize except seed corn	1	18,559

Commodity Code	Product description	Number of times it appears in our 20 tables	Total value, aggregate of our 20 countries (US$000)
120300	Copra	1	6,866
120740	Sesame seeds	2	38,054
130214	Pyrethrum, roots containing rotenone, extracts	1	24,823
150810	Groundnut oil, crude	1	62,033
160250	Bovine meat, offal, not livers, prepared/ preserved	2	25,761
160414	Tuna, skipjack, bonito, prepared/ preserved, not mince	6	377,010
170111	Raw sugar cane	6	710,716
170310	Cane molasses	1	11,245
180100	Cocoa beans, whole or broken, raw or roasted	4	1,662,251
180400	Cocoa butter, fat, oil	2	167,090
200559	Beans, prepared or preserved, not frozen/ vinegar	1	16,633
200820	Pineapples, otherwise prepared or preserved	1	45,881
200940	Pineapple juice, not fermented or spirited	1	13,168
220720	Ethyl alcohol and other spirits, denatured	1	108,782
230500	Groundnut oil cake and other solid residues	1	16,368
230610	Cotton seed oil-cake and other solid residues	1	8,045
240110	Tobacco, unmanufactured, not stemmed or stripped	3	81,527
240120	Tobacco, unmanufactured, stemmed or stripped	3	514,763
240130	Tobacco refuse	1	22,716
250410	Natural graphite in powder or flakes	1	9,931
251020	Natural calcium phosphates, ground	1	12,519
252400	Asbestos	1	57,862

Commodity Code	Product description	Number of times it appears in our 20 tables	Total value, aggregate of our 20 countries (US$000)
260111	Iron ore, concentrate, not iron pyrites, unagglomerate	1	452,529
260200	Manganese ores, concentrates, iron ores >20% manganese	2	310,285
261000	Chromium ores and concentrates	2	131,413
261690	Precious metal ores and concentrates except silver	1	124,121
262090	Ash or residues containing metals, metal compounds	1	211,662
270111	Anthracite, not agglomerated	1	93,914
270112	Bituminous coal, not agglomerated	1	1,387,901
270119	Coal except anthracite or bituminous, not agglomerate	1	315,413
270400	Coke, semi-coke of coal, lignite, peat & retort carbo	2	20,778
270900	Petroleum oils, oils from bituminous minerals, crude	4	81,470,941
271019	Light petroleum distillates	1	1,125,428
283620	Disodium carbonate	1	16,163
310520	Nitrogen-phosphorous-potassium fertilizers, pack > 10 kg	1	13,556
410110	Bovine skins, whole, raw	1	3,471
410121	Bovine hides, whole, fresh or wet-salted	1	3,115
410221	Sheep or lamb skins, pickled, without wool	1	21,030
440122	Wood in chips, non-coniferous	1	151,171
440334	Logs, okoume/obeche/sapelli/sipo/acajou d'Afrique/etc.	3	374,011
440399	Logs, non-coniferous	3	273,410
440710	Lumber, coniferous (softwood) thickness <6mm	1	15,224
440722	Lumber/okoume/obeche/sapelli/sipo/acajou/makore/etc.	4	338,286

Commodity Code	Product description	Number of times it appears in our 20 tables	Total value, aggregate of our 20 countries (US$000)
440799	Lumber, non-coniferous	1	37,741
470200	Chemical wood pulp, dissolving grades	1	234,797
470329	Chem wood pulp, soda/sulphate, non-conifer, bleached	1	92,431
470411	Chem wood pulp, sulphite, coniferous unbleached	1	3,987
520100	Cotton, not carded or combed	7	382,554
520300	Cotton, carded or combed	1	3,492
520512	Cotton yarn > 85% single uncombed 714–232 dtex, not ret	1	4,273
520942	Denim cotton > 85% > 200 g/m^2	1	11,843
530410	Sisal and agave, raw	2	19,079
560721	Binder or baler twine, of sisal or agave	1	89,900
610463	Women's, girls' trousers, shorts, synthetic fibres, knit	1	10,285
610510	Men's, boys' shirts, of cotton, knit	1	41,177
610610	Women's, girls' blouses & shirts, of cotton, knit	1	10,008
610910	T-shirts, singlets and other vests of cotton knit	3	140,239
640399	Footwear, sole rubber, uppers of leather	1	7,645
710210	Diamonds, unsorted	3	705,163
710231	Diamonds (jewellery), unworked or simply sawn, cleaved	6	738,891
710239	Diamonds (jewellery), worked but not mounted or set	3	307,881
710310	Precious, semi-precious stones unworked, partly worked	1	6,684
710399	Precious & semi-precious stones, nes, worked, not set	1	5,317
7l0812	Gold in unwrought forms, non-monetary	1	1,813,619

Commodity Code	Product description	Number of times it appears in our 20 tables	Total value, aggregate of our 20 countries (US$000)
710813	Gold, semi-manufactured forms, non-monetary	1	13,816
711011	Platinum, unwrought or in powder form	1	1,394,142
711021	Palladium, unwrought or in powder form	1	224,484
711031	Rhodium, unwrought or in powder form	1	129,554
711210	Waste or scrap containing gold as sole precious metal	1	5,021
711319	Jewellery and parts of precious metal except silver	2	26,558
711620	Articles of precious, semi-precious, artificial stone	1	2,829
720211	Ferro-manganese, > 2% carbon	1	155,795
720230	Ferro-silico-manganese	1	94,759
720241	Ferro-chromium, > 4% carbon	2	739,309
720249	Ferro-chromium, <4% carbon	1	43,572
720250	Ferro-silico-chromium	1	14,143
740200	Unrefined copper, copper anodes, electrolytic refinin	2	141,780
740311	Copper cathodes and sections of cathodes unwrought	3	696,365
740319	Refined copper products, unwrought, nes	1	65,368
750110	Nickel mattes	1	102,094
750210	Nickel unwrought, not alloyed	2	194,898
760110	Aluminium unwrought, not alloyed	2	338,493
760120	Aluminium unwrought, alloyed	1	23,778
810510	Cobalt, unwrought, matte, waste or scrap, powders	3	308,517
841191	Parts of turbo-jet or turbo-propeller engines	1	19,435
842139	Filtering or purifying machinery for gases, nes	1	106,835

Commodity Code	Product description	Number of times it appears in our 20 tables	Total value, aggregate of our 20 countries (US$000)
910811	Assembled battery watch movement, mechanical display	1	8,339
911390	Watch straps etc. and parts, of leather/ plastic/etc.	1	15,364
940190	Parts of seats	1	219,325
950341	Stuffed toys – animals or non-human creatures	1	8,166
9999AA	Commodities not specified according to kind	4	383,648

Source: Compiled by the authors.

Appendix Table 3.A6: The 25 leading six-digit categories of "exports" of our 20 African countries to the 23 importing countries in 1995

Commodity code	Product description[a]	Export value (million $)	Number of times it is a leading export
	A. RANKED BY TOTAL VALUE OF "EXPORTS"		
270900	*Petroleum oils, oils from bituminous minerals, crude*	*81471*	*4*
90111	*Coffee, not roasted, not decaffeinated*	*1817*	12
710812	Gold in unwrought forms, non-monetary	1814	1
180100	*Cocoa beans, whole or broken, raw or roasted*	*1662*	*4*
711011	Platinum unwrought or in powder form	1394	1
270112	Bituminous coal, not agglomerated	1388	1
271019	Light petroleum distilates, nes	1125	1
720241	*Ferro-chromium, > 4% carbon*	*739*	2
710231	*Diamonds (jewelry), unworked or simply sawn, cleaved*	*739*	*6*
170111	*Raw sugar cane*	*711*	*6*

Commodity code	Product description[a]	Export value (million $)	Number of times it is a leading export
710210	*Diamonds, unsorted*	705	3
740311	*Copper cathodes and sections of cathodes, unwrought*	696	3
240120	*Tobacco, unmanufactured, stemmed or stripped*	515	3
260111	Iron ore, concentrate, not iron pyrites, unagglomerate	453	1
520100	*Cotton, not carded or combed*	383	7
160414	*Tuna, skipjack, bonito, prepared/preserved, not mince*	377	6
440334	*Logs, okoume/obeche/sapelli/sipo/acajou d'Afrique/etc.*	374	3
760110	Aluminium unwrought, not alloyed	338	
440722	*Lumber, okoume, obeche, sapelli/sipo/acajou/makore/etc.*	338	4
270119	Coal except anthracite or bituminous, not aggomerate	315	1
260200	Manganese ores, concentrates, iron ores >20% manganese	310	2
810510	*Cobalt, unwrought, matte, waste or scrap, powders*	309	3
710239	*Diamonds (jewelry) worked but not mounted or set*	308	3
90240	*Tea, black (fermented or partly) in packages >3 kg*	289	5
440399	*Logs, non-coniferous, nes*	273	3

B. RANKED BY THE NUMBER OF TIMES IT APPEARS IN THE "LEADING EXPORTS" TABLES OF OUR 20 AFRICAN COUNTRIES[b]

90111	*Coffee, not roasted, not decaffeinated*	1817	12
520100	*Cotton, not carded or combed*	383	7
710231	*Diamonds (jewelry), unworked or simply sawn, cleaved*	739	6
170111	*Raw sugar cane*	711	6

Commodity code	Product description[a]	Export value (million $)	Number of times it is a leading export
160414	*Tuna, skipjack, bonito, prepared/preserved, not mince*	*377*	*6*
90240	*Tea, black (fermented or partly) in packages > 3 kg*	*289*	*5*
30613	Shrimps and prawns, frozen		
270900	*Petroleum oils, oils from bituminous minerals, crude*	*81471*	*4*
180100	*Cocoa beans, whole or broken, raw or roasted*	*1662*	*4*
440722	*Lumber, okoume, obeche, sapelli/sipo/acajou/makore/etc.*	*338*	*4*
30420	Fish fillets, frozen	176	4
620342	Men's, boys' trousers & shorts, or cotton, not knit	123	4
710210	*Diamonds, unsorted*	*705*	*3*
740311	*Copper cathodes and sections of cathodes unwrought*	*696*	*3*
240120	*Tobacco, unmanufactured, stemmed or stripped*	*515*	*3*
440334	*Logs, okoume/obeche/sapelli/sipo/acajou d'Afrique/etc.*	*374*	*3*
810510	*Cobalt, unwrought, matte, waste or scrap, powders*	*309*	*3*
710239	*Diamonds (jewelry), worked but not mounted or set*	*308*	*3*
440399	*Logs, non-coniferous nes*	*273*	*3*
60310	Cut flowers and flower buds for bouquets, etc., fresh	159	3
620520	Men's, boys' shirts, of cotton, not knit	148	3
610910	T-shirts, singlets and other vests, of cotton, knit	140	3

Commodity code	Product description[a]	Export value (million $)	Number of times it is a leading export
240110	Tobacco, unmanufactured, not stemmed or stripped	82	3
30410	Fish fillet or meat, fresh or chilled, not liver, roe	20	3
720241	Ferro-chromium, >4% carbon	739	2

[a] Product descriptions in italics indicate a product that appears in Parts A and B of the table.

[b] See Appendix Tables 3.A4 and 3.A5.

Source: Compiled by authors.

Notes

1 WTO (1997) was prepared for the WTO's high-level meeting on integrated initiatives for least-developed countries' trade development, held in October 1997.

2 "Own" export data were collected for six of the 20 African countries in Table 2.3 that are presumed to have above average quality trade statistics. Those six-digit HS data were for exports to all destinations (rather than to our 23-country aggregate) and were f.o.b., whereas our partner data are C.I.F. Even allowing for these differences (which tend to offset one another), the discrepancies between the own data and partner data were often very large. For example, the ratio of own data to partner data was in the 0.68–0.99 range for only 26 (30%) of the 86 leading six-digit categories; for 21 categories it had a value below 0.34, while 7 categories had a ratio in excess of 1.34. The 136 products, which are listed in Appendix Table 3A5, include the category 9999AA, "Commodities not specified according to kind". With respect to the HS nomenclature, it is important to keep in mind that the six-digit product groups vary enormously in terms of the value of world trade they cover. Coffee (not roasted, not decaf) and bananas each have their own six-digit category; so do cashew nuts, avocados, and brassieres (and parts thereof).

3 The list excludes category 9999AA "commodities not specified according to kind".

4 See Helleiner (1997) and Frazer and Helleiner (1997). UNCTAD has also done considerable work on the issue of non-traditional exports.

5 The work for which Douglass North received the Nobel Prize in economics could be very useful on the last point. See in particular North (1990).

6 It is interesting to note that Yeats found that while net freight and insurance payments by African countries as a group were about 15% of the value of merchandise exports (1991/92), the corresponding figure for Uganda was 71%.

7 Intuitively this point may be illustrated by noting that an individual wheat farmer in the United States, who supplies only a tiny fraction of the US wheat market, faces an infinitely elastic output demand, even though all US wheat farmers collectively face the overall

elasticity of demand for wheat (for example, –0.6). This does not mean that African exporters collectively face an infinitely elastic demand for their exports, but rather that the demand they face is more elastic – in many instances, much more elastic – than the overall elasticity of world market demand for the product in question. See Blackhurst (1973).

8 Comparing Asia, Latin America and Africa, it has been observed that in both Asia and Latin America, non-traditional crops expanded while the composition of exports from sub-Saharan Africa remained fairly stagnant (Akiyama and Larson, 1994). In Latin America, export expansion included fruits, vegetables and oilseed production. In Asia, on the other hand, production increases affected all sectors of agriculture with the largest gains coming from fruits and vegetables.

9 Only another WTO member can bring a formal complaint about non-compliance with WTO obligations. Thus as long as trading partners are willing to ignore non-compliance with WTO rules and disciplines, a country can – if it wants – get away with non-compliance.

10 Quantitative restrictions include import licensing (automatic and non-automatic), minimum import prices, quotas, tariff quotas, import monitoring/surveillance, prior authorization, state monopoly, canalized imports and bank authorization. With respect to the information on "quantitative restrictions" and "other duties and charges," the WTO Secretariat's notes to the tables observe that the information "should not necessarily be considered an exhaustive list".

11 The study also includes a few remarks on the issue of preference erosion. Referencing an OECD study ("Market Access for the Least Developed Countries: Where are the Obstacles?" TD/TC(97)19, Paris, 1997), it notes "A recent OECD Secretariat calculation suggests, as an order of magnitude, that the overall effect of the erosion of the European Community's preferences on imports from the ACP countries under the Lomé Convention could amount to between 1% and 5% of these countries' annual export earnings" (footnote on p. 5). For these countries there will also be limited losses from the erosion of the less generous GSP, as well as of other preferences, in the markets of other OECD countries.

Perhaps equally or even more important than the very limited effect (in nearly all instances) of preference erosion associated with the Uruguay Round, is the fact that not only is preference erosion a "backward looking" topic, but the reality is that very little can or will be done about it. Moreover, any new preference margins would in turn be eroded in the next multilateral negotiation on tariffs. Countries affected by preference erosion almost certainly will find that their scarce negotiating skills and political leverage are better spent working on forward looking issues they can do something about, such as preparing for the new WTO round and lobbying vigorously to get items of interest to them on the agenda.

12 This section, in particular the first part, draws heavily on Blackhurst (1998).

13 Many of the statistics in this paragraph and in the next four paragraphs are based on data in Buffle (1998).

14 There are currently 12 professionals plus the Division Director in the Technical Cooperation and Training Division. Professionals from other parts of the Secretariat participate

in technical assistance missions, but the amount of such help is severely limited by the pressure of work in the other divisions.

15 See Blackhurst (1997). Another very interesting and timely research project would be to consider the relative merits, from the viewpoint of the sub-Saharan African countries, of different types of technical assistance from the WTO Secretariat (training courses in Geneva, technical assistance missions to the countries, regional offices, assistance designed to increase participation in WTO activities in Geneva versus assistance with implementing Uruguay Round commitments, and so forth).

References

Akiyama, T. and Larson, D. 1994. "The adding up problems: Strategies from primary commodity exports in sub-Saharan Africa". World Bank Policy Research Paper # 1245.

Blackhurst, R. 1973. "Estimating the impact of tariff manipulation: The excess supply and demand approach". *Oxford Economic Papers,* March.

Blackhurst, R. 1997. "The WTO and the global economy". *The World Economy,* August.

Blackhurst, R. 1998. "The capacity of the WTO to fulfill its mandate". In A. Krueger, ed., *The WTO as an International Organization.* Chicago: University of Chicago Press.

Buffle, P. 1998. "Les activités de cooperation technique de l'OMC". Mimeo.

Elbadawi, I. 1998. "Real exchange rate policy and non-traditional exports in developing countries". Mimeo.

Frazer, G. and G. Helleiner. 1997. "Non-traditional exports and export diversification: Alternative definitions and methodologies". Mimeo.

Helleiner, G.K. 1997. "Growth, external sector and the role of non-traditional exports in sub-Saharan Africa". Mimeo.

North, D. 1990. *Institutions, Institutional Change and Economic Performance.* Cambridge: Cambridge University Press.

Sekkat, K. and A. Varoudakis. 1998. "Exchange rate management and manufactured exports in sub-Saharan Africa". Mimeo.

UNCTAD. 1997. "The post-Uruguay Round tariff environment for developing country exports". TD/B/COM.1/14.

WTO. 1996. *Annual Report,* Vol. 1. Special Topic: "Trade and foreign direct investment". Geneva: World Trade Organization.

WTO. 1997. "Market access for least developed countries". WT/LDC/HL/14. Geneva: World Trade Organization.

WTO. 1998. *Guide to the Uruguay Round Agreements.* Geneva: World Trade Organization.

Yabuki, N. and T. Akiyama. 1996. "Is commodity-dependence pessimism justified?" Policy Research Working Paper 1600, World Bank.

Yeats, A. 1997. *Did Domestic Policies Marginalize Africa in International Trade?* Washington, D.C.: The World Bank.

Yeats, A. and Francis Ng. 1996. "Open economies work better! Did Africa's protectionist policies cause its marginalization in world trade?" World Bank, Policy Research Working Paper no. 1636.

Chapter four

African Agriculture in the WTO Framework

by T. Ademola Oyejide

1. Introduction

The completion of the Uruguay Round (UR) of multilateral trade negotiations in 1993 radically changed the global environment for agriculture in terms of both the institutional setting and the rules that govern broad agricultural production policies and agricultural trade relations among countries. In particular, the UR culminated in the creation of the World Trade Organization (WTO) as the successor institution to the General Agreement on Tariffs and Trade (GATT) and thus the premier global organ for monitoring and supervising the new world trading system. In addition, by – for the first time – fully embracing agriculture, the UR placed this sector under a more formal and relatively comprehensive multilateral set of disciplines through the approval of the Uruguay Round Agreement on Agriculture (URAA).

Just as it has for other regions, the URAA is bound to have important implications for African agriculture. The more immediate implications of URAA are likely to arise from at least two directions. One would be in terms of changes in the market access conditions for African exports that the new set of multilateral disciplines can be expected to generate. The second relates to corresponding changes in the conditions for African agricultural imports.

In addition, more long-term implications can be associated with the choice of the strategy for the development of African agriculture.

More specifically, efforts to expand African agricultural output as well as to expand and diversify agricultural exports will be affected by the new WTO framework. Those involved in articulating and implementing long-term strategies for the development of African agriculture to achieve these and related objectives would need to explore how and the extent to which the WTO framework constrains or enhances a whole range of domestic policies for developing this sector. Similar concerns need to be addressed in relation to the impact on the external policy environment that must be confronted by African agriculture.

This paper is guided by the questions that are implicit in the discussion above. In addressing these issues, the paper begins, in Section 2, with a broad analysis of the structure and growth of African agriculture. This pays particular attention to the significance and contribution of the agricultural sector to the overall African economy, the structure and growth performance of agricultural production, and the structure and growth of Africa's agricultural trade.

Section 3 focuses on the identification and analysis of the key internal and external factors that seem to explain the structure and performance of Africa's agricultural production and trade. In the next section, the paper discusses the main elements of URAA and explores the effects of its different provisions on the agricultural sectors of various categories of African countries. Section 5 turns attention to an analysis of the long-term strategic issues associated with the development of African agriculture in the context of a more liberalized global trading system. This section also concludes the paper.

2. The Agricultural Sector in Africa

As the key sector in the typical African economy, agriculture carries a great deal of the economic burden of these countries, and many of their problems can be linked directly or indirectly to the performance of the agricultural sector. The sector's dominant position in African economies is indicated by its substantial contribution to the GDP, foreign exchange earnings and employment. As the main source of income and employment in many African countries, agriculture has an important and potentially pivotal role in enhancing overall economic growth and improving welfare.

Although its economic dominance has declined somewhat over the last two to three decades, agriculture continues to be the largest productive sector in many African countries and is, in aggregate, responsible for about 35% of GDP, 40% of export earnings and close to 70% of employment. There are several African countries where mineral resources challenge agriculture as the dominant sector, but overall agriculture's contribution to aggregate economic growth through the provision of foods, the supply of industrial raw materials and the provision of income to the majority of the African population ensures that aggregate economic growth remains critically dependent on the sector's performance. Viewed from another perspective, it seems clear that most African countries have not yet experienced the degree of structural transformation that would enable their economies to grow rapidly without a similarly rapid growth of their agricultural sector.

Hence, it is estimated that due to its stimulating effects on industry, transport and services, a 1% growth in agriculture generates an overall economic growth that is 1.5 times this amount in Africa (World Bank, 1993).

This close link between agricultural and overall economic growth performance in Africa, combined with the relatively sluggish growth of the agricultural sector since the mid 1960s, largely explains the focus of recent economic reforms on the sector. It is argued, in this context, that "transforming agriculture and expanding its productive capacity is a prerequisite, possibly the single most important precondition, for improving living standards in Africa (ADB, 1998: 31).

The growth of African agriculture has generally been unsatisfactory. The sector's growth performance was particularly poor during the 1970s and early 1980s when agricultural output per capital actually declined. Thus, the average annual growth rate of the volume of production fell from 2.5% during 1960–70 to 1.4% during the following (1970–80) decade. Correspondingly, average annual growth rate of per capita production, which was a mere 0.2% in 1960–70, fell further to –1.1% during 1970–80.

Over the 1980–90 decade, Africa's agricultural growth rate averaged less than 1.5% per annum. This performance compares rather poorly with the 4.7% achieved by the East Asia and Pacific countries, the 3.0% average annual agricultural growth rate of South Asian countries, and the close to 2% average annual growth rate achieved by the agricultural sector of Latin America and the Caribbean region. In the 1990s, the growth performance

Table 4.1: Agricultural value added as percentage of GDP by region, 1980–1997

Country	1980	1997
Developing countries	18	16
East Asia & Pacific	28	19
Latin America & Caribbean	10	10
South Asia	38	27
Sub-Saharan Africa	22	25

Source: World Bank, World Development Report, 1980–1997.

of African agriculture showed some improvement over the previous two decades. In particular, the agricultural sectors of many African countries achieved real average annual growth rates of over 2% during the first half of the 1990s, and by the late 1990s as many as 18 of these countries achieved agricultural growth rates of at least 4%.

While an analysis of the growth performance over time of Africa's agriculture provides important insights into the region's development profile and prospects, a comparison of a few key characteristics of African agriculture with those of other developing regions would assist in providing a more global perspective. Among these characteristics is the normally observed pattern of declining importance of agriculture as development occurs. Table 4.1 shows that between 1980 and 1997, agricultural value added as a proportion of GDP fell from 18% to 16% in the developing countries. Corresponding regional figures show a decline from 28% to 19% for the East Asia and Pacific countries, and a fall from 38% to 27% for South Asia over the same period. Latin America and the Caribbean maintained the same proportion of 10% in 1980 and 1997. But in Africa, the share of agricultural value added in the GDP actually increased from 22% to 25% over the same period. This suggests that African economies have failed to achieve the kind of structural transformation that has led to the decline in the relative significance of agriculture in the rapidly growing economies of other regions.

Table 4.2 places side by side the growth performance of GDP and agricultural value added over the 1980–1997 period. Several inferences can be drawn from the data presented in this table. First, over both 1980–90 and

Table 3.2: Growth of GDP and agricultural value added by region, 1980–1997

	GDP growth		Agric value added	
Country	1980–1990	1990–1997	1980–1990	1990–1997
Developing countries	3.0	2.8	3.2	2.9
East Asia & Pacific	7.8	9.9	4.7	3.8
Latin America & Caribbean	1.8	3.3	1.9	2.6
South Asia	5.7	5.7	0.2	2.9
Sub-Saharan Africa	1.7	2.1	1.7	4.6

Source: World Bank, World Development Report, 1998/99.

1990–97 periods, East Asia and Pacific as well as South Asia regions achieved average annual growth rates of GDP that were, at about 6% and above, much higher than the average GDP growth performance of the developing countries (around 3.5%). Second, the impressive GDP growth of these two developing country regions appears to have been underpinned by equally impressive growth rates of agricultural value added (in the range of about 3–5%). Third, Latin America and the Caribbean, as well as the sub-Saharan Africa regions that achieved below average GDP growth rates also had poor agricultural value added growth rates. Fourth, however, the growth rate of agricultural value added in Africa seems to have reversed its recent trend during 1990–97. In fact, at an average annual rate of 4.6%, its performance surpasses that of any other region, and demonstrates considerable recovery from the sector's lacklustre performance over the previous two decades.

But whether this apparent recovery can be translated into rapid and sustainable growth remains to be seen. As Table 4.3 shows, Africa's agricultural productivity remains low. In particular, the region's average agricultural value added per agricultural worker during 1994–96 was 85% of the average for the developing countries and only 17% of that of the Latin America and the Caribbean region. Similarly, Africa's average agricultural value added per hectare of agricultural land was about a third of the average for all

Table 4.3: Agricultural productivity by region, 1994–1996

	Average US$ value added per:	
Country	Agric worker	Hectare of land
Developing countries	459	206
East Asia & Pacific	2,292	116
Latin America & Caribbean	383	519
South Asia	392	68
Sub-Saharan Africa	390	67

Source: World Bank, World Development Report, 1998/1999

developing countries and only 13% of that of Latin America and the Caribbean. These figures appear to pinpoint productivity as the soft underbelly of African agriculture.

Table 4.4 presents data on two other features that are associated with agricultural productivity. In 1995, only 7% of Africa's land area was used as cropland compared with 11% for all developing countries and as much as 45% in South Asia. Similarly, Africa's cropland is the least irrigated among all developing country regions: Only 4% of the region's cropland was irrigated in 1994/96 compared with an average of 20% for all developing countries and as high as 35% for South Asia.

African exports are more dominated by agricultural commodities than those of any other developing country region. This relatively heavy reliance on agricultural exports has important implications for the region's total export earnings. Since the world market trends for Africa's traditional export crops have been largely unfavourable, particularly over the last two decades, and output growth recovery was slow up to the early 1990s, the region's total agricultural export earnings fell from over $14 billion in 1980 to about $10 billion in the early 1990s (ADB, 1998). In spite of the recovery of agricultural commodity prices in the mid 1990s, their future prospects in the world market remain uncertain while the long-term deterioration in Africa's terms of trade appears likely to continue.

Within this broad sweep, it is important to recognize some differ-

Table 4.4: Cropland by region, 1998–1996

	Cropland as % of land area	Irrigated land as % of cropland
Country	1995	1994 /1996
Developing countries	11	19.9
East Asia & Pacific	12	n.a.
Latin America & Caribbean	8	11.1
South Asia	45	35.1
Sub-Saharan Africa	7	4.0

Source: World Bank, World Development Report, 1998/1999

ences. For instance, the volume of agricultural exports declined from the early 1970s to the early 1980s. The steep rise in agricultural export unit value during the first half of the 1970s, however, fuelled the rapid increase of agricultural export earnings that occurred up to 1977. As unit value fell back and export volume failed to increase, total value of agricultural exports declined through the mid 1980s. Export volume finally picked up from 1984, but the continued decline in export unit values was such that the growth of export volume did not translate into an increase in agricultural export earnings between mid 1980 and the early 1990s. After 1993, unit export value resumed an upward movement and, together with the continued rise in export volume, agricultural export earnings were finally able to resume a rising trend.

Africa's heavy dependence on agricultural exports is made more problematic by the lack of diversification in the commodities that constitute the region's agricultural export basket. Table 4.5 shows that the same set of nine commodities accounted for over 70% of the region's total agricultural export earnings during 1970–79 and 1990–95. The top three of these commodities (cocoa, coffee, cotton) provided about 55% of total agricultural export earnings during 1970–79 and roughly 44% in 1990–95. The first five commodities (i.e., the top three plus sugar and tobacco) accounted for over 60% of total earnings during these two periods. These aggregate trends obviously hide

Table 4.5: Africa's commodity export farming as percentage of total agricultural exports, 1970–1995

Agricultural exports	1970–1979	1950–1995
Banana	0.7	1.2
Cocoa	20.6	17.7
Coffee	24.7	14.4
Cotton	9.2	11.8
Groundnut	2.4	4.3
Rubber	1.7	2.3
Sugar	5.6	9.1
Tea	2.5	4.9
Tobacco	3.1	8.9
% of total	70.4	70.7

Source: African Development Bank (1998).

significant country-level variations. Several African countries do, in fact, depend on a single export commodity for as much as 40% of their total agricultural export earnings. This level of export concentration places great strains on many African countries, which are quite literally at the mercy of fluctuations in world commodity prices (Oyejide, 1993).

Africa's heavy concentration on such a narrow range of agricultural export commodities suggests that the region has comparative advantage in producing these crops. This specialization has, however, not enabled African countries to maintain world market shares in these commodities or even gain additional market share. In fact, the opposite has happened; rather than maintain or gain market share, Africa has lost more and more of its world market share of many of its traditional agricultural export commodities.

Table 4.6 shows that between the early 1960s and the mid 1990s, Africa suffered drastic reductions in its world market share of the region's top three agricultural export commodities. For cocoa, Africa's world market share fell from 80% to 41%, a loss of almost 50%. Similarly, its world market share for coffee fell from 26% to 15%, while that for cotton declined from 20% to 13% over the same period. Among the top five commodities, tobacco maintained its share at 12% while sugar achieved a marginal increase in world market

Table 4.6: Africa's share of world trade (%), 1961–1995

Agricultural exports	1961/1963	1995
Banana	11	4
Cocoa	80	41
Coffee	26	15
Cotton	20	13
Groundnut	70	2
Rubber	7	5
Sugar	5	7
Tea	9	21
Tobacco	12	12

Source: World Bank, Commodity Trade and Price Trends; ADB (1998).

share from 5% in 1961/63 to 7% in 1995. Clearly, the most dramatic world market share loss was experienced in the case of groundnuts, from 70% to a mere 2%. Of the nine commodities, tea showed the most gain; Africa's world market share of this export crop increased from 9% in 1961/63 to 21% in 1995.

Africa's import of agricultural products has traditionally been dominated by food products, particularly cereals. Most countries of West and Central Africa are importers of grains and livestock, those in East Africa are importers of cereals, while southern Africa, previously largely self-sufficient in food has been driven by civil strife and droughts to become large-scale food importers over the last decade or so. Africa's cereal imports increased at an average annual growth rate of almost 18% in 1975–80; this growth decelerated to 3.7% during 1980–85, but rose again to almost 5% in 1985–90 and to more than double this rate over the next five years. In addition, food aid receipts by African countries experienced an average annual growth rate of close to 14% during 1975–80; the growth subsequently rose to almost 20% in 1980–85 before levelling to around 15% up to the mid 1990s.

UNCTAD (1998) shows that in Africa the ratio of trade balance to total trade in agricultural products fell systematically from 51% in 1966–68 to only 10% in 1993–95 and concludes that "this worsening of the net agricultural ex-

Table 4.7: Food production index (1979–1981 = 100) by region, 1994–1996

	1979–81	1994–1996
Developing countries	100	169
East Asia & Pacific	100	214
Latin America & Caribbean	100	144
South Asia	100	164
Sub-Saharan Africa	100	143

Source: World Bank, World Development Report, 1998/1999.

port position of Africa was due to a rapid increase in food imports exceeding the growth in earnings from export crops". But the real driving forces behind this phenomenon are probably Africa's rapid population increase in the face of sluggish food production growth. Table 4.7 shows that compared with other developing country regions, Africa lags behind in food production. Starting from a 1979–81 base of 100, the food production index for Africa rose to 143 in 1994--96; this was well below the index of 169 achieved by all developing countries and was only two-thirds of the East Asia and Pacific region's achievement. Thus, the failure of African agriculture to maintain adequate food production levels commensurate with the demand for food is generated by the rapidly increasing population in the region.

3. Explaining African Agricultural Performance

Several key contributory factors have been identified and held responsible for the weak performance of African agriculture since the 1970s. These range from the natural environment of African agriculture, through political and security problems, institutional and structural factors to the incentive structure generated by both macroeconomic and sector-specific policies.

It is generally recognized that African agriculture operates in a difficult, risky and fragile natural environment (UNCTAD, 1998). In particular, African agriculture is predominantly rain-fed since irrigation covers only 4% of cultivated area. Yet, the region has been plagued with recurring droughts; both the quantity of rain and the duration of the rainy season have declined in many parts of Africa over the last two to three decades. This makes rain-fed agriculture an inherently risky undertaking. This situation is worsened by the continued prevalence of traditional farming methods that rely on extensive cultivation techniques. Over the last three decades or so most of the agricultural production growth that Africa has achieved is ascribable to the expansion of cultivated area on which very little fertilizer is applied. Fertilizer use in Africa remains the lowest in the world: at an average of less than 10 kg per hectare, it compares poorly with India's 69 kg per hectare and China's 262 kg per hectare.

In spite of the increasing pressure to adopt intensive science and technology-based farming systems in Africa, there continue to exist significant constraints that frustrate this transformation. These include the region's weak agricultural research and extension systems whose rate of relevant technological innovation is low and which thus provide little technology that can be directly adopted by African farmers. In addition, Africa's own soil and water constraints block the direct application of imported technology. The combination of weak African agricultural research and extension systems and the inapplicability of imported technology has frustrated the extension to Africa of the knowledge-based techniques for rapid agricultural development that have been so successfully used in other developing country regions of the world.

Civil disturbances continue to displace populations and disrupt agricultural activities in many parts of Africa. In addition, many African countries lack adequate infrastructural facilities, which translates into high transport costs for both agricultural inputs and crops, especially in the many land-locked countries.

Aside from these basically structural, institutional and environmental constraints, the incentive structure that faces African agriculture appears to play a major role in the sector's performance. Specifically, it is argued that much of the poor performance of African agriculture was due to excessive (direct and indirect) taxation of farmers by African governments. In many countries, governments were involved in fixing producer prices of all major agricultural crops through the use of parastatal commodity marketing boards, and in the process ensured that farmers received substantially less than the full border prices of their products. Studies have identified at least four key mechanisms through which the incentive structure penalized traditional agricultural export commodities up to the early 1980s (World Bank, 1994).

These include over-valued currency that reduced the real domestic prices of export crops, export licensing and controls that discouraged exports, high export taxes, and marketing boards whose monopoly control over both domestic crop purchases and export sales enabled them to offer low prices to export producers. Thus, African export crop producers were explicitly penalized through producer price fixing and taxes on agricultural inputs. In addition, they were further penalized implicitly through over-valued exchange rates and high industrial protection. This series of disincentives, it is argued, has contributed to the poor performance of Africa's agricultural production and export.

A recent study of the incentive structure facing African agriculture between the late 1960s and early 1980s concludes (Oyejide, 1993: 251–2):

> ... it appears that any substantial improvements in agricultural incentives (as measured by the nominal protection coefficient) were sharply eroded by the real exchange rate appreciation between the late 1960s and early 1990s. In addition, there is a clear difference in incentives, both nominal and real, for the production of cereals and export crops. In the aggregate, although the nominal incentives for cereal production in sub-Saharan Africa increased by 51% between the late 1960s and early 1980s, in real terms, the improvement was only 9%. In comparison, the nominal incentives for export crops increased by only 2% over the same period; a level that ultimately translated into a net decline of 27% in terms of real incentives. Thus, although net positive agricultural incentives were provided through various sector-specific policies, they were not sufficiently high enough to compensate for the much stronger disincentives implicit in the macroeconomic policies simultaneously implemented over the 1970s and early 1980s.

This and other reviews of the incentive structure argued strongly that an improved domestic policy environment was crucial for the recovery and sustained growth of African agriculture. In this context, the goal would be an agricultural pricing policy that would have at least three key elements, i.e., unsubsidized and market-determined prices for inputs and outputs, neutral taxation of agriculture and other sectors, and agricultural crop prices set at border parity, where this is determined on the basis of market clearing exchange rates. This would, in turn, require the realignment of domestic producer prices with their world market equivalents, and the demonopolization and deregulation of input and output marketing channels.

Africa's agricultural and general economic policy reforms implemented since the mid 1980s have thus focused primary attention on altering the incentive structure along the lines indicated above. But these policy reforms have been implemented at a time when real producer prices for export crops were falling in the world market. Hence, their salutary effects have not been as robust as was generally anticipated. Yet, some favourable results are evident (UNCTAD, 1998). In particular, agricultural performance indicators such as productivity and output growth have generally been better since the mid 1980s than they were during the 1970s and early 1980s. These improvements remain insufficient to sustain Africa's agricultural productivity growth, however, or to increase the region's net agricultural exports and per capita food production.

Given Africa's poor infrastructure, its lack of technology, as well as its missing and imperfect markets, the extent to which liberalization (as the single policy focus) can serve as an appropriate and adequate approach for the development of African agriculture remains questionable (UNCTAD, 1998; Oyejide, 1999).

4. The Uruguay Round Agreement on Agriculture: Implications for Africa

The Uruguay Round (UR) of multilateral trade negotiations was concluded in December 1993. One of the major results of the negotiations was the Uruguay Round Agreement on Agriculture (URAA), which for the first time brought trade-related agricultural policies into the mainstream of WTO discipline by establishing a new set of rules and obligations for member countries on matters relating to agricultural trade and price policy. This represents a major achievement to the extent that it made illegal further increases in agricultural subsidies and created a general commitment to reduce agricultural support measures and to adopt a "tariffs only" regime of agricultural protection. It also represents a major departure from the past. Prior to the UR, agricultural products enjoyed a "special status" under multilateral trade rules. Under these rules countervailing actions could not be taken against agricultural products that enjoyed domestic subsidies at whatever level and of any type; some quantitative trade restrictions were permitted and rules on export subsidies for agriculture were much weaker than those for industrial goods.

URAA imposes multilateral discipline in three broad areas of agricultural trade and pricing policy. First, in the area of *market access*, the URAA establishes tariffs as the only means of protecting agricultural trade by converting existing non-tariff barriers into tariffs, prohibiting the use of such measures in future and binding the tariffs. The second area is *domestic support*, in which the URAA committed members to a progressive reduction of trade-distorting agricultural price and production support. Finally, in the area of *export competition* the URAA subjected agricultural export subsidies to quantitative reduction commitments on both budgetary outlay and quantity subsidized.

The broad commitments in each of these three areas are not without important qualifications, however. Under market access, the agreement to eliminate existing non-tariff barriers (NTBS) through tariffication and the decision that no new NTBS should be created at the same time permitted the existence of certain exempt NTBS. Prominent among these are NTBS used by developing countries under the relevant WTO balance of payments provisions, safeguard measures and special treatment measures. In addition, minimum and current access opportunities are provided for in order to ensure that the tariffication process would not unduly affect current level of imports.

The URAA's safeguard provisions are designed to protect members from sudden import surges that may accompany the import liberalization process; the remedy in such a case is an additional temporary duty to be imposed on the product concerned. Subject to these "qualifications", the URAA mandates that all the tariff rates (including the "tariffied" elements) should be reduced in equal annual instalments from the base rate to the final bound rate over the implementation period. For developed countries, the commitment should be implemented between 1995 and 2000 with average tariff reduction rate of 36% subject to a minimum tariff reduction rate of 15% for each item. For the developing countries the implementation period is 1995–2005, while the corresponding tariff reduction rates are 24% (average) and 10% (minimum).

The URAA makes a distinction between exempt and non-exempt domestic support for agriculture, and commits members to reduce their non-exempt domestic support by 20% (13.3% for developing countries) by 2000 (2005 for developing countries). This commitment applies to both monetary value and quantity of subsidized products. It also prohibits the adoption of new support measures that are not indicated in each member's commitment schedule.

The so-called "blue box" measures of agricultural support are exempt under special circumstances. Three of these may be significant. First, those support measures are exempt whose values lie within the *de minimus* provision of 5% (10% for developing countries) of the value of the product (for products-specific support) or total agricultural production (for general support). Second are direct payments under production limiting schemes. Third are the special developing country exemptions, which cover investment and input subsidies generally available to agriculture and low-income and resource-poor producers, as well as support to encourage diversification away from illicit narcotics production. Finally, "green box" measures are exempted. These are considered to have no, or at most minimal, trade distorting effects and include support measures provided through publicly-funded government programmes that do not involve transfers from consumers. Examples include general services, research and training services, pest and disease control, inspection, infrastructure services, public storage for food security purposes, income insurance, payment for relief from natural disasters, and payments under regional assistance, and environmental and structural adjustment assistance programmes.

URAA commits the developed countries to reduce their agricultural export subsidies over the implementation period by 36% for monetary outlays and by 21% for subsidized quantity. Developing countries are not required to reduce export subsidies during the implementation period.

In addition to the provisions in the three key areas discussed above, the URAA contains three other important elements. First, it imposes new disciplines on sanitary and phytosanitary (SPS) measures, mandating that they should be applied only to the extent necessary to protect food safety and animal and plant health and thus not constitute unfair technical barriers to trade. Provision is also made for possible technical assistance for developing countries to comply with the SPS standards of importing countries. Second, the URAA explicitly recognizes "special and differential" treatment for developing and least developed countries. In the case of the former group, it is permitted that the applicable reduction commitments be implemented over a period of up to ten years. For the latter group of countries, no reduction commitments are required in any of the three areas of market access, domestic support and export subsidies. Finally, the Marrakesh Declaration noted the special difficulties of least developed and net-food-importing developing countries (LDNFIDC) who may suffer sharply increased food import bills following the reduction in food export subsidies by developed countries and possible increases in food import prices. Although the commitment to provide some assistance for affected LDNFIDCS was reconfirmed at the Singapore Ministerial Conference of the WTO, no clear-cut, operational mechanism for its implementation has been articulated.

The implementation of URAA has generated several problems. In particular, the process of transforming prohibited NTBS into tariff equivalents has resulted in extremely high tariff rates for the major agricultural staple foods (such as cereal, dairy products, meat and sugar), processed foods, and products such as tobacco and cotton. These tariff peaks are as high as 35% in several developed countries. In addition, the tariff reduction formula adopted for satisfying the URAA commitments has resulted in greater tariff dispersion among agricultural products than before 1995.

In spite of these problems, however, the URAA has achieved some impressive results, viewed from an African perspective (Oyejide, 1997). While tariff reductions achieved an average 37% on agricultural products as a group, tariffs facing African agricultural exports in the markets of developing countries are down by 32–48%. In particular, average tariffs on tropical products are reduced by 43% (including 25% reduction for cereals; 35% for coffee, cocoa and tea; 40% for oil seeds, fats and oils; and 48% for cut flowers). But while these reductions look impressive they are unlikely to have a substantial impact on African export volume because they apply to existing tariff rates that are already quite low.

There are at least two areas where full implementation of URAA could have negative impact on some African countries, particularly their food import bill. Harrold (1995) exhaustively examines this issue and concludes that the negative impact is likely to be minimal – roughly 0.15% rise in the annual impact bill of Africa's net-food-importing countries. The second area of possible negative impact is the likely displacement of African producers who currently benefit from some commodity protocols in the EU market by agricultural products from temperate zone countries as a result of the prohibition of NTBS on agricultural products. Prime examples of these countries are Mauritius and Swaziland (sugar), and Botswana and Namibia (meat). Exports of these African producers are likely to suffer price declines in the EU market if the Lomé Convention protocols give way in the light of URAA provisions.

More generally, the post-UR world agricultural market is likely to constrain African agricultural exports from at least two directions. First, tariff peaks (i.e., tariff rates above 12%) will remain high for many food products and processed foods in the markets of developed countries (UNCTAD, 1997). For many of the products that are of particular export interest to Africa, peak duties are in the range of 12–30%. In addition, above quota imports into developed-country markets attract tariffs that are many multiples of these peak rates. Some examples are: imports of dried beans, peas and lentils into Japan (460–640%) and imports of garments into the USA (164%). In addition, the food industries of many developed countries account for large concentrations of tariff peaks that could constrain African exports. In the United States, for example, processed foods attract peak tariffs of 12% and more, including orange juice (31%), peanut butter (132%) and tobacco products (350%). In Japan, the highest tariff peaks are found in the processed food industry and cover such products as canned meat and meat preparations, cocoa powder and chocolate, cereal products, vegetables, fruit juices, and coffee and tea syrups.

The second direction from which an export constraining impact may be felt in Africa is tariff escalation. This may constitute a problem for many African countries seeking to diversify their exports through food processing. FAO (1997) finds that agricultural exports of developing countries are largely concentrated in the first stage of processing, while the most advanced food industry products make up 32.5% of the food exports of developed countries. Tariff escalation in the developed countries appears to be one of the major constraints to the vertical diversification of the agricultural exports of developing countries. Thus, problems associated with tariff peaks and tariff escalation have not been solved by the URAA and its implementation; they may actually have been worsened.

5. Developing African Agriculture in a Liberalized Global Trading Environment

Africa emerged from the UR multilateral trade negotiations with relatively few mandated policy changes, particularly under the provisions of the URAA. This is not to suggest that the wave of trade liberalization sweeping through the global trading system passed the region by. On the contrary, the process of trade liberalization in Africa predated the UR; the impetus for overall economic reform in Africa was essentially unilateral. Hence, the UR negotiations had no direct influence on Africa's liberalization. And although Africa participated more actively in the UR negotiations than in all previous multilateral trade negotiations (Oyejide, 1990), no concerted effort was made to link African domestic liberalization strategies with the multilateral negotiations, nor were the unilateral liberalization achievements used to bargain for better access for African exports.

In addition, Africa's agricultural trade reforms constituted an integral part of the region's unilateral economy-wide structural adjustment programmes, which combined macroeconomic reform with sector specific policy changes. The most important elements of the agricultural trade policy component of these reforms have included the elimination of most quantitative restrictions, reduction in the level and dispersion of tariffs, elimination of most export taxes, and reduction of state trading through parastatal agricultural marketing boards. The main direct effects of these reforms have been the lowering of direct and indirect taxation of agricultural exports.

In compliance with the URAA, African countries have bound 100% of their agricultural tariff lines. But most African countries have set their agricultural tariff binding at very high levels (100–300%); only a few have bound their tariffs at less than 50%. Furthermore, in all cases, Africa's bound tariff levels are several multiples of the corresponding average applied rates. This practice appears designed to provide considerable space for discretionary changes in applied tariff rates. It is a practice that does not therefore impose an effective constraint on policy reversal and, to that extent, is not likely to enhance policy credibility. It is worth noting, however, that for the African countries in the "developing country" category under the provisions of URRA, these bound rates are subject to further reduction during the 1995–2005 implementation period. In any case, Africa's very high bound rates are not entirely unlike the very high developed country rates that emerged from the process of "tariffying" prohibited NTBS.

Many of the remaining policy changes mandated under URAA place many African countries under invited obligations, essentially for two reasons. First, these obligations, e.g., on domestic support and export competition, do not cover the typical policy distortions that characterize African agricultural trade and pricing policy. Second, many African countries are classified in the "least developed country" category and are therefore exempt from URAA obligations on agricultural support policies. Export subsidies thus have little relevance for the current domestic policies of African countries, which typically focus on taxing rather than subsidizing agricultural production and exports.

Developing African agriculture in the emerging more liberalized global trading environment requires that more attention be given to measures for enhancing agricultural productivity. Increased competitiveness induced by the new environment demands no less. Part of this requirement can and should be met through further liberalization and rationalization of African agricultural trade and pricing policies. This would be a good move to make for improving the competitiveness of African agriculture, whether it is done unilaterally or through multilateral negotiations. The multilateral route could bring two additional advantages to the liberalization process: First, it could enable it to be "exchanged" for better markets for African exports in trade partner countries. Second, a multilaterally negotiated and bound liberalization enhances its credibility and could, to that extent, induce quicker and more robust output and export supply response. While Africa's traditional agricultural exports face relatively low trade barriers in the developed country markets, the region's attempts to diversify and expand its agricultural export basket by processing more of these commodities and by expanding into non-traditional agricultural products would be frustrated in the absence of further negotiations aimed at substantially reducing the existing peak tariffs and eliminating tariff escalation in the developed countries. Credible offers by African countries to further lower their agricultural trade barriers will probably be needed in exchange.

This said, it should also be recognized that appropriate domestic policy reforms in the areas of agricultural trade and pricing regimes constitute only necessary but by no means sufficient conditions for developing an internationally competitive African agriculture. As shown previously, African agricultural production for exports is constrained by several other structural, institutional and natural/environmental factors. Key among these are infrastructural facilities, particularly in the form of transportation and irrigation systems; education, training, and research and development through which knowledge about new production technologies and crop varieties can be widely disseminated; pest and disease control systems; and land reform. Concerted efforts to deal with these constraints could, in turn, enhance the capacity of Africa's agricultural producers to respond more effectively to the opportunities provided by a more liberalized domestic agricultural trade and pricing policy and by improved access to foreign materials.

Such efforts will require increased resources from African governments, and this kind of support would not violate the commitments mandated by one URAA. It can also be combined with policies aimed at directly supporting domestic agricultural producers, although this latter form of support will not be allowed in the post-URAA world agricultural trading system. But Africa's least developed countries are not obliged to undertake the relevant URAA commitments and most other African countries still have a limited window of opportunity to use these support measures, where appropriate, up to 2005. But for its lack of productivity-enhancing technology, Africa's low input and largely unsubsidized agriculture would have been in an enviable competitive position as URAA obligations forced down agricultural subsidies in other parts of the world. Hence, the appropriate response to the challenge of global liberalization may not be to subsidize in the pre-URAA sense but to identify and use the measures for eliminating the infrastructural, institutional and technological constraints that hold down agricultural productivity in Africa.

References

Africa Development Bank (ADB). 1998. *African Development Report 1998*. Oxford: Oxford University Press.

Food and Agricultural Organization of the United Nations (FAO). 1997. "The impact of the Uruguay Round on tariff escalation in agricultural products". ESCP no. 3, FAO, Rome.

Harrold, P. 1995. "The impact of the Uruguay Round on Africa: Much ado about nothing?" World Bank Conference on the Uruguay Round and The Developing Countries, 26–27 January, Washington, D.C.

Oyejide, T.A. 1990. "The participation of developing countries in the Uruguay Round: An African perspective". *The World Economy*, vol. 13: 427–444.

Oyejide, T.A. 1993. "Effects of trade and macroeconomic policies on African agriculture". In R.M. Bautista and A. Valdes, eds., *The Bias Against Agriculture: Trade and Macroeconomic Policies in Developing Countries*. ICEG/IFPRI. San Francisco, California USA: ICS Press.

Oyejide, T.A. 1997. *Africa's Participation in the Post-Uruguay Round World Trading System*. PSID Occasional Paper, WTO Series no. 6, The Graduate Institute of International Studies, Geneva.

Oyejide, T.A. 1999. "Markets and economic growth in Africa". Paper prepared for the AERC collaborative research project on Explaining African Economic Growth Performance, presented at the Harvard Conference, 26–27 March.

UNCTAD. 1997. "The Post-Uruguay Round tariff environment for developing countries", TD/B/COM.1/14. Geneva: UNCTAD.

UNCTAD. 1998. *Trade and Development Report, 1998*. New York and Geneva: United Nations.

World Bank. 1993. *A Strategy to Develop Agriculture in Sub-Saharan Africa and a Focus for the World Bank*. Technical Dept, Africa Region. Washington, D.C.: The World Bank.

World Bank. 1994. *Adjustment in Africa: Reforms, Results and the Road Ahead*. Washington D.C.: The World Bank.

Chapter five

Opportunities and Challenges Facing Africa in the Development of Key Export Sectors Under the WTO Agreement – A Focus on Mining, Manufacturing and Services

by Colin McCarthy, Department of Economics, University of Stellenbosch

1. Introduction

Escalating economic growth and development form part of the anticipated African renaissance. Many analysts see a greater integration of African economies into the global economy through export-oriented growth as a prerequisite for this development. Will the agreements of the World Trade Organization (WTO) play an important or even decisive role in African's renaissance? This paper – with its focus on the economies of sub-Saharan Africa (SSA), the least developed ones in particular – addresses this question. The conclusion is that the primarily demand-oriented WTO agreements will have little direct impact on countries that face severe supply constraints.

In contrast to the seven earlier rounds of the General Agreement on Tariffs and Trade (GATT) negotiations, developing countries actively participated in the Uruguay Round. For these economies the Round represented an important and necessary episode in the development of their trade policies. In the course of the 1980s a large number of developing countries liberalized trade in the process of adopting outward-looking development policies. This change in strategy was accompanied by the growth of developed economies' defensive protection through non-tariff measures in particular. Having been converted to outward-looking growth policies, in many cases somewhat forcefully through structural adjustment programmes, developing countries became active participants in the Uruguay Round to enhance their integration into the world economy. They made significant concessions "in the hope of obtaining improved access to international markets and greater disciplines on unilateral measures against their exports" (Agosin, et al., 1995: 2).

The Uruguay Round agreements are of special interest to developing countries since they not only extended the conventional scope of GATT beyond the border protection of goods, but in this category also placed greater emphasis on agricultural products. The extension of trade liberalization was effected by the adoption of the General Agreement on Trade in Services (GATS). This acknowledged the fact that the service sector is now the largest sector in most developed and developing economies and one of the fastest growing components of world trade. Developing countries are also strongly affected by the Agreement on Trade-Related Aspects of Intellectual Property Rights (TRIPS), which covers substantive intellectual property rights and their protection, as well as measures for enforcement. Since developing countries are more likely to include interventionist support measures in their trade and industrial policies, they also have a potentially stronger exposure to the tighter disciplines of the Uruguay Round agreement on the direct and indirect subsidies governments provide to assist agricultural and industrial producers. The same applies to the Agreement on Trade-Related Investment Measures (TRIMS), which explicitly acknowledges that certain investment support measures have restrictive and distortive effects on trade; TRIMS, therefore, set out to govern these measures.

The updated GATT 1994 and a further 12 side agreements such as the agreements on subsidies and countervailing measures (together these make up the Multilateral Agreement on Trade in Goods), the General Agreement on Trade in Services, and the Agreement on Trade-Related Aspects of Intellectual Property Rights,[1] represent the core of the WTO. They are of special significance for developing countries since the Final Act represents a "single undertaking". This means that all countries, including developing countries, that join the WTO sign up to all three agreements. Under the regime created by the Tokyo Round, countries could be selective about the codes they acceded to. This ability to pick and choose agreements has now been denied developing country governments, since the only agreements members of the WTO can now decline to accede to are the plurilateral trade agreements (see note 1).

In addition to the removal of agreement on code selectivity, the special and differential treatment (SDT) in favour of developing countries has also been changed drastically. The SDT dispensation of the earlier regime survives in principle, with the only asymmetry being that the developing countries are allowed longer phase-in periods. However, real exemptions with a SDT for the least developed countries still exist. For other developing countries a major outcome of the application of the subsidies agreement, for example, is that they do not have the option of replicating the export promotion policies used by the Republic of Korea and Taiwan during the 1960s and 1970s (Rodrik, 1995b).

On balance, the outcome of the Uruguay Round does not represent much for developing countries (Agosin et al., 1995). Market access is a key issue, but while tariffs on products of special interest to developing countries have been cut, they remain at higher levels than those on goods mainly traded among developed countries. The textile industry is of special importance to the industrial development of the developing world, and the integration of these sectors into the WTO, with the staged phasing out of the Multi-Fibre Agreement (MFA) over a period of ten years, is important. However, as will be argued later on, the phasing out of the MFA will not unambiguously favour sub-Saharan African economies. Tariff escalation, although reduced, also remains in place, thus inhibiting the competitive processing of primary commodities in developing countries. Furthermore, food importers will lose because of the price increases that are likely to result from the elimination of agricultural subsidies for developed country food producers. However, in considering the net impact on developing countries, it is worth noting Rodrik's (1995b: 46) view: that "The more important and potentially highly significant gains will come indirectly, from the strengthening of multilateral discipline in the areas of safeguards, anti-dumping and, above all, dispute settlement". Simultaneously, it needs to be considered that the Uruguay Round agreements have created a force of discipline over national policy with the curtailment of the room for discretionary changes in national industrial and trade policies. This discipline forms the basis for Rodrik's (1995b) contention that WTO membership and its commensurate commitments can play an important role in improving economic policy.

But, as will be argued below, neither the curtailment of special and different treatment nor the relatively weak improvement in market access and other benefits are as serious for sub-Saharan Africa as for the developing world in general. In both respects, least developed countries are mainly excluded. Most sub-Saharan African countries fall in this category. Other sub-Saharan African countries that are excluded are Cameroon, Congo, Côte d'Ivoire, Ghana, Kenya, Nigeria, Senegal and Zimbabwe.

Clearly, international obligations and opportunities have changed under the new WTO disciplines and commitments. While the implications of the new dispensation for African development have been fairly adequately researched and commented on, little attention has been given to the proactive measures that can be taken under the new circumstances to encourage diversified growth on the basis of manufactured exports, foreign direct investment and technology development. Against this background, this paper considers the position in Africa of the mining, manufacturing and services sectors, specifically:

- Their performance and growth potential.
- The constraints to market access that confront them when output and exports are expanded.
- The key elements of the WTO agreements that inhibit the development of these sectors in African economies, specifically the constraints placed on the ability of governments to implement policy measures in support of national development strategies.

A major theme of the paper is that the access to markets, which is what the WTO agreements are primarily about, is not the major constraint on the diversified and sustainable growth of the typical or "average" African economy. One observer concluded that "... the problem of African producers is not the lack of market access but excessive production costs, inadequate knowledge of markets, poorly developed product ranges and the obstacles placed in the way of export oriented manufacturing industry by states incapable of reform" (Kappel, 1996: 38). This is a harsh judgement, but one that deserves consideration.

Since the focus of the paper is sectoral, the conceptual framework that will be used is the division of economic activity into tradeable and non-tradeable production, with the tradeable component further divided into exportables and importables. The primary focus of the paper is the tradeable goods sector, exportables in particular, and the implications of the WTO agreements for the development of this sector. Primary sector production, both agriculture and mining, and manufacturing are the main tradeable components. However, services are increasingly brought into the tradeable sphere, hence the importance attached to services in the Uruguay Round negotiations and in the subsequent WTO agreements. This paper excludes agriculture; a complementary paper is being prepared on the agricultural sector.

2. Marginalization and the Development Challenge

Anne Krueger (1977: 1) introduced her Presidential Address at the 1997 meeting of the American Economic Association with the following observation: "The improvement in living standards, life expectancy, and economic growth prospects in developing countries ranks among the most important economic success stories since the Second World War". This improvement in living standards has been firmly based in the benefits developing countries have derived from the growth in world trade and capital flows in recent years. Developing countries increased their share of world trade from 23% in 1985 to 29% in 1995; at the same time their trade linkages deepened and diversified. The share of inter-developing country trade in total developing country trade increased from 31% in 1985 to 37% in 1995. During the same period the share of manufactured products in their exports increased from 47% to 83% (IMF, 1997).

These encouraging developments unfortunately do not reveal the wide disparities among developing countries and developing regions. Virtually a whole continent, Africa, by and large missed out on the advances made by the developing world. For many developing countries, especially in Latin America and Africa, the 1980s proved to be a poor decade for economic growth and development. These regions, and Africa in particular, were

Table 5.1: World output growth (%), 1980–1997

	1980–90[a]	1991	1992	1993	1994	1995	1996[b]	1997[c]
World Developed	2.9	0.6	1.4	1.4	2.8	2.4	2.8	3.8
Market economies	1.8	0.9	1.6	1.0	2.9	2.0	2.3	2.3
Developing countries	2.8	2.9	3.6	5.0	4.8	4.8	5.6	5.6
Africa	1.6	1.9	0.7	-0.6	1.4	2.8	3.9	3.9

Notes: [a] Annual average. [b] UNCTAD estimate. [c] UNCTAD forecast.
Source: UNCTAD (1997a).

hard hit by the deterioration in terms of trade of the 1980s. During 1980–91 the annual average terms of trade loss was equivalent to nearly 25% of the value of commodity exports in 1980. According to Maizels (1994: 1686–7) this loss was "significantly greater than the equivalent experience during the Great Depression of the 1930s when the annual average terms of trade loss of the present group of developing countries over 1930–38 amounted to some 16–17% of the pre-recession (1929) level of their commodity exports". Because the commodity sector is relatively more important for African economies, the terms of trade loss, in relation to GDP, was much greater for African countries than for the other developing regions. The loss for Africa (excluding Nigeria and other oil exporters) was, on a cumulative basis, as much as 25% of GDP. This was much more of a severe drain on resources than the 12% for Asia and 14% for Latin America (Maizels, 1994).

In most sub-Saharan African countries the poor growth performance continued into the 1990s (see Table 5.1), despite the numerous structural adjustment programmes implemented to bring about a turnaround in the economic welfare of the continent. But economic recovery began in 1994, with growth accelerating to 3.9% in 1996. UNCTAD (1997a,b) has noted as important contributing factors to this improvement: favourable commodity prices, improved weather conditions, reductions in political instability and civil unrest, and the continued and deepened implementation of economic reform programmes. But UNCTAD (1997a,b) also cautions that many of these factors are of a once-off nature and, therefore, cannot be expected to increase output indefinitely.

The declining growth performance of sub-Saharan Africa (always bearing in mind that there are some important exceptions, which, however, should be regarded as outliers) has led to the apocalyptic emphasis on the marginalization of sub-Saharan Africa in the global economy. There is no paucity of information to illustrate Africa's marginalization. A few examples will suffice to make the point.

In 1973, sub-Saharan Africa contributed 1.7% to the world GNP. This share increased to 2.3% in 1983 but then declined sharply to 1.1% in 1994. In 1973 the GNP per capita of sub-Saharan Africa came to 21% of world GNP per capita. This increased to 25.4% in 1983 but then more than halved to 10.9% in 1994. During the 1970s, sub-Saharan Africa's real GDP average annual growth of 3.8% was lower than that for developing countries as a whole (5.2%), but marginally higher than for the world (3.6%). During 1980–93, sub-Saharan Africa's average growth dropped to 1.6%, which was significantly lower than the 2.9% of developing economies and the world (Africa Institute, 1997). The share of sub-Saharan Africa in world manufacturing output decreased from 0.6% in 1970 to 0.5% in 1980 and 0.3% in 1990 and 1995 (UNCTAD, 1997a).

During 1992–94, Africa's exports on average represented only 2.4% of the world total (see Table 5.2). Although agriculture, as will be shown below, dominates most African economies, this dominance does not find expression in a large share of world agricultural trade; during 1992–94 this share came to only 3.7%. A characteristic of sub-Saharan Africa's export trade is its high level of country concentration. As shown in the Appendix, South Africa contributed 40.1% to sub-Saharan Africa's exports in 1995 and oil-producing Nigeria contributed 16.4%. No other country accounted for more than 5% of the region's exports. During 1980---1990, sub-Saharan Africa's exports shrank by an annual average of 1.4%, improving to a growth of 1.5% during 1990–96. During 1990–93, exports declined by 3.4% annually. Imports declined by 1.3% per year during the 1980s, but increased by 1.6% during 1990--93 (WTO, 1995, 1997a).[2] In 1994, sub-Saharan Africa's exports grew by 3.1%. However, if South Africa's export growth of 4.4% is excluded, the growth for the remainder becomes negligible. Africa's intra-regional trade is also very low. In 1994 it was 9.1%, compared to the 20.2% for Latin

Table 5.2: Africa's share in world merchandise trade 1992–1994

Agricultural products	3.7%
Mining products	1.6%
Manufactures	2.4%
Total merchandise exports	2.4%

Note: Merchandise exports to unspecified destinations are excluded.
Source: WTO (1995).

America, although this ratio does represent an increase of 8.0% in 1992. But again, if South Africa's substantial contribution and very rapid growth of exports to African countries were to be excluded, the picture would be even less rosy.

Production in Africa is supported (constrained) by a notoriously weak infrastructure. Africa's electricity generating capacity is 0.14 MW per 1,000 population, compared with the world total of 0.55 MW per 1,000 persons. Electricity output per capita is 503 kWh in Africa compared with 2,692 kWh in the world. Only 20% of the African road network was paved in 1990. Some 19 telephones existed per 1,000 population, compared with 130 per 1,000 persons for the world (Africa Institute, 1997). In studies on the impact of the Uruguay Round outcomes on the economies of Ghana, Malawi and Namibia, UNCTAD encountered a common complaint from the private sector about the constraints that infrastructural deficiencies – covering services such as finance, transport, telecommunications, electricity, water supply and road maintenance – placed on export growth (UNCTAD, 1997d). These constraints apply in other sub-Saharan African countries as well, with the possible exception of South Africa. An aggravating factor is that 14 of sub-Saharan Africa's 42 continental states are landlocked, which introduces further problems as far as transport and communications are concerned. Being landlocked creates extra costs and administrative hassle, and could make an economy dependent on the poorer infrastructure of a neighbour. With trade mostly concentrated in low value, high bulk commodities and products, airfreight cannot be an affordable substitute for surface transport.

In 1990–92, Africa received one-thirtieth of the net inflows of FDI to developing economies and 0.6% of portfolio equity inflows. Malaysia, alone, received three times as much FDI and five times as much portfolio capital (Easterly, 1996).

While one cannot ignore marginalization, especially if sub-Saharan Africa's declining share in world trade is taken as a criterion, it should be borne in mind that the post-apartheid inclusion of South Africa in sub-Saharan Africa renders marginalization less emphatic. The South African economy – though not booming, but with stable and positive real growth and significant growth in manufactured exports – can hardly be described as a marginalized entity. If one also includes in the group of non-marginalized sub-Saharan African economies the consistent outliers (Botswana, Lesotho, Swaziland, Namibia and Mauritius) as well as those African economies that during recent years have been bucking the marginalization trend (e.g., Uganda, Ghana, Ethiopia), it would appear that the largest component of sub-Saharan Africa's gross production is not generated in marginalized circumstances. Of course, should population and not output be taken as the relevant criterion, the spectre of marginalization remains firmly in place for sub-Saharan Africa, with very little relief from poverty in sight for the vast majority of Africa's population.

A turnaround in Africa's economic decline in the post-Uruguay era will require some appreciation of the causes of the decline. An important starting point is to understand that the decline was neither predictable nor inevitable, but rather contingent. The point is often made that at independence in the 1960s Africa was in better economic shape than the less developed Asian economies (Ndlovu, 1996).[3]

A number of studies that used a dummy variable to account for differences in economic growth performance among different geographic groups established that a dummy variable for Africa consistently yielded a significant and negative coefficient.[4] From a historical perspective, being an African economy introduces the likelihood of poorer economic performance, much of which can be ascribed to misguided policies. Easterly (1996) found that three policy variables – financial depth, the black market premium over the official exchange rate and government surplus (manifesting as, respectively, financial repression, over-valued exchange rates and excessive budget deficits) – explained a loss of aggregate income for 1989 equal to about $800 billion. This was approximately four times the total external debt in Africa. It is also generally accepted that weak policies for the provision of infrastructure and education contributed to Africa's malaise. However, having accounted for policy as contributing factor, a large part of Africa's poorer growth (compared with that of Southeast Asia) remains unexplained. Ethnic diversity fills part of the gap and so does contagion, that is, the impact of neighbours' policies and growth performance on your own. Easterly (1996) found a remarkably strong relationship, with slower growth by 1.0 percentage point, in the neighbours reducing the home country's growth by 0.34 to 0.55 percentage points.

Contagion is important for development. One can theorize about the explanation of the contagion effect but if accepted at face value it can provide valuable pointers to development strategies that could be adopted in Africa. Two immediate elements come to mind. The first is that regional cooperation takes on a new meaning. Regional integration does not have a good track record in Africa and the large number of failures could lead to integration agnosticism. However, the potential for negative or positive contagion should strengthen the argument for regional cooperation. Over-optimistic plans for integration need not be the focus of the exercise; regional cooperation and institution building that would enhance the development of a regional identity and cohesion, as well as policy coordination, can provide an important framework for the transmission of positive signals. The second element, which can be linked to the first, is the positive impact on neighbours of continental success stories. In East Asia, Taiwan was the first to abandon inward-looking policies in favour of development through exports. Korea adopted a similar strategy in 1960 and, according to Krueger (1997: 17), "the favourable experience of Taiwan undoubtedly facilitated the willingness of decision makers to try the new approach". Focusing on continental success stories and their contagious impact re-affirms the importance of good policy. In this respect the study by Savvides (1995: 454) of the economic factors that contribute to the diverse performance across African economies confirmed "that the policies promoted in other parts of the globe, namely macroeconomic stability and outward orientation, are conducive to economic growth in Africa. ... the factors making for greater economic growth in Africa are no different from those elsewhere". It may be emphasized that Savvides's research results indicate "African nations that have experienced greater political freedom appear to have grown faster in comparison to other African nations". It is not unrealistic to envisage a general improvement in Africa's economic performance if a number of countries could implement policies that would serve as role models for neighbouring states.

3. Development Strategies – An Overview

The situation that faces sub-Saharan Africa requires rapid economic growth, since growth, although not a sufficient condition for the amelioration of poverty, is a necessary one. The main objective of this paper is to briefly review export-oriented growth policies from a sectoral perspective and to do so within the context of the WTO multilateral trading system. The sectoral focus of the paper requires some comment to explain the underlying theme of the story I tell, namely the need to expand tradeable production across all economic sectors.

The information summarized in the Appendix allows the identification of certain characteristics of the typical sub-Saharan Africa economy.

The great majority of sub-Saharan African countries are poverty-stricken and have economies that are small, in terms of both population and GDP. Only six countries in sub-Saharan Africa have a GNP per capita in excess of $1, 000. The aggregate of the GDPs listed in the Appendix is $276,427 million, which is roughly the size of Belgium's GDP in 1995. If South Africa, which contributes approximately 49% to the GDP of sub-Saharan Africa, is excluded, a GDP of $140,035 million is obtained, which in size approximates that of Norway or Hong Kong. The largest concentration of least developed economies (LDCs) is found in sub-Saharan Africa; of the 48 countries listed by UNCTAD as least developed, no fewer than 33 are in sub-Saharan Africa, which means that 69% of sub-Saharan Africa falls in the category of least developed economies. Domestic commercial markets in sub-Saharan Africa, therefore, tend to be relatively small.

In general, the economies of sub-Saharan Africa are primary-producing, mostly in agriculture, with only ten of the economies' agricultural sectors contributing less than 20% to GDP (Appendix). For most of the countries in sub-Saharan Africa, manufacturing contributes less than the 13% weighted average share of this sector in the GDP of low-income economies (China and India excluded) as classified by the World Bank (World Bank, 1997b). If the share of the labour force in agriculture is taken as indicator, the dominance of this sector is even more pronounced, even in those countries where agriculture is not the most prominent contributor to GDP. For example, in oil and diamond-producing Angola, agriculture contributes 12% to GDP, but 74% of the labour force is active in this sector. In mineral-rich Botswana the respective shares are 5% and 46% and in Zimbabwe 15% and 71%. The large overall discrepancy between the contribution of agriculture to the GDP and the share of the sector in the labour force reflects the low productivity of agricultural production in sub-Saharan Africa.

A number of sub-Saharan African countries can also be classified as mineral-rich economies. On the basis of the minerals' contribution to merchandise exports and the GDP in 1991 and a mineral dependence index, Davis (1995) identified 33 developing countries as mineral-based economies, of which 14 were sub-Saharan African countries.[5] In 1970 only six sub-Saharan African countries fitted this description. There are six countries that largely depend on oil exports: Nigeria, Angola, Congo, Gabon, Cameroon and Equatorial Guinea.

In view of these characteristics, the first inference would be that the development of the agricultural sector must be a first priority. The majority of economically active people depend, at low levels of productivity, on agriculture for their livelihood and, hence, growth in agricultural productivity will be the most direct way of raising standards of living. Where exploitable mineral resources exist, it can be assumed that these are the surest means of attracting foreign direct investment; creating employment and cash income; providing government with a significant source of revenue; and earning foreign exchange. From a development point of view the mining sector introduces a number of important issues. The first is that in sub-Saharan Africa, South Africa excluded, the exploitation of mineral resources has mostly been undertaken by foreign mining companies. Experience, supported by theory, shows that FDI in the minerals sector, compared with manufacturing, is influenced by a different set of factors. The reason for this is that mining is resource – and therefore location – bound, while manufacturing, by comparison, is footloose. Since mineral deposits are exhaustible the distribution and use of encashed mineral rents will determine the impact of mining on economic development. This issue will be discussed in Section 4.

If export orientation is introduced as an element of development, most sub-Saharan African economies face a predicament that has been summarized in a succinct description by the WTO secretariat: "The dependence of least-developed countries on exports of a narrow range of largely unprocessed primary commodities and raw materials, which are susceptible to price volatility on world markets, whose price and income elasticity of demand is low, and whose growth has been far more sluggish than world trade overall, is one of the main factors hindering their export performance. It also limits severely the stimulus that the export sector can provide to the domestic economy through backward linkage activities" (WTO, 1997b: 5). It is widely believed that the only solution to these problems is the diversification of economic activity and exports into manufactures. However, this does not mean that room does not exist in many instances for export diversification into non-manufactured tradeables in primary commodities and services, tourism in particular.

There are sub-Saharan African economies (for example, South Africa, Zimbabwe and Côte d'Ivoire) that already have significant manufacturing sectors and they, as well as the African LDCs who would be making progress on the basis of their primary sectors, will have to either increase the extent and rate of industrial development, or, in the case of the LDCs with the smallest presence of industrial activity (for example, Ethiopia, Uganda and Guinea), encourage manufacturing growth. For many of the latter economies, the processing of primary commodities may represent the most viable first steps in industrial development. Since mineral beneficiation, in general, depends on the existence of exploitable resources and also tends to be highly capital intensive, it may be expected that the processing of agricultural products (mainly foodstuffs for which a domestic market will exist) will provide the most likely means of increasing domestic value added.

Manufacturing is generally regarded as the engine of economic growth, and industrialization the appropriate road to sustainable diversification, but this sector is too capital intensive to provide the growth in jobs that sub-Saharan African economies require. For many sub-Saharan African economies, services may be the sector that will enhance income and employment creation. The potential for tourism-related growth in services (transport, accommodation, promotion and commerce) specifically should not be underestimated.

Special consideration should also be given to the development of the financial services sector in view of its contribution to economic development. Through its role in mobilizing savings and channelling these to investors, a good financial system allocates these savings to high-return investments. In addition, it manages the payments mechanism of the economy and plays an important part in risk assessment. Although some progress has been made, financial systems, as will be argued in Section 6, remain weak in most sub-Saharan African countries.

4. Mining Industry

One of the major constraints to economic growth and development in sub-Saharan Africa is that saving and investment rates, particularly those of the private sector, are significantly lower than those of other developing countries. During 1986--1994, gross investment in sub-Saharan Africa on average constituted 17% of GDP and the average private savings rate 13%. This investment rate is significantly below the 25% investment–GDP ratio that is the estimated ratio required to sustain real GDP growth at about 6% (IMF, 1995). Mineral resources have the potential to close this gap, as well as the foreign exchange gap that arises because of the importation of capital and other goods required for investment and growth. Closing the gap is achieved by the export-oriented nature of mining and by the fact that in sub-Saharan Africa, South Africa excluded, mining activity is usually the outcome of foreign direct investment (FDI). This means that both the current and the capital account of the balance of payments benefit.

As shown in Table 5.2, sub-Saharan African mining industry contributed 1.6% to world merchandise trade during 1992–1994. Since mining products during this period represented 11.4% of world trade, sub-Saharan Africa's share is quite significant. Two observations about trade in mining products are in order: First, in certain important products sub-Saharan Africa has experienced a decline in its share of world production, and second, mining production tends to be concentrated in a few countries in the region.

Table 5.3 summarizes the share of sub-Saharan Africa in the world output of gold and silver, the base metals copper, lead, zinc and tin, as well as uranium and platinum, and uranium platinum metals. With the exception of the latter metal group, sub-Saharan Africa's share in the world output of these metals has significantly declined since 1988. In all these cases the decline in relative contribution has been accompanied by a fall in the volume of production. The second characteristic of sub-Saharan Africa's mining

Table 5.3: The contribution of sub-Saharan Africa to the volume of selected world mining production, 1988–96 (%)

	1988	1990	1992	1994	1996
Gold	44.5	34.7	31.2	30.3	26.9
Silver	3.4	3.1	2.4	2.2	1.6
Copper	17.7	15.5	8.9	7.0	5.8
Lead	6.4	4.5	3.4	4.4	3.8
Zinc	5.3	4.4	2.3	1.7	2.2
Tin	3.8	3.8	2.7	–	–
Platinum & uranium					
Platinum metals	66.9	69.2	74.7	78.1	79.8
Uranium	23.5	21.8	18.9	12.7	12.6

Source: Financial Times Energy Yearbooks, Mining, 1994 and 1998, London.

activity is the high country concentration of output: 87.6% of sub-Saharan African gold output in 1996 was produced in South Africa, 71.4% of silver in South Africa, 56.5% of copper in Zambia and 55.1% of uranium in Namibia. The same of course applies for oil, with its concentration in countries like Nigeria and Gabon. Nevertheless, mineral production is an important factor in many sub-Saharan African economies. Some 14 sub-Saharan African countries were included in a group of 33 countries identified as mineral dependent economies, defined as such on the basis of the contribution of minerals to GDP, merchandise exports and government revenues (Davis, 1995). Cognizance must also be taken of the fact that sub-Saharan Africa has substantial mineral reserves, which will lead to growth in mineral output as the current pace of exploration increases.

Mining development can have a beneficial impact on income creation and foreign exchange earnings. But mining has other characteristics that are not so favourable from a development point of view (Lewis, 1984). Mining projects tend to be capital intensive and generally very "lumpy". They often involve capital investment over a long gestation period, with capacity output for the mine reached in a short period, thus resulting in rapid growth of physical output and jumps in export earnings and measured GDP. The high capital intensity is reflected in high capital/output and capital/labour ratios. South African data for 1990, for example, reveal a real capital/output ratio in mining of 2.89 compared with 1.54 in manufacturing; that is, the ratio for mining is 88% higher than for manufacturing. The fixed capital stock per worker was 45% larger in mining than in manufacturing (South African Reserve Bank, 1997). Even if allowance is made for the capital intensity of deep-level goldmining, which, in any case, is somewhat neutralized by the capital intensive nature of the South African manufacturing industry, these figures confirm the general impression of mining as a capital intensive activity. Therefore, the share of labour in value added is typically low, with a large fraction of value added going either to the government or to multinational corporations responsible for the investment. Mineral markets also tend to be unstable internationally and, given the export-oriented nature of mineral production, substantial instability of export earnings and government revenue may be expected.

These characteristics would seem to justify the argument that mineral wealth can be more of a liability than an asset in the process of economic development. Intuitively it is difficult to accept that a developing country with rich mineral resources will be better off without these resources or that the discovery of mineral resources must be regarded as a blow to the development prospects of a poor economy. Questions about the real benefit derived from mineral wealth arise from the use made of "encashed" mineral rents and the impact of this on economic development policy. Assuming that a fair agreement is reached between the government of the host country and the multinational corporation about the distribution of ensuing mineral rents, the key questions concerning the exploitation of the mineral resource are how fast to utilize the resource and how to divide mineral rents between current consumption and investment in income-producing assets, that is, future consumption (Lewis, 1984).

The thesis that mineral resources might rather be a curse than a blessing derives from the observed tendency of mineral-rich countries to make poor decisions about them. Often mineral rents are consumed through the growth in public sector employment and salary bills. But perhaps the greatest damage is done by inappropriate policy decisions related to the channelling of part of mineral revenues into other economic sectors. This is an important issue since mineral resources are finite and once they are exhausted other economic activities must be in place to generate output that can serve as a substitute for the exhausted minerals. This process of channeling revenues into other sectors may take on different forms, but the primary aim should be to invest a substantial share of mining rents in the productive non-mining sectors of the economy, that is, outside general government sectors (Lewis, 1984). A number of options exist:

- The constraint of a weak infrastructure on growth and development was emphasized earlier. In most mineral-rich sub-Saharan African economies it should be an imperative to allocate a part of encashed mineral rents to investment in infrastructure that will support the agricultural and manufacturing sectors in particular.
- For most developing countries, and for those in sub-Saharan Africa in particular, a lack of human capital is a binding constraint to development. Using mineral rents to alleviate this problem through investment in education, training and health services would be a wise investment in favour of diversified economic growth in the long run.
- Mineral rents can also be absorbed into the development of the tradeable sector in an effort to diversify the economy. This can be achieved through the protection of either import-competing or export-oriented industries through tariff and non-tariff protection, which can include direct subsidization, especially in the case of infant exporters. Funds could also be allocated to a development bank for the financing of investment in productive private enterprises.
- It can also be negotiated that the mining company use part of its mineral rents to enhance the links between the mining operation and the domestic economy. In order to prevent an enclave-type development, mine operators can be expected to recruit local workers as far as possible, thus restricting expatriate workers to a minimum, purchase production inputs of domestic origin wherever feasible, and invest in social and physical (long-term) infrastructure (housing, health services, education and training, road systems, airports, and harbour facilities).

Unfortunately, elements of the use of mineral rents are taken to extremes and beyond a reasonable duration as far as protection of domestic industries is concerned. Rich natural resource endowments have been associated with lax macroeconomic policies, over-valued exchange rates, the protection of industries (often of a highly capital intensive nature) without maturation within a reasonable period, and the development and toleration of rent-seeking groups (Auty, 1994). These experiences should not be interpreted as economic law. Auty (1994: 24) has described them "as merely a strong tendency" that can be avoided through prudent policies.

The experiences of many developing countries testify to the positive impact of the exploitation of an economy's mineral wealth. Davis (1995), in his analysis of the impact of mineral resources, refers to the experience of Chile, one of a number of mineral-based economies, where the mineral industry developed the first railways and modernized agriculture through direct investment linkages, and where the investment of the mining elite contributed to urban development, banking and wine-making. There can also be little doubt that sub-Saharan Africa's largest and most sophisticated economy, South Africa, owes much of its development to the mining industry. The mining revolution, which started in the late nineteenth century in South Africa, not only directly created thousands of jobs, income, foreign exchange earnings and government revenue, but also encouraged the development of the transport and communications infrastructure. For example, in 1861 there was only a single railway line of three kilometres in South Africa (on the Cape Peninsula); in 1891, 24 years after the discovery of diamonds in 1867 and five years after the proclamation of the Witwatersrand as a gold-producing area in 1886, the railway system covered 4,067 kilometres. Mining purchases of inputs like mineworker uniforms, wooden sleepers and explosives also encouraged domestic industrial development. To these backward linkages can be added the indirect encouragement of manufacturing and agriculture through the production of import-competing products that, in meeting a growing domestic demand, enjoyed the natural protection afforded by the long distance of South Africa's mining areas from the coast.

The contention that mining is beneficial for economic development also finds support in the comparative analysis of the experience of mineral-rich economies. In a comparison of 22 economies (which he classified as "persistent mineral economies") with the performance of a comparison group of 57 developing economies, Davis (1995) found that over the period 1970 to 1991 the mineral economies significantly outperformed the non-mineral economies in terms of growth in GNP per capita. The same appears to be the case if outcome-based indicators of development are taken as indicators. Davis (1995: 1773) concluded that "the mineral rents appear to have been used for substantial health and educational development, even in severe Dutch disease economies such as Nigeria". In the evaluation of the long-run performance of the two groups of economies, Davis also found no evidence that the mineral economies consistently suffered from the mismanagement of mineral rents and that the non-mineral economies therefore failed to catch up. For a number of development indicators such as life expectancy at birth, infant mortality and adult literacy, Davis (1995: 1773) found that "the percentage change in the performance of the mineral economies is comparable to or exceeds the comparison group in nearly all cases". Recalling Auty's conclusion, referred to earlier, that the resource curse is not a law but a tendency that can be avoided through prudent policy, Davis' (1995: 1777) empirical observation needs to be noted: "Mineral economies as a group are not cursed, have not performed poorly in the long run, and have not been decimated by the Dutch disease that may or may not in practice accompany mineral booms".

As far as the WTO agreements are concerned, mining products that are exported in unprocessed form do not present any problem. The absence of an entrepreneurial cadre with the expertise and capital required to extract the resources also does not present an economy with insurmountable obstacles since multinational mining corporations are prepared to invest if profitable opportunities exist. If the natural resource is rich enough these corporations will not be prevented from investing by constraints like weak infrastructure. A part of the mineral rent will be used to create the required infrastructure. However, it follows as a matter of course that the more favourable the investment environment is – for example, with infrastructure in place, skilled workers readily available and public services of relatively high quality provided – the more inclined foreign investors will be to invest in the extraction of lower grade resources.

The WTO agreements do become relevant if economies move toward the adding of value to mining output through further processing and manufacturing of downstream products. Adding value takes the analysis into the sphere of economic activity where the conventional distinction between primary and secondary activity can be somewhat vague. For the purposes of this paper it is useful to discuss processing as part of the manufacturing process because of, among other reasons, the phenomenon of tariff escalation, which has survived the Uruguay Round negotiations.

5. Manufacturing Development in the Growth of Sub-Saharan Africa

The Appendix shows that manufacturing does not make a substantial contribution to the GDP of most sub-Saharan African economies. Bearing in mind that the weighted average of manufacturing's contribution to the GDP of the World Bank's category of low-income developing economies (China and India excluded) was 13% in 1995, the (unweighted) average of 11.5% for the economies listed in the Appendix is quite low. With the exception of economies such as Mauritius, South Africa, Swaziland, Zambia and Zimbabwe, the contribution of most sub-Saharan African economies' manufacturing sectors to GDP is in the low teens or below 10%. No fewer than 16 economies had a manufacturing GDP lower than 6%. The lack of diversification of sub-Saharan African economies is also reflected in the composition of exports. In other developing regions the share of manufacturered goods in total exports has grown since 1980; in sub-Saharan Africa, however, it shrank in 12 out of the 30 sub-Saharan African countries for which data are available (UNCTAD, 1997b).

It should also be borne in mind that for most sub-Saharan African economies, manufacturing activity is restricted to relatively unsophisticated processing activities demanding few skills and with low levels of value added to primary products or intermediate inputs.[6] Section 3 emphasized the role that agriculture can play to improve the living standards of the population. This is true, but it is also true that the economic emancipation of sub-Saharan African countries to high levels of economic development and welfare will require industrialization. Africa, of course, has experienced its share of serious efforts to industrialize. This is briefly reviewed in the next section, after which the discussion shifts to manufacturing growth on the basis of primary processing (vertical diversification), horizontal diversification into manufacturing and the likely impact of the WTO agreements on the prospects for manufacturing growth in sub-Saharan Africa.

Early policies of import-substituting industrial development

Reference has already been made to the contribution of inappropriate domestic policies to economic failure in Africa. When African countries gained their independence, a major aim was to catch up with the developed world. To achieve this, the focus fell on industrialization as the engine of economic development. In line with structuralist thinking, the governments of African countries, as primary-producing economies, believed that they would face severe development problems if they depended on primary commodity exports as their source of growth. Locked into a pattern of primary product exports and manufactured imports, African economies faced declining terms of trade and hence the prospect of immiserizing growth.

Economic diversification through industrialization held out the solution to this problem. The obvious target, when viewed from the demand side of the growth process, was to produce for the ready market identified by imports, which means that import-substituting industrialization suggested itself as the logical route to follow. Exports could also provide the opportunity for manufacturing growth, but structuralist thinking was firm in the contention that the markets of the developed economies would not be accessible to developing countries' manufactured exports and also that the manufacturers of the developing world would not be able to compete against the established producers of the developed countries – hence, the need to protect developing country industries during their initial phase of production for the domestic market. In adopting this approach, African economies were not out of line with the general thinking of economists. As Krueger (1993: 43) summarized it: "Seizing upon the desire for industrialization, and supported in part by the suspicion of the international economy, most development economists endorsed import substitution as a means for developing domestic industry". Between the early 1960s and the early 1980s many African countries established highly protectionist trade regimes noted for restrictive import licensing systems, high tariffs, escalated or cascading tariff structures consisting of several layers, import prohibitions, and tight foreign exchange controls (Oyejide, 1997).

The infant industry argument can be used to justify protection. With lower cost producers established abroad, protection for domestic industries with the potential to develop seems reasonable. Given the existence of dynamic externalities, a private producer would not find it profitable to produce under free trade circumstances. Protection would allow establishment subject to the condition, in theory at least, that the industry have the potential to develop to a competitive level and that the cost of the import-competing domestic product would fall below the cost of the import to such an extent that it would provide a return on the cost of protection.

Although the infant industry argument featured prominently in the approach of the Lagos Plan of Action, with its emphasis on trade integration as the means to enhance opportunities for import-substituting industrialization, it is doubtful whether African countries explicitly grounded their infant industry trade and industrial policies on the proactive identification and subsequent protection of industries with the potential to benefit from temporary protection. During the first decades of the post-colonial era, protectionism was rather based on a general preference for interventionism and protectionism, with an added dose of pragmatism to be found in the use of tariffs as an important source of government revenue. Because of this general policy attitude, interventionism was also extended to the export side of trade policy with explicit and implicit taxes on exports. The result was, in the words of Ademola Oyejide (1997: 24), "the rather haphazard, incoherent and internally inconsistent nature of the trade regimes".

Many African governments also did not favour the development of private industry and hence sought import substituting industrial development through the establishment of state-owned enterprises.[7] The dominance of inefficient parastatals and the absence of a dynamic private sector became the hallmark of African efforts to industrialize. As Douglas Rimmer (1989:182) put it: "Economic diversification seems often to have been attempted with scant regard for economic gain or loss, or on the basis of extravagant implicit valuations of externalities". In the world of African development policy, no real efforts were made to identify the dynamic externalities that were supposed to be associated with the infant industry argument. Also, protection became a permanent feature of infants that never grew up. A preference for large-scale heavy industries further indicated that the question of a potential to develop to maturity was never an important consideration.

A general lack of concern for the theoretical niceties of the infant industry argument does not mean that no notice was taken of the need to consider economies of scale in production. In fact, the small size of the typical African economy prompted African states and African development agencies to adopt another element of Latin American structuralism, namely the argument that regional integration could provide the means to create larger markets within which import-substituting industrialization could derive scale economies. Lower unit costs to improve the opportunities for the growth of large-scale manufacturing industries were more achievable in the protected market of a customs union than in the domestic market of the typically small African economy. This rationale and the vision of an African common market led to the adoption of regional integration as the cornerstone on which industrial development, envisaged in the Lagos Plan of Action, was built.

The broad inward-looking development strategies adopted in sub-Saharan Africa have produced an outcome that cannot be regarded as conducive to outward-looking development in the globalized economic setting:

- Sub-Saharan Africa has not been successful in diversifying its tradeable goods production. The Appendix shows that the concentration of these goods is still strongly in primary commodities. To the extent that manufacturing development has taken place the adopted route of import substitution has not led to the creation of a viable and competitive industry in importable goods production and it has also not, as noted earlier, led to growth in Africa's share in world manufactured output.
- In many instances the production of importables was placed in the hands of parastatals. Consequently, a private sector in manufacturing was not nurtured and developed. Those of a structuralist persuasion may see in this an important inflexibility built into the economies that would constrain adjustment to the signals of a market-oriented society in the post-Uruguay environment. Had import substitution taken the route mainly of facilitating the

development of private enterprise in the importable goods sector, the argument would be that a corps of entrepreneurs would now at least exist that could react to the challenges of participation in the global economy.

- It stands to reason that protectionist strategies have created uncompetitive structures that are biased against export production The issue will be to assess the ability of sub-Saharan African economies to meet the demands of the new global trading environment, making full use of available measures to counter this bias.

If the excessive protection of domestic industry in sub-Saharan Africa is taken as the main issue, the questions that need to be addressed are: What can be done to change the situation around to greater international competitiveness and export orientation? More specifically, what is the role of the WTO agreements?

Export-oriented development and the capacity to produce

The forces of structural adjustment and globalization have contributed to the realization that policies of protectionism and inappropriate import substitution do not contribute to the creation of competitive economies. Greater export orientation requires a reasonable degree of neutrality in the markets facing export and import-competing producers. This means that a producer should not face a set of relative prices and incentives that create a bias in favour of the domestic market, as is the outcome of protectionist strategies. Two broad approaches can be taken to remove the bias caused by protectionism: the one would be to liberalize the trade regime and the other would be to neutralize through input subsidies and other mechanisms – such as duty drawback – the higher domestic cost facing export producers because of protection. In sub-Saharan Africa there has been little effort to use such schemes; subsidies create a drain on constrained treasuries, and complicated mechanisms like duty drawbacks require an administrative capacity within governments that does not exist in most sub-Saharan African countries. Many sub-Saharan African countries have consequently chosen the route of trade liberalization, in many instances geographically confined to export processing zones. The general provision that applied in the Uruguay Round was that LDCS were to liberalize their trade regimes more slowly than other WTO members.

Recent years have seen a marked change in sub-Saharan Africa's trade and industrial policies, and in sketching the history of the inward-looking strategies one is drawing only half the picture. Many African states have been compelled to liberalize trade unilaterally as part of structural adjustment programmes (SAPS). Between 1980 and 1992 a total of 35 sub-Saharan African countries were subjected to IMF and/or World Bank-sponsored adjustment programmes, which produced 162 high conditionality, policy-based programmes (UNCTAD, 1993). No other region in the world has had SAPS applied more intensely and frequently than sub-Saharan Africa. Eighteen sub-Saharan African countries have virtually eliminated their non-tariff barriers, a further nine have substantially reduced them and many have reduced their tariff rates.

The underlying contention of trade liberalization is that it reduces to world market levels the cost of imports for export producers, which allows exporters to become competitive on world markets. The economy is then expected to grow on the basis of investment and production growth in the export-producing sectors. This is also the only viable option for small economies, of which there are many in sub-Saharan Africa, since a small domestic market does not allow significant inward-looking opportunities for growth.

Should sub-Saharan Africa be successful in converting to a route of export-oriented economic diversification, the impact on growth and development could be dramatic. If, using 1995 data as a benchmark, sub-Saharan Africa could over a period of time increase its share of world exports from 1.5% to 2.5% (that is, a single percentage point) the value of exports would be $47.6 billion higher, which amounts to 16.5% of sub-Saharan Africa's GDP.[8] Such a quantum change in gross output could have a substantial impact on economic growth.

Interpretations of Africa's experience with SAPS vary widely in their conclusions on the process and outcome of adjustment. That many African countries had raised their protection to excessive levels without much impact on the development of infant industries is widely accepted. The removal of this protection, however, has not, by and large, led to growth in export production that could produce substantial growth and compensate for the disruption caused by the removal of protection. In its 1993 Trade and Development Report, UNCTAD (1993: 109) had no hesitation in identifying its view on the cause of this failure: "The reason for the failure in sub-Saharan Africa was structural. The region's industrial basis is weak and the scope for switching to exports limited". The WTO Secretariat, on the other hand, is quite confident "that those African countries that have undertaken substantial liberalization of their trade policies are seeing their efforts repaid in higher growth" (WTO, 1998: 4).

Comparative studies on industrialization and economic growth tend to confirm the stylized view of a threshold of development that developing countries have to reach if they wish to catch up on development. It is widely acknowledged that technological spillover gives developing countries the opportunity to raise productivity quickly and to grow faster than developed economies. However, for the least developed economies there appears to be a threshold created by poor infrastructural development, insufficient physical and human capital, and too little domestic demand for the areas of production where technological advance is concentrated, to bridge the gap to accelerated economic growth. These economies are consequently left in a state of malaise below high- and middle-productivity countries. In a comparative study that included, as a third group, 29 very poor economies (almost all African), Dowrick and Gemmell (1991: 274) identified the inability of the poorest economies to catch up in industrial technology and a threshold of structural poverty in world development: "Once over this threshold countries are able to follow the route of modernization and catch-up through industrialization. Below this threshold it is extremely difficult to sustain sufficient growth in per capita income to generate the savings and investment, and perhaps to moderate population growth, which might allow further economic development".

Elements of the threshold argument also feature in the work of Owens and Wood (1997) on export-oriented industrialization through primary processing. Following Owens and Wood, it is useful to divide tradeable products into three categories: primary products, processed primary products and narrow manufactures. In terms of the standard international product classifications, processed primary products represent the middle ground that is included in conventions that define the Standard International Trade Classification's (SITC) primary products as SITC 1–4 plus 68, with SITC

5–8 minus 68 being defined as manufactures. The International Standard Industrial Classification (ISIC), however, includes processed products in its definition of manufactured goods (ISIC3).

Using the three-category classification as a point of departure, the main issue is to determine where the emphasis of sub-Saharan African economies should fall with respect to export-oriented growth. The point was made earlier that mineral production in sub-Saharan Africa is export oriented; the issue at stake is whether export orientation should be driven through primary processing (adding value to the primary commodity), which can be described as vertical diversification, or through the production for export of narrow manufactures, which represents horizontal diversification. This question concerns the comparative advantage in international trade of the typical sub-Saharan African economy, and to address the issue it is useful to identify the principal features of these categories of products and to link these to alternative development approaches. The following production characteristics are relevant:

- Processed primary products:
  - capital intensive, or not particularly labour intensive
  - resource intensive and resource bound in terms of locality
  - skill intensive
  - optimum levels of production at high levels of output (economies of scale)
- Narrow manufactured goods:
  - skill intensive
  - labour intensive (potential to be)
  - footloose in location (not resource bound)

Linking these characteristics to the fact that sub-Saharan Africa is capital and skill poor but relatively well endowed with natural resources, leads to the conclusion that sub-Saharan Africa does not have a comparative advantage in either narrow manufactured goods or in the processing of primary products. Owens and Wood (1997) recently extended the research by Wood and Berge (1997), who tested the hypothesis that countries with high skill/land ratios tend to export manufactured goods (defined in the narrow sense as explained above), while those with low skill/land ratios tend to export primary products (defined to include processed primary products). Using the three categories of narrow manufactured goods, processed primary goods and narrow primary commodities, their econometric work on cross-sectional data led Owens and Wood (1997: 1467) to the conclusion that "the combination, as in Africa, of low skill per worker and moderate or high land per worker causes a comparative disadvantage in broad manufacturing or, in other words, a comparative advantage in narrow primary production". The absence of skills is regarded as the major constraint on industrial development. This applies not only to industrial growth paths that focus on the narrow definition of manufacturing, but also to the processing of primary commodities.

According to Owens and Wood (1997: 1467): "... our results suggest that whether a country with extensive natural resources can produce and export processed primary products depends on the skills of its workforce. If the level of skill per worker is high, the country will have a comparative advantage in primary processing; if the level of skill is low, its exports will be concentrated on narrowly defined (unprocessed or less processed) primary products". Consequently, they concluded that the future:

> ... for countries with low skill/land ratios, but moderate levels of skill per worker, epitomized by much of Latin America, is a positive one. Although they lack a comparative advantage in the sorts of manufactures in which East Asia specialises, these countries can, through primary processing, produce and export other sorts of manufactures. For countries which have both low skill/land ratios and low levels of skill per worker, *epitomized by much of sub-Saharan Africa*, the message ... is a more negative one. Countries in this situation have no stronger a comparative advantage in primary processing than in narrowly defined manufacturing. They thus have little chance of exporting large amounts of any sort of manufactures, unless or until they can raise the skill level of their workers (not just absolutely, but relative to the rest of the world), which will require, first and foremost, large increases in the coverage and quality of basic education, and is bound to be a slow process. (Emphasis added.)

According to this analysis, countries with an abundance of land (representing natural resources) and low levels of education and skills should seek their growth opportunities within the category of narrow primary commodities.

The lack of skills ties in with all the other constraints such as poor infrastructure and governmental support systems to create a threshold to export manufacturing that many sub-Saharan African countries find difficult to cross. Malawi is such a case. After having analysed the impact of the Uruguay Round on Malawi, an UNCTAD (1996) report had the following to say:

> A more serious concern for Malawi would seem to be the structural and socio-economic deficiencies that impede growth in the economy and the extent of export opportunities. A perception exists among the commercial community that there are already trade opportunities in Malawi's main markets (the EU and the United States) that domestic producers cannot realize. The claim is made that factors such as the high cost of materials, finance, transport and the uncertain supply of water and electricity are limiting the expansion of exports. ... These comments indicate that the major challenge facing Malawi is to overcome the deficiencies within the domestic economy, in order to take advantage of the trade opportunities resulting from the Uruguay Round. Indeed, domestic policies to combat institutional and infrastructural weakness may be more decisive than externally induced changes, in influencing future growth.

On the view that sub-Saharan Africa's problem is structural and the industrial basis too weak to provide the basis for diversifying export-led growth, the question remains whether trade liberalization on its own will succeed in pushing the economy over the threshold into export-oriented economic diversification. One does not have to subscribe to the view that industrial targeting is an appropriate strategy to appreciate that a significant degree of government intervention will be required to facilitate the establishment of an industrial base that can react positively to liberalization measures.

The experience of East Asia has shown, and intuition-driven logic would support the contention, that in general only firms that are established in the domestic market can become competitive exporters.

It is also clear that a quantum increase in investment will be required to lift sub-Saharan African economies over the threshold. This is in line with Rodrik's (1995b) conclusions on the Korean and Taiwanese experience. These economies, he argued, managed a sharp economic take-off because their governments in the early 1960s and thereafter "managed to engineer a significant increase in the private return to capital", and that the importance of the export-oriented policies derived from the fact that "they enabled a steady rise in imported capital goods" (Rodrik, 1995b: 57, 97). Growth in investment rates is an important prerequisite for accelerated economic growth. In his study of long-term growth, Angus Madison (1989: 23) observed that "none of the countries which had accelerated post-war growth has done so without an increase in investment rates, and the highest rates are generally found in the countries which have had the fastest growth". Investment in these countries provided the "big push", the "critical minimum effort" or the "take-off" of the development literature, or in the context of this paper on African economies, the "shove over the threshold".

In Africa, the investment in physical capital will also have to be complemented with a substantial increase in investment in human capital through education, training and investment in productivity-enhancing social infrastructure. Economic diversification through industrialization, whether it happens to be through import substitution – that is, competing with importables – or export production, will require a broader skill base in the labour supply.

The WTO *agreements and export-oriented diversification*

In sub-Saharan Africa the challenge is to identify the impediments to private investment, the development of skills and provision of adequate infrastructure, and then to put policies in place that will address these obstacles. Since these impediments are mainly on the supply side of production, the required policy framework will not be as demand-side oriented as one would expect it to be if the WTO agreements are taken as primary focus. Of course, the WTO agreements remain crucial. In the first place, supply-side measures and the growth in the capacity to produce tradeable goods cannot be separated from the market absorption of the larger output, and second, there are WTO agreements that have a direct bearing on the measures that are available to encourage investment and productivity growth. This means that the WTO agreements have an impact on both the demand and supply side of industrial development and economic growth, but less so on the latter.

The supply side of industrial and economic growth refers to the capacity to produce tradeable goods. The argument thus far has been that with the exception of economies like South Africa, Kenya, Mauritius, Botswana and Zimbabwe, the economies of sub-Saharan Africa have a particular constraint in this respect: Most sub-Saharan African countries are trapped behind the threshold of development discussed earlier and to escape the process of marginalization will require a quantum change in investment in human and physical capital, thereby establishing a capacity for the competitive production of tradeables for the domestic and foreign market.

It is difficult to conceive of any element of the WTO agreements that may prove to be a supply-side constraint to the establishment of this capacity. Since government subsidies could be used to encourage the required capacity creating investment, it may at first glance appear that the Agreement on Subsidies and Countervailing Measures could serve as a constraint. However, supply-oriented direct and indirect subsidies (such as fiscal measures designed to encourage research, the training of labour and management, technological development and adaptation, productivity improvements, and privatization) and other measures to increase the productive capacity of the economy have no direct bearing on export prices and are therefore regarded as non-actionable subsidies.

In an indirect way the WTO agreements and the new regime that applies in international trade and in the global economy can also have an impact on the supply-side of growth through the policy environment that is created. The realization is taking place "that special preferences for developing countries have largely not worked in the past, and are even less likely to be put to a good test in the future" (Rodrik, 1995a: 49). Even for the LDCs the message should be clear: growth will require participation in the global economy and this will demand an improvement in the quality of governance. Accountability and transparency in the formulation and implementation of economic policy have become deciding, albeit subtle, factors in the establishment of a competitive productive capacity.

The demand side of export-oriented growth is obviously more susceptible to the impact of the WTO agreements. Market access is a major consideration, and here two dimensions can be distinguished: the first is intervention by trading partners, which could have an influence on market access, and the second is the measures implemented by the exporting country to provide its exportables with a price advantage.

In the first category, considering the raison d'être of the Uruguay Round negotiations and the greater participation of developing countries, the general impression is that developing countries would have less restricted access to the major markets of the world. The situation has improved, and will be improving even more as time proceeds. However, while the reduction in tariffs on industrial products will be significant, the reductions will on balance be less favourable to developing countries since goods that they, in particular, export will experience lower reductions than other goods.[9] Primary-producing developing economies that can adopt the processing route to industrialization will also face the constraint of the continued existence of tariff escalation (Agosin et al., 1995). However, tariff de-escalation has occurred over a wide range of commodities with the exception of jute and cocoa, where tariffs on intermediate products were reduced more than those on the final stages of the production chain (Safadi and Laird, 1996).

For most developing countries, the least developed economies of Africa included, textiles and clothing represent the most viable entry point into export manufacturing. This is illustrated by the experience of many developing countries that have achieved substantial industrial growth through the establishment of export production capacity in the clothing and textile industry. Some 22% of all developing country industrial exports (more than 20% for as many as 30 developing countries) consist of clothing and textile exports (Weston, 1995). In view of this the phasing out of the quantitative restrictions embodied in the MFA would at first glance appear to be a major change in favour of the prospects for developing countries to diversify their export production. However, as noted earlier, the tariff substitutes agreed on are relatively high, and even less favourable is the way in which the quantitative restrictions will be phased out: the integration into GATT will take place over a ten-year period in a back-loaded process that will allow nearly half of the liberalization to be delayed until the last day of the ten-year period.

But for African economies that have duty-free access to the European market in terms of the Lomé Convention, the phasing out of the MFA could be bad news because it will introduce competition from other non-ACP developing country producers with more developed and more competitive industrial sectors. These latter producers will now have a competitive edge that did not exist previously. In a textile and clothing market that is only constrained by MFN tariffs, a major change in the distribution of export production in favour of low-cost producers, such as China and others from Asia, can be expected (Safadi and Laird, 1996).

Although it is uncertain what will replace the current Lomé Agreement in 2000, there can be little doubt that the deterioration of the special preferences African countries now enjoy will have a detrimental impact on the room for export-oriented growth. Sceptics, however, can point out that with the exception of economies like Mauritius and, to a lesser extent, Lesotho, African countries have in the past not made good use of the competitive room Lomé created and that its loss is only of academic importance. However, for some countries like Lesotho the loss will not be academic. This small country, totally landlocked within South Africa, has been very successful in raising its manufacturing production through the attraction of export-oriented foreign investment. Closer analysis, however, shows that this investment has mostly been in clothing and textiles,[10] and furthermore that it has been dominated by Taiwanese firms who use Lesotho as a production base to circumvent the quotas on Taiwanese clothing and textile exports, with the added benefit of exporting from a Lomé Convention country. With the constraint of quantitative restrictions removed, it is likely that the efforts to attract new investment may suffer and that footloose clothing manufacturers may leave Lesotho.

In addition to the MFA, export restraint arrangements on industrial goods (voluntary export restraints, for example) are to be phased out in four years in a way that allows each country to maintain one restraint until 2000. While this achievement of the Uruguay Round will, according to Safadi and Laird (1996: 1229), "go a long way towards levelling the playing field in sectors where developing countries enjoy a major comparative advantage", it is unlikely, within the time frame that applies, to be of benefit to any African economy, South Africa included. Only a small number of the more advanced developing country and some developed country exporters of footwear, travel goods, electronics and steel will benefit (Weston, 1995).

As far as the ability of African economies to intervene and provide their export producers with a price advantage is concerned, export subsidization and the Agreement on Subsidies and Countervailing Measures immediately come to mind. Interventions that can be classified as "prohibited" or those that could be termed "actionable" in terms of the agreement will not be available as elements of export-oriented industrial development strategies. As noted earlier, the restrictions placed on the ability to subsidize export industries are interpreted as an effective constraint on the part of developing countries to adopt the strategies used by the East Asian economies in their export-oriented growth. For the more developed African economies this is true. South Africa, for example, was forced by its WTO commitments to terminate its export subsidy scheme. Consequently, a WTO friendly supply-side development approach to encourage the export-oriented growth in manufacturing production has been adopted (McCarthy, 1998). But by far the largest number of sub-Saharan African economies will not be affected by the prohibition of trade-related subsidies since countries with a per capita income of less than $1,000, the so-called Annex VII countries, are allowed to maintain export subsidies. The exemption does not apply to any product in which the Annex VII country has achieved a situation of "export competitiveness", which is defined as a share for two consecutive years of 3.25% or more in the world trade of the product concerned. Once a developing country graduates to an income level above $1,000, it has eight years in which to phase out export subsidies.

As is clear from the Appendix many sub-Saharan African economies, such as Zimbabwe, Nigeria and Kenya, which have a fairly substantial industrial capacity, have considerable room to use export subsidies should they wish to do so. The following points are worth considering:

- Countries with low per capita incomes hardly have the revenue to afford subsidies. However, subsidies may be indirect and implicit when they are designed as tax incentives, artificially low rates of interest, or differentiated and discriminating pricing policies in the provision of services by public utilities. The last two lay claim to scarce resources and need to be considered carefully. Tax incentives in favour of export production, however, can be designed in a way that will not cause government revenue to be sacrificed; revenue forgone of course represents a claim on scarce resources. If the tax incentive is structured in a way that will encourage the growth of production and profits, the revenue forgone argument does not apply since, without the incentive, the revenue would not have existed. Nevertheless, if considered in a general equilibrium framework, export-oriented incentives will affect the allocation of resources of which the final outcome cannot be foreseen clearly.

- The second point to consider is the comparative benefit of export subsidies. Considering the line of argument that the capacity to produce tradeable goods is the real stumbling block, it would seem to be more sensible to target policy measures, including incentive systems and public expenditure, on the supply side of diversifying output growth.

To conclude: the WTO agreements, by and large, can in the long run only benefit African economies in their efforts to encourage export-oriented industrial growth. Comparing pre- and post-Uruguay world trade environments, the fact is that world markets for industrial goods are more accessible, bearing in mind, however, that in some selected but important sectors, such as clothing and textiles, the impact of the phasing-in of trade into the WTO system may be negative. But the WTO agreements are in a direct sense not really the issue when it comes to the export-oriented industrialization of African economies. The WTO – and what it embodies – has created an environment of trade liberalization that is focused on trade as a source of growth for economies participating in the global economy. To escape poverty and marginalization, sub-Saharan African economies will have to trade more, but the major constraint in this respect is found on the supply side of output growth. Since the WTO agreements are primarily concerned with demand-side influences, these agreements are of lesser importance in most African economies.

6. Services as a Source of Export-Oriented Growth

The importance of services in economic activity was alluded to earlier. Services have become a major contributor to income and job creation in national economies, and in some developed economies the cause of or counter to de-industrialization. They are also a growing component of international trade, a factor that has forced analysts to change the conventional practice of regarding them as non-tradeable.

Services are not only important because of their direct contribution to economic activity and trade, but also in the indirect sense of facilitating growth and development. Earlier, the importance of investment as a source of capacity-creating growth was highlighted. An analysis of the impediments to investment will identify limited entrepreneurship (as an outcome of past, and in some cases present, tendencies of governments to favour public at the cost of private enterprise) and constraints on private capital accumulation as major stumbling blocks. It is in the latter respect that one service industry, the financial sector, comes into its own as a facilitator of growth.

Investment is strongly influenced by the efficiency of the financial system in accumulating private domestic and foreign savings and in converting these into productive investment. The perception of the role of the financial sector in development has undergone substantial change and it is now understood that an economy's financial sector is a significant indicator and facilitator of development. Although there are important exceptions (notably in southern Africa), sub-Saharan Africa's financial system is too poorly developed to provide the essential services demanded by investment growth and the development of a modern and productive economy. This lack of development is reflected in the financial deepening ratios for the selected countries (listed in Table 5.4). It is highly unlikely that the current providers of financial services in sub-Saharan Africa have the skills, expertise and entrepreneurial talent to transform the financial sector to the required levels of competence.

At this point one could argue the case for a market failure and therefore the need for the government to intervene, as happens in many African countries, to provide development and commercial finance services. This is not the place to argue the merit of such intervention. What is important within the context of this paper is to make the case for opening the financial service sectors to foreign service providers.

In broad terms, developing countries, and African economies in particular, could derive several advantages from this opening up to foreign financial service providers (Agosin et al., 1995):

- Most African economies are characterized by a dearth of the financial services that any export-oriented economy will require. Foreign trade financing, insurance and sophisticated merchant banking services are not available from domestic financial institutions. Expanding the range of available services will allow goods producers to be more competitive in foreign markets.
- The introduction of these services and the accompanying technologies and skills will spill over to domestic financial institutions.
- Finally, the participation of foreign financial institutions in the domestic market will also increase the potential for the host economy to have access to new sources of foreign finance. Access to the use of foreign savings to finance production for export could allow the host economy to escape the constraint introduced by its inability to generate sufficient savings.

Table 5.4: Financial deepening (money plus quasi-money/GDP) in selected sub-Saharan African and other countries, 1993–1994(%)

Botswana	29.1
Cameroon	18.7
Chad	14.2
Côte d'Ivoire*	28.4
Ethiopia	44.6
Ghana*	17.2
Kenya	40.0
Lesotho	42.4
Malawi	22.7
Mauritius	72.3
Namibia	36.3
Nigeria*	23.7
Senegal	21.5
South Africa	53.4
Uganda	10.1
Zimbabwe*	31.7
Canada	59.2
Belgium*	48.3
Portugal	81.5
Korea	42.8
Australia	61.3

Notes: *The ratio applies to the most recent two years prior to 1993/94.

Significant participation by foreign financial service suppliers can make any developing country, especially the least developed ones, susceptible to the vagaries of foreign capital flows. Although the annex on financial services in the General Agreement on Trade and Services (GATS) provides for host countries to protect themselves against some of the negative impacts, it is open to question whether a small developing economy will be able to take a stand against large multinational financial institutions. On balance though, the need for access to financial services, in the absence of adequate domestic suppliers, will outweigh the possible negative outcomes.

Financial services were specifically considered in the GATS, as were telecommunications, transport, professional services, labour mobility, construction and engineering, transport, audio-visual services, and tourism. Within the ambit of the broader services industry there is clearly a potential to assist development in agriculture, mining and manufacturing through the provision of supporting infrastructure and business services. Tourism, however, provides an independent source of employment-creating growth that in its own right can contribute significantly to economic growth. The commercial, transport and accommodation services that are required for tourist-led growth are in turn impeded by the lack of entrepreneurship, private investment and infrastructure. Because of these constraints tourism is virtually absent in many sub-Saharan African countries or regionally confined, that is, limited to a specific region or place in the country. Most African countries, however, have a comparative advantage in tourism, especially with the increasing focus on eco-tourism. Without the supporting infrastructure this potential for the development of an autonomous source of export-oriented growth will not be realized.

7. Concluding Remarks

An African renaissance will remain a dream unless the continent improves its economic growth record and its share in the economic activity of a global economy that is becoming increasingly integrated. One does not have to subscribe to the view that export growth drives economic growth to appreciate that nations wishing to import can only do so by exporting. Creating the capacity to produce tradeable goods will require a sharp increase in investment in physical and human capital, which in turn will require a substantial expansion of imports. Export growth, therefore, becomes essential to improved growth performance, either as the engine that drives economic growth, or as the facilitator of growth in avoiding the balance of payments constraint.

The theme of this paper is that Africa's economic revival must in the first place be sought in the capacity to produce tradeable goods. The WTO agreements, by and large, are relevant to the demand side of economic growth since they are mainly concerned with access to markets and the effective price at which goods trade internationally. One could therefore argue that for Africa's low-income economies the WTO has comparatively little direct relevance. Even those agreements that could affect supply-side policies, for example, the prohibition on subsidies, do not apply to most of the countries of sub-Saharan Africa. This does not mean that the WTO agreements are unimportant. In a perverse way they could even have a detrimental impact as a demand constraint on Africa's ability to create capacity in important industries, specifically clothing and textiles. However, the WTO agreements have created an international trade regime that ensures improvement in market access and dispute settlement and is more transparent in its operation and in the rules that apply.

Contemplating the full range of policy measures that could be used to create a productive capacity takes one beyond what was intended with this paper. Export growth in non-traditional sectors is an essential objective in the overall aim to improve the economic position of African economies. Diversifying export growth will require the creation of a capacity to produce tradeable goods competitively. Greater competitiveness will require a stable macroeconomic environment and an improvement in productivity, which can be brought about by higher investment in infrastructure, production structures and human capital in order to deepen and broaden the skills base of the economy. Countries that are fortunate enough to be well endowed with mineral resources must avoid the policy temptations that could convert the blessing of mineral wealth into a curse, for example, by channelling a significant part of encashed mineral rents into investment in infrastructure, training and education as well as in primary health care. Mineral-generated resources can also serve as a source of funding for development banks, which can supply fixed investment finance in economies where venture capital markets do not exist or are poorly developed.

There exists no quick fix that can provide the competitive production capacity needed in sub-Saharan African economies. It can also be envisaged that finding the appropriate mix of policy measures will be controversial. But, to conclude with a point made earlier in the paper: The factors that will contribute to Africa's economic growth are not different from those that applied elsewhere.

Appendix 5.A1 Sub-Saharan Africa: Selected economic indicators, 1995

	Population (mil.)	GND per capita US$	GDP mill. US$ 1995	Man. GDP / GDP (%)	Share in SSA exports (%) (1993)	Agric GDP / GDP (%)	Share of labour force in agric	Service / GDP (%)
Angola	10.8	410	3,722	3	4.7	12	74	28
Benin	5.5	370	1,522*	8*	0.2	34*	60	53*
Botswana	1.5	3,020	4,318	4	2.8	5	46*	48
Burkina Faso	10.4	230	2,325	21	0.2	34*	92	39*
Brundi	6.3	160	1,062	12	0.1	56	91	26
Cameroon	13.3	650	7,931	10	2.5	39	79*	38
Cape Verde	0.4	960	108	–	–	–	27	–
Central African Rep.	3.3	340	1,128	–	0.2	44*	78	43*
Chad	6.4	180	1,138	16*	0.2	44*	81	35*
Comoros	0.5	470	174	5	–	39	75	–
Congo Dem Rep.	43.5	120	–	11*	0.6	30*	66	–
Congo Rep.	2.6	680	2,163	6	1.9	10	62*	51
Côte d'Ivoire	14.0	660	10,069	18	4.4	31	65*	50
Dijibouti	0.6	–	–	5	–	3	–	–
Equatorial Guinea	0.4	380	168	14*	0.1	50	73	–
Eritrea	3.6	700	–	11	–	11	79	–
Ethiopia	56.4	100	5,287	3*	0.3	57*	85	33*
Gabon	1.1	3,490	4,691	5	3.2	–	75*	–
Gambia	1.1	320	384	7*	0.1	28*	80	58*
Ghana	17.1	390	6,315	6	1.7	46	59*	38
Guinea	6.6	550	3,686	5	1.0	24	85	45
Guinea-Bissau	1.1	250	257	7	–	46	84	30
Kenya	26.7	280	9,095	11	2.2	29	81*	54
Lesotho	2.0	770	1,029	18	0.1	10	39	34

	Population (mil.)	GND per capita US$	GDP mill. US$ 1995	Man. GDP / GDP (%)	Share in SSA exports (%) (1993)	Agric GDP / GDP (%)	Share of labour force in agric	Service / GDP (%)
Liberia	2.7	–	–	–	0.3	–	70	
Madagascar	13.7	230	3,198	13	0.4	34	70	53
Malawi	9.8	170	1,465	18	0.5	42	86	31
Mali	9.8	250	2,205	6	0.6	46	84	37
Mauritania	2.3	460	1,068	13*	0.8	27*	49	43
Mauritius	1.1	3,380	3,919	23	2.1	9	16*	58
Mozambique	16.2	80	1,469	–	0.2	33*	81	55*
Namibia	1.5	2,000	3,033	9	2.2	14*	43*	56*
Niger	9.0	220	1,860	7*	0.5	39*	89	44*
Nigeria	111.3	260	26,817	5	16.4	28	48*	18
Rwanda	6.4	180	1,128	3*	0.1	37	91	46
Sao Tome & Principe	0.13	350	59	7*	–	23*	–	–
Senegal	8.5	600	4,867	12	1.0	20	81*	62
Seychelles	0.07	6,620	–	–	0.1	–	–	–
Sierra Leone	4.2	180	824	6	0.2	42	67	31
Somalia	9.5	–	–	5*	0.1	65*	94	26*
South Africa	41.5	3,160	136,035	24	40.1	5	13*	64
Sudan	26.7	–	–	9*	0.8	–	68	–
Swaziland	0.9	1,170	1,075	46*	1.1	13*	74*	38*
Tanzania	29.6	120	3,602	8	0.7	68	83	24
Togo	4.1	310	981*	9	0.4	38*	62	41*
Uganda	19.2	240	56,655	6	0.3	50	83	36
Zambia	9.0	400	4,073	30	1.7	22	74	37
Zimbabwe	11.0	540	6,522	30	2.6	15*	71*	48*

Notes: Most recent year before 1995 for which data are available.

Sources: World Bank (1997b); UNCTAD (1997c); Africa Institute (1997); WTO (1995).

Notes

1 In addition to the three core trade agreements, the Final Act of the Uruguay Round also provided the WTO with a dispute settlement mechanism, embodied in the Understanding on Rules and Procedures Governing the Settlement of Disputes. The fifth element of the WTO framework is the plurilateral trade agreements, namely the Agreement on Trade in Civil Aircraft, the Agreement on Government Procurement, the International Dairy Agreement and the International Bovine Meat Agreement.

2 Note that the shares in world exports and imports are those for Africa as a whole. For sub-Saharan Africa, these figures would be less than 2%. In 1993 sub-Saharan Africa was responsible for 67% of African exports and 64% of the continent's imports.

3 Although a single example cannot tell us much about the general situation, a comparison of Ghana and Korea is revealing in illustrating the impacts of different growth strategies. In 1960 the following applied (World Bank, 1980): (a) gross domestic investment was 24% of GDP in Ghana, compared with 11% in Korea; (b) Ghana's exports were 28% of GDP and Korea's only 3%; in Ghana manufactured exports other than textiles, clothing, machinery and transport equipment contributed 10% to total exports, compared with 6% in Korea; and (c) manufacturing contributed 10% to Ghana's GDP and 12% to Korea's GDP. But the situation soon changed, with investment in Korea growing at an average annual rate of 23.6% during 1960–70, compared with -3.2% in Ghana. Korea's exports grew at an average annual rate of 35.2% during the 1960s while Ghana's exports stagnated at an annual growth rate of only 0.1%. In Ghana the contribution of the component of manufactured exports referred to above decreased to 6%; in Korea its share grew to 36%. GDP increased at an annual rate of 8.5% in Korea during the 1960s while Ghana produced a growth rate of only 2.1%. During the 1970s and 1980s the comparative position of Ghana worsened even further, leaving the country far behind Korea, which grew to achieve the status of a newly industrialized country.

4 For a list of relevant references to these studies see Savvides (1995).

5 The 14 countries are Nigeria, Botswana,, Gabon, Zambia, Congo, Angola, Guinea, Namibia, Niger, Democratic Republic of Congo (Zaire), South Africa, Mauritiana, Cameroon and Togo. The sequence here is in terms of the level of the mineral dependence index, which is the mean percentage contribution of minerals to GDP, merchandise exports and government revenues.

6 Another way of looking at this issue is in terms of the distinction of standardized product categories. The ISIC is much broader in its definition of manufactured goods through its inclusion of processed primary products. The SITC is narrower, excluding processed goods and only including SITC 5–8 (minus 68). Sub-Saharan African economies, to the extent that they have developed an industrial base, have done so mostly in the primary processing components of the ISIC.

7 When Ghana gained its independence in 1957 the first independent government adopted a policy of direct government intervention in the productive sectors of the economy. Not only were many state enterprises set up in manufacturing, but state farms featured prominently in agriculture, a state fishing corporation was established and, in the services industry, the National Trading Corporation, a state shipping line, the Ghana Airways Corporation and the state transport corporation. Allocation of resources was primarily undertaken through controls and licensing and the economy took on all the

structures of a 'command economy'. (See UNCTAD, 1996a). This experience would fit into Anne Krueger's observation that many African leaders were explicitly 'socialist' and focused upon industrialization through public sector activity as a means for achieving development" (1993: 51).

8 These rough estimates are based on a GDP of US$276.4 billion for sub-Saharan Africa, world merchandise exports of US$4,404.6 billion and sub-Saharan African exports of US$64.4 billion.

9 Products in this category include textiles and clothing, leather, rubber and footwear, fish products, and transport equipment. Should one look outside processed and manufactured goods, tropical agricultural products are also important in the category of lower tariff cuts (Agosin, et al., 1995).

10 In 1994, Lesotho exported 17.7 million square metres of clothing and textiles to the USA, which was slightly more than Kenya's 17.1 million square metres. Clothing and footwear contribute more than 80% of Lesotho's manufacturing exports (World Bank, 1995).

References

Africa Institute of South Africa. 1997. *Africa at a Glance: Facts and Figures 1996/1997.*

Agosin, M.R., D. Tussie and G. Crespi. 1995. "Developing countries and the Uruguay Round: An evaluation and issues for the future". In International Monetary and Financial Issues for the 1990s, vol. 6. Geneva: UNCTAD.

Auty, R.M. 1994. "Industrial policy reform in six large newly industrializing countries: The resource curse thesis". *World Development*, 22 (1).

Davis, G.A. 1995. "Learning to love the Dutch disease: Evidence from the mineral economies". *World Development*, 23 (10).

Dowrick, S. and N. Gemmell. 1991. "Industrialization, catching up and economic growth: A comparative study across the world's capitalist economies". *The Economic Journal*, March.

Easterly, W. 1996. "Why is Africa marginal in the world economy?" In G. Maasdorp, ed., *Can South and Southern Africa Become Globally Competitive Economies?* London: Macmillan Press.

Financial Times Energy Yearbooks, Mining, 1994 and 1998, London.

International Monetary Fund. 1995. *World Economic Outlook*. May.

International Monetary Fund. 1996. International Financial Statistics Yearbook.

International Monetary Fund. 1997. *World Economic Outlook*. May.

Kappel, R. 1996. "Africa's marginalization in world trade – A result of the Uruguay Round agreements". *Intereconomics*, Jan/Feb.

Krueger, A.O. 1993. *Political Economy of Policy Reform in Developing Countries*. Cambridge, Massachusetts: The MIT Press.

Krueger, A.O. 1997. "Trade policy and economic development: How we learn". *American Economic Review*, vol. 87 (1).

Lewis, S.R. 1984. "Development problems of the mineral-rich countries". In M. Syrquin, L.Taylor and L.E. Westphal, eds., *Economic Structure and Performance*. Orlando: Academic Press.

Madison, A. 1989. *The World Economy in the 20th Century*. Paris: OECD.

Maizels, A. 1994. "The continuing commodity crisis of developing countries". *World Development*, vol. 22 (11).

McCarthy, C. 1998. "South African trade and industrial policy in a regional context". In L. Peterson, ed., *Post-Apartheid Southern Africa, Economic Challenges and Policies for the Future*. London: Routledge.

Ndlovu L. 1996. "Constraints to manufacturing production". In S. Ellis, ed., *Africa Now*. London: James Currey.

Owens, T. and A. Wood. 1997. "Export-orientated industrialization through primary processing?". World Development, 25 (9).

Oyejide, Ademola T. 1997. "Regional integration and trade liberalization in sub-Saharan Africa". AERC *Special Paper* No. 28. Nairobi: African Economic Research Consortium.

Rimmer, D. 1989. "Africa's economic future". *African Affairs*, vol. 88.

Rodrik, D. 1995a. "Developing countries after the Uruguay Round". In *International Monetary and Financial Issues for the 1990s*, vol. 6. Geneva: UNCTAD.

Rodrik, D. 1995b. "Getting interventions right: How South Korea and Taiwan grew rich". *Economic Policy*, April.

Safadi, R. and S. Laird. 1996. "The Uruguay Round Agreements: Impact on developing countries". *World Development*, vol. 2d(7): 1223–42.

Savvides, A. 1995. "Economic growth in Africa". *World Development*, 23 (1).

South African Reserve Bank. 1997. *Quarterly Bulletin*, June.

Wood, A. and K. Berge. 1997. "Exporting manufactures: Human resources, natural resources, and trade policy". *Journal of Development Studies*, vol. 34(1): 35–59.

UNCTAD. 1993. *Trade and Development Report 1993*. New York and Geneva: United Nations.

UNCTAD. 1996a. Impact of the Uruguay Round on Selected African Countries - Ghana Country Study, undertaken by P.E. Donovan and I. Osei, RAF/94/A34. Geneva: United Nations.

UNCTAD. 1996b. Impact of the Uruguay Round on Selected African Countries - Malawi Country Study, undertaken by P.E. Donovan and J.R.M. Chigaru, RAF/94/A34. Geneva: United Nations.

UNCTAD. 1997a. *Trade and Development Report 1997*. New York and Geneva: United Nations.

UNCTAD. 1997b. UNCTAD's Contribution to the Implementation of the United Nations New Agenda for the Development of Africa in the 1990s: African economic performance, prospects and policy issues. Aug TD/B/44/12. New York and Geneva: United Nations.

UNCTAD. 1997c. *The Least Developed Countries 1997 Report*. Geneva and New York: United Nations.

UNCTAD. 1997d. The Uruguay Round and its Follow-Up: Building a Positive Agenda for Development. Report on a workshop convened by the Secretary-General of UNCTAD, 3–4 Mar 1997. New York and Geneva: United Nations.

Weston, A. 1995. "The Uruguay Round: Unravelling the implications for the least developed and low-income countries". In *International Monetary and Financial Issues for the 1990s*, vol. 6. Geneva: UNCTAD.

World Bank. 1980. *World Development Report 1980*. New York: Oxford University Press.

World Bank. 1995. Lesotho Poverty Assessment. Report No. 13170 LSO.

World Bank. 1997a. "Lesotho's garment exports: Attracting foreign direct investment". Findings, January.

World Bank. 1997b. *World Development Report 1997*. New York: Oxford University Press.

World Trade Organization. 1995. International Trade - Trends and Statistics 1995, Geneva: WTO.

World Trade Organization. 1997a. *WTO Focus*. April. Geneva.

World Trade Organization. 1997b. *WTO Focus*. November. Geneva.

World Trade Organization. 1998. *WTO Focus*. January. Geneva.

Chapter six

Costs and Benefits of "Special and Differential" Treatment for Developing Countries in GATT/WTO: An African Perspective

by T. Ademola Oyejide

1. Introduction

"Special and differential" (henceforth S&D) treatment covers the set of rights and privileges provided in the framework of the General Agreement on Tariffs and Trade (GATT) and its successor institution, the World Trade Organization (WTO) for its developing and least developed country members, and from which the developed countries are excluded. In essence, these rights and privileges endow these countries with a unique status by granting them more favourable access to the markets of the developed countries while also giving them substantial policy discretion in their own domestic markets. Thus, S&D treatment in the GATT/WTO context combines, in varying proportions, a right of enhanced access by developing and least developed countries to the markets of the developed countries with the right of developing and least developed countries to limit the access of developed countries to their own markets.

In operational terms, the first of these S&D rights is exercised through trade preferences granted to developing and least developed countries in developed countries markets, while the second right is secured by the maintenance of trade barriers at home. The second element of the S&D rights is, in some sense, broader than the use of trade barriers to protect the domestic markets of the developing and least developed countries. It includes, as well, substantial exemption from several important GATT/WTO disciplines that apply to developed country members. In particular and prior to the changes agreed to during the Uruguay Round of multilateral trade negotiations, S&D treatment covered various additional rights. For example, it permitted developing countries to use quantitative restrictions for infant industry protection and balance of payments purposes, to create preferential regional and global trading arrangements among themselves without extending such preferences to non-members in accordance with the most-favoured-nation (MFN) principle of GATT/WTO, and to benefit from multilateral trade negotiation agreements, in accordance with the MFN principle, without being obliged to observe reciprocity.

An analysis of Africa's position in the WTO framework and a review of the region's current trade patterns, features and prospects suggests that S&D treatment for developing countries in global trading arrangements should be of particular relevance to Africa. It is worth noting, to begin with, that Africa provides about a quarter of the membership of WTO, while the region contains the largest number (compared with other developing regions) of the least developed countries recognized by the WTO. Any trading rule or arrangement that sets aside specific rights and privileges for developing and least developed countries is thus likely to be significant for the African region.

The relevance of S&D treatment, especially preferences, for Africa emanates primarily from the overall significance of developed country markets for African exports. Approximately 80% of these exports find markets in Organization of Economic Cooperation and Development (OECD) countries; and the European Union, as a unit, accounts for over 50% of all African exports. World merchandise exports grew rapidly, in both volume and value, during the 1980–95 period; recovering from a 1% average annual decline during 1980–85, world merchandise exports grew by an annual average of 12% over 1985–90 and 7.5% over 1990–95 (WTO, 1996).

The Africa region failed to share in this virtually global trade expansion; its exports declined by an annual average rate of 8% over 1980–85, recovered enough to grow at an annual average of 5% during 1985–90, but fell back to zero growth rate during the 1990–95 period. As a result, Africa's share of world merchandise exports fell almost two-thirds from approximately 6% in 1980 to about 2% in 1995. The decline in Africa's share of world merchandise exports was a dramatic 50% between 1985 and 1995. In addition, compared with other regions, Africa has a small share of total exports derived from manufactured products. In 1995, the share was 28% for Africa compared with Asia's 83%, Latin America's 50% and the world average of 76%. Correspondingly, African exports contain a much larger share of primary commodities; this was 64% in 1995 as against Asia's 15%, Latin America's 49% and the world average of 24%. Africa's unusually heavy reliance on primary commodity exports clearly influences the region's perspectives regarding S&D treatment for developing countries in the global trading system.

For all participating countries, developed, developing and least developed, there exists, presumably, a shared common interest in a global trading system that delivers benefits at a reasonable cost. More specifically for developing and least developed countries, one of the central concerns of trade policy for development is the terms of access of their exports to the markets of the developed countries. In addition, these countries cling to the right to offer special governmental support to their infant industries and to deal with their balance of payments problems, using various trade policy measures that may have the effect of restricting imports. These concerns raise important issues regarding the extent to which developing and least developed countries need to be accorded S&D treatment in the global trading system and whether a claim to S&D treatment could compromise the achievement of other (and perhaps more significant) benefits.

Even when the idea that developing countries should receive S&D treatment in the global trading system is widely accepted, based partly on the understanding that the more developed and richer countries should transfer income to the poorer countries and partly on the recognition of the special difficulties of the latter countries, two other issues for debate also surface. First, it is not necessarily self-evident that income transfers should be made through S&D treatment; other mechanisms that may be more efficient could be available. Second, it is worth examining whether S&D treatment provides appropriate incentives for developing and least developed countries to pursue policies that do in fact more rationally promote their development.

It is in this context that the question of whether S&D treatment for developing countries has yielded much benefit in concrete terms becomes pertinent. This question, in turn, has several dimensions. One focuses on the actual consequences of S&D treatment for developing countries and is aimed at determining what gains are realizable therefrom. Another concerns itself with estimating the actual costs associated with those gains, and a third dimension examines the extent to which the realized gains are likely to outweigh the costs incurred. In other words, a cost-benefit analysis of S&D treatment would determine not only whether there are accruable benefits but also whether these benefits are large enough to swamp the costs involved. This analysis would, in turn, assist in answering the ultimate question: Is clinging to S&D treatment in the best interest of the developing and least developed countries, or could they obtain better and more durable results from the global trading system by giving up their claims to S&D treatment and accepting to participate on the same basis and subject to the same set of rules as the developed countries?

This paper focuses on many of the issues and questions raised above, and does so specifically from the perspectives of African countries – against the background of the special features of their economies, their trade policy and development experience, and their experience within the global trading system. In the process, Section 2 traces the origins and tracks the evolution of S&D treatment for developing countries in the GATT/WTO framework and indicates its current status after the Uruguay Round of multilateral trade negotiations. Sections 3 and 4 deal, respectively, with the benefits and costs of various elements of S&D treatment and Section 5 concludes the paper.

2. Origins and Evolution of "Special and Differential" Treatment

The guiding principles

S&D treatment of developing countries in the global trading system derives its origins from several inter-related ideas and pressures dating back to the early 1950s. Prominent among these were the recognition by the developed country members of GATT that the trade problems of their developing country counterparts were in certain ways fundamentally different from their own, the desire to keep developing countries within the framework of trade rules established under GATT, and the prevailing intellectual climate regarding development that provided strong support for trade intervention as a legitimate and potent instrument of development. Subsequent changes in each of these perspectives, particularly in the 1970s and 1980s, have weakened the apparent consensus on the need for S&D treatment for developing countries. As a result, the conceptual foundations and operational principles of the special treatment of developing and least developed countries in the GATT/WTO framework have been subjected to sustained attack and erosion.

An implicit assumption upon which GATT was based was that its effective operation as a body of rules designed to guide international trade relations would automatically lead to the economic growth and development of all participants, developed and developing countries alike. This assumption rested on the premise that GATT would provide an environment in which the most efficient industries in developing countries would be able to expand by finding markets all over the world and would, therefore, enhance the achievement of the development goals of these countries (UNCTAD, 1985).

The observed realities of the 1950s and 1960s failed to validate these assumptions. It became clear that developing countries were not deriving much benefit from various GATT multilateral trade negotiations and that very few of these countries actually participated in the GATT process (Hindley, 1997; Blackhurst, et al., 1995). A 1956 GATT report on international trade provided strong confirmation of this trend by demonstrating that a disproportionate increase in exports accrued to the developed country members of GATT. This, in turn, led GATT to appoint a group of experts with the mandate to examine international trade trends with particular reference to the performance and prospects of developing countries. This expert group produced the Haberler Report (GATT, 1958), which concluded, first, that various domestic policies in the developed countries contributed significantly to the decline in the exports of developing countries and, second, that the developing countries were experiencing special difficulties in the GATT negotiating process (Whalley, 1989; Hindley, 1997). On the first count, the report demonstrated that high tariffs faced exports of developing countries on a wide range of products in which they probably had comparative advantage. On the second count, developing countries were handicapped in negotiating reductions of those high tariffs because they were often not the principal suppliers of many of the products.

Furthermore, a study of the barriers against the exports of developing countries conducted during 1960/61 by a GATT committee concluded that these countries often had little or nothing to offer in return for requesting developed countries to lower the tariffs on products of particular export interest to them. Hindley (1997) suggests why developing countries had little to offer in multilateral trade negotiations aimed at reducing tariffs. First, the imports they regard as essential for their development, such as intermediate and capital goods, carried zero or minimal tariff duties. Second, they needed to impose substantial tariffs on the remaining imports, given their heavy dependence on trade taxes as sources of government revenue in the absence of alternative tax handles. These concerns imply that developing countries could not effectively participate in the normal GATT negotiation process.

Their willingness and ability to participate were further constrained by their limited leverage in the globalized negotiating framework and the structural features of their economies. Compared with the developed countries, the developing countries were economically small while their exports were typically concentrated on a limited number of commodities. The latter feature of the typical developing country economy rendered it particularly vulnerable to greater terms of trade volatility and greater susceptibility to external shocks in general. As a result, the nature of their balance of payments problems could be more long term and thus call for extended use of trade restrictions. They could, of course, place greater reliance on exchange rate changes for restoring external balance. But in reality, their usually thin foreign exchange markets could not be relied on to sustain appropriate exchange rate changes without causing some potentially large dislocations in the domestic economy.

In essence, therefore, the perspective that was apparently ascribed to the developing countries during the 1950s and 1960s implies that while the GATT framework could assist in enhancing their growth and development, their economies have peculiar characteristics that constrain their trade prospects and these should justify their being given special status under the global trading rules and arrangements embodied in GATT. In particular, the peculiar features of their economies show up most prominently in four key areas:

- Their balance of payments problems tend to be endemic and long-term and may call for the use of trade restrictions.
- Their trade prospects are poor because their exports are relatively income inelastic; special access to developed country markets may be needed to enhance their export prospects.
- Their growth and development could be significantly enhanced through industrialization and export diversification which, it was believed, could be achieved through domestic protection.
- In the absence of more viable alternative sources of government revenue, they are obliged to rely quite heavily on trade taxes.

For these reasons, elements of special status for developing countries in the GATT framework would include considerable domestic autonomy in the use of trade policy to deal with balance of payments problems, promote industrialization and raise government revenue. In addition, these elements would also include preferential access to developed country markets as a means of offsetting their poor export prospects.

Hudec (1987) argues convincingly that the peculiar features of developing country economies cited as a basis for according them special status under GATT had been recognized and acknowledged even before GATT was established. In particular, in negotiating the original charter of the International Trade Organization (ITO), the stillborn predecessor of GATT, the United Nations Economic and Social Council voted an amendment to the draft resolution requiring the negotiations to (Hudec, 1987: 9):

> ... take into account the special conditions which prevail in countries whose manufacturing industry is still in the initial stages.

According to Hudec (1987: 15), not only did the negotiations acknowledge the legitimacy of the claim "that the special position of developing countries justified some dispensation from the GATT-ITO legal discipline; this principle was recognized from the very beginning of the drafting process". In effect, the discussion leading to the establishment of GATT explicitly acknowledged that developing countries were at a significant disadvantage in relation to the developed countries particularly in terms of competing in manufactured exports where comparative advantage could be influenced by economies of scale, learning-by-doing and other externalities. This recognition also subsequently gave birth to the concept of generalized trade preferences in favour of developing countries in developed country markets – a key component of S&D treatment designed to enable developing countries to expand their manufactured exports and, in the process, encourage industrialization. In this context, preferential tariffs on imports from developing countries would reflect the fact that they are at a lower level of development and establish equality of treatment between them and domestic producers in developed country markets (UNCTAD, 1985).

The origins of several key S&D components can also be traced to the prevailing view of development in the 1950s and 1960s. As will be shown below, various aspects of this view cover the growth and overall economic management concerns of developed countries as well, at least in the early stages.

In broad terms, this view implies that developing country economies could derive some benefits from trade protection. The infant industry argument provides one such area of benefit. It begins with the proposition that comparative advantage can be enhanced or changed through learning-by-doing, suggests that government assistance may be necessary to overcome market imperfections that constrain appropriate investment in the learning process, and concludes that import protection could be a mechanism for enhancing learning. Clearly, the market system in typical developing countries contains a substantial amount of imperfections and distortions that could make purely market directed investments sub-optimal (Stiglitz, 1996). In such circumstances, it would be possible to improve the situation by using properly managed government intervention. Because of the inherent difficulties of using more appropriate intervention instruments, developing countries are often obliged to use trade protection (Rodrik, 1992). Thus, a development strategy that embodies this view would regard as acceptable or even desirable the use of trade policy instruments (including tariffs and quantitative restrictions) to restrain imports. In addition to their use in support of the infant industry rationale, however, trade protection can also serve as an important source of government revenue and may be used to curb conspicuous luxury consumption.

This development strategy has two other dimensions that have significant implications for trade policy. First, the strategy suggests that by prioritizing among imports so as to favour imports of intermediate inputs and capital goods that are regarded as particularly critical to development, higher rates of productive investment can be sustained and, hence, more rapid growth can be achieved. Second, a development strategy that embodies an infant industry component requires long-term commitment regardless of the occurrence of external shocks to which developing economies are particularly susceptible. This suggests the need to insulate key industries from external shocks. Both sectoral prioritization and insulation from external shocks can be achieved by an appropriate use of import restriction measures.

To the extent that these arguments are valid and the development strategy based on them feasible, developing countries would be led to demand from the global trading system the right to maintain control over their own trade policy and to vary this in ways that assist in promoting their industrialization, expanding their manufactured exports and hence their overall economic growth and development. This right would not, in fact, be fundamentally different from the dispensation that developed countries also gave themselves in both the GATT and the ITO charter. Hudec (1987) shows that the very large number of exceptions provided for the benefit of producers in developed countries in these documents amounts to an endorsement of the view that trade restrictions could be used as legitimate and appropriate instruments for facilitating development. In particular, these exceptions included the right to use quantitative restrictions in agricultural imports, to use export subsidies, and to impose discriminatory import restrictions as a means of dealing with balance of payments problems.

Not only were these rights acquired, they were actually used quite liberally. According to Hudec (1987: 25), as of 1 January 1954, 16 of the 20 developed country members were restricting imports for balance of payments reasons and 9 out of the 14 developing countries were doing likewise". Moreover, virtually all of these 25 countries (developed and developing alike) were using discriminatory quantitative import restrictions. The major difference between the developed and developing countries in this regard emanates, apparently, from changes in their respective economic situations. Thus, as developed countries gradually pulled out of their postwar balance of payments crisis, they were better able to refrain from resorting to the exceptions built into GATT; on the other hand, the balance of payments situation of many developing countries failed to show such dramatic improvements. This may have induced the developing countries to cling even more tenaciously to these exceptions.

The evolution of various elements of S&D treatment for developing countries in the global trading systems has broadly reflected the motivations and origins discussed above. In particular, the build up, and expansion processes of specific S&D provisions in GATT that culminated in the establishment of the generalized system of preferences (GSP) closely followed the intellectual support for import substitution industrialization policies that prevailed in many developing countries through the 1960s and 1970s. Similarly, the failure of these policies, the realities of development in the 1980s and early 1990s, and the emerging consensus in support of outward-oriented development strategies are associated, broadly, with the winding down and narrowing of the scope of S&D treatment.

Pre-Uruguay Round S&D status

At the launch of the Uruguay Round of multilateral trade negotiations in 1986, several key elements characterized the S&D treatment of developing countries in the GATT framework. Prominent among these were the right to impose quantitative import restrictions to protect infant industries and combat balance of payments problems, exemption from the obligation to offer reciprocal concessions as a condition for benefiting on an MNF basis from concessions made by developed country GATT members, eligibility under the GSP to enjoy lower rates of duty on their exports to preference-granting developed country markets, and the right of developing countries to grant one another preferential tariffs without extending these to other countries on an MNF basis. Each of these provisions evolved in specific sequences over time; the evolutionary process reflected some of the broad considerations alluded to above.

Article XVIII was the first concrete attempt by GATT to incorporate into its basic law a major element of the concerns of its developing country members. Along with Article XII (for developed country members), this provision permits members to use trade restrictions when their foreign exchange reserves reach unacceptably low levels. The 1954/55 review of GATT articles made a number of significant changes to Article XVIII that in effect specified separate conditions under which trade restrictions could be used to protect infant industries and to deal with balance of payments problems. As a result, Article XVIII acquired three major component parts. Part A permits developing countries to modify previously negotiated tariff bindings in order to assist the establishment of a particular industry. But when this provision is invoked, compensation is expected to be offered or, in the alternative, retaliation may result. Part B permits the use of trade restrictions for combating balance of payments problems, and Part C permits developing countries to use quantitative import restrictions for infant industry protection. Like Part A, however, the use of Part C is subject to compensation or retaliation in the absence of a negotiated agreement.

The decision of developed countries not to insist on full reciprocity from the developing countries for the concessions being made to them is reflected in Article XXVIII bis(3), which indicates that the needs of developing countries to use import duties for general economic development and fiscal purposes should be borne in mind during tariff negotiations.

In spite of the S&D rights created for developing countries in the GATT framework up to and including the 1954/55 review of GATT articles, their trade problems continued to generate concern. In this context, the 1963 GATT ministerial meeting recognized the need for a formal institutional framework for dealing more effectively with these problems. The meeting also approved a declaration accepting the objective of duty-free access for tropical products without expecting reciprocity from developing countries. Finally, it set up a working party to explore the issue further.

While the study by the GATT working party concluded against extending tariff preferences to developing countries in 1965, the meeting of UNCTAD I had, in 1964, discussed the proposal advocating free entry into the developed country markets of developing country exports of manufactures for an initial period of ten years. Due partly to pressures from outside the GATT itself, the continued emphasis on the trade and development problems of the developing countries induced a further revision of the GATT in 1965 by the addition of a new Part IV.

This addition did not provide any new S&D rights for developing countries, but it did offer a permanent form in the text of GATT for some of the existing appeals for special treatment. More specifically, Part IV adds three articles to the 35 articles in parts I–III of the GATT and, as its title suggests, it focuses primarily on trade and development issues. Article

XXXVI recognizes the development needs of developing countries and the importance to them of improved market access. It concludes with a restatement of the principle of non-reciprocity. Article XXXVII suggests that trade negotiations should give priority attention to products of special interest to developing countries, and Article XXXVIII provides for joint action in studying the export potentials of developing countries.

Part IV was largely a diversion, but it failed to stem the pressure for trade preferences in favour of developing countries. Finally, in 1968, during UNCTAD II, the principle and objectives of a generalized and non-reciprocal system of trade preferences for developing countries received approval. The objectives of this initiative were to increase their export earnings, promote their industrialization and accelerate their rates of economic growth. These objectives were to be achieved by granting to the developing countries tariff preferences in the markets of developed countries without reciprocity, on all products.

The GATT provided legal backing for this agreement by its decision of 25 June 1971, to waive the provisions of its Article I for a period of ten years, thus making it legally possible for its developed country members to offer trade preferences to developing countries without offending the MFN principle.

S&D treatment for developing countries in the GATT framework probably reached its peak in the Tokyo Round. At the launch of this Round, developed country members of GATT accepted the idea that existing S&D treatment would serve as the basis of the participation of developing countries in the trade negotiations. The Tokyo Round produced, in 1979, a framework agreement entitled "Differential and More Favourable Treatment, Reciprocity and Fuller Participation of Developing Countries, also known as the "Enabling Clause", which refined or redefined some elements of S&D treatment. In particular, it provided permanent legal cover for the continuation of various GSPs beyond the original ten years indicated in the waiver of Article I granted in 1971. It also identified the "least developed countries" as a separate category of members that should be accorded even more favourable treatment than the group of developing countries, and it specified the S&D elements of various codes agreed to in the Tokyo Round. Finally, the Enabling Clause codified the "graduation" principle by which developing countries would be expected to take on more and more of the obligations of GATT membership as their economies grew stronger. This has generally been interpreted to mean that developing countries will progressively give up various components of S&D treatment as they achieve higher levels of economic development (Laird and Sapir, 1987), although the Enabling Clause itself contains no specification of appropriate criteria for graduation.

S&D provisions contained in the Tokyo Round codes are in three categories. One type consists of offers of technical assistance meant to help developing countries comply with the new rules. A second category provides developing countries with rights to weaker discipline in certain respects, and the third group provides exemptions from the new obligations based, largely, on the presumed limitations of administrative capacity of developing countries. Thus, in the subsidies code, the prohibition of export subsidies on non-primary products was not applicable to exporters from developing countries. Similarly, both the standards and valuation codes either excused developing countries from using standards they consider inappropriate for their development needs or permitted them to set aside particular provisions on a transitional basis.

Post-Uruguay Round S&D status

The next major event to have significant implications for the evolution of S&D treatment for developing countries in the GATT framework was the Uruguay Round. This Round did not start with an agenda to modify any S&D provision – the entire issue was not even on the agenda. When the Uruguay Round (UR) was launched in September 1986, the launch statement contained an explicit promise that the developing countries would be accorded S&D treatment in the negotiations in accordance with the terms of the framework agreement established in 1979 at the Tokyo Round. As the UR negotiations proceeded, however, significant elements of S&D treatment came up for discussion and modification. Most of the changes in S&D provisions that occurred during the UR can be traced to one institutional innovation that was adopted as a guiding principle for the round. This is the "Single Undertaking" principle, which requires that all members of GATT/WTO would be bound by more or less the same set of rules. The acceptance of this principle automatically reduced the scope of many of the existing S&D provisions. In particular, the developing countries are called upon to meet virtually the same standards on a broad range of market access issues as the developed countries. In other areas, S&D provisions have been reformulated essentially in the form of longer time periods within which developing countries should implement the newly negotiated agreements. But for the new category of least developed countries, quite a few of the post-Tokyo Round S&D provisions have survived the UR changes and therefore remain in place. Perhaps the single most important S&D provision to survive the UR without modification for both developing and least developed countries is the GSP. Appendix A presents a fairly comprehensive description of the changes. This forms the basis of the analysis below.

An important area in which the standard of behaviour of developing countries is expected to match that of developed country members of GATT/WTO relates to the use of quantitative import restrictions and special assistance to producers. There are instances, under the new agreements, in which the pendulum appears to have swung the other way round. In other words, in these instances developed country members now have greater advantage in the use of certain otherwise prohibited instruments. For example, developed countries can use quantitative import restrictions virtually without challenge in textiles and for safeguard actions. Similarly, the agreement on subsidies intrinsically favours developed countries by allowing their use for basic research and development, labour training and environmental protection that are more appropriate for developed countries and prohibiting their use for items such as product development that could be more relevant for developing countries.

Prior to the UR, S&D provisions covered two key issues in the general area of market access. One was the binding of tariffs and the other was reciprocity. Both have been modified significantly. Tariff binding has now become mandatory for developing countries as it has always been for their developed counterparts. What continues to exist is difference in the level of tariff binding; because there has been much greater trade liberalization in developed countries, their tariffs are bound at much lower levels than those of developing countries. The result with respect to the second issue is less clear cut. Although the UR did not explicitly revoke the pledge of developed countries not to expect reciprocity from the developing countries, many developing (including African) countries actually made significant concessions during the round (for details, see Harrold, 1995).

S&D provisions regarding the use of quantitative restrictions for dealing with balance of payments problems were radically modified by the results of the UR. The new understanding imposes more restrictive rules and procedures for using quantitative restrictions beginning with the commitment to publicly announce time schedules for the removal of existing import control measures taken for balance of payments purposes. Key elements of these new rules and procedures include the agreement to give preference to "price-based measures" (such as import surcharges, import deposit, etc.) and thus avoid the use of quantitative restrictions unless price-based measures fail to restore the external payments position. Where the use of quantitative restrictions is justified, it must be limited in duration and restrict imports on a non-discriminatory basis. There are two exemptions to the across-the-board rule, and both relate to "essential" imports, i.e., import of products that satisfy basic consumption needs and those that help to improve the external payments position by enhancing output and exports such as capital and intermediate goods.

The right of developing countries to use export subsidies under pre-UR S&D provisions has also been sharply curtailed. Under the new subsidies agreement, developing countries, except those with per capita income below $1,000, are required to eliminate export subsidies within eight years. With respect to sectors and issues such as agriculture, services, trade-related investment measures and intellectual property protection, the remaining elements of S&D treatment for developing countries amount to lower levels of concessions and longer transition periods before compliance is achieved. But, in each of these cases, least developed countries continue to have access to the full S&D provisions.

The agreements relating to technical barriers to trade and safeguards appear to preserve the pre-UR S&D rights of developing countries. Under the former, the developing countries are not required to use international standards that are not appropriate for their needs or which may hinder the preservation of indigenous technology. In the latter case, a developing country's exports to a market cannot be countervailed as long as its share of total imports of the product is 4% or less. In addition, developing countries are exempt from safeguard actions if their share of total imports is 3% or less.

It should be clear that in the post-UR era S&D treatment for the developing countries reduces essentially to extended transition periods over which the same levels and scope of obligations as those relating to developed countries would be assumed. This compares with what was, in several key cases, a permanent derogation of basic GATT/WTO obligations. For the least developed countries, however, S&D provisions pre- and post-UR are not too far apart. For both categories of countries perhaps the single most important element of S&D treatment that survived the UR reforms without any significant change is the GSP.

3. Benefits of S&D Treatment

Various S&D provisions were inserted into the GATT/WTO framework as part of the desire to deal, in a systemic way, with several characteristics and deficiencies that, more or less, define the economies of developing countries. An approach to identifying and assessing the benefits of these provisions should, presumably, link the benefits to the special features and deficiencies at which the provisions are targeted. This is the focus of the analysis that follows.

Nurturing infant industries

A key element of S&D treatment for developing countries recognized the need to nurture their infant industries. GATT Article XVIII, Section C, enabled these countries to take appropriate measures to protect infant industries. It is not uncommon to view industrialization as a major indicator of economic development; hence rapid industrialization has been a goal of economic policy in many developing countries. Active economic policy to speed up the development process has also involved efforts to develop a country's technological capabilities, build up its domestic capacity to manufacture a range of products, and promote exports.

Active policy to alter the speed and character of industrialization is justified by the existence of specific market failures and externalities that could cause a sub-optimal share of the economy's resources to be allocated to the industrial sector, in the absence of corrective measures (Rodrick, 1992). In other words, manufacturing investment and capacity could remain too small relative to the economy's resource endowments if the negative effects of these market failures and externalities are not corrected by appropriate policy interventions. The pervasiveness in developing countries of pronounced market failures, as well as such phenomena as learning-by-doing, economies of scale and other externalities that are inherently tied up with modern manufacturing and service activities, provides strong support for interventionist and non-neutral policies, including the use of various measures to protect and promote infant industries.

The market failures that are likely to be of special significance in developing countries emanate from various sources (Rodrik, 1992; Stiglitz, 1996). In the early stages of development, markets may be missing or not sufficiently well developed to provide good signals for resource allocation. The existing private markets typically have inadequate incentives for investing in the production and acquisition of information and expertise needed to boost the level of technology at which the developing economy operates. In addition, when the increasing returns and learning-by-doing associated with modern manufacturing are combined with shortage of capital, the small firms in the typical developing country may be stunted. In these circumstances, infant industry protection and support are important means of ensuring that the young firms can gain the experience required to lower their cost of production and eventually become fully competitive. The backwardness of developing countries (broadly measured by their distance from the international technology frontier), the market handicaps that characterize their economies at the start of the development process, and the time required to establish and nurture markets and marketing institutions, and to acquire and build up the capacities to compete with advanced country firms, all point in the direction of a necessary period of infant industry protection as a prelude to rapid industrialization and overall economic growth.

It is widely recognized, in this context, that subsidies may play an important role in the development programmes of developing countries. In particular, subsidies granted contingent upon export performance or use of domestic in preference to imported inputs in the production process could be valuable instruments of trade and industrial policy. Such performance-based incentive systems are associated with important benefits. Stiglitz (1996: 157) argues that "government intervention through a performance-based reward system ... provides strong growth-oriented incentives..." When such a system is based on exports, it could serve as an objective and efficient selection mechanism for the award of subsidies. Since export markets are more likely to be competitive and firms competing in international markets gain from spillovers in marketing and production know-how, a firm that succeeds in the export market is more likely to be economically efficient. Thus, a performance-based subsidy award system is likely to promote efficiency and ensure that only industries with real long-term growth prospects are provided with infant industry protection and support.

The benefits to developing countries of the S&D provision for infant industry protection go well beyond theoretical arguments. The mechanism through which local firms are protected in a captive home market subject to an export performance target, enabling them to make high profits that in turn finance higher rates of investment, to learn by doing and to improve the quality of their products, is one that has been aggressively, effectively and successfully used by the East Asian countries (Singh, 1995). Their experience suggests that trade and industrial policies that take advantage of the S&D provision on infant industry protection could not have been successful without the imposition of export performance standards.

Protecting the balance of payments

GATT Article XVIII, Section B, provided developing countries with the flexibility to impose quantitative import restrictions to protect their balance of payments. This S&D provision is a recognition of the special difficulties that the developing countries have often had in maintaining balance of payments equilibrium as they pursue their development goals. Given the volatile terms of trade and the greater susceptibility to external shocks that characterize many developing countries, especially those that are heavily dependent on the export of primary commodities, these economies may suffer from undesirable "stop-go" cycles associated with recurring balance of payments crises. The S&D provision under discussion enables developing countries to use discretionary trade and payments controls for dealing with short-term balance of payments problems and hence permits them to commit themselves to a long-term development strategy without having to change direction abruptly at the onset of a balance of payments crisis.

A development strategy that includes strong elements of infant industry protection and import substitution is not necessarily or inherently prone to external payments instability or "stop-go" policy cycles. Macroeconomic stability and external balance are not incompatible with any degree of trade protection. Regardless of its trade orientation, appropriate fiscal and exchange rate policies should enable an economy to maintain external balance. However, the typically thin foreign exchange markets of developing countries may impose serious constraints on the efficacy of exchange rate policy in dealing with abrupt and large external imbalances. Similarly, the other important objectives of fiscal policy often preclude its exclusive focus on balance of payments concerns. In these circumstances, many developing countries have found the flexibility provided by GATT Article XVIII, Section B, particularly useful in dealing with abrupt external imbalances.

Macroeconomic stability (which includes external balance) is widely recognized as a necessary condition for fast and sustainable economic growth. Hence, a feasible development strategy would aim at ensuring a current account balance while simultaneously achieving a rate of growth that is as high as possible. The balance of payments may be viewed, in this context, as the main constraint to fast economic growth. It can be argued (see, for example, Singh, 1996) that when trade and industrial policy instruments such as import controls and export promotion are effective in relaxing the balance of payments constraint, they directly promote macroeconomic stability and thus enhance the prospects for long-term growth.

Non-reciprocity

Non-reciprocity is the S&D provision that confers on developing countries the benefits of trade liberalization in developed countries without requiring them to similarly open up their own trade regime. The beneficiary developing countries would obviously gain, in terms of improved exports, from additional and enlarged access to the liberalized markets of developed countries. The liberalization of their own trade regimes would also bring welfare gains to the developing countries but these can be associated with significant fiscal costs when a developing country is heavily dependent on trade taxes as a source of government revenue. As Rodrik (1992: 312) points out, "practical and administrative considerations dictate that trade taxes will be an important source of revenue for a poor country; the poorer the economy, the higher the reliance on trade taxes". By implication, the lower a country's level of development, the more significant may be the non-reciprocity S&D provision.

Trade preference schemes

The acknowledged need of developing countries for special assistance to gain access to the markets of developed countries is met through the S&D provision embodied in the GSP schemes. The GSP arrangement has often been cited as the major element of S&D treatment for developing countries in the GATT/WTO framework that produces concrete benefits (Whalley, 1989).

The GSP was designed with three objectives in view: to provide generalized, non-reciprocal, and non-discriminatory system of preferences in favour of developing countries as a means of increasing their export earnings, promoting their industrialization and accelerating their rates of economic growth. Assessments of GSP benefits have typically focused on the first of the three objectives, the implicit assumption being that the achievement of this first objective would probably be associated with the attainment of the other two. Based on this perspective, there has emerged a broad consensus that the reduction of trade barriers by developed countries, through various GSP schemes, is economically beneficial for developing countries.

In principle, the GSP can be shown to yield benefits to developing countries through several channels. First, since the GSP implies the reduction or elimination of an import duty, it can be expected to increase the volume of exports from beneficiary countries. Second, even if the volume of export is not significantly affected, the GSP could still boost the returns to the exporters from developing countries. Third, if the GSP applies in a case in which beneficiary countries also enjoy comparative advantage over all other producers, the resulting positive trade effects are the same as those commonly associated with non-preferential tariff reductions. Fourth, when GSP applies in the case where the beneficiary countries do not have comparative advantage over other producers, the preferences generate trade diversion but the developing countries still derive benefits. In particular, such benefits may feed into more dynamic long-term effects to the extent that they enable infant industries to grow and ultimately permit the evolution of comparative advantage. In sum, any trade induced by the GSP would generate, from the perspectives of beneficiary developing countries, a higher return on the resources used than would ordinarily be available without preference.

Various studies (e.g., Baldwin and Murray, 1977; Sapir, 1981; Karsenty and Laird, 1986; Langhammer and Sapir, 1987; Laird and Sapir, 1987) have attempted to estimate the actual quantitative trade benefits derived by developing countries from various GSP schemes. In general, these estimates relate potential trade benefits to the volume of dutiable imports of preference granting developed countries and the product coverage of each GSP scheme. The latter variable determines the level of imports eligible for GSP treatment. While the levels of GSP-eligible and GSP-receiving trade provide an indication of trade benefits, a more correct indicator is the additional trade, emanating either from trade creation or trade diversion or some combination of both, that results from the preferential scheme.

The studies generally show that the various GSP schemes have yielded benefits to the preference-receiving countries. According to Laird and Sapir (1987), roughly 50% of dutiable imports in OECD countries up to the early 1980s were GSP-eligible; of this, only 50% actually received GSP treatment. Hence, only 26% of the dutiable imports of the OECD countries from beneficiaries of their schemes actually enjoyed GSP treatment. In its review of the first decade of GSP schemes, UNCTAD (1985) broadly confirms this general result for 1982. According to this source, total imports of OECD preference-giving countries from developing countries amounted to $267 billion, out of which only $63 billion (or 24%) were eligible for GSP treatment and only $28.2 billion (or 10.5%) worth of imports actually received preferential treatment. A decade later, UNCTAD (1995) shows that in 1993, total imports of preference-giving countries from GSP beneficiaries amounted to about $439 billion, of which approximately $305 billion (or 69.5%) were dutiable. But only $172 billion (or 56.3%) were GSP-eligible and, of this, only $82 billion (or 47.9%) actually received GSP treatment. In other words, only 27% of all dutiable imports were granted preferential access.

For 1983, Laird and Sapir (1987) estimated that up to $4.6 billion worth of imports by OECD countries could be attributed to various GSP schemes. While this gain was due mostly to trade creation, it represented only 8% of beneficiary country exports to OECD markets and less than 4% of dutiable OECD imports. Over the 1976–93 period, the total value of preferential imports under various OECD GSP schemes increased at an average annual growth rate of 12.7%, from $10.4 billion to $79 billion (UNCTAD, 1995: 6).

Since the GSP schemes cover mostly manufactured products, developing countries with wider industrial and more diversified manufactured exports have gained more than those relying on exports of agricultural products and raw materials. Hence, up to the early 1980s, there was a remarkable concentration of GSP benefits among a few developing countries; the top three (Hong Kong, South Korea, and Taiwan) accounted for as much as 45% of total GSP gains. The concentrated nature of GSP benefits remained largely unchanged through the early 1990s. UNCTAD (1995) reports that in 1992 between 6 and 12 of the largest beneficiaries accounted for 71%–80% of the preferential imports of Japan, the United States and the European Union. In summary, it is clear that GSP schemes provide some benefits to preference-receiving countries. The gains so derived are relatively small, however, when compared with the total exports of developing countries and are heavily concentrated in a few beneficiary countries.

Preferences and African trade

Yeats (1994) offers a comprehensive analysis of special trade preferences and their consequences for African trade. This analysis shows that as a result of Lomé preferences, as much as over 95% of each African country's exports enter the EU duty-free. In addition, and as Appendix Table 6.A2 shows, non-oil exports from six African countries (Congo, Gabon, Guinea, Niger, Sierra Leone and Tanzania) face a zero duty rate in the EU market; Uganda faces the highest duty rate of 0.6%, while Togo and Zambia follow with a rate of 0.5%. Non-oil exports from other African countries attract EU import duty rates ranging from 0.1% to 0.4%.

These relatively low preferential tariff levels provide African countries with pre-Uruguay Round preference tariff margins that are several percentage points lower than those facing non-preference receiving exporters of similar products in the EU market (again, see Table 2). The smallest preference tariff margins (i.e., less than 2 percentage points) apply to non-oil exports from Ethiopia, Liberia and Sudan; the highest (almost 5 percentage points) applies to exports from Swaziland. For the majority of African countries, non-oil exports enjoy preferential tariff margins of 2 to 4 percentage points in the EU market.

Lomé trade preferences are not without restrictions, which inherently limits their impact. In particular, the ability of many African countries to effectively and fully utilize the available Lomé preferences is diminished by ceilings, quotas and other non-tariff barriers that apply apparently independently of the preference scheme. In addition, in several instances rigid rules of origin have also frustrated attempts to use the preferences.

The various preferential trade arrangements (including Lomé) that have been designed to benefit African trade have, on the whole, had a rather disappointing impact. They have clearly failed to help Africa expand and diversify its exports or even to maintain the region's share of EU or world export markets. In spite of the trade preferences enjoyed by many African countries, the region has continued to rely on a few primary commodities; it started to lose its market share internationally from the 1970s and over 20 years of special trade preferences have not succeeded in turning this trend around. The region certainly derives some value from the preferences but when related to the experience of other regions, it seems reasonable to suggest that trade preferences that are not associated with outward-orientation and export-enhancing policies in the recipient countries may be neither a necessary nor a sufficient condition for good export performance.

While this suggestion appears to be consistent with Africa's aggregate performance, it is important to note that several African countries have derived important gains from special trade preferences. Mauritius derived as much as 6% of its GDP over 1990–94 from transfers linked to the price stability and guaranteed market access provided by the sugar protocol of the Lomé convention. Similarly, Botswana received annual payments averaging 24 million ECU from its export of beef to the EU under the beef and veal protocol of the Lomé Convention. In the same way, Lomé preferences have played a significant role in those sub-Saharan African countries exporting tobacco and other products covered by the protocols. In addition, several countries (including Mauritius, Kenya and Zimbabwe) that have succeeded in diversifying into non-traditional exports (such as clothing, processed fish, horticultural products, etc.) have achieved significant gains that can be closely associated with the special trade preferences.

When fully implemented, the Uruguay Round agreements will significantly reduce trade barriers and the resulting tariff reductions will, no doubt, erode the preferential tariff margins currently enjoyed by many African countries. To the extent that they suffer significant erosion of their trade preferences, they would also incur trade losses as their competitive positions deteriorate in the OECD markets and their exports are displaced by those from other countries.

While it is generally agreed that the generalized reduction of tariff barriers resulting from the Uruguay Round will endanger Africa's preferential tariff margins, estimates of the corresponding loss in exports vary. For example, one set of estimates (Yeats, 1994) suggests that complete liberalization of most-favoured-nation tariffs in the EU would generate total trade losses of over $250 million in Africa; for the 30 major sub-Saharan African exporters, these losses would represent as much as 2% of their current export values. According to this estimate, the big losers would be Côte d'Ivoire ($57 million), and Mauritius and Kenya (with $25 million each). These estimates thus suggest that African countries will likely experience large net trade losses as a result of the impending Uruguay Round tariff cuts that virtually eliminate their preferential tariff margins.

These estimates probably reflect the worst case scenario, however. Other estimates (e.g., Harrold, 1995) offer reasons why African trade losses resulting from the erosion of their tariff preferences are unlikely to be very large. Preferential tariff margins on many manufactured products are already quite small. In any case, manufactures constitute only a small proportion of Africa's total exports. The predominant proportion of trade preferences benefit agricultural products and, as they apply to agriculture, Uruguay Round agreements are unlikely to generate a great deal of liberalization in the immediate future. Preferential access to EU markets will, in many cases, be safeguarded through allocation of minimum access quotas to qualifying African countries, at least until the expiration of Lomé IV. Thus, preferential gains derivable from the agricultural protocols, fishing agreements and textiles will still be available. Based on these considerations, Uruguay Round changes are expected to inflict a trade loss of $5.25 million on African countries in the EU markets. Note that even these lower estimates still indicate that African countries will suffer significant trade losses as a result of the erosion of their Lomé trade preferences.

The estimates of trade losses resulting from the erosion of Africa's Lomé preferences do not take explicit account of the possible effect on export supply response of recent policy reforms and the increasing shift towards an outward-oriented development strategy in many African countries. An important factor behind Africa's ineffective utilization of the market access opportunities provided by Lomé preferences is clearly inadequate export supply response, especially with respect to manufactured products. To the extent that the emerging shift to greater outward-orientation is accompanied by more robust export response, the *potential* African trade losses associated with the region's preference erosion could be much larger than any of the current estimates suggests. This point has a second and equally important implication. Many African countries have been embarking on difficult structural adjustment and policy changes aimed ultimately at altering incentives to favour outward orientation and the promotion of a diversified basket of exports on the assumption that preferential market access is guaranteed under the Lomé framework. Any fundamental and adverse change in this basic assumption – whether caused by significant preference erosion or the unraveling of the Lomé framework itself – could have disastrous consequences for overall policy reform in Africa.

4. Costs of S&D Treatment

Critique of S&D provisions in the GATT/WTO framework comes from several directions. Sometimes, the critique reflects the belief that there is nothing special about developing or low income countries that could set them apart for any S&D treatment, particularly in the area of trade policy. At other times, the critique is based on the idea that trade-restricting development strategies impose an unnecessary cost on developing countries instead of assisting to speed up their development process. Whether specific S&D provisions give developing countries an undeserved "free ride" in the global trading system or permit them to suffer from the self-inflicted pain of wrong-headed policies, various criticisms of these provisions imply that they are associated with certain costs that are borne either by the "beneficiary" developing countries themselves and/or by the global trading system as a whole.

Costs of infant industry and balance of payments protection

Focusing specifically on S&D provisions relating to infant industry and balance of payments protection, Hudec (1987) considers them harmful on at least two counts; first, they permit developing countries to take "market-distorting" measures, and second, they amount to the abandonment of any real effort to limit or control the use of such measures by these countries. To the extent that the use of such "market-distorting" measures are, indeed, counterproductive, they could impose a cost on the developing countries themselves. This basic criticism can be (and has been – see Whalley, 1989) taken further. The continued justification for the S&D provision on balance of payments protection is questioned in the belief that, in the current economic environment, exchange rate changes supported by appropriate macroeconomic policies should be adequate for balance of payments adjustments. Thus, the continued use of quantitative import control measures to deal with external imbalances when more effective price-based and non-market-distorting alternatives are available would impose a resource allocation inefficiency cost on the economy.

Both strands of this basic criticism ignore or assume away those special features of developing and low income countries whose explicit recognition gave birth to the S&D provisions in the first place. When appropriate markets are missing or underdeveloped for various reasons, price-based measures are unlikely to provide correct signals for efficient resource allocation decisions. Notions of inefficiency costs associated with inappropriate policies in the context of well functioning markets with full information do not typically carry over into situations where these assumptions are patently violated.

Less fundamental objections to these S&D provisions have also been raised. Balance of payments justification for quantitative import restrictions may have a hidden sectoral protection intent. Thus, because of more stringent procedural requirements of GATT Article XVIII, Section C, compared with those of Section B, some developing countries appear to have found it relatively easier to obtain GATT "cover" for infant industry protection under the guise of balance of payments protection. In making this supposition, Anjaria (1987) argues that in a large majority of developing countries that declared Article XVIII B restrictions, the measures covered less than half of import categories; moreover, if these restrictions were truly for balance of payments purposes, they would cover all import categories.

This argument misses an important rationale of balance of payments protection in developing countries. Typically, the goal is to maintain current account balance at a rate of economic growth that is as high as possible. In this context, imports of capital and intermediate goods are treated as "essential" and are thus protected from import control measures. As a result, quantitative import restriction measures taken for balance of payments purposes tend to cover "non-essential" consumer goods primarily, not necessarily because there are any existing industries in this sector to be protected, but simply because they constitute the "discretionary" imports that can be curtailed without derailing the country's development programme.

The down side of non-reciprocity

The S&D provision that grants non-reciprocity rights to developing countries can, in principle, be associated with at least two different types of costs. First, lack of reciprocity may make it more difficult for developed countries to reduce trade barriers to exports from developing countries. Second, absence of obligatory and binding reciprocity may preclude the GATT/WTO from serving as an "agency of restraint" for developing countries and thus make it more difficult to resist the claims of local protectionist interest groups.

The second type of cost may be particularly significant. As Wolf (1987: 664) argues, "a principal reason for participation in GATT negotiations is not just to obtain improved access abroad but to make it politically easier to liberalize at home". A reciprocally bargained international agreement can, in this context, strengthen the hands of a developing country that wishes to resist undesirable protectionist measures championed by local producers. It is not necessarily the case, however, that the non-reciprocity S&D provision removes the right of any developing country to use the GATT/WTO institutional framework as an agency of restraint, since the provision does not prevent developing countries from reducing and binding their tariffs.

The fist type of cost associated with non-reciprocity assumes that developed countries would treat exports from developing countries more liberally if a mutually reciprocal relationship was established (Hudec, 1987). There may be some substance to this assumption. It appears that certain restrictions on the coverage of various GSP schemes as well as pressures to "graduate" certain product groups and developing countries out of the GSP are not entirely unrelated to lack of reciprocity. For the majority of developing countries, however, it does not seem clear that their commitments to reduce trade barriers against exports of developed countries play a significant role in determining the amount of market access they can expect in return.

The disadvantages of trade preferences

Criticisms of various GSP schemes focus largely on their many limitations, which preclude the realization of the full benefits that they could generate if they had been implemented, as originally conceived, as "generalized and non-discriminatory" preferential systems. In effect, the costs associated with the GSP emanate largely from these limitations.

First, since the GSP provisions are non-contractual and therefore subject to unilateral modification or withdrawal at the pleasure of preference-granting countries, they may not provide a reliable and stable basis for investment decisions. Long gestation types of investments made in developing countries on the basis of incentives provided by the GSP may be jeopardized by sudden changes and modifications to the system. Second, Wang and Winters (1997) argue that trade preferences impose significant costs that could ultimately subvert long-term development. It is suggested, in particular, that the desire to retain the privileges of GSP schemes open preference-receiving countries to immense pressures to accept various conditions imposed by preference-granting countries, while the incentives generated by GSP schemes tend to create inefficiencies in production and trade, divert resources from critical sectors and encourage rent-seeking instead of productive investment.

5. Concluding Comments

The various S&D provisions that evolved in the context of the GATT/WTO framework were established in response to the special problems of developing countries and against the background of the prevailing views of the development process. Many of these special problems, especially those emanating from underdeveloped and missing markets, imperfect information, and economies of scale, continue to be relevant, particularly in the developing countries of Africa. The underlying philosophical view of trade policy and its role in the development process has undergone more dramatic changes. Common policy thrusts, reflecting current thinking, generally emphasize the opening of developing country economies to world markets and elimination of anti-export biases in domestic policies. Yet, in the light of significant market failures that remain in many developing countries, there continues to be an important role for trade and industrial policies aimed at building the domestic capacity to manufacture a range of products, developing technological capabilities to support this effort, and promoting exports. Both theoretical considerations and the practical experience of East Asian countries suggest both that government intervention is often necessary and that a performance-based reward system can serve as an efficient subsidy allocation system.

Viewed from this perspective, the interests of developing countries would be better served by an analytically based deliberative process in the context of which each of the various S&D provisions is reviewed and, where necessary, suitably reformed. A dispassionate analysis of accumulated development experience would not support the total elimination of the S&D provision for infant industry protection; what it might suggest could be a tighter formulation of the rules and enhanced surveillance of their implementation. A preference for price-based measures over quantitative control measures for dealing with balance of payments problems makes sense in circumstances where foreign exchange markets can be relied on to restore external balance without causing large domestic dislocations. In other words, the thinness of the typical developing country markets and the greater terms of trade volatility to which such countries are susceptible deserve careful consideration in reformulating an S&D provision on the management of balance of payments that would not only be efficient but also effective and equitable.

Following the conclusion of the Uruguay Round, non-reciprocity in its full sense has probably receded into the status of a non-issue. Many developing countries have been engaged in the unilateral liberalization of their trade regimes, they made some tariff concessions during the round and have agreed to bind their tariffs. It should be clear, however, that reciprocity does mean that developed, developing and least developed countries will have the same tariff levels. It is not unreasonable for developing and least developed countries to retain the discretion for the disciplined use of appropriate trade and industrial policies for the purposes of protecting and promoting infant industries, dealing with chronic balance of payments problems and deriving fiscal revenue.

In spite of the severe limitations that rob it of its full potential, most studies of the GSP scheme confirm it has yielded over time small but significant benefits, particularly to those developing countries that had acquired the appropriate supply-response capabilities. Interestingly enough, such major GSP beneficiaries have not, in fact, suffered from any of the "costs" theoretically associated with the scheme. This suggests that the reform of the system should focus specifically on those limitations – product coverage, graduation criteria, rule of origin and safeguards – with regard to which multilaterally negotiated changes might further enhance the benefits derivable from the scheme.

Appendix Table 6.A1: Post-Uruguay Round S&D Provisions

Subject	Developing countries	Least developed countries
1. Safeguards	• Measures extendable for an additional duration of 2 years beyond the general limit of 8 years	• Same as for developing countries
	• Can re-apply measures more often	" "
	• No safeguard action can be taken against a product originating in a developing country if its share of imports is less than 3% or not more than 9% for a group of developing countries.	" "
2. Balance of payments	• Simplified consultation process applies	" "
3. Subsidies – export	• Not prohibited for LDCs with per cap. income <$1,000	• Not prohibited
– import substitution	• Not prohibited for 5 years from 1995	• Not prohibited for 8 years from 1995
4. Anti-dumping	• Special consideration when action is contemplated	• Same as for developing countries
5. TRIMS	• Temporary deviation allowed for balance of payments protection	• Same as for developing countries
	• Elimination of prohibited measures within 5 years from 1995	• Elimination of prohibited measures within 7 years from 1995
	• Time extension can be requested	• Time extension can be requested
6. Technical barriers to trade	• Developing country members not bound to use international standards	• Same as for developing countries
	• Technical assistance to be provided	• Same as for developing countries

Subject	Developing countries	Least developed countries
7. Customs valuation	• May delay implementation for a maximum period of 5 years	• Same as for developing countries
8. Agriculture – Tariff reduction	• Lower levels of reduction over longer period	• No commitment required
– Domestic support	" "	• No commitment required
– Export subsidy	" "	• No commitment required
9. Textiles and clothing	• More favourable treatment for small producers	• More favourable treatment
10. Services	• Special considerations	• Same as developing countries
	• Technical assistance	" "
11. TRIPS	• Longer transition period: 5 years, extendable to 10	• Longer transition
12. Dispute settlement process	• Obligatory provision for good offices, conciliation for mediation	

Appendix 6.A2: The incidence of OECD tariffs on selected sub-Saharan African countries

	OECD average		European Community		Japan		United States	
Exporting country	African tariff	Preference margin	African tariff	Preference margin	African tariff	Preference margin	African tariff	Preference margin
Angola	0.2	-1.5	0.3	-3.2	1.8	0.0	0.1	-0.04
Botswana	0.3	-2.8	0.1	-2.9	0.0	-2.1	3.5	-1.1
Cameroon	0.4	-2.5	0.1	-2.8	0.0	0.0	2.1	-1.1
Central African Republic	0.2	-2.2	0.2	-2.3	0.0	0.0	0.0	-1.1
Chad	0.4	-2.7	0.2	-2.9	2.5	0.0	1.6	0.0
Congo	0.1	-1.4	0.0	-2.2	0.0	0.0	0.3	-1.6
Côte d'Ivoire	0.7	-3.1	0.3	-3.3	1.2	-0.5	3.3	-2.0
Ethiopia	0.7	-1.3	0.1	-1.9	1.5	-1.3	2.0	0.4

	OECD average		European Community		Japan		United States	
Exporting country	African tariff	Preference margin	African tariff	Preference margin	African tariff	Preference margin	African tariff	Preference margin
Gabon	0.6	-2.0	0.0	-2.7	0.0	0.0	2.9	0.7
Ghana	1.0	-2.2	0.1	-3.1	2.3	0.0	2.6	-0.9
Guinea	0.6	-2.3	0.0	-2.9	1.8	-1.9	1.9	-1.0
Kenya	0.5	-3.3	0.2	-3.5	2.4	-1.1	3.1	-2.3
Liberia	0.6	-1.7	0.3	-1.9	0.0	-0.3	2.5	-1.1
Madagascar	0.5	-2.0	0.4	-2.7	0.8	-0.2	0.8	-1.0
Malawi	1.1	-2.4	0.1	-3.5	0.0	-0.1	5.4	-0.6
Mali	0.4	-3.4	0.2	-3.5	0.0	-1.6	3.1	-2.2
Mauritania	1.7	-2.3	0.2	-3.9	3.6	-0.4	1.2	-1.6
Mauritius	1.3	-3.1	0.2	-3.4	4.8	-1.1	6.4	-1.8
Niger	0.1	-3.0	0.0	-3.0	0.0	0.0	3.3	-1.6
Nigeria	2.7	-0.9	0.1	-2.6	3.7	-0.8	5.2	0.7
Senegal	0.5	-3.3	0.3	-3.5	3.6	0.1	4.9	-1.2
Sierra Leone	0.5	-3.1	0.0	-4.0	2.6	-0.7	2.3	-0.2
Sudan	0.1	-1.5	0.1	-1.9	0.0	0.0	0.7	-1.0
Swaziland	0.8	-4.4	0.5	-4.9	6.7	-3.0	3.5	-1.9
Togo	0.3	-2.8	0.2	-2.8	9.8	-0.8	0.2	-2.8
Uganda	0.9	-2.4	0.6	-3.0	0.0	0.0	2.1	-0.3
United Republic Tanzania	0.1	-2.3	0.0	-2.5	1.4	-1.0	0.0	-2.4
Zaire	0.3	-2.1	0.1	-2.4	0.0	-0.5	1.3	-1.1
Zambia	0.3	-1.7	0.5	-2.9	0.0	-0.6	1.4	-1.4
Zimbabwe	0.9	-2.5	0.2	-3.3	1.2	-1.0	4.0	-1.0

Notes: 1. Negative values show the average preferential tariff margins (in points) that the African exporter has over all other exporters of the same goods.

2. Positive values indicate that the exporter faces a higher than average tariff due to preferences other countries receive.

Source: Yeats (1994).

References

Anjaria, S.J. 1987. "Balance of payments and related issues in the Uruguay Round of trade negotiations", *The World Bank Economic Review*" vol. 1, no. 4 (September) 1(A): 669–88.

Baldwin, R.E. and T. Murray. 1977. "MFN tariff reductions and developing country trade benefits under the GSP". *Economic Journal*, 87(345): 303–46.

Blackhurst, R., A. Enders and J. Francois. 1995. "The Uruguay Round and market access: Opportunities and challenges for developing countries". World Bank Conference on The Uruguay Round and the Developing Economies, 26–27 January.

GATT. 1958. *Trends in International Trade: Haberler Report*. Geneva.

Harrold, P. 1995. "The impact of the Uruguay Round on Africa: Much ado about nothing?" *The Uruguay Round and the Developing World*, World Bank Conference, Washington, D.C.

Hindley, B. 1997. "Different and more favourable treatment … and graduation". In Finger and Olechowski, eds., *The Uruguay Round: A Handbook on the Multilateral Trade Negotiations*. Washington, D.C.: The World Bank.

Hudec, R.E. 1987. *Developing Countries in the GATT Legal System*, Thames Essay No. 50. London: Gower.

Karsenty, G. and S. Laird. 1986. "The generalized system of preferences: A quantitative assessment of the direct trade effects and of policy options". UCTAD Discussion Paper 18. Geneva: United Nations.

Langhammer, R. and A. Sapir. 1987. *Economic Impact of Generalized Tariff Preferences*. London: Gower.

Laird, S. and A. Sapir. 1987. "Tariff preferences". In Finger and Olechowski, eds.

Rodrik, D. 1992. "Conceptual issues in the design of trade policy for industrialization". *World Development*, vol. 20, no. 3: 309–320.

Sapir, A. 1981. "Trade benefits under the EEC generalized system of preferences". *European Economic Review*, vol 14: 339–55.

Singh, A. 1995. "The Post-Uruguay Round world trading system, industrialization, trade and development: Implications for the Asia-Pacific developing countries". In UNCTAD, *Expansion of Trading Opportunities to the Year 2000 for Asia-Pacific Developing Countries*. Geneva: United Nations.

Stiglitz, J. 1996. "Some lessons from the East Asian Miracle". *The World Bank Research Observer*, vol. 11, no. 2: 151–178.

UNCTAD. 1985. *The History of UNCTAD 1964–1984*. New York: United Nations.

UNCTAD. 1995. *Policy Options and Proposals for the Revitalization of the Generalized System of Preferences*, Report No. TD/B/SCP/13. Geneva: United Nations.

Wang, Z.K. and L.A. Winters. 1997. "Africa and the global economy". Paper presented at the plenary session, AERC research workshop. 24–29 May, Nairobi.

Whalley, J. 1989, *The Uruguay Round and Beyond*. London: Macmillan.

Wolf, M. 1987. "Differential and more favourable treatment of developing countries and the international trading system". *The World Bank Economic Review*, vol. 1, no. 4: 647–68.

WTO. 1996. *Annual Report, 1996*. Geneva: World Trade Organization.

Chapter seven

Africa and the "New Issues" in the World Trade Organization Framework

by Patrick Low, WTO Secretariat

1. Introduction

The multilateral trade agenda has grown in complexity and diversity in the last five years, creating major challenges for most governments as they struggle to absorb new issues, evaluate their implications and set priorities. For the first thirty years of its existence, the General Agreement on Tariffs and Trade (GATT) concerned itself mainly with reducing tariffs on goods, against a background of rules whose primary objective was to protect the market access value of tariff commitments. The early GATT rules went beyond tariff bindings to cover such measures as quantitative restrictions, anti-dumping actions, contingency protection and subsidies, but all these rules basically concerned policy conditions at the frontier. The Tokyo Round (1973–79) focused on deepening the rules, but beyond the establishment of new rules for government procurement,[1] did little to expand the scope of the multilateral trading system. The Tokyo Round's contribution in the rules area was to clarify and in some cases extend the reach of rules already incorporated within the GATT framework.

The real expansion of the trade agenda was foreshadowed to a degree in various work programmes instituted in the early 1980s, but only took place in the Uruguay Round and its aftermath. The Uruguay Round brought trade in services and trade-related intellectual property rights into the system, and instituted a work programme on trade and the environment. The Singapore Ministerial Declaration added work programmes on trade and investment, trade and competition policy, certain aspects of government procurement, and trade facilitation. It is hardly surprising that such a rapid expansion of the agenda has raised questions about the capacity of some governments to implement their legal commitments in a timely and adequate manner. For most developing countries, especially those whose participation in the Uruguay Round was limited, the adoption of the Uruguay Round results as a "single undertaking" is severely testing the absorptive capacity of governments in both a political and administrative sense. Some governments, including in Africa, have expressed misgivings about the manner in which the WTO agenda is being shaped and have complained of marginalization from the decision making process. These kinds of concerns can only begin to be addressed if governments are adequately informed of the nature of the issues involved and have developed a coherent perception of where national interests lie.

Why did the multilateral trade agenda burgeon so with the Uruguay Round and the establishment of the WTO? The most obvious answer is that the trading system had been left behind, and needed to catch up with the trend of globalization in the world economy if it was to retain its relevance. This is a process that will continue, as new issues are explored and perhaps become part of a negotiating agenda, and as governments strive to improve the substance of what they have been able to agree so far in particular areas. And why has WTO membership expanded so markedly, from around 100 countries at the end of the Tokyo Round to 132 today, with another 31 countries negotiating for WTO membership. To some extent this is because there are more sovereign states than ever before, but it is also because of heightened interest in the trading system in a world of growing interdependence.

Africa's relationship to the world economy in the last two decades or so has been different from that of any other region. Setting aside for the moment the important distinctions that should be made among African countries, the continent taken as a whole has disengaged in recent years from the international economy. While world trade has consistently outpaced world GDP growth in the post-war period, raising the ratio of exports to

GDP from 8% in 1948 to 26% in 1997, the same pattern has not prevailed in Africa throughout this period. In the 1980s, the exports of sub-Saharan Africa grew at an annual average rate of 0.4%, whereas GDP grew by 2.4% (Collier, 1997). In the period 1985–90, Africa accounted for 2.0% of foreign direct investment (FDI) inflows on average, and this share had dropped to 1.4% in 1996. African FDI stocks were 2.4% of world stocks in 1980 and only 1.8% in 1996 (UNCTAD, 1997). Aggregate output growth figures confirm the overall picture of sub-Saharan Africa being left behind: developing countries as a group grew at an annual real average rate of 4.3% between 1971 and 1988 and 5.8% from 1989 until the present, while the comparable figures for sub-Saharan Africa are 2.3% and 2.9%, respectively (Vockey, 1997). It must be emphasized that the picture across the continent is far from uniform, and that some African countries have recorded significantly higher rates of growth. Moreover, the average growth rate for sub-Saharan Africa has improved recently, exceeding 4% in 1996 and 1997, and was forecast to do the same in 1998.

Notwithstanding the improved performance of certain countries, and seemingly favourable prospects for the continent as a whole, there can be no denying the concern of many policy makers and observers about the elusiveness of "convergence" — in other words — the remoteness of the possibility that rapidly increasing living standards in poorer countries, especially in Africa, will allow these countries to "catch up" in economic terms. The prospect of continuing or even aggravated marginalization remains real unless the trends of the last two decades are reversed. It is not the purpose of this paper to enter into the debate about the root causes of Africa's under-performance, in particular between those who attribute much of the problem to policy factors and those who look to other explanations, such as resource endowments, geography, climate and other "initial" conditions as the relevant variables.[2]

Suffice it to note for present purposes that a discussion of the new WTO issues and the options they present for African governments is only relevant if one accepts that the behaviour of these governments in the WTO, including in respect of the new issues, makes a difference to their growth and development prospects. An underlying assumption of this paper is that appropriate and full participation in the WTO is an important element of any strategy that calls for engagement rather than retreat from the international economy. Given the increasingly multi-faceted and intrusive reach of the WTO, the argument behind this assumption is reinforced by the conclusion of a growing body of literature that a range of interacting policy factors determines growth.[3] According to this analysis, economic performance will be compromised if crucial policy complementarities are ignored in the design of reform packages.

The remainder of this paper is divided into sections that deal with seven new issues on the WTO agenda. The issues covered – trade in services, investment, intellectual property rights, competition policy, government procurement, trade facilitation, and trade and environment – are not sharply distinguished between those that already form part of the system and those that are only being discussed in working groups. The list does not include the subject of labour standards, which, although raised for discussion in the context of the Singapore Ministerial Meeting, does not form part of the WTO work programme.[4] Given the number of new issues covered in this paper, it is impossible to provide an extensive treatment of any of them. The purpose, rather, is to identify the most salient aspects of the issues from a policy perspective, explain how they are being dealt with in the WTO context, and consider their relevance for African economies.

In reading this paper, it is important to bear in mind its limitations. Neither the full complexity of the issues involved, nor the diversity of individual country experience, can be adequately captured in a paper of this length. The paper can only hope to introduce the issues and outline their implications in broad terms for African countries. A natural next step for the analysis would be to look at these issues individually in terms of what they mean for the policies and interests of particular countries. Two points of importance suggest themselves in this connection. First, there is a need to establish clear priorities from a domestic policy perspective. It is obvious that not everything on the WTO's agenda can be of equal importance in terms of the stage of development and the policy challenges prevailing in a given country. A focused and more selective approach will yield better results. But account should also be taken of the fact that governments may wish to influence the direction of discussion in the WTO in areas that are not of immediate relevance to the existing situation, but which could become important later.

All countries face resource constraints when it comes to participating in organizations like the WTO, but these constraints are more pressing for African countries than for most. Reference has already been made to growing concerns over implementation. These arise directly from the fact that an expanded and growing agenda places a heavy strain on already stretched resources. In essence, the concern is that having assumed wide-ranging commitments in the Uruguay Round, countries are now hard pressed administratively to implement, which in some cases may lead to WTO-inconsistent actions or policies. This problem is not emphasized in the present paper, since for the most part no obligations treated by the paper have yet been assumed (such as investment, competition and trade facilitation), or they concern subjects where commitments have been taken with grace periods for implementation (intellectual property).

Second, the analysis needs to be firmly rooted in an adequate overall appreciation of governments' underlying policy objectives. This means that the way issues are treated in the WTO environment matters. Most importantly, positions must be judged in terms of the domestic policy framework. External policy conditions are important for a country's development prospects, but the domestic policy framework is even more important, and a country's posture and activities in the WTO should be tailored as much to an emphasis on the latter as on the former. The sometimes adversarial approach adopted by countries in the WTO is perhaps inevitable, but it does not always ensure that national interests will take precedence over political postures. This is why involvement in the WTO must be clearly seen in terms of national policy objective and priorities.

2. Trade in Services

African countries differ widely in terms of the share of services activities in GDP. On the one hand, the share of services is within the 20–30% range for countries like Burundi, Nigeria and Tanzania. On the other, the share reaches 70% or more for Djibouti and Eritrea (World Bank, 1997). Differences are partly explained by resource endowments, but the share of services activities in GDP typically rises with increases in national income. For this reason, industrial countries on average have higher services-to-GDP ratios than developing countries, and the policy regime a government chooses for services assumes increasing importance over time. In retrospect, it is perhaps surprising that it took until the early 1990s for governments to agree on multilateral rules for trade in services. On the other hand, it is only with more recent developments in information technology – that is, in telecommunications, computer technology and software – that services have become more tradeable and also more readily "disembodied" from goods in certain sectors. And even with greater tradeability, the establishment of multilateral rules on trade in services entailed acceptance of disciplines on investment as well as on cross-border transactions (see below).

Two features of services that distinguish them from production and trade in goods deserve emphasis at the outset, and help to explain what made the negotiation and final shape of the General Agreement on Trade in Services (GATS) so different from the GATT. First, production and consumption of a service may occur simultaneously, since no possibility exists of storing certain services produced now for consumption later. Hair-cutting is an obvious example of this class of service. In such cases, a transaction requires that the producer and the consumer must be in one location. For other services, such as construction, arms-length supply is impossible because the service is not transportable, modern telecommunications notwithstanding. A physical presence is therefore necessary. This implies that if a government grants market access rights to foreign suppliers for non-storable or non-transportable services, it may have to accept either that foreign enterprises can establish a commercial presence in its territory, or that the service suppliers in question may enter its territory, if only on a temporary basis.[5]

The delivery of many services is not so intrinsically restricted, and arms-length supply across frontiers is feasible, although not necessarily desirable from the point of view of the seller and the consumer.[6] Thus, even where establishment or temporary presence is not essential to an exchange, a preference may exist for the physical presence of the supplier in the territory of the consumer, or vice-versa. The essential point here is that either through force of circumstance, or because of the nature of an activity, trade in services cannot be promoted without a willingness on the part of governments to contemplate multiple modes of delivery, involving the movement across national jurisdictions of the services themselves, or of producers or of consumers. These realities are reflected in GATS.

Second, services tend to be subject to a greater degree of regulatory supervision than physical goods. In part, this reflects concerns about consumer protection, or in the case of financial services, prudential issues. Since fraud, sharp practice and substandard output may be difficult or impossible to detect and prevent before the damage is done, governments feel obliged to control supply ex ante rather than output on an ex post basis. Another consideration is that some service sectors, like banking, have economy-wide externalities, so that regulation erring on the side of caution is considered necessary to avoid the widespread damage that would be caused by specific sectoral failures. Moreover, in making the comparison with goods, it should be borne in mind that the GATS covers service suppliers (i.e., production) as well as services, whereas in GATT only products are covered.

Heavy regulation may also reflect protectionist policy, where for one reason or another governments are unwilling to countenance foreign competition. Either way, the relative intensity of regulation in many service industries contributes to the complexities of promoting trade liberalization. The focus of negotiations on trade in services is upon sectors, although there is undoubtedly room to do more by way of developing principles applicable to all services trade, regardless of the degree of sector-specific liberalization that governments are willing to countenance. Given the greater necessity of regulation from a consumer protection perspective in the sphere of services, progress in trade liberalization should not be judged merely by reference to the pace and degree of deregulation.

A final point worth making concerns the severe dearth of information available to policy makers and analysts about service transactions. For the most part, governments have not collected data on international service transactions in a systematic fashion, save in a highly aggregated and not always internationally comparable form in the balance of payments accounts. Attempts are being made by the OECD, Eurostat and the International Monetary Fund to improve the standard of data collection in services (World Bank, 1995), but these efforts will take several years to bear fruit. Moreover, problems will still arise because of a (growing) range of intra-firm electronic service transactions that are not recorded in conventional balance of payments statistics. A further limitation of data on services transactions is that so-called "establishment" trade – the sales of foreign-owned enterprises in the host country – is not recorded under most existing statistical methodologies.[7] Finally, as Jagdish Bhagwati pointed out over ten years ago, services statistics will be influenced by economic structure (Bhagwati, 1984).

For example, where a manufacturing firm maintains in-house advertising services, advertising will be recorded as goods production; but a manufacturer who buys advertising from an agency triggers a transaction that will be recorded in national output statistics as advertising services. Specialization that leads to out-sourcing of service inputs into manufacturing is referred to as "splintering".

The structure of GATS

The GATS is crafted cautiously,[8] in that it provides signatories with ample scope to condition their multilateral commitments. Only some of the provisions of the GATS framework relate to the universe of trade in services, as defined under the agreement, while others are restricted to those service activities subject to specific, scheduled commitments. Several provisions clearly reflect the pervasiveness of regulations in many service sectors, and the intent to prevent the protectionist abuse of such regulations. The specific schedules indicate which service sectors each signatory has been willing to subject to non-general obligations under the GATS. The schedules also provide for qualifications to the national treatment and market access commitments that otherwise apply to sectoral commitments.

The scope of the agreement, the definition of trade in services and the sectoral coverage are laid out in Part I of the GATS. Trade in services is defined in Article I in terms of four modes of supply. The first mode involves the cross-border (arms-length or long-distance) supply of a service from one jurisdiction of suppliers.[9] Tourism is a good example of this mode, involving the movement of (mobile) tourists to (immobile) tourist facilities in another country. The third mode of supply is through the commercial presence of a supplier in the jurisdiction of consumers. This is the investment mode, which caused so much difficulty in the early stages of the services negotiations. Some developing countries argued that commitments on service transactions under this mode of supply were tantamount to a surrogate obligation on foreign direct investment, and they expressed unwillingness to tie in their investment regimes in this manner. Finally, the fourth mode entails the movement of natural persons from one jurisdiction to another. This is the mode under which the sensitive issue of the movement of labour is addressed. The fourth mode relates both to independent service suppliers and to employees of juridical persons supplying services.

The conceptual approach underlying these modes was first developed in the academic literature (Sampson and Snape, 1985) as a heuristic device to explain the nature of international transactions in services. Differentiation by modes of supply later formed the basis on which governments defined market access commitments under GATS in their schedules, permitting a choice to be made from among alternative modes. The use of modal distinctions is a reflection of the manner in which liberalization is defined under the agreement, and the possibility of applying different policy regimes to different modes of supply is a potential source of economic distortion (DeAnne Julius, 1994). Despite early reservations about commercial presence, a tendency to encourage this mode is discernible in the schedules of commitments (see below). In some cases, this may be because countries have attempted to use the GATS as an instrument for encouraging foreign direct investment. In others, it reflects the desire to avoid "regulatory competition" between different jurisdictions. Furthermore, where regulatory control is considered important, as in prudential controls in banking, for example, governments find it easier to impose and enforce regulations in their own territories. The extent to which the absence of modal neutrality under GATS is the source of distortion is an empirical question well beyond the scope of this paper.

The GATS, like the GATT, is based on the most favoured nation (MFN) principle, designed to prevent members from discriminating among their trading partners. In order to attain final agreement on the MFN principle, and to avoid the wholesale exclusion of sectors from GATS coverage, limited exemptions to MFN are permitted under the agreement. The MFN exemption provisions reflected the concern of some larger countries that by granting MFN access to their markets, they would be losing the opportunity to exchange their relatively open access for further liberalization in other markets. In other words, these countries were arguing that "free riding" would occur in the absence of an effective instrument to ensure reciprocity. Some 70 countries have taken MFN exemptions.

A fundamental feature of GATS is the principle of progressive liberalization. It reflects the reality that governments were neither willing nor able simply to open up their services markets to international competition from one day to the next. Progressive liberalization implies a gradual approach, and the structure of the GATS accommodates such gradualism. Three aspects of the GATS are crucial determinants of the pace and reach of liberalization under GATS. First, governments determine in the course of negotiations which sectors or activities to include and which to exclude from market-opening in their schedules of specific commitments. Few GATS obligations apply unless a sector and the associated modes of delivery have been made subject to specific commitments in the schedule of a member. The MFN principle in Article II and the transparency commitments in Article III are the main general obligations of the agreement. The notable gaps in general application, which have the effect of reducing the reach of GATS, are those relating to domestic regulation and national treatment.

The second aspect concerns the manner in which market access limitations are expressed in schedules of specific commitments. Four of the six possible ways in which market access may be limited under GATS (Article XVI) are expressed in terms of quantitative limitations – the number of suppliers, the value of transactions or assets, the number of operations or quality of output, or the number of natural persons that may be employed. The other two market access limitations refer to restrictions on types of legal entity and participation of foreign capital. Reliance on quantitative rather than price-based market access limitations carries well-known efficiency costs and distribution implications, and is likely to imply less liberalization than a price-based approach.

The third aspect, already noted above, relates to the role played by the national treatment commitment under GATS – that is, the requirement of equal treatment of foreign and domestic supplies and suppliers in the domestic market. In contrast to GATT, national treatment under GATS is not a general principle. Rather, it is a matter for negotiation. National treatment applies to scheduled commitments unless an explicit indication is given to the contrary. One reason why governments may have been unwilling to see national treatment play the same role in GATS as in GATT, or the role that MFN plays in GATS as a general principle, is that under the commercial presence and movement of natural persons modes of supply in GATS (modes 3 and 4), full national treatment is equivalent to free trade – it would guarantee unlimited investment rights for foreign service suppliers. While governments were willing to guarantee this treatment in some sectors where they made scheduled commitments unencumbered by national treatment limitations, it is difficult to imagine the circumstances in which governments would have been willing to do this across the board.

Liberalization commitments

The gradualist approach to liberalization under GATS has produced diverse range of commitments among WTO members in terms of sectoral coverage and the degree of market opening. Many countries have been cautious and considerable scope remains for liberalization initiatives in the future. Governments have recognized this, and Article XIX of GATS calls for successive rounds of negotiations, the first of which is scheduled to begin in the year 2000. Unfortunately, the nature of trade in services, the dearth of reliable data and the structure of market access commitments under GATS make it very difficult in many cases to assess the significance of what has been committed so far by way of trade liberalization. When a sector or activity is not omitted altogether from a schedule, it may be specified without any market access or national treatment limitations under all four modes of supply. Otherwise, the limitations that are specified must be judged in terms of their restrictiveness, and the information requirements can be prohibitive.

Another aspect of the assessment of the value of a specific commitment requiring detailed information is its worth in relation to the actual policies pursued by a government. If a specific commitment ties a member to a policy regime that is less open than the regime applied, then it has less value for trading partners than a commitment that reflects the policy status quo. And a commitment that corresponds to the policy status quo at the time it is made is less valuable than one that promises further trade liberalization, although such a commitment still has value in that it ensures against any increase in protection. Many specific commitments under GATS are at or below the status quo, and this has led observers to question the degree to which the GATS has so far led to actual liberalization. The more recently concluded negotiations on basic telecommunications and financial services, however, have entailed significant liberalization moves on the part of many members (Low and Mattoo, 1997; Mattoo, 1998).

Specific service commitments by country are summarized in Appendix Table 7.A1. Because of the constraints on making accurate assessments of what has been committed, the Annex takes a simple approach that presents a very partial picture.[10] If a member has made any commitment whatsoever in one of 12 highly aggregated sectors, this is indicated, and such commitments are summed. The most significant information the Appendix gives is where countries have omitted to make any market access commitments at all in sector – no quantitative statements can be made where commitments have not been made. But this crude approach is still quite revealing. For all WTO members and all possible commitments measured in this way, the Appendix shows that only 47% of the total possible commitments have been made. The comparable figure for African countries is 34%. Africa's commitment levels are particularly high in tourism and related travel services (95%) and particularly low in distribution services, educational services, environmental services, and health and related social services.

Options for Africa

Even with very crude measurement methods, it is obvious that considerable scope exists for increasing commitment levels in trade in services. This does not apply only to Africa, but more generally. Once a government determines how much liberalization it wishes to undertake and at what pace, the question is what WTO commitments can do to support and sustain liberalization efforts. WTO commitments sometimes seem to be looked upon as concessions that carry a cost, unless they are matched by comparable commitments from trading partners. In economic terms, reciprocity plays a positive role only in narrowly drawn conditions that are unlikely to apply to most African countries in most circumstances – namely, that the liberalizing country will suffer a deterioration in its terms of trade. Bearing this in mind, along with solid empirical evidence that the welfare gains from liberalization accrue primarily to the liberalizing country,[11] and that countries that have pursued more open policies have performed better, it is difficult to see an economic argument based on reciprocity demands for refraining from making binding liberalization commitments under the WTO.

Binding international commitments serve to tie in policies that are susceptible to pressure from adversely affected domestic interests. In the specific case of investment, or commitments under the third and fourth GATS modes of supply, they can also provide a positive signal to foreign investors and guarantee a commitment to policy continuity. Adequate investment in infrastructural industries, for example, is a key ingredient of growth and development. Clear GATS commitments in such sectors as telecommunications, health, education, financial services and transport could contribute to increased investment.[12]

Finally, although the economic case for not binding liberalization commitments is weak or nonexistent for the most part, political economy considerations – in particular the natural resistance to liberalization from those that stand to lose from it – may make it easier to liberalize in the context of joint action under a multilateral negotiation. This is an argument for more effective engagement in multilateral processes under the WTO. A related argument for such engagement is the fact that when new negotiations on trade in services start in the year 2000, they are likely to involve the design of rules as well as liberalization commitments. All member countries have an incentive to ensure that the rules of the system accommodate their interests.

3. Trade and Investment

Trade related investment measures

Efforts made by some countries during the Uruguay Round to bring the subject of investment into the multilateral trading system were of limited success. The Agreement on Trade-Related Investment Measures (TRIMS) reiterates the applicability of GATT provisions on national treatment and the prohibition of quantitative trade restrictions to certain TRIMS. The agreement does not address the treatment of investments or investors, but rather focuses on trade measures that are linked to investment policies. An illustrative list annexed to the TRIMS agreement contains examples of measures inconsistent with national treatment or involving quantitative trade restrictions, including local content requirements, trade-balancing requirements and measures that have the effect of restricting imports.

The agreement establishes grace periods within which these and any other non-conforming measures must be brought into conformity. All inconsistent measures were to have been notified within 90 days of the entry into force of the agreement. Phase-out periods for these measures were set at two years for developed countries, five years for developing countries and seven years for least developed countries. Transition periods can be extended for developing and least developed countries if they face difficulties in eliminating TRIMS. A standstill clause requires that existing TRIMS are not intensified during the transition period. A special provision permits the imposition of TRIMS on new enterprises during the transition period if that is considered necessary in order to avoid any disadvantage against established enterprises already subject to TRIMS. Notifications of TRIMS were received from 34 members, mostly developing countries. Among African countries, notifications of measures were received from Egypt, Nigeria, Uganda and South Africa, while Mauritius and Zambia notified that they had no non-conforming measures. In proportionate terms, notifications from Africa were far fewer than those from Latin America and Asia, raising the question whether this is because less frequent use has been made of TRIMS in Africa, or whether more notifications should have been made.

The Working Group on the relationship between trade and investment

The limited scope of the TRIMS agreement has not discouraged some countries from continuing to press for the inclusion of investment on the multilateral agenda. A peg upon which these efforts have been hung is the provision in the TRIMS agreement calling for an examination within five years of the question whether the agreement should be complemented by provisions on investment and competition policy. For reasons discussed below, the initiative to launch a comprehensive work programme at the Singapore Ministerial Conference in December 1996 proved controversial.

The agreement that finally emerged involved the establishment of a working group to examine the relationship between trade and investment. The mandate stated that this exercise did not prejudge whether negotiations would be launched in the future, and that if any such negotiations were eventually launched, this would only occur after an explicit consensus decision was taken to that effect by WTO members. These preconditions reflected concern on the part of some developing countries that they might be pressurized into a negotiation exercise they did not support. Other developing countries have expressed support for negotiations. Provisions attached to the working group's mandate seek to ensure that the interests of developing countries are fully reflected in the discussions. A decision will be made in two years upon how the work should proceed.

At its first meeting, the working group adopted a detailed work programme, bearing in mind that its mandate was exploratory, and of a fact-finding and educational nature. Four items were identified around which the work is being organized. The first addresses the relationship between trade and investment in terms of its implications for growth and development. Issues taken up in this context include foreign investment and technology transfer, the effects of foreign investment on the balance of payments, investment and competition, and the relationship between investment and employment. The second item examines the economic relationship between trade and investment, including the determinants of foreign direct investment and the nature of the interaction between trade flows and investment flows. Third, the working group is examining existing international arrangements involving or impinging upon trade and investment, including in the WTO. Finally, the fourth item on the working group's agenda addresses issues relevant to an assessment of the need for possible future initiatives, such as commonalities and differences in existing international instruments dealing with investment and obligations between home and host countries and between investors and host countries.

The case for multilateral cooperation on investment

The debate about the desirability of extending multilateral rules on investment is taking place against the background of two inter-related factors, one economic and the other institutional.[13] The first of these relates to the dramatic expansion that has occurred in international capital flows in recent years.[14] Foreign direct investment (FDI) flows averaged $50 billion per annum between 1980 and 1985, and had reached $50 billion by 1996[15] – a seven-fold increase. At the same time, a growing number of countries, especially developing countries, are involved in these capital flows.

Secondly, as a result of the growing prominence of FDI and of globalization trends more generally, international cooperation on investment matters is increasing and new agreements are being drawn up all the time. Bilateral investment agreements (BITS) have expanded dramatically. There were some 1,160 BITS in existence by mid 1996 (Ha Yeung, 1997), two-thirds of which were signed in the 1990s. Some 256 of these agreements involved African countries. Typically, BITS provide for non-discriminatory treatment of foreign investors and investments, and also provide guarantees against expropriation and for the transfer of funds. These agreements focus primarily on the conditions of operation at the post-entry stage, and do not stipulate entry or establishment conditions for FDI. A growing number of regional agreements include investment provisions – indeed, there is probably no regional integration agreement signed over the last decade or so that does not incorporate some investment provisions. In addition, the WTO itself already has investment provisions in the services area (see previous section), and rules relevant to investment in the TRIMS agreement, the Agreement on Trade-Related Aspects of Intellectual Property Rights, the Agreement on Subsidies and Countervailing Measures, and the Agreement on Government Procurement. The OECD has developed a number of instruments dealing with investment and for several years has been trying to negotiate a Multilateral Agreement on Investment. These institutional developments are a logical consequence of global FDI trends, and raise the question whether it would not make sense to seek a more comprehensive and coherent set of rules.

Increased capital flows, like other features of globalization, are not only attributable to technological advances and innovative business sector behaviour – policy has also played an important role. Many governments used to be more inclined than they are today to ration and condition the entry of FDI into their markets. They have become less confident that they are better placed than markets to deliver economic prosperity. Outward-oriented trade policies have emphasized the need to compete on world markets, which in turn requires new investments in modern plant and continuing upgrading of human skills. It is also the case that many developing country governments have lost at least part of their earlier mistrust of transnational corporations (TNCs) and the fear that if not restrained, these enterprises would act contrary to national economic interests. The capacity of TNCs to behave monopolistically can be attenuated through trade liberalization, so that enterprises have to compete in contestable markets rather than prospering behind government-granted market entry barriers.

As corporations have become increasingly internationalized, with production processes located in different parts of the world, trade and investment have tended to complement rather than substitute one another. Tariff-jumping investments, designed to secure access to a market through a domestic production presence rather than through trade, are becoming less important relative to investments that complement trade flows. Competitive imperatives increasingly require that international businesses both trade and invest, in an overall production/marketing cum market access strategy. Economic policies that frustrate such strategies will carry higher economic costs as the globalization process continues. In sum, the case for international investment liberalization is the same as that for trade liberalization – to reap the welfare gains from international economic specialization.

Developing country concerns

Notwithstanding the observations made above about growing reliance on the international economic and market-oriented policies, many countries, especially developing countries, continue to have misgivings about an uncritical and undifferentiated approach to foreign investment. In some of the WTO discussions, such misgivings have sometimes found expression in the argument that it is impractical to work on investment because the agenda is already overloaded. While the greatly enlarged dimensions of the WTO's post-Uruguay Round agenda has posed significant implementation challenges for many governments, the more substantive concerns that have been expressed about multilateral rules on investment can be summarized under five headings.

First, even though TRIMS may have lost some of their lustre, many governments still wish to use elements of "industrial policy" to influence resource allocation decisions, including in relation to investment. Investment policy, involving a mixture of controls and incentives, has been deployed by many countries to promote specific objectives, such as technology transfer, industrialization more broadly, regional development and export expansion.[16] As discussed above, the TRIMS agreement circumscribes some of the measures deployed for these purposes. In general, however, these provisions focus on measures that can be substituted for more efficient fiscal interventions, should such interventions be deemed to make any sense in the first place. A domestic content requirement, for example, could be replaced by "equivalent" tariffs on the competing imports against which the domestic content rule was aimed.

It can be shown that in certain second-best situations, a domestic content requirement could increase welfare. Under standard competitive assumptions in final and intermediate goods markets, however, and in the absence of other government interventions, a domestic content requirement is unambiguously welfare deteriorating (Grossman, 1981). The economic proposition that a domestic content requirement can improve welfare has led some to argue for them (Balasubramanyam, 1991), while others have emphasized uncertainty about the outcome and the fact that this kind of policy will induce wasteful rent-seeking behaviour.

As far as subsidies are concerned, the Agreement on Subsidies and Countervailing Measures prohibits subsidies contingent upon exportation or the use of domestic over imported inputs. The agreement also provides for remedies against subsidies that while not illegal, are actionable because they have adverse effects. Non-specific subsidies are exempted from the disciplines of the agreement and are not countervailable.[17] The emphasis here is on subsidies that are less distortionary because they are not narrowly focused on a particular activity or firm. Certain subsidies made generally available for the purposes of regional development, for example, or for research or environmental purposes, are non-actionable. One important point to note about the WTO subsidy disciplines is that they are designed first and foremost to deal with subsidy practices affecting trade in goods, and they will not always apply easily to investment incentives. One area that could be of immediate interest to most countries would be the prospect of disciplining fiscal incentives designed to influence investors' location decisions. Such incentive packages can prove costly for governments, and may well amount to fruitless competition among national treasuries, with little resulting effect on location decisions or on the total supply of investment funds.

In sum, the TRIMS and subsidies rules seek to eliminate the most economically distorting interventions that governments might be tempted to make in the name of investment policy, but existing WTO rules do not prohibit these policies altogether. Disciplines in these areas have, however, become more strict over the years. Any multilateral investment agreement would have to address the question of whether existing disciplines require modification. The matter may not prove straightforward, considering that in the OECD Multilateral Agreement on Investment (MAI), no provisions are included on fiscal measures, except insofar as these overlap with other specific provisions, such as transparency commitments or protections against expropriation.

The second category of concern in multilateral investment rules involves competitiveness considerations. This issue will be taken up later in a broader discussion of competition policy. The concern is that if a multilateral investment agreement sets about constraining the behaviour of governments and guarantees access and attractive operating conditions for investors, it may neglect the abuse by enterprises of their monopolistic positions in ways that reduce national welfare in the host country. It was concerns about such anti-competitive behaviour that led to efforts in UNCTAD to establish a Set of Multilaterally Agreed Principles and Rules for the Control of Restrictiveness Business Practices in 1980. The question of what the WTO might do to control anti-competitive behaviour emanating from the private sector is subject to discussion in the Working Group on the Interaction Between Trade and Competition Policy (see below).

The case for ensuring that TNCs do not abuse monopoly positions is strong, but identifying the appropriate policy prescription for doing so may be just as important.[18] Before choosing the best remedy for anti-competitive behaviour, it would be important to identify the source of a TNC's monopoly power. Sometimes these kinds of market advantage are the direct result of government policy. If a market is protected, for example, and then an investor is invited in to supply the market through domestic production, competition could be stifled. In such a case, a government may want to consider whether it should use trade liberalization as a vehicle for inducing competition, rather than to allow a monopolist to survive and then seek to restrain anti-competitive behaviour. A suitable alternative remedy could be to allow additional investment in the sector. In some instances, pro-competitive regulation or the application of competition laws might be the only solution, but it should be borne in mind that implementing such policies could involve considerable administrative costs, not to mention the risks associated with unproductive rent-seeking behaviour.

Third, concern has been expressed over the environmental implications of liberal investment regimes. This issue became a prominent plank in the opposition of some non-government organizations to the OECD's MAI. Incorporating the necessary provisions in an investment agreement to address environmental externalities, and ensuring that such interventions are the most efficient available, would seem relatively straightforward in theory. In practice, differences among governments on these issues would make for a challenging negotiation.

Fourth, the question of the timing and place of liberalization would need to be determined in a multilateral investment agreement, and some governments argue for a gradual approach. The arguments here are similar to those that arise with trade liberalization. A slower pace of liberalization might allow domestic producers to prepare for new competition and for more orderly adjustment where domestic production is displaced by imports. But gradualism also carries the risk that the liberalization process will be frustrated more easily by vested interests. Similar considerations apply in the case of investment. A balance must be struck. Those arguing for gradualism favour the GATS model, which emphasizes progressive liberalization and allows members to decide the pace and content of their liberalization commitments. As discussed above, the GATS has not been a dynamic instrument of liberalization in many sectors.

Finally, arguments about the need to safeguard national sovereignty, strategic considerations, and protection of the cultural heritage cannot be evaluated on economic grounds. A public policy "override" driven by any of these rationales should be made explicit and defended on its own terms. All that economic analysis can offer is an analysis of the costs of such policies in conventionally measured welfare terms. These kinds of "carve-out" provisions can be found in many agreements.

Options for Africa

If the rationale for liberalizing investment inflows is essentially the same as that for trade in goods and services, then existing trends towards opening up to FDI (UNCTAD, 1997) should continue. Legitimate questions arise as to the pace at which the liberalization process should be conducted, but in deciding how quickly to move, it is important to bear in mind the downside risks of not moving quickly enough. There may be grounds for applying investment incentives in pursuit of clear, broad-based policy objectives, but detailed interventions at the sectoral, sub-sectoral or even firm level are likely to carry the same high costs as trade protection. Public policy objectives can be safeguarded in a multilateral setting, provided governments involve themselves actively in discussions, and ultimately in negotiations should these take place. Africa as a whole has not been markedly successful in attracting foreign investment in recent years, and the policy framework is a key determinant of performance.

4. Trade-Related Aspects of Intellectual Property Rights

The TRIPS agreement

The Agreement on Trade-Related Aspects of Intellectual Property Rights (TRIPS) and the General Agreement on Trade in Services (GATS) were the two most significant extensions of the agenda of the multilateral trading system that emerged from the Uruguay Round.[19] The TRIPS agreement aims to do three things. First, it defines the substance of intellectual property rights in seven distinct areas, building on several pre-existing international agreements for the protection of intellectual property. The areas covered are copyright, trademarks, geographical indications, industrial designs, patents, lay-out designs of integrated circuits, and undisclosed information (trade secrets). Second, the TRIPS agreement creates obligations for the enforcement of intellectual property rights at the national level. Third, it forms part of the WTO's integrated dispute settlement system, providing for enforcement of the agreement at the international level.

The TRIPS agreement provides phase-in periods for various of its provisions. Developing countries are allowed up to five years to phase in most provisions, excluding the most favoured nation (MFN) and national treatment obligations (one year). They are permitted a further five years in cases where patentable technology was not protected at the date of entry into force of the agreement. In the case of least-developed countries, a phase-in period of 11 years is foreseen (except for MFN and national treatment), with the possibility of further extensions. For most developing countries, therefore, a TRIPS-consistent system of intellectual property right protection is supposed to be in place by the turn of the country. This requirement is going to prove a significant challenge for many countries, given all that is needed in the way of laws, institutions and procedures.

Economic considerations and the cost-benefit calculus

The area of intellectual property in the WTO has been contentious. As with trade liberalization, there are winners and losers from reforms. But the situation is more complex in the case of intellectual property rights, and it is less easy to argue that all the losers can be adequately compensated in some foreseeable future, or that national welfare in the aggregate will always be augmented in the medium to long term, especially when the initial redistributive effects of introducing intellectual property involve one country gaining and another losing. Much depends on the circumstances of the country concerned. Moreover, the policy default is different in the TRIPS area: While trade and investment liberalization involve the withdrawal of governments from markets, in TRIPS governments are entering markets to protect the returns of a subset of economic agents. Notwithstanding these uncertainties, however, it would be difficult to argue convincingly that countries with their own innovative capacity and that have achieved a certain level of development and technological sophistication could possibly gain from the denial of intellectual property rights to creators and inventors. As Primo Braga (1995) has argued, the fundamental challenge facing developing countries is to convert the granting of intellectual property rights from a rent transfer mechanism to an effective instrument for technological development.

From an economic perspective, there are essentially two reasons why governments may wish to grant producers the exclusive rights embodied in intellectual property protection, both of which turn on the presence of market failure. First, to the extent that investments in knowledge generation – that is, the fruits of research and development and other creative activity – cannot be recouped through some kind of exclusivity of access to the returns from such investments, they will be under-supplied. Potential innovators will not innovate, nor creators create, thereby arresting technological progress and cultural development. The market fails to align social and private costs and benefits in these circumstances, providing justification for arrangements to ensure that producers of intellectual property are permitted to recoup the outlays involved.

Second, the provision by governments of intellectual property rights may be designed to eliminate information asymmetries in the market, or in other words to protect consumers from their ignorance about the characteristics of particular products. Trademarks are the most relevant property right in this context. They provide consumers with a guarantee of the quality of products. While it is easy to state these propositions in abstract terms, a complex welfare analysis underlies any judgement as to what level of protection should be permitted, and for how long. Indeed, some would argue that for all practical purposes, the answers to these questions are indeterminate – the optimum outcome can only be approximated by a decision making process infused with power politics. Furthermore, from a national welfare standpoint, the ideal level of intellectual property protection would vary from country to country, depending on such factors as income levels, degree of skills development and the extent of indigenous capacity for technological innovation. When these uncertainties are added to the sensitivities inherent in the redistributive implications of interventions to protect intellectual property rights, it is not surprising that this is a contentious policy area.

Three key benefits flow from intellectual property protection. First, it can encourage local innovation and technological and cultural enrichment. Second, foreign owners of intellectual property are more likely to invest in a jurisdiction that protects their rights over that property, thus augmenting both the amount and quality of foreign investment. Third, technology transfer and diffusion are likely to be greater under a stronger system of intellectual property protection than a weaker one.[20]

Against these considerations, five categories of cost or potential cost can be identified. It is important to note, however, that a number of these costs are of a transient or once-off nature, and that there will be circumstances in which net costs become negative when matched to benefits over the medium and long term. The first cost to be noted is simply that of payment for the exploitation rights of intellectual property. Second, it may be the case that prices for products that are subject to intellectual property protection rise when this protection is granted. This is most probable in circumstances where the protection is granted to products with low price elasticities in markets where rent appropriation is easiest. Third, effective implementation of intellectual property rights in the field of trademark infringement, in particular, can lead to falls in output and employment. On the other hand, substitution in consumption for unbranded products of comparable quality to counterfeit goods may mitigate such effects, and more investment may also be forthcoming from trademark holders if they have greater confidence in the intellectual property protection system.

Fourth, producer and consumer costs may arise from the negative effects on the diffusion of technological knowledge that can accompany the granting of exclusive rights. The strength of this effect depends on how well developed a market is, whether the protection of proprietary knowledge creates significant structural bottlenecks in the economy, and how the intellectual property owner uses the exclusive right. Finally, many countries, especially developing countries, will encounter significant administrative costs as they set up the institutional and legal machinery necessary to comply with the TRIPS agreement. The agreement recognizes this difficulty in part through the phase-in periods it foresees, and also through its encouragement of technical assistance.

Options for Africa

Compliance with the TRIPS agreement poses major challenges for many African countries, and the agreement carries with it a number of uncertainties as to the cost–benefit calculus involved in full compliance. The considerable complexities associated with TRIPS suggest the need for technical assistance, as well as close attention to discussions on implementation as they unfold in the WTO.

Two general points should be borne in mind. The first is that governments can influence the severity of the downside associated with intellectual property protection through other policies. The more open markets are to trade and investment, the less likely are owners of intellectual property to be able to appropriate economic rents. Obviously the size of potential rents is affected by underlying elasticities, but governments can make a contribution to reducing monopolistic abuses by making markets competitive through liberalization and, where necessary, through pro-competitive regulation. Second, net long-term cost problems linked to intellectual property regimes are likely to be the most acute in countries with limited technological development, where technology transfer and knowledge diffusion are limited, and where local innovation has yet to take off. The policy implications of this are clear – policies that support the development of human skills, technology and knowledge diffusion are essential to reducing these costs. One particular area where concerted action could have significant returns is in the field of telecommunications and information technology based on computers.

5. Trade and Competitive Policy

The Working Group on the Interaction Between Trade and Competition Policy

Ministers agreed at their meeting in Singapore in December 1996 to establish a working group to study issues relating to the interaction between trade and competition policy, including anti-competitive practices. The mandate was established in parallel to that on trade and investment, and stated that the exercise did not prejudge whether negotiations would be launched in the future, and that if any such negotiations were eventually launched, this would only occur after an explicit consensus decision was taken to that effect by WTO members. These preconditions reflected both the realization that this was a complicated policy area, about which there was limited understanding in many quarters, and the concern on the part of some countries that they might be pressured into a negotiating exercise they did not support. Other provisions attached to the working group's mandate seek to ensure that the interests of developing countries are fully reflected in the discussions. A decision will be made in two years upon how the work should proceed.

As noted in Section 3 above, international efforts had been made previously to address competition-related issues in an explicit way, notably through UNCTAD's 1980 efforts to establish a Set of Multilaterally Agreed Principles and Rules for the Control of Restrictive Business Practices. The interest in exploring competition policy in the WTO context – a possibility that had been foreshadowed in the Uruguay Round TRIMS agreement – is attributable to a number of factors. As trade and investment liberalization efforts have intensified, the possibility that private sector behaviour alone can frustrate competition and influence markets has become a greater concern to governments. Attention has been focused on anti-trust or competition policy in a domestic setting for many decades in developed countries, but the international dimension is more recent.

The concerns of completion policy

Globalization, or the growing integration of the world economy, has given competition policy a transborder dimension that was largely absent previously, and has already led to various forms of bilateral cooperation, mostly involving comity-type arrangements for information sharing and consultation. Some more recent bilateral arrangements have gone further, and anticipate the possibility of one competition policy authority asking another to act on its behalf. An additional influence on the decision to look at competition policy in an international context is interest in ensuring that any discussion of possible rules on investment flows be adequately balanced by work on the competition side to guard against the anit-competitive abuse of a market position by enterprises.

In considering competition policy, it is important to remember that many different policies influence the conditions of competition in a market.[21] Trade liberalization, more open procurement arrangements, control of the protectionist abuse of technical standards and the removal of subsidies are examples of policies that affect the conditions of competition. They can all be characterized as pro-competitive policies that enhance efficiency and increase economic welfare, and therefore act in the same direction as explicit competition policies targeted more directly on firm behaviour or market structures.

Whether directed at firm behaviour or market structure, competition policies can have ambiguous welfare effects, especially in a temporal sense. A government might decide, for example, to allow a merger in the name of greater productive efficiency or competitive capacity internationally, while at the same time recognizing that the merger will lead to higher prices for customers. The need for such trade-offs helps to explain why a distinction is made in practice between *per se infringements* of competition laws, which are outright illegal, and *rule of reason* judgements, where the competition authorities have to decide whether or not a practice or a proposed merger, for example, should be permitted. As the practice of competition policy becomes more sophisticated, and the capacity to analyse probable outcomes improves, governments are becoming less certain about what can be treated in a straightforward per se fashion, leaving only the most egregious types of price-filing and exclusionary behaviour in this category.

The case for and against international competition policy

It is easy to see how these difficulties are compounded in an international context. Take, for example, a welfare analysis of a competition policy decision by a national competition authority involving, say, a merger. It may transpire that national welfare would be enhanced in the country whose enterprises were merging, but at the expense of consumer welfare in other countries. In an international setting, what welfare standard should apply? In the case just described, the welfare cost to the affected country could exceed the gain to the country permitting the merger. In this case a national welfare standard would favour action, but a global standard would not. If the welfare gain were greater than the welfare loss, a national and a global welfare standard would yield consistent conclusions, but still at the expense of consumers in another jurisdiction. Governments may have difficulty in subscribing to a global welfare standard, and accepting associated judgements that could always be challenged in relation to the welfare calculus, where this standard will often either sanction a welfare loss in one country or prevent another country from reaping a welfare gain.

A further complication arises from differences in national approaches to competition policy. In the United States, for example, considerable emphasis is placed on the protection of consumer welfare, strict prohibition of a range of per se prohibitions, the use of criminal penalties, and effective enforcement, including by private citizens. The European Union, on the other hand, has placed greater emphasis on integrating the European market, including through the extensive use of block exemptions to permit agreements among firms and practices that would otherwise be prohibited. The EU approach is more broad-based than many, incorporating state aids to industrial and regulatory structures that distort competition, as well as private business practices.

Both the discretionary nature of much competition policy and the existing differences in national approaches make it unlikely that governments would agree easily to a strong form of multilateral commitment, such as harmonized rules and multilateralized decision making in competition policy decisions. Alternative approaches, such as commitments on the implementation of national laws and regulations, minimum standards, or community-based cooperation, might stand a better chance of prospering.

The arguments, in summary, in favour of multilateral competition rules can be broken into four broad categories (Hoekman and Mavroidis, 1994). First, the absence of national competition rules and resulting trade distortions might provide grounds for international action. Second, differences in national regimes and omissions in these regimes could be usefully eliminated through international rules. The elimination of the exemption of export cartels from national competition laws, for example, would enhance competition in increasingly integrated international markets. Third, as transnational corporation (TNCs) increasingly operate in multiple jurisdictions, international cooperation would help control abuses of market positions that cannot be easily addressed by a single authority. Multilateral cooperation would also lower transaction costs for TNCs, who have to deal with different national competition authorities that do not necessarily pronounce in a consistent fashion.

Fourth, international cooperation on competition policy could provide an avenue for moderating what is perceived in some quarters as a growing problem in international trade – the use of anti-dumping measures. While sometimes presented as a pro-competitive policy instrument, anti-dumping actions generally have the effect of making markets less contestable. Anti-dumping actions typically benefit domestic producers at the expense of foreign suppliers and domestic consumers, as does any protection policy. To the extent that anti-dumping actions seek to respond to the consequences of uncompetitive conditions in export markets, international cooperation in the field of competition policy could provide a more appropriate framework than anti-dumping. In reality, however, it is unlikely that governments would agree to substitute anti-dumping rules with multilateral competition rules in the foreseeable future. This is because for many countries, the anti-dumping apparatus functions at least in part as a safety valve when liberalization takes place, displacing in such cases the regular safeguard mechanism provided in the WTO. The anti-dumping question will be addressed in its own terms, and not as a by-product of competition policy disciplines. Moreover, experience also suggests that anti-dumping might disappear altogether only in circumstances of deep integration, such as in the European Union.

A reason for thinking carefully about the role for competition policy in an economy before investing in the necessary legal and institutional machinery relates to the point made earlier about the array of policies that can be brought to bear upon the conditions of competition in a market. There is a risk that competition policies could be used as a surrogate or indirect means of dealing with problems of abusive market behaviour that are in themselves made possible by other government policies. Trade protection, anti-dumping actions and investment restrictions, for example, can all render markets less competitive. Does it make sense to apply the band-aid of competition policy and regulation in cases where the problem only exists because the government allows it to exist through other policy interventions? It is important for governments to be clear on this point both in terms of domestic policy, and before they become embroiled in any possible future international competition policy commitments. The key question to ask is how far will open markets render explicit competition policy redundant. Will open trade and investment policies ensure competition? The answer may well be affirmative for many industries, but not for all. In network industries like basic telecommunications, for example, it is clear that liberalization alone does not remove the scope for suppliers to abuse their market position. Pro-competitive regulation is also required.

The argument that competition policy should not be adopted uncritically, without an analysis of alternative ways in which markets can be rendered more competitive, is reinforced when the risks of regulatory capture are taken into account (Neven et al., 1993). The relationship between the regulators and the regulated is always complicated, at the level of both design and implementation. On the other hand, a well-designed and well-run competition policy authority could serve a useful role in pointing out the anti-competitive consequences of other government policies, acting as a kind of watchdog on government's role in influencing the conditions of competition in national markets.

Options for Africa

Only eight African countries have adopted anti-monopoly or competition legislation,[22] and another seven have either started to prepare such legislation or have the matter under serious consideration[23] (WTO, 1997). Before competition policy legislation is adopted, governments should consider carefully why they want it, what priority it should have and whether alternative policy approaches can do more to address particular instances of anti-competitive behaviour by private business. The necessary competition policy or regulatory interventions can then be designed to meet specific needs that cannot be addressed through improved policy design elsewhere. Capacity building needs, including the framing of legislation, regulations and qualified administrators, will be considerable. As far as international efforts to address competition policy are concerned, close monitoring of the discussions in the WTO working group would be useful in developing an understanding of the issues involved, including the desirability of possible future commitments in this area.

6. Government Procurement

Government procurement has never been in the mainstream of the GATT or the WTO. It was explicitly excluded from the national treatment provisions of the GATT, and similarly carved out of the GATS.[24] In the Tokyo Round (1973–1979) an agreement on procurement was reached. This agreement was amended in 1988 and then replaced by a new Agreement on Government Procurement (GPA) in the Uruguay Round. The GPA has only 26 signatories[25] out of the total WTO membership of 132, and several reasons have been put forward for why the GPA did not attract more signatories.[26] Many governments have opted for maintaining procurement arrangements that favour domestic suppliers over foreign ones, something not permitted by the national treatment provision of the GPA. Another argument is that the procedures involved are excessively cumbersome and costly for countries with limited administrative resources. The disciplines of the GPA apply only to the governmental entities indicated by a signatory and it has been asserted that prospective signatories have found the demands of existing signatories with respect to the entities to be covered too enacting. Another consideration is that many developing countries believe that for competitive reasons they cannot bid effectively for foreign procurement contracts, and so they attach little importance to international procurement disciplines.

Ministers agreed at their meeting in Singapore in December 1996 to establish a working group with the mandate "to conduct a study on transparency in government procurement practices, taking into account national policies, and based on this study, to develop elements for inclusion in an appropriate agreement".[27] The Working Group on Transparency in Government Procurement is open to all members and any eventual agreement in this area would apply to the full WTO membership, and not just to a subset of countries. The initiative to promote this work was taken by developed countries, in particular the United States. Along with the mandate on trade facilitation (see Section 7 below), this exercise can be seen in part as an effort to address governance or corruption issues.[28] Government procurement has been shown time and again in different countries, both developed and developing, to be a major source of government patronage and corruption.

In addition, procurement is worth a significant amount. Estimates of its value vary from 7–12% of GDP at the upper bound to 2.75–4.25% at the lower bound (Trionfetti, 1997). Procurement therefore offers major scope for liberalization gains and the creation of new market opportunities for foreign suppliers. It is interesting to note that according to the analysis of the value of procurement markets undertaken by Trionfetti (1997), smaller countries and developing countries spend proportionately more of their GDP on procurement than large industrial countries.

The working group on transparency does not focus on the issue of protection in procurement, but only on the transparency of procedures and the public availability of relevant information. Among the elements of transparency that have been identified in the working group on the basis of national practices and the provisions of other international procurement agreements[29] are information on national legislation and procedures, prior information on procurement opportunities, tendering and qualification requirements, conditions for fairness, accountability and integrity in evaluation procedures, and surveillance and enforcement mechanisms. A significant point about transparency requirements is that they must be seen to be applied – putative transparency is not enough.

It remains uncertain whether a transparency agreement on procurement will be concluded under the auspices of the WTO, since the mandate may be interpreted to envisage the possibility but not to entail a commitment to that effect. If this does happen, there would eventually be a question as to whether a further step would be taken to address preferences and various "offset" requirements that are now commonplace in procurement.[30] Judging from the exceptions and partial coverage of the GPA, the elimination of preferences and other national objectives from procurement activities seems some way off. In any event, it is difficult to imagine that there would be an ex ante exclusion of the possibility that developing countries could use some measure of preference in government procurement. On the other hand, pressures are mounting for improvements in procurement practices in developing countries, both as a condition demanded by international financial institutions and because of budgetary circumstances that call for maximum efficiency in the use of government revenue. These considerations militate in favour of active engagement in the WTO process, so that governments can be adequately informed and influence outcomes.

7. Trade Facilitation

Ministers agreed at Singapore in December 1996 to direct the Council for Trade in Goods "to undertake exploratory and analytical work, drawing of the work on other relevant organizations, on the simplification of trade procedures in order to assess the scope for WTO rules in this area". Trade facilitation refers to practically any aspect of trade or trade-related activity where government requirements exist, but in its wider conception also includes consideration of such matters as harnessing new information technology in order to accelerate transaction times. The interest in increasing efficiency in trade has been heightened by the fact that other barriers to trade have been falling in the last few years, making delays at borders, cumbersome and excessive documentation requirements, and a lack of automation relatively more costly. These additional cost factors may often exceed tariff levels.

Several international organizations have been working on these questions for many years. The WTO also contains provisions relevant to trade facilitation, including the rules on transit traffic, fees and formalities, customs valuation, and publication of regulations. Separate agreements also exist on customs valuation, technical barriers to trade, sanitary and phytosanitary measures, import licensing procedures, rules of origin, and preshipment inspection. The Singapore Ministerial Conference mandate provides the opportunity to take a comprehensive look at these provisions from the perspective of trade facilitation.

Some governments are already pressing for a formal agreement on trade facilitation in the WTO, while others prefer to wait and deal with the issue in a broader negotiating context. Among the main elements where improvements could be made in the name of trade facilitation are streamlining of documentary requirements, improved automation and use of information technology, more transparency in procedures, and better risk assessment and audit based techniques of control in customs. Considering the welfare gains that could accrue from improvements in these areas, especially in countries where such problems are pervasive and carry high costs for the economy, the WTO trade facilitation exercise would seem to justify active participation.

8. Trade and Environment

Work in the WTO on trade and environment

Growing concerns among various governments and non-government organizations, especially from the early 1990s onwards, about environmental protection and the relationship between trade and environment, led to the establishment of a GATT work programme on this subject.[31] This mandate was replaced at the time of the completion of the Uruguay Round by a new one. The Committee on Trade and Environment (CTE) was established with the twin objectives of identifying the "relationship between trade measures and environmental measures in order to promote sustainable development" and making "appropriate recommendations on whether any modifications of the provisions of the multilateral trading system are required, compatible with the open, equitable and non-discriminatory nature of the system". The CTE has carried out an extensive programme of background analysis and discussions, which is continuing. Certain recommendations emerged from the CTE for the Singapore Ministerial Meeting, but no conclusion has been reached on the central question of whether any modifications of WTO provisions are required.

Ministers at Singapore noted that the CTE would continue to examine, among other things, the scope of the complementarities among trade liberalization, economic development and environmental protection. They stated that the full implementation of the WTO agreements would make an important contribution to achieving the objectives of sustainable development. Ministers also noted the importance of policy coordination at the national level on these issues, and recognized the contribution of government experts in the work of the CTE.

Trade policy and environmental policy

One of the most obvious links between trade policy and environmental policy is the role that trade liberalization can play in improving environmental quality. In the case of agriculture, for example, protection in industrial countries can lead to capital and input-intensive agricultural production techniques that are less environmentally friendly than the alternative of allowing countries with more suitable resource endowments and propitious environmental conditions to undertake agricultural production. Trade liberalization in these circumstances would imply improvements in environmental quality.

Unless trade itself is identified as the direct source of an environmental problem, and such a determination would require a comprehensive analysis taking fully into account the general equilibrium effects of alternatives, then the association of trade restrictions with improved environmental quality is likely to be erroneous. In practice, trade policy is often invoked as a means of persuasion, or as a threat. Trade policy in these circumstances serves as a mechanism for punishing governments that do not comply with certain environmental standards. Such standards may be set cooperatively, as for example in a Multilateral Environmental Agreement (MEA), or they may be developed unilaterally and then applied to other jurisdictions.

In either case, the immediate point here is that trade restrictions are typically not an efficient intervention from an environmental perspective because they do not attack the environmental problem at source. Import restrictions on a scarce natural resource, for example on tropical timber, will not guarantee the preservation of tropical forests. The incentive effects of such a measure may simply be to increase domestic consumption of the natural resource, or so cheapen its price in the market as to induce agriculturalists to clear the forests and use the land for other purposes. The optimal intervention is to manage the resource directly, and by assigning of property rights, fiscal measures or some other kind of intervention, address the externality that is resulting in socially costly depletion of a natural resource. The challenge of identifying economically optimal policy interventions to deal with environmental quality externalities is not always relished by environmental groups, some of whom prefer to reject the idea of scarcity and opportunity cost, and others of whom relish trade policy because of its coercive promise in an international setting.

An additional pressure in the trade and environment debate emanates from protectionist interests. It is attractive for those seeking protection from foreign competition to be able to point to concerns over the state of the environment as a reason for blocking trade. In effect, to the extent that protection lowers the incomes of those seeking to sell in export markets, it may indirectly have a negative effect on the environment. The demand for improved environmental quality typically rises as incomes increase.

Demands for internationally harmonized environmental standards may emanate from environmentalists or from protection-seekers. While perhaps a superficially attractive idea, the notion that environmental problems could be solved by ensuring that all countries subscribe to identical standards, or to agreed minimum standards, tends to overlook the practical difficulties of settling on such standards. Moreover, there are good environmental reasons why standards may differ, associated with the absorptive capacity of different locations. And as noted previously, different income levels are likely to result in different priorities when it comes to fixing environmental standards, which means that additional incentives may be needed to ensure some given level of environmental standard. Pressures for harmonization can be particularly imposing when they go beyond the characteristics embedded in products themselves and cover non-product related process and production methods (PPMS).

Whatever the outcome of deliberations on the best approach to standard-setting in the environmental field, a point that has been emphasized by most members in the CTE is that standards, and suitable remedies against non-compliance, should be decided through a cooperative process and not through unilateral determinations. If governments decide in a multilateral environmental agreement (MEA), for example, that they want to use trade restrictions as a remedy for non-compliance with agreed environmental norms, this is a decision that trade specialists might not always see as optimal, but it would represent a consensus. A consensus agreement of this nature, with a specific environmental focus in a MEA, would be more likely to lead to a desirable environmental outcome without trade restrictions than a unilateral approach without any basis in prior commitments from other countries. Trade restrictions have been written into relatively few MEAS and no instance of their use has been the subject of a WTO dispute to date. This observation reinforces the argument that the best place to deal with environmental issues that have international dimensions is in MEAS. The idea of making the WTO responsible for policies in this area is neither good for the environment, nor beneficial to the WTO and the legitimate trade interests of potentially affected countries.

Options for Africa

One issue brought before the CTE, which has its origins in GATT discussions going back to the early 1980s, is that of the export of domestically prohibited goods. This issue is important for many African countries, for whom the export of inferior or dangerous goods from countries in which the sale of such goods is prohibited, has been a source of environmental damage, health hazards and other economic costs. Specialized inter-government organizations are helping to resolve the problems that arise here. WTO members should be encouraged to support these efforts, including through the provision of technical assistance that would strengthen the technical capacity of the affected countries to monitor and control when necessary the imports of domestically prohibited goods.

Other concerns that appear of particular interest to developing countries are to ensure that environmental arguments are not appropriated for protectionist ends, that spurious harmonization objectives are avoided, and that the global responsibility for safeguarding environmental quality is equitable shared. African countries might also press for further liberalization in such areas as agriculture, where positive environmental spin-offs would be forthcoming. In the longer term, it is in the interests of all countries, as well as of the multilateral trading system, that growth and development be sustainable. But good environmental policy is much more likely to secure this objective than bad trade policy.

**Appendix Table 7.A1:
Summary of specific services commitments by country**

Countries	01	02	03	04	05	06	07	08	09	10	11	12	Total
Angola							*		*	*			3
Antigua and Barbuda	*						*		*	*	*		5
Argentina	*	*	*	*			*		*				6
Australia	*	*	*	*	*	*	*	*	*	*	*		11
Austria	*	*	*	*	*	*	*	*	*	*	*	*	12
Bahrain							*						1
Bangladesh									*				1
Barbados	*	*					*			*			4
Belize	*							*					2
Benin	*						*		*		*		4
Bolivia								*	*	*			3
Botswana	*	*							*				3
Brazil	*	*	*	*			*		*		*		7
Brunei Darussalam	*	*					*				*		4
Bulgaria	*	*	*	*	*	*	*	*	*	*	*		11
Burkina Faso									*				1
Burundi	*		*	*				*	*				5
Cameroon	*								*				2
Canada	*	*	*	*		*	*		*		*		8
Central African Rep.	*	*				*			*	*			5
Chile	*	*					*		*		*		5
Colombia	*	*	*			*	*		*				6
Congo									*	*			2
Congo RP	*	*	*		*				*	*			6
Costa Rica	*				*			*	*	*	*		6
Côte d'Ivoire	*		*						*		*		4
Cuba	*	*	*				*		*	*	*		7
Cyprus	*						*						2
Czech Republic	*	*	*	*	*	*	*	*	*	*	*		11
Djibouti	*	*							*	*			4

Countries	01	02	03	04	05	06	07	08	09	10	11	**12**	**Total**
Dominica		*					*		*	*			4
Dominican Republic	*	*	*				*	*	*				6
Ecuador	*	*	*	*		*	*	*	*	*	*		10
Egypt			*				*		*		*		4
El Salvador	*	*				*	*		*		*		6
European Community	*	*	*	*	*	*	*	*	*	*	*	*	12
Fiji									*				1
Finland	*	*	*	*		*	*		*	*	*		9
Gabon	*		*				*		*				4
Gambia	*	*	*	*	*	*	*	*	*	*	*	*	12
Ghana			*		*		*		*		*		5
Grenada		*					*		*	*			4
Guatemala	*						*		*		*		4
Guinea	*					*		*	*		*		5
Guinea-Bis-sau									*	*			2
Guyana	*	*					*		*		*		5
Haiti	*		*		*		*		*				5
Honduras	*						*		*		*		4
Hong Kong	*	*	*	*			*		*	*	*		8
Hungary	*	*		*	*	*	*	*	*	*	*		10
Iceland	*	*	*	*		*	*		*	*	*		9
India	*	*	*				*	*	*				6
Indonesia	*	*	*				*		*		*		6
Israel	*	*				*	*		*				5
Jamaica	*				*		*	*	*	*	*		7
Japan	*	*	*	*	*	*	*	*	*	*	*		11
Kenya		*					*		*		*	*	5
Korea RP	*	*	*	*		*	*		*		*		8
Kuwait	*		*	*		*	*	*	*	*			8
Lesotho	*	*	*	*	*	*	*		*		*	*	10
Liechten-stein	*	*		*	*	*	*		*	*	*		9
Macau	*						*		*				3
Madagascar	*												1

Countries	01	02	03	04	05	06	07	08	09	10	11	12	Total
Malawi	*		*				*	*	*				5
Malaysia	*	*	*				*	*	*	*	*	*	9
Maldives	*												1
Mali					*				*				2
Malta							*		*		*		3
Mauritania									*				1
Mauritius		*							*				2
Mexico	*	*	*	*	*		*	*	*		*	*	10
Mongolia	*	*	*	*			*		*				6
Morocco	*	*	*			*	*		*		*		7
Mozambique							*						1
Myanmar									*		*		2
Namibia	*								*				2
New Zealand	*	*	*	*	*		*		*		*		8
Nicaragua	*	*					*		*		*		5
Nigeria		*					*		*		*		4
Norway	*	*	*	*	*	*	*		*	*	*		10
Pakistan	*	*	*				*	*	*				6
Panama	*	*	*	*	*	*	*	*	*	*	*		11
Papua New Guinea	*	*	*				*		*		*		6
Paraguay							*		*				2
Peru	*	*		*			*		*	*	*		7
Philippines	*	*					*		*		*		5
Poland	*	*	*	*	*	*	*	*	*		*		10
Qatar	*	*	*			*	*		*				6
Romania	*	*	*	*		*	*		*		*		8
Rwanda	*				*	*			*	*			5
Saint Kitts & Nevis		*					*		*	*	*		5
Saint Lucia							*	*	*	*	*		5
Saint Vinc. & Gren.							*	*	*	*	*		5
Senegal	*	*		*					*	*	*		6
Sierra Leone	*	*	*		*	*	*	*	*	*	*		10
Singapore	*	*	*				*		*	*	*		7

Countries	01	02	03	04	05	06	07	08	09	10	11	**12**	**Total**
Slovak Republic	*	*	*	*	*	*	*		*		*		9
Slovenia	*	*	*	*	*	*	*	*	*	*	*		11
Solomon Islands	*		*				*		*				4
South Africa	*	*	*	*		*	*		*		*	*	9
Sri Lanka									*				1
Suriname									*		*		2
Swaziland	*							*	*				3
Sweden	*	*	*	*		*	*		*	*	*		9
Switzerland	*	*	*	*	*	*	*		*	*	*		10
Tanzania									*				1
Thailand	*	*	*	*	*	*	*		*	*	*		10
Togo			*						*	*			3
Trinidad and Tobago	*		*		*		*	*	*	*	*		8
Tunisia							*		*				2
Turkey	*	*	*		*	*	*	*	*		*		9
Uganda									*				1
United Arab Emirates	*	*	*			*	*		*				6
Uruguay	*	*					*		*	*	*		6
USA	*	*	*	*	*	*	*	*	*	*	*		11
Venezuela	*	*	*				*		*	*	*	*	8
Zambia	*		*					*	*				4
Zimbabwe		*					*		*				3
Total all countries	87	69	58	36	30	38	86	32	110	47	67	9	669
Total – Africa	22	14	14	5	7	8	16	7	37	11	13	4	158
% of possible commitments – All countries	73	58	49	31	25	32	73	27	93	40	57	8	47

Key:
- 01 Business services
- 02 Communication services
- 03 Construction and related engineering services
- 04 Distribution services
- 05 Educational services

06 Environmental services
07 Financial services
08 Health and related social services
09 Tourism and related travel services
10 Recreational, cultural and sporting services
11 Transport services
12 Other services

Source: WTO Services Database.

Notes

1 These rules were subscribed to by only a handful of developed country governments. Moreover, much of what was negotiated in the Tokyo Round by way of elaborations on the trade rules applied to a subset of the GATT membership, excluding many developing countries.

2 For an excellent summary of this debate, and advocacy of the view that Africa's economic difficulties are rooted primarily in policy factors, see Collier (1997) and references cited therein.

3 See, for example, Williamson (1993) and Aziz and Wescott (1997).

4 Ministers at Singapore affirmed the commitment of all members to observance of internationally recognized core labour standards and stated that these standards should be addressed by the ILO. They noted that labour standards are promoted by growth and development, which in turn is fostered by trade liberalization. Ministers also expressed their rejection of the use of labour standards for protectionist purposes and agreed that the comparative advantage of countries must in no way be put into question. If the issue is present again for inclusion in the work of the WTO, developing countries and others would certainly be concerned about the risk that arguments relating to labour standards would be appropriated for protectionist motives.

5 Some internationally traded services, such as telephone conversations, may also involve instantaneous production and consumption, but in this case the transaction takes place across a frontier and is therefore similar to cross-border exchanges of goods.

6 Where repeated transactions are required, such as in after-sales services, a continuing local presence is obviously more desirable than long-distance supply.

7 The implied allocation of locally generated output as domestic sales of foreign trade on the basis of the ownership of the equity responsible for production appears to have limited economic relevance. Yet under GATS, governments have assumed obligations in respect of production attributable to foreign equity.

8 Relatively few analyses exist of GATS. See Hoecman (1995), Hoekman and Sauvé (1994), Altinger and Enders (1995), on a Sauvé (1994).

9 Both a service supplier and a service consumer could, of course, move to a third jurisdiction. Under GATS, this would be treated as two separate transactions from the point of view of the host country.

10 More sophisticated attempts at measurement have been made by Hoekman (1995),

Altinger and Enders (1995), and Mattoo (1997), but they all suffer from severe information constraints and rest on heroic assumptions.

11 See, for example, Martin and Winters (1996) and WTO (1998), which contain or report upon various studies of the gains from liberalization under the Uruguay Round.

12 Support for this view can be found in UNCTAD (1996).

13 The WTO's 1996 Annual Report contains an extensive analysis of the relationship between trade and investment.

14 The WTO discussions described above are primarily about foreign direct investment, and not short-term capital flows. The latter have been the subject of much scrutiny recently because of the Asian financial crisis.

15 See UNCTAD's annual World Investment Report (various years) for the most comprehensive data available on foreign direct investment.

16 See, for example, Maskus and Eby (1990).

17 A subsidy is considered non-specific if access to it is not limited to certain enterprises, and if prior objective and neutral criteria of an economic nature determine access to the subsidy.

18 Should rules be required, this could be done within an investment agreement or as part of a stand-alone agreement on competition policy.

19 Two good papers providing an analytical overview of the TRIPS Agreement are Primo Braga (1995) and Subramanian (1995). In addition, the World Intellectual Property Organization commissioned papers from several authors in 1995. These papers provide useful background, analysis and policy guidance. See Sherwood (1996), UNCTAD (1996), and the Institute for Economic Research (1996). These papers contain extensive bibliographies.

20 For some empirical evidence on these points, see Mansfield (1995).

21 The 1997 WTO Annual Report contains a detailed analysis of trade and competition policy (WTO, 1997). The report includes an extensive bibliography on a wide range of issues raised in the competition policy debate.

22 Algeria, Côte d'Ivoire, Gabon, Kenya, Mali, South Africa, Tunisia and Zambia.

23 Cameroon, Egypt, Ghana, Madagascar, Malawi, Morocco and Zimbabwe.

24 Negotiations are taking place under Article XIII of GATS on government procurement in services. The work is still at a preliminary, exploratory stage.

25 Canada; the European Community and member states; Hong Kong, China; Israel; Japan; Korea, Liechtenstein; Netherlands for Aruba; Norway; Singapore; Switzerland; the United States.

26 For a discussion of this and many other aspects of government procurement, see Hoekman and Mavroidis (1997)

27 See Kulacoglu (1997) for a description of the working group's activities.

28 For a discussion of corruption and procurement, see Economic Commission for Africa (1997).

29 The latter include the UNCITRAL Model Law, the World Bank Guidelines on procurement and the GPA.

30 Such offsetting requirements may involve requirements expressed in terms of such things as technology transfer, counter-trade, R&D, exports, local content, training, national subcontracting, and investment.

31 See Low (1992) for surveys of these issues. New work from the World Bank on trade environment issues is under preparation.

References

Altinger, L. and A. Enders. 1995. "The scope and depth of GATS commitments". *The World Economy*, vol.

Aziz, J. and R. Wescott. 1997. "Policy complementarities and the Washington Consensus". International Monetary Fund Working Paper 129, August.

Balasubramanyam, V.N. 1991. "Putting TRIMS to good use". *World Development*, vol. 19: 1215–24.

Bhagwati, J. 1984. "Splintering and disembodiment of services and developing nations". *The World Economy*, vol. 8: 133–44.

Anderson, K. and R. Blackhurst. 1992. *The Greening of World Trade Issues*. Ann Arbor: University of Michigan Press, and London: Harvester Wheatsheaf.

Collier, P. 1997. "Globalisation: What should be the African policy response?" Centre for the Study of African Economies, Oxford, November Mimeo.

DeAnne Julius. 1994. "International direct investment: Strengthening the policy regime". Paper prepared for IIE Conference on Managing the World Economy of the Future: Lessons from the First Fifty Years After Bretton Woods. Washington: Institute for International Economies.

Economic Commission for Africa. 1997. "Practices and procedures of government procurement in Africa". Working Paper Series ECA/ESPD/WTO/97/10, December.

Grossman, G. 1981. "The theory of domestic content protection and content preference". *The Quarterly Journal of Economics*, vol. 96, no. 4: 583–603.

Ha Yeung, D. 1997. "Africa in the face of a likely multilateral framework on investment: Elements of a common African position". Discussion paper commissioned by the OAU/African Economic Community, Addis Ababa.

Hoekman, B. 1995. "International capital markets: Development, competition policy and the GATT". *The World Economy*, vol. 17, no. 2: 121–50.

Hoekman, B. and P.C. Mavroidis. 1997. "Law and policy in public purchasing: The WTO agreement on government procurement". Studies in International Trade Policy, The University of Michigan Press.

Hoekman, B. and P. Sauvé. 1994. "Liberalizing trade in services". World Bank. Discussion Paper No. 234, Washington, D.C.

Institute of Economic Research. 1996. "Study on the financial and other implications of the implementation of the TRIPS Agreement for Developing Countries", prepared for the World Intellectual Property Organization. Mimeo. September.

Kulacoglu, V. 1997. WTO Government Procurement Regime and Related Activities. Mimeo.

Low, P. 1992. "International trade and the environment". World Bank Discussion Paper, No. 159, Washington, D.C.

Low, P. and A. Mattoo. 1997. "Reform in Basic Telecommunications and the WTO Negotiations: The Asian Experience". World Trade Organization.

Mansfield, E. 1995. "Intellectual property protection, foreign direct investment, and technology transfer". International Finance Corporation, Discussion Paper No. 27.

Maskus, K.E. and D.R. Eby. 1990. "Developing new rules and disciplines on trade-related investment measures". *The World Economy*, vol. 13: 523–39.

Mattoo, A. 1998. "Financial services and the WTO: Liberalization in the developing and transition economies. Mimeo.

Neven, D., R. Nuttal and P. Seabright. 1993. *Merger in Daylight: The Economics and Politics of European Merger Control*, London: CEPR.

Primo Braga, C.A. 1995. "Trade-related intellectual property issues: The Uruguay Round Agreement and its economic implications". Paper presented at the World Bank Conference on The Uruguay Round and the Developing Economies, Washington, D.C.

Sampson, G. and R. Snape. 1985. "Identifying the issues in trade in services". *The World Economy*, vol. 8: 171–81.

Sauvé, P. 1994. "The General Agreement on Trade in Services: Much ado about what?" In Daniel Schwanen, ed., *Trains, Gains and Automobiles: Canada and the Uruguay Round*. Toronto: C.D. Howe Institute.

Sherwood, R.M. 1996. "Study of the financial and other implications of the implementation of the TRIPS agreement for developing countries". Mimeo prepared for the World Intellectual Property Organization, September.

Subramanian, A. 1995. "Trade-related intellectual property rights and Asian developing countries: An analytical view". Paper presented at the

Conference on Emerging Global Trading Environment and Developing Asia, Manila, Philippines, 29–30 May.

Trionfetti, F. 1997. "The government procurement agreement and international trade: Theory and empirical evidence". Mimeo. Harvard University, Cambridge, Massachusetts USA.

UNCTAD. 1996. "Study on the financial and other implications of the implementation of the TRIPS agreement for developing countries". World Intellectual Property Organization, September Mimeo.

UNCTAD, *World Investment Report* (various years).

Vockey, M. 1997. "Investment implications of selected WTO agreements and the proposed multilateral agreement on investment". Mimeo prepared for the World Intellectual Property Organization.

Williamson, J. 1993. "Democracy and the Washington Consensus". *World Development*, vol. 21: 1320–36.

World Bank. 1995. *Global Economic Prospects.* Washington D.C.: The World Bank.

World Bank. 1997. *World Development Indicators.* Washington, D.C.: The World Bank.

WTO. 1996. Annual Report.

WTO. 1997. Annual Report.

WTO. 1998. *Guide to the Uruguay Round Agreements.* Geneva: WTO and Kluwer Law International.

Chapter eight

Development Policy Option for Africa in the Context of the World Trade Organization (WTO) Agreements

by Charles D. Jebuni, Centre for Policy Analysis (CEPA) and Samuel M. Wangwe, Economic and Social Research Foundation (ESRF)

Acknowledgements

We would like to thank the African Economic Research Consortium (AERC) for initiating and sponsoring this study. The first draft of the study was presented in a workshop held in Accra in October 1997. At that workshop we received very useful comments from the participants. In particular, we would like to thank Dr. Charles Gore of the United Nations Conference on Trade and Development (UNCTAD) for his rich comments as a discussant at that workshop. His comments were useful to us in producing the final version of the paper. To all those who facilitated the completion of this work we are very thankful. As usual we accept responsibility for the opinions and for any errors that may remain in the paper.

1. Introduction

The world is changing and with it ideas about African development strategy. Developments in economic theory and research, coupled with empirical experiences both within Africa and in the rest of the world, are shaping

African perceptions of the continent's development options. From the dirigism of the 1960s and 1970s, there is an evolution towards a market-friendly approach. There is increasing acceptance of a shift from a state-led, import substitution-based development strategy to a private sector-led, outward oriented development strategy.

Shifting technological and market conditions influence the position of Africa and the role it may play in the world economy. Globalization has been characterized by changes in patterns and organization of production, distribution, marketing and financial flows. All this has led to greater openness and intensification of competition in the world market. Many of the negotiations in the Uruguay Round (UR) were an attempt to come to terms with these globalization trends. The agreements reached at the Uruguay Round and the formation of the World Trade Organization (WTO) signify to a large extent the formalization of the processes of globalization.

These developments have implications for both the requirements and the development policy options available to Africa.

In this paper, we provide a brief summary of the emerging challenges for African development options and the implications of the emerging external environment for these options. In Section 2, we discuss the background of the African development strategy of the 1960s and 1970s as an input into the appreciation of the extent of change taking place in Africa. In Section 3, we review the emerging consensus on the current development policy options/strategy, and in Section 4 we discuss the WTO and the implications of the agreements for the African development policy options. Section 5 addresses regional integration in the WTO world and Section 6 concludes.

2. The Old Development Strategy and the Current Challenges

Whatever the method by which African countries gained independence, it occurred on the basis of promises of economic transformation presumed to have been hindered by colonialism. Rapid transformation of their economies was therefore an imperative of post colonial African states. The emerging development strategy was based partly on certain premises in development economics theory as well as on the colonial heritage.

Development through outward orientation, it would appear, was ruled out because of the new states' production structures or world market conditions. The production structure of African countries, as in other developing countries, was heavily concentrated on primary commodities. Engagement in free international trade, it was presumed, would lead to a specialization in these products. Prospects for expansion and development through such specialization were deemed dim because of the low income elasticity of demand for them in the industrial countries (Nurkse, 1961) or because of a tendency for their terms of trade to decline (Prebisch, 1950; Singer, 1950). Exports of manufactures were also considered impossible because of either the perceived difficulties of producing them efficiently domestically or the protectionism of the industrial countries. "Pessimism about the trade prospects of developing countries was soon formalized into so-called 'two-gaps' models of development" (Lal, 1983: 24). These models, combined with the presumed non-responsiveness of African peasants to incentives, provided a rationale for fixed exchange rates, exchange controls and the need for external aid inflows. Capital accumulation was seen as the predominant means to growth and development. The traditional microeconomic concern with the efficient allocation of resources became irrelevant.

In any case, the price mechanism or its working was to be replaced by various forms of direct state involvement. Either the workings of the price mechanism would be too slow for the rapid transformation desired, or "market failure" justified state intervention.[1] In the specific case of Africa, because of its colonial history, we did not have either accumulated capital or the entrepreneurial class. The state was therefore to play the role of both entrepreneur and regulator.

The resulting development strategy involved industrialization through import substitution behind high protective barriers. With almost no exception, African countries adopted this strategy, which appeared so justified it also secured exceptions under international trade rules:

> The premises underlying import-substitution policies were so widely accepted that developing country exceptions were even incorporated into the General Agreement on Tariffs and Trade (GATT) articles. Article XVIII explicitly protected the developing countries from the "obligations" of industrialized countries and

> permitted them to adopt tariff and quantitative restrictions. They were also entitled to "special and differential treatment" in other regards under GATT (Krueger, 1997: 5).

The failure of this development strategy to generate the much hoped for economic transformation and improvement in the standard of living led to economic crisis in one African country after another. At the same time, the experience of other countries, in particular the East Asian countries, that pursued an outward-oriented development strategy provided evidence of the success of an alternative path. Interpretations of this experience, of course, differ.[2] However, the rapid growth, transformation and improvements in the standard of living of these countries were attributed, among other things, to the pursuit of policies designed to encourage exports, the reversal of import-substitution strategies, the opening up of their economies and the uniformity of incentives across the board (Krueger, 1997).

At the theoretical level, the breakdown of the Keynesian consensus, and the rise of monetarist and rational expectations schools, led to questions about the efficiency of policy interventions and greater faith in the superiority of markets (Killick, 1989). The findings of Little et al. (1970), the theory of rent-seeking (Krueger, 1978) and the growth retarding effects of rent-seeking in Africa (Gallagher, 1991) all demonstrated the high real costs of the state-led import substitution strategy of development.

As economic crises deepened, African countries increasingly turned to the Bretton Woods institutions for economic reform programmes. The commonality of the source of the advice and similarity in policy instruments led Williamson (1994) to describe this view of the set of policy prescriptions as "the Washington Consensus".

3. Emerging Consensus on Development Policy Options?

The change in development strategy in Africa from the dirigism of the earlier period to a private sector based, outward-oriented development strategy implies the acceptance of a number of principles. Though subject to debate, the emerging consensus suggests that Africa has accepted:

- That a market-friendly approach will be taken to development and economic management. This means a roll back of the state and wherever possible and practicable, greater reliance on the market. The extent to which the state should be rolled back is subject to debate and in particular the role of the state in industrial policy is contentious.

- That the private sector will be the engine of growth.
- That growth will be export led, implying an internationally competitive production base and in particular a diversified export base.
- That a growth-based approach to poverty alleviation in the long run will supersede the consumption/distribution based approach of the earlier period. In the short to medium term, however, programmes and projects may be designed to provide some safety nets.

There is broad consensus on the need for fiscal and monetary prudence and an outward-oriented trade policy combined with a commitment to maintain a competitive exchange rate. Thus the maintenance of macroeconomic stability and the avoidance of real exchange rate misalignment are considered the fundamentals for the success of this strategy. Various forms and measures of trade liberalization are essential to trade policy. In general the objective is to avoid domestic policy distortions, open up the economy to world markets and achieve a neutral trade regime. This implies that in the long run, trade policy aims to create uniform incentives for all industry whether producing for domestic or foreign sales.

The extent of trade liberalization and the speed with which the process takes place will naturally vary according to different local conditions. Many sub-Saharan African countries depend, to a considerable extent, on trade taxes. It has been argued that substantial import liberalization will lead to fiscal revenue losses that might reduce governments' capacity to function and threaten the reform process as a whole. At the same time, import liberalization in an import compressed economy could lead to a surge in imports with possible adverse effects on the balance of payments (Oyejide, 1997).

The consensus on the extent and speed of liberalization will also vary from country to country. This consensus is broader than the Washington Consensus, which recommends specific levels of tariffs. In view of the differences in the sensitivity of the balance of payments and dependence of individual countries on trade revenues, no specific levels of tariff can be recommended. The basic guiding principle is to pursue what may be called sustainable country-specific trade liberalization.

Africa's experience with inward-looking import substitution strategies points to the need to re-conceptualize the development problem. The challenges of a more open world economy suggest that the process of restructuring African economies will also need to take a more open approach. In the context of new technologies and rapidly changing world market conditions, the process of restructuring for export orientation is going to pose a challenge to African countries. The questions that need to be addressed are what constraints are likely to be encountered and what opportunities could emerge for these economies in this restricting process.

African countries, it is argued, are justifiably concerned about the survival and future development of an efficient manufacturing sector as an important component of their development. In this context, some level of temporary, time-bound protection may be needed for traditional infant-industry reasons (Oyejide, 1997). There are also additional arguments for protection in the presence of scale economies and imperfect competition arising from developments in the new trade theory.

Whatever position one takes, the general levels of protection implied would be much lower than during the earlier period of import substitution. The general principle of the emerging development strategy is to keep the levels of protection low.

While the macroeconomic controversy has been resolved largely in favour of orthodoxy, there is still debate over the scope for beneficial intervention within an orthodox policy framework (Auty, 1994). Some extremists will argue that macroeconomic management is the key to industrialization and will eschew any form of sectoral targeting or intervention. This will imply that financial markets will determine the pattern of investments. The past experience of state intervention in industry and agriculture, the dangers of adverse selection, and the political use of resources would seem to justify minimal state intervention. There is, however, increasing recognition that an important component of the East Asian miracle was the extensive use of inducements to domestic firms based on satisfactory export performance. It is now accepted that governments contributed in a variety ways to facilitate the process of industrial and economic development (Wade, 1990). In applications of these lessons to Africa it must be recognized that the issue of state capacity and institutions to ensure their effectiveness is of critical importance (Harrold, 1996).

The strategy and methods will have to differ from the import substitution strategy and move much more along the lines of what is referred to as competitive industrial policy (CIP). This strategy "provides a package of market information, credit, tax breaks and trade incentives for new entrants to set up infant industries" (Auty, 1994: 15). While providing support, the strategy demands that firms must rapidly achieve economic and technological maturity in terms of international competitiveness.

4. WTO and African Development Policy Options

For a continent undergoing the kind of economic reforms taking place in Africa, a favourable external environment is a helpful development. In particular, for countries pursuing an export-led growth strategy, a favourable world trading environment provides a boost to their efforts. To that extent, the Uruguay Round of GATT negotiations seeking to generate a freer world trading system must be a boost to Africa's efforts. On the other hand, the extent to which any country can benefit from the external trading system, irrespective of how liberal, depends on domestic economic policies and their success in developing a competitive production base. It is in this context that this section examines the effects and issues raised by the WTO provisions and disciplines and their implications for African development policy options.

The provisions of the Uruguay Round Agreements

The Uruguay Round altered the world trading environment to a greater extent, many analysts believe, than any other agreement since the original General Agreement on Tariffs and Trade (GATT) talks in 1947. Africa must be sure that it is aware of the implications of the arrangements and that it has poised itself to take the best advantage of them.

The Uruguay Round Agreements (URAS) resulted in:

- Improvement of the rules of GATT and its associate agreements. The Round has brought about further liberalization of trade.
- The adoption of the General Agreement on Trade in Services (GATS).

- The adoption of agreements on trade related measures (TRIMS) and trade related intellectual property rights (TRIPS).

One of the other achievements of URA is the establishment of the WTO, which entered into force on 1 January 1995; GATT thus ceased to be a separate institution and became part of WTO. WTO is responsible for the surveillance of the implementation of the rules of URA by its members and is also responsible for arranging continuing negotiations for the liberalization of trade among its member countries.

In general, therefore, the WTO world is expected to be a world of an improved framework of multilateral rules governing international trade and further improvements in access to foreign markets for both goods and services.

Multilateral trade liberalization and market access

Market access negotiations reached agreement on:

- Cutting tariffs and instituting tariffication.
- Phasing out the Multi-Fibre Agreement (MFA) in ten years.
- Bringing trade in agricultural products under GATT discipline and liberalizing trade in agriculture. The agreement on agriculture establishes a programme for a fair and equitable market-oriented agricultural trading system by requiring countries to adopt new discipline governing both the use of border measures to control imports and the use of export subsidies and other subsidies to protect farmers' incomes. Developed countries are required to reduce tariffs by 37% in six years and developing countries to reduce tariffs by 24% in ten years. Least developed countries are not required to reduce them.
- Reducing tariffs by developing countries and transitional economies for both industrial and agricultural products.
- Expanding the proportion of bound tariffs.

The agreement in general seeks to bring about further global trade liberalization and expansion of world trade in goods and services through improvement in access to markets by the reduction and elimination of tariffs and non-tariff barriers. It is estimated that on average, tariffs on developed country imports from all sources would decline from the pre-Round level of 6.4% to about 4.0%, representing a 38% reduction. Tariffs on imports from less developed countries are expected to decline from 6.8% to 4.5%, representing a 34% reduction. There is also expected to be an increase in duty free developed country imports from 20% of imports to 43% of industrial products (United Nations, 1994).

At the sectoral level, bindings on manufactures will rise from 68% to 87% of tariff lines, and almost 100% for developed countries, and tariffs on African industrial exports will fall by an average of 31%. Trade in agriculture will be more bound, as 100% of all agricultural products will be covered by bindings by both developed and developing countries. There is to be a "tariffication" of quantitative restrictions and a reduction of both export and domestic subsidies on agricultural products (Harrold, 1995).

WTO provides for specific needs of least developed countries (LDCs) and the adoption of positive measures to facilitate the expansion of trading opportunities in favour of the LDCs. In order to ensure effective participation of LDCs in the trading system, the Ministerial Decision on Measures in Favour of the LDCs has rightly called for advancement of the implementation by developed countries of tariff and non-tariff concessions agreement in the Uruguay Round for products of export interest to the LDCs (UNCTAD, 1997).

The WTO agreement imposes obligations relating to tariff bindings that may result in higher import bills for basic foodstuffs in the medium term. In view of this possibility the ministers agreed to establish appropriate mechanisms to ensure that the availability of food aid is maintained at a level that continues to meet the food needs of LDCs and net food-importing developing countries. Among other measures it was agreed to provide technical and financial assistance to LDCs and net food-importing developing countries to improve their agricultural productivity and infrastructure. In addition, it was agreed to ensure that any agreement relating to agricultural export credits provides for differential treatment in favour of these countries.

The commitments by sub-Saharan African countries in the Uruguay Round are summarized in Table 8.1; it can be seen that tariff bindings agreed to in the Round are quite high. Whatever the motive for the very high bounds by African countries, "Sub-Saharan African countries have not taken advantage of the opportunity offered by the Uruguay Round to bind domestic reforms to an international anchor to improve credibility of these reforms in Africa" (Harrold, 1995: 32). This could send a bad signal to potential third-country investors, creating greater credibility problems for the African reform effort than its actual policy stance will justify. The expected foreign investment required by Africa may not materialize in spite of the reforms and yet aid is falling off and savings ratios are low. Tying to an external anchor could also have reduced the pressures from domestic lobbyists (Collier and Gunning, 1994).

In general, these agreements should increase both market access and the security of markets for African exports. The bindings imply that tariffs in those lines cannot be increased but they can be reduced. If Africa's emerging development strategy is to succeed, it must result in increased trade with the rest of the world and in particular exports, since this is expected to be the engine of growth. The expected increase in total world trade, the increased market access and the enhanced security should provide markets and increase total African exports.

It is argued that the success of this development strategy requires a diversification of exports from the traditional raw material exports into non-traditional exports, particularly manufactured exports. Escalation of tariffs according to level of processing has been perceived as a hindrance to such exports. The WTO provisions will result in important reductions in tariff escalation with potential beneficial effects for African exports.

Diversification into manufactured exports in several cases started with the matured, relatively low-skill intensive industries of textiles, garments, leather products, etc. These sectors usually provide the springboard for exporting and for creating a disciplined workforce. While the Multi-Fibre Agreement (MFA) is to be phased out and brought under GATT rules, average tariffs in these earlier lines of industrial export development remain high. These received below average tariff reductions, with rates standing at 10.2% for garments and textiles, 11.4% for fish products, and 2.1% for leather.

A major implication of the WTO agreement is that the preference margins that Africa used to enjoy will be eroded and there will be increased competition for African exports from other developing countries. The lowering of tariffs will decrease the preference margin for Africa from EU and other OECD countries from which Africa enjoyed some advantages.

Table 8.1: Summary of commitments in the UR by sub-Saharan African countries

			Agriculture		Industry		
Country	GATT status	Average rate of tariff binding %	Average applied rates	Previous bindings (% of lines)	Share of lines round in UR (%)	Average bound level in UR (%)	Average applied rates (%)
Benin	LD	80		29X	1.4	69	
Burkina Faso	LD	150		29X	1.2	150	
Cameroon	D	310		0	0.1	177	
Congo	D	30		0	3.2	15	
Côte d'lvoire	D	215		29X	0.4	257	
Gabon	D	260		?	1.3	206	
Ghana	D	98	22•	0	1.1	33	16*
Kenya	D	100	44•	0	1.6	54	35*
Madagas-car	LD	280		?	11.1	280	
Mali	LD	110		29X	2.8	110	
Mauritania	LD	54		29X	1.3	45	
Mauritius	D	135		0	1.6	82	
Namibia	D	40		31+	68.0	17@	22!
Niger	LD	132		29X	65.0	100	
Nigeria	D	230	47•	0.1	7.0	128	36*
Senegal	D	180	44•	29X	2.4	180	34*
South Africa	IND	40	7•	31+	68.0	17@	22!
Swaziland	D	40		31+	68.0	17@	22!
Tanzania	LD	240		0	0.1	240	
Uganda	LD	80		0	2.7	50	
Zambia	LD	124		?	4.0	42	
Zimbabwe	D	161	24•	8	0.8	66	31*

• From GATT Trade Policy Reviews, latest available.

@ Reduced from 24% to 17%.
! Trade weighted average.
x Assumes countries with (x) applied same schedule as Senegal as former French colonies.
\+ Assumed same as South Africa.

Source: Harrold (1995); Table 7.15.

Consequently, on the basis of current costs, Africa will lose "competitiveness". This raises questions about Africa's development strategy relating to the role of the external environment in the development of African exports and to the nature of domestic trade policy to increase competitiveness.

The reductions of tariffs on manufactured goods, the tariffication of non-tariff barriers in agriculture and commitments to reduce the levels of agricultural protection as well as production and export subsidies, the phasing out of the MFA and the elimination of VERs are all designed to lead to a more liberalized world trading system.

Two issues are raised here: the role of demand-side concessions in African exports development and Africa's response to increased world competition.

First, in spite (indeed perhaps because) of the concessions received by Africa, her exports remain undiversified in terms of both commodity composition and direction. Africa's exports are dominated by food and raw materials. In extreme cases, such as Uganda, Somalia, Malawi and Chad, over 90% of exports are agricultural products. As Table 8.2 shows, over 50% of African exports go to Europe. The EU-ACP arrangements offering concessions to African countries are no longer consistent with the WTO requirements and will have to be brought in line with those arrangements after the year 2000. The principles underlying the agreement also imply that special cases will be increasingly difficult to justify.

Second, Africa has also lost competitiveness in world markets, with her share of total world exports dropping by 50% between 1985 and 1995 in spite of the preferential treatment. From a share of 4.2% in 1985, Africa's share of total world exports was only 2.1% in 1995. The EU–ACP framework provides one of the most comprehensive sets of preferences to Africa. However, as Table 8.3 indicates, Africa lost competitiveness and market share even in the EU market. From 6.0% of EU imports in 1976, Africa's share of the EU market

Table 8.2: Sub-Saharan Africa: Structure of merchandise exportsa, 1995

	$ bn	% of sub-Saharan exports	% of world exports
Total[b]	103	100.0	2.1
Intra-regional	10	10.0	0.2
Inter-regional	90	87.0	1.7
Europe	57	56.0	1.1
North America	15	14.2	0.3
Asia & Australia	14	13.5	0.3
Latin America	2	1.7	0.0
Middle East	2	1.6	0.0

[a] Includes North Africa.

[b] Includes unspecified destinations.

Source: EIU: World Trade Report 3rd Quarter 1997.

declined to 3.3% in 1992 (Hewitt and Koning, 1994). Africa, it seems, had cocooned itself within this framework into remaining specialized in primary products, in the event actually losing competitiveness in these very product lines as a result of more aggressive efforts particularly from non-ACP Asia.

The role of bloc markets such as the EU has been argued elsewhere and their importance to African development has been overplayed. There has never been an explicit demonstration of the importance of these markets to African development. Ignoring extreme positions, the development of African exports has never been constrained seriously by tariffs and other world market conditions. Neither have African exports been promoted by the type of preferences sought and received.

The studies based on general equilibrium models have shown that the preference erosion resulting from the URA will amount to a loss of 0.1% in total African LDC exports to the European Union market (CIDA African Studies, 1995). The small size of the loss probably reflects the fact that most African exports are more supply constrained than market constrained. It should also be recognized that African economies are heterogeneous in both their economic structure and their trade interests. The average loss

Table 8.3: Value of EU imports from ACP states in billion ECU and share of total EU imports, 1976–1992

	1976 bn ECU	%	1980 bn ECU	%	1985 bn ECU	%	1990 bn ECU	%	1992 bn ECU	%
Africa	9.4	6.0	17.2	6.3	24.3	6.0	20.1	4.4	16.0	3.3
Caribbean	0.8	0.5	1.6	0.6	1.6	0.4	1.4	0.3	1.5	0.3
Pacific	0.2	0.1	0.4	0.1	0.7	0.2	0.4	0.1	0.4	0.1
Total ACP	10.5	6.7	19.4	7.2	26.8	6.7	21.9	4.7	18.0	3.7
of which: ACP non-oil exports	6.6	6.1	9.7	5.3	13.9	4.8	13.5	3.5	12.3	2.9

Note: All EU imports mentioned in this study are extra-EU imports, excluding intra-EU trade.
Source: Eurostat data.

may conceal considerable differences depending on the extent to which a country is a net exporter of tropical products, a net importer of temperate products, an exporter of textiles and clothing, or a net food importer.

African economies are less barrier-restrained in exports and more restrained by domestic supply bottlenecks and capacity constraints. Most of them rely on preferential trade agreements such as the Lomé Convention and the Generalized System of Preferences (GSP) that include rights to export various products such as sugar and beef to the market concerned at well above world prices. Many countries in sub-Saharan Africa are net food importers and may suffer higher import bills arising from increases in agricultural prices.

The impact of URAS would to a large extent be influenced by the way development policy options are used to create the preconditions by which Africa could exploit emerging opportunities and avert potential threats that may arise in the WTO world. In particular, the need to create the capacity for supply response to new trading opportunities will be a principal objective for most sub-Saharan African (SSA) countries whose major problem is supply capacity (as manifested in low quality products and lack of competitiveness) rather than market access.

An important aspect of building supply capacity and competitiveness is the improvement of infrastructure. Infrastructural deficiencies such as finance, transport, telecommunications, electricity and water supply hinder the growth of volume of exports and their competitiveness.

New investments will play a crucial role in the creation and realization of new trading opportunities in the WTO world. A substantial part of these investments could come from the private sector, provided the governments put in place appropriate policy frameworks for the private sector (local and foreign) to respond to and pursue the new trade opportunities. Given that primary products dominate exports from sub-Saharan Africa, the greatest opportunities in the WTO world will mainly arise from new high value-added products destined for new markets. Efforts to develop new export products on the basis of dynamic comparative advantage and to develop new markets should form an important component of the development policy options.

Africa's response to increased world competition will have to be further domestic policy changes, especially trade policy within a supportive or enabling macroeconomic framework, in order to develop a competitive production base and a change in the nature of the concessions it seeks from the world system. As latecomers into the world market the skills composition of African exports may have to be higher than those of the earlier developers. In other words, in view of changing tastes and technological developments, Africa cannot expect to benefit substantially from the export of unskilled-labour-intensive products, although the upward climb of the ladder by the early birds may provide easy opportunities. Furthermore, globalization may imply that cheap unskilled labour will become less important in firms' location decisions (Sander, 1994). African exports, even for the clothing and textiles industry, will have to be relatively more skill intensive. This will require, in addition to changes in trade policy, the development of human capital through appropriate education, training and research.

The nature of concessions that Africa requires from the world system will also have to shift from demand related to supply related ones. For example, Azita Amjadi et al. (1996) conclude that "transport costs have a significant negative impact on African exports or the location of manufacturing activity in Africa, which is more important than generally recognized. Freight rates for African exports are often considerably higher than those on similar goods originating in other countries and these charges often conceal very high rates of effective protection for processed goods. A point that significantly reduces incentives for new investment in export-oriented production activity". Concessions on the supply side will have to be identified and negotiated in the next round.

The experience of the past two years (1994–96) has shown that the WTO system needs to improve the rate at which the substantive commitments on market access are implemented. Monitoring of implementation would be enhanced by the timely availability of trade and tariff data. In particular, greater transparency and follow up is needed for commitment on reduction of tariffs and tariffication of NTBs, the agriculture agreement, compliance of contingency protection measures with WTO principles, and the integration process relating to MFA. In view of the quasi-judicial nature of the Textile Monitoring Body (TMB), greater transparency should be achieved in providing a rationale for TMB findings and recommendations. The responsibility of the Goods Council in overseeing the functioning of the Agreement on Textiles and Clothing (ATC), whose implementation is being supervised by the TMB, will need to be emphasized.

The phasing out of the MFA may affect textile and clothing production that has relocated to Africa from Asia as a result of quota restrictions under the MFA. As the MFA is phased out, quota restraints will be removed on large Asian exporters, a situation that could return the quota-hopping investment to those countries from which it originated. The emerging textile and clothing industries in Africa could be adversely affected by the receding investment and by intensified competition.

Subsidies and protection provisions

Much more critical to the emerging development strategy for Africa are the WTO disciplines that affect Africa's options for the development of a competitive production base. As indicated earlier, outward orientation may involve active policies in industry and agriculture. Temporary subsidies, whether in terms of credit or for purposes of socializing part of the risk associated with investing in Africa, may have to be used. The agreement on subsidies and countervailing measures imposes new disciplines on the type of incentive packages that can be used to encourage industry. The agreement prohibits export subsidies and subsidies that encourage local content. This prohibition is expected to apply to all countries except the least developed ones and other developing countries with per capita GNP below $1,000, except for products in which they achieve export competitiveness defined as a share in world trade of 3.25% for two consecutive years.

URA urges countries to keep protection of their industries at low levels and to provide it through tariffs. An important exception permits countries in balance of payments difficulties to restrict imports in order to safeguard their external financial position. This exception provides greater flexibility to developing countries to use quantitative restrictions if necessary.

URA also divides subsidies into prohibited and permissible subsidies. Prohibited subsidies include export subsides, but developing countries have a transitional period of eight years to conform to the rule. This rule does not apply to LDCS or to developing countries with GNP per capita of less than $1,000. Permissible subsidies are not prohibited; they can be actionable (subject to countervailing duties if they cause damage to the importing country) or unactionable.

The agreement recognizes, however, that some subsidies may be required at the initial stages of development. As a result, the least developed and low income countries are exempted. As far as Africa is concerned, about 43 countries will be exempted from the disciplines of these provisions. These consist of the 33 countries in Table 8.4 and 8.10 other countries with per capita GNP below $1,000 (Cameroon, Congo, Côte d'Ivoire, Egypt, Ghana, Kenya, Morocco, Nigeria, Senegal and Zimbabwe). In the case of subsidies linked to the use of domestic inputs, these must be phased out in eight years by the least developed countries and five years by all others.

URA provides special flexibility to developing countries to take safeguard measures to restrict imports, for temporary periods, in order to promote the development of new or infant industries. A large proportion of the tariffs of member countries have been bound against further increases. Where more protection is needed, the government will be required to invoke the provisions on "safeguard actions for development purpose". WTO grants approval if member countries are satisfied that higher protection will help the industry to become internationally competitive within a reasonable period.

Agreements on safeguards also authorize importing countries to restrict imports for temporary periods to protect domestic industry from serious injury. The intention is to give the affected industry time to prepare itself for the increased competition that it will have to face after the restrictions are removed. The temporary period may not exceed eight years. Developing countries can impose such restrictions for up to ten years.

As argued here, the issue of subsidies is the one area that directly affects Africa's options in terms of developing its supply capabilities. While non-discrimination in the application of any subsidy schemes on the basis of nationality of the firm may be acceptable, it is doubtful that the same rationale should apply to source of input. It is clear that the early industries and the stepping stones to international competitiveness tend to be resource intensive. Government decisions to support such industries are constrained by these provisions. Africa may need to go back to negotiations to defend its right to encourage the use of certain domestic resources. This will also be consistent with other treaty provisions related to national treatment.

Concern has been expressed that anti-dumping actions were proliferating and risked becoming a problem for exports to both developed and developing countries. There was also a risk that increased use of countervailing actions would counter the special and differential treatment allowed to developing countries on subsidies. Countervailing and anti-dumping duties are permissible in response to unfair trade practices where exported goods benefit from subsidies or when exports are dumped in foreign markets.

There is pronounced fragility in most export manufacturing firms. Detailed enterprise level analyses suggest that the fragility and lack of competitiveness largely arise from the enterprises operational characteristics (or factors internal to the enterprises), although for some firms the external environment (trade and fiscal policy, markets) is more important. This distinction is important in determining how to support enterprises. What is clear is that reinforcement will be needed both at the level of the enterprises and in the environment within which enterprises are operating.

Agreements on Trade in Services (GATS)

The General Agreement on Trade in Services (GATS) consists of a framework of rules (most favoured nation and national treatment principles) and liberalization commitments specific to the service sectors. The objective of GATS is to promote the economic growth of all trading partners and the developing countries through the expansion of trade in services.

Table 8.4: Africa: Least developed countries

1	Angola	18	Madagascar
2	Benin	19	Malawi
3	Burkina Faso	20	Mali
4	Burundi	21	Mauritania
5	Cape Verde	22	Mozambique
6	Central African Republic	23	Niger
7	Chad	24	Rwanda
8	Comoros	25	Sao Tome & Principe
9	Djibouti	26	Sierra Leone
10	Equatorial Guinea	27	Somalia
11	Eritrea	28	Sudan
12	Ethiopia	29	Tanzania
13	Gambia	30	Togo
14	Guinea	31	Uganda
15	Guinea Bissau	32	Zaire
16	Lesotho	33	Zambia
17	Liberia		

Source: UNCTAD.

Other important provisions of the GATS framework are rules that require transparency in the regulations applicable to service industries and activities and those that aim to ensure the increasing participation of developing countries in trade in services. Increased participation of developing countries is expected to be brought about by:

- Giving priority to liberalization in the modes of supply and service sectors of export interest to developing countries.
- Allowing developing countries to have the flexibility to open fewer sectors to import competition and to liberalize fewer types of transactions.
- Allowing developing countries to impose conditions requiring

foreign suppliers to set up joint ventures or better access to their technology.

Unlike goods, which can be protected through tariffs, services are protected largely by national domestic regulations on FDI and the participation of foreign service suppliers in domestic industries.

The challenge for Africa is to develop an efficient and competitive service sector.

Agreement on Trade-Related Investment Measures (TRIMS)

The agreement on TRIMS requires countries to phase out TRIMS that have been identified as inconsistent with GATT rules on national treatment and the rules against the use of quantitative restrictions. The phasing out period is two years for developed countries, five years for developing countries and seven years for transitional economies (with effect from 1 January 1995).

Four TRIMS have been identified in this context:

- Local content requirements.
- Trade-balancing requirements (e.g., obliging imports to be equivalent to a certain proportion of exports).
- Exchange restrictions resulting in restrictions on imports.
- Domestic sales requirements involving restrictions on exports.

Countries are allowed to invoke the banned TRIMS only for balance of payments purposes (Agosin et al., 1995).

Under TRIMS, African countries must be prepared to pursue economic policies that attract investments and allow foreign investors to operate under conditions that are not less favourable than those of local investors. Negotiation of TRIMS concentrated on the GATT compatibility of measures imposed on investors with an effect on trade, i.e., domestic content and trade balancing requirements. This essentially widens the scope of international jurisdiction over domestic policies.

The TRIMS agreement does not contain rules to regulate flows of FDI, although it provides for a review of its possible extension to include investment and competition policies within five years of entry into force of the WTO. The pressure for action in WTO on these issues has increased following the decision of the OECD to negotiate a Multilateral Agreement on Investment (MAI). Attempts to harmonize country investment policies along the lines of MAI are likely to affect the scope of national policy objectives and overall strategies for a country's development. MAI could limit the formulation of policies relating to selective investment incentives, performance requirements for development of local technological capabilities and encouragement of skills training.

Concern has been expressed that the OECD's Multilateral Agreement on Investment (MAI) focuses more on the needs of the providers of investment. Host country problems such as increasing competition to offer concessions to attract investments are not receiving attention. African countries should identify and make more effective use of instruments that are permissible under WTO and coordinate their efforts to offer concessions. Because FDI is an important source of non-debt creating investment finance, transfer of technology, productivity increase and integration into the world economy, appropriate investment policy instruments should be used effectively to realize industrialization and enhancement of competitiveness in the WTO world.

The emphasis on enhancing and defining competition has come to the fore as a result of trade liberalization and the focus on private sector led development. There is need for African countries to formulate appropriate competition policies, yet most countries do not have domestic laws for such policy.

The narrow coverage of TRIMS has led some countries to argue that the agreement should be reviewed within five years and that the review should consider the desirability of complementing it with provisions on investment and competition policy. Africa should take stock of the experience with TRIMS so far and put forward its interests. In particular, problems experienced with restrictive business practices and other anti-competition behaviour that poses a threat to international trade should be put on the agenda.[3]

The abolition of local content requirements may have impact on ancillary industries that are benefiting from the protection provided. However, these industries are already facing competitive pressure under open trade policies. Those that deserve protection can continue to enjoy protection within the framework of the WTO rules.

Agreement on Trade-Related Aspects of Intellectual Property Rights (TRIPS)

The TRIPS agreement lays down minimum standards of protection for intellectual property rights (IPRS) as well as the procedures and remedies for their enforcement. It establishes a mechanism for consultations and surveillance at the international level to ensure compliance with these standards by member countries at the national level.

The provisions of the agreement apply to patents, copyrights and related rights, trademarks, industrial designs, lay-out designs of integrated circuits, undisclosed information, and geographical indications.

TRIPS provides a transitional period of one year for developed countries and five years for developing countries and for transitional economies (up to 1 January 2000) to bring their IPR legislation into conformity with the provisions of the Agreement. For least developed countries the transition period is 11 years.

TRIPS has implications for the development of trade on three grounds:

- Manufacturers of research and technology intensive products are more willing to sell in markets where their patent rights are adequately protected to enable them to recoup their R&D expenditures.
- The willingness of investors, especially FDI, to manufacture patented products under license or within joint ventures depends on how assuring the IPR system of the host country is.
- Weak IPR systems encourage production and trade of counterfeit and pirated goods.

One implication of TRIPS is that importers of technology would face increased royalty payments for the use of patented technology under license and higher prices for the products so manufacture.

TRIPS builds on existing international conventions on IPR and further provides higher protection. Five main groups of provisions are made under TRIPS:

- Basic principles and general obligations.

- Minimum standards of protection.
- Restrictive business practices.
- Enforcement of IPRS.
- Transitional arrangements for implementation of IPR rules at the national level.

On the positive side, TRIPS may encourage transfer of technology on commercial terms by:

- Attracting FDI in technology transfer especially those producing products that are prone to imitation (e.g., electronic and computer products).
- Increasing the number of patents registered in Africa. Disclosure of technical information in the patents may enable local technical personnel to reconstruct the inventions and develop processes and products that differ from those patented.
- Encouraging FDI in joint ventures for research and development work in Africa.

These benefits, however, are tenable where the adopted development policy option favours building of technological capabilities (human, institutional and necessary infrastructure).

TRIPS may also bring under control trade in counterfeit goods. This may be an advantage where counterfeit and pirated goods are of dubious quality. It may also encourage subcontracting or production by MES in Africa to take advantage of low labour costs. This would enable small and medium enterprises in Africa to produce such items under license and have them marketed internationally under known brand names.

TRIPS presents two challenges to African countries. First, African countries will have to build the capacity to put in place stronger IPR regimes and enforcement mechanisms. Patent protection systems will not only have to be instituted but will have to be extended to new areas, e.g., pharmaceutical and chemical products; the period of patent protection will have to be extended to 20 years for most cases and systems put in place for protection of plant varieties (sui generis systems). Second, TRIPS will make it more difficult to acquire and build technological capacities through reverse engineering and imitation, which have been an important source of technology for many small and medium enterprises.

During the transition period African countries would need assistance in the elaboration of judicial procedures for enforcing law and establishing a commensurate administrative framework including customs procedures. The task here will involve upgrading existing arrangements. In some cases it will also involve establishment of additional administrative arrangements for areas not currently covered.

African countries face the challenge of having to relate the IPRS to their development objectives and of fostering dynamic competition to cope with the requirements of globalization. The design and application of IPRS should be aimed at improving technological innovation systems, carefully striking a balance between incentives to invent and innovate and the need for diffusion of knowledge. Strong IPR regimes that are sufficiently focused on promoting appropriate forms of investments can be a powerful instrument for encouraging many investments in technology.

Case studies carried out by UNCTAD in six developing countries (UNCTAD, 1996) came out with three main findings:

- The implementation of the TRIPS agreement would involve changes in existing IPR regimes. The extent and scope of these changes will be influenced by the level of development of current laws and regulations.
- The strengthening of IPR regimes will require substantial resources from the least developed countries.
- There is an urgent need for better understanding of the implications of implementing the TRIPS agreement.

A recent report of WTO on the Ministerial Conference in Singapore on 9–13 December 1996 indicated that during the previous 24 months (1994 to 1996) the efforts of the least developed countries to implement notification requirements and comply with other aspects of MTA were hampered by the paucity of human resources and weak institutional infrastructure.

The wide-ranging nature and complexity of concepts, principles and rules of the WTO instruments have contributed to the delay in putting into effect the provisions in favour of the developing countries (WTO, 1996).

Most African least developed countries have yet to incorporate provisions contained in the Uruguay Round agreements and the Marrakesh Ministerial Meeting in their favour into their trade policy measures and development programmes. Such failures imply that these countries would have missed some benefits ensuing from the agreements (WTO, 1996).

Article 31(b) (k) of the TRIPS agreement states that if there is a national emergency, patents can be ignored. What, then, constitutes a national emergency? In sub-Saharan Africa, about a third of the population does not get enough food (170 million people), and 15% of newborn babies are underweight. Counterfeit pharmaceutical products from, for example, China or India, provided they are up to standard, could be considered, and defended with article 31 (b) (k). The economic consideration relevant to this observation is that the LDCs' hands are not as badly tied as might initially have been suspected. In effect, the government has the option of taking advantage of this emergency clause. If this is treated carefully, it could be a strong bargaining point when negotiating licensing fees. There may be limits to its use, however, as its indiscriminate application is likely to invoke the disapproval of the World Bank, IMF and large corporations, damage important FDI and joint ventures accordingly, and reduce prospects of other sources of resource inflows into Africa.

There are other areas where the TRIPS agreement is open to some interpretation, especially articles 7 and 8. Article 7 talks of "mutual advantage", "social and economic welfare", and the "balance of rights and obligations". As Correa writes, "Under these provisions, national legislation can provide for a variety of measures that promote competition and balance, to some extent, the interests of the title holders with the users of the technology. Such measures may include parallel imports, non-patentability of substances in nature and of animals and plants; compulsory licences of various types; reverse engineering of computer programs, among others." Correa also points out that "it should be noted that the TRIPS agreement does not limit (except for semi-conductor technology) the grounds under which compulsory licenses can be granted, but only defines the conditions therefore". As mentioned before large deviations from the accepted WTO intentions are likely to result in retaliation in the form of barriers to trade, but their use is still an option.

There is need to harmonize competition policies relating to international transactions, including intellectual property issues, with efforts to counter restrictive business practices by TNCs.

5. WTO and Regional Integration

Regional integration according to the 1980 Lagos Plan of Action is not only a means for African development, but an objective in itself. Under Article XXIV, the WTO rules allow for regional free trade arrangements provided they cover substantially all trade and do not raise external trade barriers on balance, and that they achieve free trade within a certain period. In theory, therefore, the WTO rules are consistent with African regional integration aspirations. WTO monitoring should engender some pressure, but in practice it is doubtful that WTO would be effective in monitoring. However, the general rules making for freer global trade raise the broader issues of multilateral trade liberalism versus regional trade liberalization or regionalism (Bergstern, 1997).

In theory, the multilateral trade liberalization implied by the WTO rules will reduce the margin of preferences within a customs union. This reduces the extent to which concessions within the union would be trade creating and also reduces the extent to which they would be trade diverting. In the case of Africa, regionalism has never been effective in liberalizing trade among member countries. What has occurred in terms of increased intra-regional trade has been regionalization induced by unilateral trade liberalization.

The current geographic destinations of many sub-Saharan African countries' exports of manufactured products underline the significance of regional markets for the growth of current exports and development of new export products (UNIDO Studies on Africa, 1996).

Africa has demonstrated the slowest progress in developing regional integration and cooperation arrangements (UNCTAD, 1993b). The challenge that emerges is whether regional cooperation arrangements can be designed for Africa to facilitate (through investment, joint technological activities and trade) the process by which firms and other institutions in Africa build up technological capabilities. The African Economic Community and existing subregional economic cooperation arrangements should accord high priority to promoting trade expansion, based on both exports and imports, by removing distortions, avoiding the duplication of large investments where national markets are small, reducing transaction costs (e.g., by trading arrangements that guarantee market access, regional marketing intelligence, improvements in the marketing infrastructure), and redirecting trade flows.

Regional cooperation may also be useful in importing technology. The collection of information on sources of equipment and technology is an expensive business; institutions to serve groups of countries could marshal more resources than those confined to the smaller individual economies. Once imported, the technology could be adapted to local needs by regional technology institutes. This would be a highly skill-intensive task, where the regional sharing of the cost and benefit would clearly make economic sense.

Africa needs to recognize these trends and respond to these changes by putting greater effort into exploring possibilities of beneficial inter-firm linkages with TNCS from the North and from the South. It would appear that if the potential benefits from TNCS are to be realized, domestic policies concerning development of the technological capabilities of domestic firms, education and vocational training, investment, trade, technology adaptation, and R&D can play a crucial role in that process. However, the context of the emerging work market and new technologies demands new forms of networking with TNCS. Identifying the conditions under which the role of TNCS could be complementary and supportive of sub-Saharan Africa's efforts to develop international competitiveness deserves special attention. The guiding question here should be: In what ways can African firms forge inter-firm linkages and cooperation arrangements that are conducive to the development of the technological and other capabilities necessary for making gains in international competitiveness?

Promotion of South–South inter-firm linkages and cooperation arrangements should be viewed as complementary to the kinds of benefits that can be obtained from inter-firm networks and cooperation arrangements with TNCS from the North, and not necessarily as substitutes. The Abuja declaration on the establishment of the African Economic Community is an encouraging step. Its implementation, however, should involve taking first steps towards establishing the institutional framework to spearhead the development of these kinds of inter-firm linkages and cooperation arrangements not only within Africa but between Africa and other regions.

6. Conclusion

The emerging development strategy requires freer and growing world markets. The WTO agreements provide opportunities for African countries in terms of security and access to world markets. The emerging competition for African countries implies deeper economic reform including both unilateral and regional trade liberalization.

However, expected increased competition and the demand for reciprocity also imply that the nature of concessions that Africa needs will have to change. Hitherto, concessions have been in terms of the demand side. These are perhaps less important now, and in any case have not been effective. The greater requirements for the success of the African development strategy will be supply-related. These will include among other things negotiated technology and investment related concessions and possibly negotiated agreements to secure lower transportation, freight and other service charges for African exports. Africa faces challenges of:

- Taking fuller advantages of opportunities in the WTO world, including more effective use of rights and compliance with obligations.
- Effectively pursuing the built-in agenda, particularly the further liberalization of trade in agriculture and services.
- Engaging more effectively in the WTO debate on the new trade agenda, especially relating to trade and investment and competition policy.
- Striving to bring about a better balance in the rules of the game in support of development. Greater access to markets should be accompanied by greater access to technology to develop competitive supply capacities. The state and the market must be actively used in a complementary manner to build effective supply capacities. The challenge is to develop the capacity to adjust government policy and engage policy options for national development within the framework of the WTO world.

It has been noted that most developing countries were largely unaware of potential gains from the active use of the dispute settlement mechanism as an option that could replace bilateral negotiations, where small countries often lack bargaining power (UNCTAD, 1997). WTO has made some concessions and allows for support programmes targeted to sub-Saharan Africa (SSA). Yet sub-Saharan Africa has not been taking advantage of such provisions probably for lack of information or for lack of the capacity to tap the advantages in those provisions. There is need to build the capacity to understand the rules and issues in WTO agreements and how best to benefit from the provisions and trade assistance programmes.

The experience of Uruguay Round (UR) negotiations shows that most developing countries were not adequately prepared (UNCTAD, 1997). One of the main reasons for the difficulties encountered with notifications is that it was only later that many developing countries realized the implication of what they had accepted and signed. In the Singapore Conference of December 1996 the same problem of lack of preparation surfaced again.[4] This suggests that there is need to build the capacity for preparation and understanding of the implications of developments in regional and world trade systems for the interests of developing countries. It also implies that the development policy options Africa should consider must reflect a positive agenda for trade liberalization in ways that are consistent with the interests of Africa in the context of the WTO world. This way Africa can achieve integration within the world trading system in relation to its ability to formulate and pursue development policy and strategy options within the framework of multilateral trade obligations.

Concern has been expressed about tendencies of developed countries to challenge developing country rights that had been provided for under URAS, for example, the right to apply quantitative restrictions as a defense for balance of payments if facing growing pressure. There has also been growing bilateral pressure on developing countries to draw up IPR legislation under which they would give up the right to apply special and differential treatment provided to them under the TRIPS Agreement. In addition, certain investment measures might face challenges, although they are not specifically prohibited under the TRIMS Agreement (UNCTAD, 1997).

Many sub-Saharan African countries have weak institutions for designing and implementing trade policies and are weak in monitoring the trade policies of developed countries and their implications for sub-Saharan Africa. In this context, the WTO Trade Policy Review (TPR) mechanism could provide useful information with which sub-Saharan African countries could make their own assessments of policy implications. The capacity for undertaking such analyses will need to be built and necessary technical assistance for that purpose may have to be sought in the area of policy advice to complement domestic capabilities – which should also be used more effectively.

Technical assistance (TA) is necessary to enable sub-Saharan African countries to cope with some of the requirements of WTO. However, sub-Saharan Africa should strive to have better coordinated TA that builds on local capacities rather than replacing them. The proposed integrated programme of TA by IMF, World Bank, UNDP, UNCTAD, ITC and WTO is a welcome initiative for attaining more coherent and better coordinated TA.

In response to WTO requirements, there is need to strengthen policy coordination among government agencies and to improve liaison between government policy makers and the business sector.

The heavy debt burden is likely to limit sub-Saharan African countries' ability to implement WTO agreements and build the capacity to compete. External debt relief and the transfer of new resources coupled with domestic policy efforts are the key to sustained recovery in Africa.

Notes

1 See Killick (1989) for the theoretical basis and shifts with respect to the role of the state.

2 See Wade (1990) for the different theoretical underpinings of different interpretations of the experience.

3 Business Guide to the Uruguay Round. Abstract for Trade Information Services. International Trade Centre, UNCTAD, WTO, Commonwealth Secretariat, Geneva & London, 1995.

4 Noted in the introductory remarks by Rubens Ricupera, Secretary-General of UNCTAD, as they appear in UNCTAD (1997).

References

Agosin, M.R., D. Tussie and G. Crespi. 1995. "Developing countries and the Uruguay Round: An evaluation and issues for the future". In United Nations, *International Monetary and Financial Issues for the 1990s*, Volume VI. Geneva: UNCTAD.

Auty, Richard M. 1994. "Industrial policy reform in six large newly industrializing countries: The resource course thesis". *World Development*, vol. 22, no. 1: 11–26.

Azita Amjadi, U. Reincke and Alexander J. Yeats. 1996. "*Did external barriers cause the marginalization of Sub-Saharan Africa in World trade?" World Bank Discussion Paper* No. 348. Washington, D.C.

Bergstern, C. Fred. 1997. "Open Regionalism". Institute for International Economics, Working Paper No. 97–3. Washington, D.C.

Bliss, Christopher. 1987. "The new trade theory and economic policy". *Oxford Review of Economic Policy*, vol. 3, no. 1.

Collier Paul and Jan W. Gunning. 1994. "*Trade policy and regional integration: Implications for the relations between Europe and Africa*". Discussion Paper No. 1012. Centre for Economic Policy Research, London.

Economic Intelligence Unit. 1997. *World Trade Report*. 3rd quarter.

Gallagher, Mark. 1991. *Rent-Seeking and Economic Growth in Africa*. Boulder, Colorado: Westview Press.

Harrold, Peter. 1995. "The impact of the Uruguay Round on Africa: Much ado about nothing?" Paper presented at the Uruguay Round and the Developing Economies, World Bank Conference. January, Washington, D.C.

Harrold, P., M. Jayawickrama and D.B. Bhattasali. 1996. "Practical lessons for Africa from East Asia in industrial and trade policies". World Bank Discussion Papers, Africa Technical Department Series, No. 310. Washington, D.C.

Hewitt, Adrian and Antonique Koning. 1994. "The survival of special preferences under the Lomé Convention: The ACP countries and the European Union after the Uruguay Round". In H. Sander and A. Inotai, eds., *World Trade After the Uruguay Round: Prospects and Policy Options for the Twenty-First Century*. New York: Routledge.

Killick, Tony. 1989. *A Reaction Too Far: Economic Theory and the Role of the State in Developing Countries*. London: Overseas Development Institute.

Krueger, A. 1970. *Liberalization Attempts and Consequences*. New York: National Bureau of Economic Research.

Krueger, Anne. 1997. "Trade policy and economic development: How we learn". *American Economic Review*, vol. 87, no. 1 (March): 1–22.

Krugman, P. 1984. "Import substitution as export promotion". In H. Kierskowski ed., *Monopolistic Competition and International Trade*. Oxford University Press.

Lal, Deepak. 1983. *The Poverty of Development Economics*. London: The Institute of Economic Affairs.

Little, I.M.D., Tibor Scitovsky and Maurice Scott. 1970. *Industry and Trade in Some Developing Countries*. Oxford: Oxford University Press.

Nurske, R. 1961. *Equilibrium and Growth in the World Economy*. Cambridge, Massachusetts: Harvard University Press.

Owens, T. and A. Wood. 1997. "Export oriented industrialization through primary processing?" *World Development*, vol. 25, no. 9 (September): 1453–70.

Oyejide, T. Ademola. 1997. "Trade policy and regional integration in the development context: Emerging patterns, issues and lessons for sub-Saharan Africa." Plenary Session, African Economic Research Consortium Workshop. 25 May, Nairobi.

Prebisch, Raul. 1950. *The Economic Development of Latin America and its Principal Problems*. New York: United Nations.

Rodrik, Dani. 1995, "The Uruguay Round: Unravelling the implications for the least developed and low-income countries". In United Nations: International pp. 61–98.

Sander, Harald. 1994. "Multilateralism, regionalism and globalization: The challenges to the world trading system". In H. Sander and A. Inotai, eds., *World Trade After the Uruguay Round: Prospects and Policy Options for the Twenty-first Century*. London: Routledge.

Singer, Hans. 1950. "The distortion of gains between borrowing and investing countries". *American Economic Review*, May.

UNCTAD. 1996. *The TRIPS Agreement and Developing Countries*. New York and Geneva: United Nations.

UNCTAD. 1997. "The Uruguay Round and its follow-up: Building a positive agenda for development". Report on a Workshop Convened by the Secretary-General of UNCTAD. Geneva, 3–4 March.

United Nations. 1994. "The Uruguay Round of multilateral trade negotiations: A preliminary assessment of results". In H. Sander and A. Inotai, eds., *World Trade After the Uruguay Round: Prospects and Policy Options for the Twenty-First Century*. London: Routledge.

Wade, Robert. 1990. *Governing the Market: Economic Theory and the Role of Government in East Asian Industrialization*. Princeton, New Jersey: Princeton University Press.

Weston, A. 1994. "The Uruguay Round. Unravelling the implications for the least-developed and low-income countries". Report prepared for UNCTAD by the North-South Institute. Ottawa, August.

Williamson, John. 1994. "In search of a manual for technopols". In John Williamson, ed., *The Political Economy of Policy Reform*. Washington, D.C.: Institute for International Economics.

Wood, Adrian and Berge Kersti. 1997. "Exporting manufactures: Human resources, natural resources and trade policy". *Journal of Development Studies*, vol. 34 (Oct.): 35–59.

World Bank. 1993. *The East Asian Miracle: Economic Growth and Public Policy*. New York: Oxford University Press.

Chapter nine

African Development in the Context of New World Trade and Financial Regimes: The Role of the WTO and its Relationship to the World Bank and the IMF

by Ibrahim A. Elbadawi, African Economic Research Consortium and Gerry Helleiner, Department of Economics, University of Toronto

---

The authors are grateful for comments on an earlier draft by Benno Ndulu and participants in the workshop organized by the AERC collaborative project on "Africa and the New World Trading System", on 27–29 April 1998, in Mombasa, Kenya. We would also like to acknowledge the research assistance of Rajal Upadhyaya.

1. Introduction

The quest continues for the deep, sustained and equitable growth that will permit sub-Saharan Africa (hereafter Africa) to address its grave poverty and other social and economic development problems. Both African governments and the international development community increasingly perceive the need for new development strategies – broader than economic adjustment – in order to achieve such growth. At the same time, the rapid pace of globalization in international trade and finance, aided by tremendous progress in information technology, has started to affect Africa's macroeconomic and financial performance and policies. It is likely to have substantial impact on the course of Africa's development in the future. Globalization, all agree, presents Africa with both opportunities and risks.

Some see globalization as inherently beneficial for Africa – provided that its governments open up their economies, substantially reduce transaction costs and develop mechanisms for increasing the credibility of their policy reforms. They then see a brighter African future through the attraction of substantial private capital and the export of manufactures (e.g., Collier, 1997). Some are less sanguine about the African prospect and foresee continuing "marginalization" and instability.

Globalization and "deepening" international economic integration have brought increasing calls for improved institutions and modalities for global economic governance (e.g., Culpeper and Pestieau, 1996). In the wake of the Mexican and East Asian crises, these have been particularly forceful in the spheres of macroeconomic and financial management. In international trade and related issues, however, the inauguration in 1995 of a world-wide intergovernment organization – the World Trade Organization (WTO) – with a mandate to formalize, interpret and police earlier (General Agreement of Tarriff and Trade, GATT) and prospective rules, already marked, in the view of some, an important and positive "watershed in the international economic system" (Henderson, 1998: 107; quoting Jackson, 1995: 25).

Others are more wary, both about the implications of globalization and about the potential role of international regimes. Ferrer (1997: 178–85), for instance, in a Latin American context, has noted the many "myths" behind "the fundamentalist view of globalization", e.g., that it has no historical precedent, that national economic space has dissolved into a purely global order, that the only viable policies are those of market deregulation, and that economic development and equitable distribution will look after themselves. With or without globalization or the WTO or other institutions of global governance, he argues, *national* policies are still "decisive for economic development" (p. 181). The UN Conference on Trade and Development (UNCTAD) has noted that, "While full integration into the global economy should be the ultimate objective of each and every economy, liberalization and deregulation need to be carefully and appropriately managed, phased and tailored to the level of economic development and the capacity of existing institutions and industries" (Ricupero, 1997: 3; see also UNCTAD, 1997; UNDP, 1997, chapter 5; and, in an African context, Helleiner, 1999).

Accession to the WTO certainly involves commitments on the part of national policy makers – in a very wide (and evidently still expanding) range of policies. It can have "profound implications" for strategies and policies for industrialization and development in that "it presents both opportunities and constraints" (Soludo, 1997: 16). A recent UNCTAD (1996: 25) report observes that

> It is undeniable that the global economy is currently going through significant changes. The new trading regime under the WTO has reduced the scope for using some measures ... trade-related subsidies, lax enforcement of intellectual property rights, and strategic conditions imposed on foreign investments, which were integral parts of the East Asian development strategy. Certainly the more generalized protection which provided a backdrop for targeted policies in East Asia is no longer possible, and many of the export promotion policies no longer appear permissible. It may also be true that the changes will reduce the scope for policy manoeuvre for the developing countries which wish to pursue a strategy involving vigorous infant industry protection and export subsidies.

The International Monetary Fund and the World Bank have, of course, been around for much longer than the WTO. In the new global economy, both are searching for new – and central – roles in their respective spheres. The IMF aspires to an increased and important role in global macroeconomic and financial management. The World Bank seeks global intellectual leadership in development policy and a continued important role in the provision of long-term development finance to justify it. These international financial institutions (IFIs), unlike the WTO, have already had profound effects on African development and development policies. These effects have been the result of their advice, their finance, their "signalling" role for others (particularly aid donors), and – above all – the conditionality attached to their lending and associated pressure for policy reform.

While mindful of the potentially positive consequences of globalization for Africa, this paper posits that conscious policies are required to ensure that trade openness and increased private capital inflows lead to enhanced and sustained growth. Despite the pressures from external sources of essential finance and external policemen enforcing new global rules, African economic policy makers still have important options as they address the future of their countries' relationships with the world. They need not mindlessly submit to the forces of globalization by total abandonment of any role in the mediation of national links to the world economy.

We begin with a review, in Section 2, of the recent evolution of the world's trade and financial regimes from a primarily African perspective. In Section 3, we offer our perspective on the role of external sector policies – of various kinds – in African development. Section 4 provides a review of the African experience in the areas of trade and capital account policies in the context of the analytical framework of Section 3. This sets the stage for the analysis in Section 5, which explores the interactions between the WTO and the two Bretton Woods' institutions in the areas of trade and capital account policies, and draws potential implications for Africa's future development. This section attempts to set out some modalities for collaboration among the WTO, IMF and the World Bank that, in our view, could provide better multilateral institutional support for African development and calls attention to the real problems in achieving such useful cooperation/coordination between the three institutions. Section 6 concludes.

2. The New World Trade and Financial Regimes

The ultimate impact of the new trade and financial regimes will depend, in large part, on the nature of the interactions among the existing multilateral institutions – especially the WTO, the World Bank and the IMF – and their capacities (as organizations) to fulfil their mandates. In a recent analysis of the linkages between and the relative competencies of the three institutions, Vines (1998) argues that the prospects for formal cooperation between the WTO and the other two multilateral institutions depend on three organizational characteristics: the objectives these institutions were created to achieve, their relative competencies, and the future challenges/agendas they have to address.

The IMF, as an institution, has experienced a major evolution from an organization that administered the international monetary system according to specified rules (anchored around a fixed exchange rate regime) to an organization that provides short- to medium-term programme loans and policy advice to individual – primarily less developed – countries in a context of (policy-based) conditional lending. The IMF's considerable expertise and research capacity in macroeconomics give credibility to its policy advice and loan conditionality. Its lending generates the net income to finance the research and gives the institution its basic financial independence. According to Vines (1998: 65), the two core activities of policy advice and conditional lending in a relatively well-defined area comprise an "extraordinarily coherent package". The IMF's ability to bring these two features together may have made the IMF, in his view, "the most effective international organization in history".

The role of the IMF in Africa, and in the poorest developing countries elsewhere, has also changed significantly over the years. Until the 1970s, the IMF was relatively inactive as a source of balance of payments finance for these countries. During the 1970s and up until the debt crisis of the early 1980s, the IMF provided it to scarcely anyone else. The IMF plunged significantly into Africa for the first time in the early 1980s. From then on, while the IMF significantly increased the concessionality of its lending to Africa it basically just "rolled it over" rather than expanding it any further.

At present, the enhanced structural adjustment facility (ESAF) is the IMF's primary instrument for providing finance to the poorest countries. Today's ESAF is a highly concessional loan facility, offering longer term finance than the IMF has traditionally provided, and using both a broader range of conditionality and more cooperation with the World Bank (which has typically been much more intrusive into domestic policies) than was ever the norm in the past. After years of emphasis on its purely monetary role and steadfast unwillingness to consider itself a development institution, the IMF now finds itself offering medium-term finance at highly concessional rates, and involving itself in the "structural" problems of development. Its primary orientation remains, however, both shorter term and more geared to macroeconomic stabilization, particularly the reduction of inflation, than that of the World Bank. Moreover, in Africa, the IMF's principal role in the provision of finance has been indirect – signalling to aid donors (and Paris Club creditors), with much more finance to offer, that recipients can effectively use their assistance.

The World Bank has a much wider and more challenging set of objectives than the IMF. Again Vines (1998: 67–78) provides a succinct characterization: "the World Bank now owes its strength and distinctiveness to bringing together into one organization a number of activities. The core International Bank for Reconstruction and Development (IBRD) function bundles together lending, development research, and development assistance – all glued together by the Bank's ability to exercise conditionality. The International Development Association (IDA) function is similar except that the lending is 'concessional' and is effectively aid. The Bank is now best thought of as a multilateral organization that enables richer countries to assist with the development problems of the poorer countries without entering into direct bilateral political power relations with them; we might say that by doing this the Bank sustains what is an implicit 'global development policy' regime".

The role of the World Bank in Africa has been well described in the monumental (and independent) new history of the Bank (Kapur, et al., 1997). "The scale and scope of the Bank's engagement in sub-Saharan Africa over the past twenty-five years has been substantially different from that elsewhere" (Kapur et al., 1997: 684). "The period from 1980 onward witnessed economic decline in most of sub-Saharan Africa and unprecedented power being wielded by the Bretton Woods institutions" (p. 766). "By the mid-1980s, the Bank had established itself as the preeminent external actor in sub-Saharan Africa" (p. 751). Although the IMF retained its role as financial gatekeeper and senior partner in the preparation of "policy framework papers", it was "its dominance of the intellectual discourse that solidified the Bank's preeminent role. ... Other multilaterals, even the IMF, were simply not in the same league as the Bank in terms of the sheer volume of analysis on the continent" (p. 764).

By the mid 1990s, however, and not just in Africa, the World Bank's list of "programme priorities ... had been stretched almost beyond recognition" (Kapur et al., 1997: 1215). It seemed to feel that "it was part of being the 'world's leading development promotion agency' to reach into one new field after another" (p. 1216). In Africa, the Bank was by now being led "into areas and issues where it had historically little competence or comparative advantage, a consequence of changing fashions and pressures from donor governments, Western NGOs and activist sections of its staff" (p. 800). Its management and owners, by this time, badly needed to develop their own "*policy* of self-restraint" (ibid.).

Relations between the IMF and the World Bank have been governed broadly by an agreed division of labour between them – as between the support of macroeconomic stabilization and the support of development. But, particularly in Africa, and as the range of conditions on IMF lending expanded, this division became increasingly blurred; differences over policy recommendations and conditionality sometimes followed. (Some of the differences between the IMF and Bank staff in the African context are reviewed by Kapur et al., 1997: 764; on IMF–Bank relations, see also Polak, 1994, and Feinberg, 1988.)

Finally, Vines (1998: 70) contrasts the mandate and objectives of the WTO with those of the IMF and the Bank:

> Quite unlike the Fund, whose primary output is adjustment assistance (advice and loans) to individual countries, or the Bank, whose primary output is development assistance (advice and loans) to individual countries, the primary output of the WTO is rule writing and enforcement of an explicit global regime. It is an organization that writes rules and, in so doing, makes laws with which its contracting parties agree to abide. Unlike the Fund and the Bank, whose effectiveness ultimately stems from a combination of an internal knowledge base and an ability to exert conditionality on individual countries, the effectiveness of the WTO rests upon its combination of a global forum in which rules can be brokered and a dispute settlement process in which they can be enforced.

Both the IMF and the Bank are vigorous in their promotion of more liberal and market-friendly approaches to development policy than have, until recently, been the norm in Africa. In this respect, their policy approaches are quite consistent with those implicit in the rules of the WTO.

The IMF and the World Bank are faced with major challenges that may force some changes in their modes of deploying conditionality, and perhaps also in their mandates. These challenges are, by and large, related to increased global capital market integration and the substantial rise in private capital flows to many middle-income countries. The IMF has increasingly been drawn into initiatives to enhance international macroeconomic policy coordination and crisis response, e.g., after the Mexican crisis in 1994 and the current East Asian crisis. However, the IMF may lack both the mandate and the relevant competencies to undertake this task: "there are deep problems as to agreement on appropriate policies, on monitoring, on enforcement, and on conditions" (Vines, 1998: 66). As for the Bank, there are two main challenges. First, high-growth middle-income countries have increasingly resorted to the private capital market as an alternative source of finance to the Bank's conditional lending. Second, even in the case of concessional development finance (by IDA), as discussed below, the effectiveness of policy conditionality as an instrument for enhancing reform has come under increasing criticism (e.g., Collier, 1991, 1996; Helleiner, 1998a).

On the other hand, the WTO has just begun the process of addressing its agenda – with much less technical in-house capability than the other two organizations (Blackhurst, 1998). The WTO is, perhaps by design, still a fragile body – essentially a contract among governments – with limited research expertise or interpretive capacity. Its organizational structure was likely adequate for meeting the requirements of overseeing the originally-charted principles of its predecessor, the GATT: notably most favoured nation (MFN) and national treatment. However, the widening of the GATT agenda – and its formalization in the WTO mandate – to include a range of new areas (e.g., liberalization of financial services, intellectual property rights, anti-dumping, etc.) has stretched the WTO organization beyond the limits of its capacities (Vines, 1998).

To remain credible and effective, both the Bank and the IMF will need at least formally to cooperate with the WTO in a way that will allow them to enhance the quality and effectiveness of their policy conditionality. One hopes that such improvements may emerge within the more reciprocal and participatory context that the WTO can provide. On the other hand, the WTO would need enhanced research capabilities to be able to cooperate with these two institutions on a comparable, if not on equal, footing. Moreover, the IFIS will always retain the powers of their purses. These are therefore unlikely to be equal partnerships, and WTO influences over processes or policies may be fairly limited.

A further element in the emerging global regime for international trade and finance is the Multilateral Agreement on Investment (MAI) proposed by OECD. Although originally to be applicable only to OECD members and now, in any case, ground down in intra-OECD disputes, the draft MAI provides a clear indication of what many major powers want in the way of an international regime for foreign investment. The proposed agreement includes an all-encompassing definition of "investment" (including, for instance, intellectual property and portfolio capital), sweeping and legally binding restraints on government performance requirements, and the requirement of national treatment for foreign investors both before (which is radically new) and after establishment in the host nation; but no disciplines on government investment incentives or any of the many aspects of investor behaviour that were the subject of extensive (and ultimately unsuccessful) international negotiations on "codes of conduct" for TNCs in an earlier period (Correa, 1998; Ganesan, 1998). It is also quite clear that the pressure on developing countries to "restrain" their policies toward OECD property owners will be unrelenting, with or without an agreed new multilateral investment regime (which will still be sought in one forum or another). Apart from its substantive content, an MAI raises important new jurisdictional issues between the IMF, the WTO and any new investment-focused agreements or institutions.

3. External Sector Policies and African Development

African governments make policies relating to their countries' economic relationships with the rest of the world in several different dimensions – notably in trade (and other current account) relationships; in the treatment of international capital flows; and in the overall management of their external balance of payments. As they do so, they not only interact bilaterally and directly with their trading partners and particular owners of foreign capital (both private and public), but they must also deal, as has been seen, with multilateral institutions that "govern" the global trading and financial systems – the IMF, the World Bank group, the WTO and possibly an eventual MAI. Additionally, their dependence on foreign capital (and general external friendliness and support) subjects African governments to policy conditionality on a wide range of other issues as well, including such highly political matters as the institutions of domestic governance and the role of the state.

It would be idle to pretend that there is universal agreement as to appropriate development strategy for all of the varied countries of Africa.

(At this point, and throughout the rest of this paper, we assume that development strategy builds on a pre-existing situation of reasonable, or at least "normal", macroeconomic stability.) It is generally accepted, however, that in the pre-industrial phase of a country's development, industrial import substitution (IS), normally confined to non-durable consumer goods, can be both very rewarding and relatively easy to execute. Domestic production of such manufactures constitutes the first attempt at modernization that does not require high technical skills or complicated strategic state interventions to resolve the market coordination failures that normally characterize modern sector production. To support such import substitution, restrictive trade policy and hence more appreciated currencies (in real terms) are typically deployed. Apart from the industrial policy considerations behind trade (especially import) restrictions, high tariffs on imports and modest taxation of traditional exports are also the main sources of tax revenue at this early stage of a country's development. The overall trade regime consistent with this first (easy) phase of the IS strategy is therefore essentially biased against exports. However, even in this phase, since traditional exports are the main source of foreign exchange for the economy, some minimum threshold of export performance has to be secured, to allow for the import of sufficient key intermediate and capital goods to support the strategy. Thus, even as IS is just getting under way some direct export promotion (EP) measures may be required to neutralize, at least partially, the deleterious incentive effects of direct export taxation and the indirect incidence of import taxation on exports.

In a small economy, the domestic market for non-durable consumer manufactures is inherently rather limited, and therefore the labour absorption capacity of the sector is also limited. This suggests that the easy phase of IS cannot be sustained for long. At some point it will be necessary consciously to switch into a strategy of EP of simple manufactures, based initially on the capacity for producing them that was created in the easy IS phase.

As far as trade policy issues are concerned, there is indeed already a remarkable consensus in Africa on the need for significantly improved export performance, and sufficient incentives and other supports to induce increased and sustained investment in export-oriented activities. The rationales for such "export promotion" vary. They include:

- The possibility of using existing productive capacity more fully and effectively.
- The purported productivity-enhancing effects and positive externalities from non-traditional export-oriented production.
- The potential for attracting fresh foreign investment to profitable exporting opportunities.
- The productivity-enhancing effects of the imports of capital goods, intermediate inputs and technology that the foreign exchange earned by exporting can finance.
- The sheer absence of plausible alternatives for profitable investment in small economies (Helleiner, 1995).

It would be wrong to think of export expansion and import substitution as necessarily mutually exclusive, but in small countries, after some point, exports are what must drive the process (Williamson, 1997a: 18).

The import liberalizing implications of such a switch towards an export-orientation strategy could eventually be substantial, but the move toward a *generally* more open trade regime may, and probably should, take some time. On the other hand, the immediate implications of such a shift in strategy for exchange rate policy are usually much more dramatic. Its inauguration has typically involved real currency depreciation (with subsequent stability) and direct support for exports (e.g., through rebate of tariffs levied on inputs to exports, or tariff exemptions for such inputs, or even direct subsidies). Only later, typically, is this followed by tariffication of QRs, and then reductions and rationalization of tariffs (Helleiner, 1995).

In order to overcome the initially limited capability for exporting manufactures – and sufficiently enough to stimulate new investment in export-oriented production – the real value of the currency may have to depreciate quite considerably, overshooting its eventual equilibrium value (Williamson, 1997a). It is likely to have to remain under-valued for several years, before sufficient productivity growth in the traded sector is generated to bring with it secular real currency appreciation (Balassa, 1964; Samuelson, 1964). In the current era of global capital market integration, the temptation to abandon (or the inability to maintain) this real currency depreciation prematurely – before the economy is sufficiently developed to sustain real appreciation – has proved to be quite formidable in many developing countries. The recent Asian financial crisis makes clear that even the most successful developing countries may fall victim to this problem. The recent, and in our view premature, opening of capital accounts in many reforming African countries (mainly based on advice from the IMF) has resulted in a rise in (mainly short-term) private capital inflows to these countries and consequent real currency appreciation. Given the speculative and unsustainable nature of these capital flows and the likelihood of frequent occurrence of financial crisis, the real exchange rate (RER) can be expected to experience *major* swings (increased RER instability) around a more appreciated currency value. (Some degree of short-term variation around the "target zone" for the RER is, of course, inevitable.)

An alternative strategy available to larger economies is to extend IS to consumer durables, intermediates and capital goods; but, to be sustainable, there must be continued incentives for profitable investment. Rodrik (1994) credits the successful coordination of investment demand (and associated booms of capital goods imports), rather than exports per se, for the phenomenal economic growth of Korea and Taiwan; this, in his view, facilitated even more remarkable export expansion as a by-product of the investment (and import-led) growth. However, even under this strategy (or interpretation of strategy) there is a clear recognition of the important role of exports, though "not necessarily as the critical vehicle for technology transfer but more significantly as the primary source for financing the indispensable bottleneck-breaking and technology-bearing imports, especially in the absence of adequate capital inflows" (Oyejide, 1997a: 7). A striking piece of evidence revealed in Rodrik's analysis is that despite the substantial and sustained export expansion in the two countries, the profitability of exports – as proxied by the RER – remained highly stable.

This analysis suggests that through a combination of direct EP measures and real exchange rate policies, the overall structure of incentives should never be allowed to be *grossly* biased against exports. Moreover, experiences with IS elsewhere suggest that successful strategies (most notably in East Asia) have been characterized by two further important design features: First, the levels of protection were relatively moderate, to minimize adverse impacts on resource allocation and second, protection was time-bound, so that the ultimate survival of an infant industry rested with its ability to compete effectively, in both the domestic and international markets (Oyejide,

1997a). Early across-the-board import liberalization was not typical of other developing countries' successful EP strategies. It is also clear from experience elsewhere that an appropriate and stable real exchange rate is of paramount importance to the encouragement of exports.

4. Trade, Exchange Rate and Capital Account Policies in Africa

Trade and payments liberalization in recent experience

Prior to independence, African economies typically defended fixed nominal exchange rates and enjoyed fairly liberal trade (and payments) regimes. During the 1960s and 1970s, the efforts of newly independent governments to accelerate industrialization and development generated increasing tax burdens and more activist trade policies. As balance of payments pressures emerged, rather than adjusting exchange rates African governments typically introduced or tightened foreign exchange and import controls. By the mid 1970s, most African countries had acquired fairly closed trade regimes and over-valued currencies. Many had not only high import tariffs but also import prohibitions and quantitative restrictions, and exorbitant (explicit as well as implicit) export taxes.

In the 1970s in particular, trade policies were basically used as macroeconomic instruments in response to sustained adverse external shocks, for restoring public revenues or to stem current account deficits. Industrial policy considerations had little, if any, effect on African trade regimes during this period (Oyejide, 1997a).

In the 1980s substantial currency devaluations and trade liberalization reforms were effected in several African countries. These reforms helped shape Africa's trade and exchange regimes in a number of important ways:

- Exchange controls – especially in relation to current account transactions – were eliminated in most countries.
- Export taxes were eliminated or substantially reduced in almost all countries.
- Tariff rates were reduced and harmonized, and tariff policies became more transparent (Africa's average tariff rates declined from 30% in the early 1980s to 21% in the late 1980s).

- Non-tariff barriers were either eliminated or tariffied in many countries.
- By and large, trade policy was less frequently used to address balance of payments problems as exchange rates were freed or became more flexible.

While substantial reforms were implemented by many African countries in the 1980s, compared with other developing regions, Africa's average tariff rates were still high in 1990. In terms of non-tariff measures, the gap between Africa and other regions was even wider (Rodrik, 1997: tables 4 and 5). Trade liberalization efforts in Africa were also often short-lived and lacking in credibility. In a recent comprehensive paper on trade policy and economic performance in Africa, Rodrik (1997: 5) provides the following evaluation: "successful instances like Botswana and Mauritius notwithstanding, trade reform in Africa has generally been erratic and marked by reversals and lack of credibility".

An important further fact about trade liberalization attempts in Africa is that they have been almost exclusively unilateral, mainly implemented in the context of the World Bank's structural adjustment programmes (SAPS) and their policy conditionality. African trade liberalization reforms were thus, by and large, implemented as parts of comprehensive macroeconomic reform packages. They were not part of binding and reciprocal liberalization processes such as characterized GATT/WTO negotiations. Actual tariff levels in Africa are typically much lower than the levels at which they are "bound" in the WTO, where they are bound at all. This suggests that there may be deeper considerations behind the erratic and apparently "incredible" record of trade liberalization in Africa than those traditionally highlighted in analyses of such policy reforms, such as the role of interest groups and lobbying in "public choice".

First, not the least of the problems of African adjustment programmes is now generally believed to be their frequently limited degree of national "ownership". The problem of ownership is highlighted in the most fundamental critiques of reform programmes tied to conditional lending, in which policy-based lending is seen as both ineffective and "incredible", not only in the area of trade liberalization but in other areas as well. According to Collier (1991, 1996) and Collier and Gunning (1993), for example, such lending cannot be an effective "agency of restraint" against policy reversals because it suffers from time inconsistency problems – lending is given before reforms are implemented. In addition, they argue, it is not credible because it is inherently "alien" – administered and monitored by outside institutions. Instead, they propose domestically-built agencies of restraint or more effective external collective threat-making mechanisms.

In particular, to the extent that further trade liberalization is required for Africa, these authors argue in favour of a reciprocal multilateral framework, such as that of the WTO, or a regional agreement that allows further reductions of tariffs to be tied, for example, to increased access to major Northern trading partners' markets. Liberalization within a framework of reciprocity and in the context of "open regionalism", they say, may not be simply complementary but actually preferable to further SAP-inspired unilateral trade liberalization in that:

- It would achieve as much as Africa can achieve from unilateral liberalization.
- It would establish credibility of trade reform.
- It would serve a defensive purpose, ensuring that Africa would not be left out of trade blocs if WTO rules were insufficiently enforced.
- It might be politically easier to achieve than unilateral reform.
- It might facilitate the adoption of useful institutions at the regional level.

Second, in terms of their substantive content, SAP-inspired trade liberalization attempts, like the control regimes before them, suffered from the fact that they were not explicitly and appropriately linked to an EP development strategy (Oyejide, 1997a). A vast body of literature, drawn from a variety of trade liberalization experiences, suggests that strong prior export expansion – based on proactive export promotion policies – is critical for sustaining trade liberalization (Oyejide, 1997a; Lall, 1996; Helleiner, 1994, 1995). "Introducing other export policy reform shortly before, or at least at the same time as, import reforms permits an earlier export supply response and allows unification of the tariff structure to proceed without burdening exporters" (Nash, 1992: 63). This helps to address the "sharp distributional consequences of trade reform" that Rodrik (1997: p. 5), among others, emphasizes as "at the heart of the difficulties [of trade reform]". Rodrik has sensibly urged packaging and sequencing trade reforms with other reforms so as to offset or dilute the distributional consequences of trade liberalization, and proceeding in stages so that winners can emerge early and provide political support. Accordingly, export promotion and special export incentives should now be the top priority for African trade policy reform.

Private capital flows and the capital account

Africa has not as yet been fully integrated into the newly globalized markets for capital. This is mainly because borrowers from this region, whether sovereign or private, have been considered poor credit risks by bankers and bond markets. Moreover, if anything, the poor economic performance of most of Africa has worsened perceptions of creditworthiness, even for good performers, due to the contagion effect of their "bad" neighbourhood. In particular, as long as the perceptions about the region remain, foreign direct investment will not be forthcoming, even for countries that undertook economic and political reforms some considerable time ago, except in highly profitable sectors, e.g., mining and petroleum, and in "protected" circumstances. The region's reputation causes investors to attach a high weight to the possibility of policy (or political) reversals, and therefore leads them to exercise the option to wait. This creates a sort of market coordination failure that may require some strategic external intervention to resolve. Given the substantial exodus of capital from Africa during the 1970s and 1980s, Africa should attempt at least to repatriate its lost capital.

Most of the current capital inflows to Africa – and those in the foreseeable future – are likely to be short-term and of a somewhat speculative nature. Such flows are responsive to high domestic interest rates, which are themselves very much linked to national fiscal and monetary policies. Large capital inflows to some African countries in recent years (e.g., Ghana, Kenya, Uganda, Zambia and Zimbabwe, among others) were mainly triggered by sharp rises in real interest rates brought about by IMF-inspired policies of severe macroeconomic restraint together with financial liberalization when the fiscal positions were still weak (Asea and Reinhart, 1995; Kasekende and Martin, 1995). Such surges of private capital, wherever they occur, result in real appreciation of the currency, and associated problems both for short-term macroeconomic management and for longer-term development (particularly of exports and import substitutes) (Helleiner, 1997, 1998b). Analysis of real exchange rate experience in Africa and elsewhere attributes significant misalignment (real currency over-valuation) to unsustainable capital inflows in Ghana (1994–95) and, to a lesser degree, in Mauritius (1994–95) and Tanzania (1995) (Elbadawi, 1998). Thus despite the currently low levels of capital inflow, African governments need to develop suitable approaches to global financial markets and, in particular, to consider the capital account effects of domestic fiscal and monetary policies.

In small open economies, such as are typical of Africa, the most important single "price" is generally acknowledged to be the relative price of tradeables to non-tradeables, or the real exchange rate (RER). Economies that are vulnerable to exogenous long-term influences and short-term shocks, e.g., in the terms of external trade, external capital flows, weather, etc., can expect to experience significant exogenously-determined changes (or pressure towards changes) in the RER, over the longer run and in the short run, respectively, regardless of national economic policies. As the underlying "fundamentals" of RER determination change, the RER must avoid undue "misalignment" or risk serious resource misallocation, macroeconomic imbalance and resulting social costs. At the same time, reasonable RER stability is required to avoid disruption and uncertainty in the economic signalling system. Appropriate RER policy, based on appropriate balance of payments management (including the capital account) and macroeconomic policy, is therefore critically important to African development prospects.

Trade policies – import or export taxes, subsidies or controls – themselves influence the "equilibrium" RER; other things being equal, restraining imports will raise the real value of the currency (and thus implicitly tax exports). But trade policies have typically been much more stable than RERs, and their effects have been relatively smaller. In any case, there has been significant, though some would say still not enough, trade liberalization in Africa in recent years. Export and development prospects in Africa now seem much more likely to be influenced by the RER and the macroeconomic policies that influence it than by trade policies narrowly defined.

In recent years African central banks have typically been concerned primarily with the control of price inflation. Where they have lost such control, as in Ghana, Uganda and Tanzania, the consequences were dire; their principal objective was, properly, to restore some stability to the value of the currency. Monetary restraint has typically been their main policy instrument with the exchange rate left, except in the Franc Zone, to find its own level in the market. Central bank intervention in foreign exchange markets outside the Franc Zone has typically been limited, and more directed toward the support of the national currency (albeit with limited reserves for the purpose) than to the modification of its appreciation. Only in a few cases has there been debate about the potential desirability of intervention for purposes of moderating movements in the real exchange rate; in Uganda, for example, where this has been addressed, there have been doubts expressed about its practical feasibility.

African investment and export prospects thus depend greatly upon the maintenance of stable and appropriate real exchange rates at the national level. Volatile short-term capital flows, through their exchange rate effects, seriously threaten Africa's development. It follows that advice to open up the capital account *totally*, such as often flows from the IMF, needs to be carefully weighed against the counter-arguments. International financial integration poses major risks for small countries with fragile domestic banking and financial systems. While on the one hand, it may increase the efficiency of the financial services sector and diversify its overall portfolio and thus its risks (though perhaps via external ownership and control), it also increases vulnerability to the turbulence of foreign financial markets and constrains the potential for independent monetary and exchange rate policies. Further, there may be serious difficulties in the transition from a controlled system to an open capital account. Marrying a very thin, immature and therefore volatile set of domestic financial markets to the notoriously volatile (and huge) global financial and exchange rate system may be foolhardy.

There are thus powerful arguments for the use of capital controls, direct or indirect or both, over both inflows and outflows, as part of the armoury of African macroeconomic and/or development (notably fiscal) policy instruments. At a minimum, they can "buy time", like reserves, for the deployment of other more fundamental policy instruments.

Of course, restrictions and controls – whether direct or indirect – also involve social (as well as private) costs: notably the costs of the administrative systems they require, microeconomic/allocative "distortions", and increasing resort to illegal or informal financial transactions. It is well known that controls over the external capital account or cross-border payments taxes are difficult to police and that the new technologies in international financial markets have probably increased the difficulties. The efficacy of such controls or taxes also probably declines over time as market participants find new avenues for evasion. But it does *not* follow that they therefore cannot work *at all* and/or that they need immediately to be eliminated and governments forever foresworn against their future use.

Securing the competitiveness of the economy via conscious real exchange rate policy need not be at the expense of adequate integration into the global capital market. In this connection the experience of Chile offers potentially important lessons for Africa. This country has successfully influenced the overall size and type of private capital inflows, mainly through indirect measures (notably reserve requirements against foreign deposits and other liabilities) – and it has done so in the context of an essentially open capital account regime. Long-term capital was encouraged while short-term and speculative capital was discouraged and aggregate capital inflows were kept close to sustainable levels consistent with real exchange rate competitiveness (Le Fort and Budnevich, 1997). On the other hand, many now attribute the current difficulties of East Asian countries, at least in part, to their premature liberalization of the external capital account (e.g., Sachs and Radelet, 1998); certainly the recent financial and exchange rate crises had their macroeconomic genesis in appreciated and over-valued currencies.

Chile's capital account policies assisted it to maintain a competitive real exchange rate in support of rapid growth and diversification of exports, and to avoid financial crisis despite the potential for massive private capital flows. Obviously, the efficacy of alternative instruments of control over (or other policy response to) unwelcome surges of capital, in or out, needs to be studied in the context of specific African situations. When formal financial institutions are simple and few, there may be considerable macroeconomic policy mileage in the deployment of some direct controls as well.

5. Implications of the New Trade and Financial Regimes

The possibilities for new approaches

New approaches to trade and financial regimes arise from the evolving roles of the World Bank and the WTO in the area of trade and the relationships among the Bank, the IMF and the WTO in the area of capital account policies.

The new trade regime: The World Bank and the WTO

The influence of the World Bank in opening up economies of developing countries has come both from its role as an intellectual leader in the development debate and from its policy conditionality. Unilateral trade liberalization has been a major policy thrust within World Bank supported structural adjustment programmes (SAPS), in both Africa and elsewhere. (Some World Bank insiders argue that trade issues should assume even more prominence in future Bank research and policy interventions [Nogues, 1998].) The Bank seeks to remain active in the area of trade – when the WTO is emerging as a major player on trade issues – first, to ensure that trade policy remains linked to a development context, and second, to further enhance its current "informal" collaborative relationship with the WTO.

The Bank and the IMF are in full agreement on the desirability of further trade liberalization in Africa. Such liberalization is likely to lead to some import and export expansion, but by itself it will not necessarily increase overall economic growth (Rodrik, 1997). In our view, further trade liberalization is usually *not* now a top priority for most African countries seeking to improve their policies for more rapid, sustainable and equitable development (though, as always, there is great variety in recent experiences and current policy priorities). Indeed a thorough stocktaking of trade barriers would uncover ongoing difficulties and complexity (and controversy) in the implementation of current import regimes, e.g., the extensive use of ad hoc tax concessions on imports of intermediate inputs and capital goods as "sweeteners" for foreign investors and NGOS, widespread tax evasion and corruption in the collection of customs duties, instances of significant negative effective protection in some sectors, and continuing heavy fiscal dependence on taxes on trade. A review of such issues should certainly precede any national-level plunge into further import liberalization.

As argued above, once macroeconomic stabilization has been attained, as far as trade and related policies are concerned, priority should more typically be assigned instead to (1) the achievement and maintenance of an appropriate and broadly stable real exchange rate; (2) special incentives and supports for investment in export-oriented productive activities, particularly by local firms; and (3) full domestic development, management and "ownership" of development programmes. These priorities are not those at present typically espoused in the WTO, IMF and World Bank, or in the proposed MAI, in all of which the push for across-the-board liberalization in all spheres and completely level playing fields remains in vogue, and "tight leash" conditionality remains its principal supportive instrument.

Indeed, strategic interventions for resolving market failures or building technological capabilities, the so-called "second generation" trade issues, are specifically targeted for elimination (or "standardization") and international surveillance under the WTO. Some strategic (and selective) interventions, particularly, in support of investment in export activities and by local firms, are likely to be helpful in Africa, given the prevalence of market failures, the disadvantages of "late starters", and the structure of African industry – among other adverse factors. (For a recent review of these issues, see Soludo, 1997.) Some analysts in the World Bank appear to support – at least at the intellectual level – some flexibility to allow countries to adopt different development policies, including policies of intervention. In particular, the current Chief Economist of the Bank argues persuasively that the East Asian countries, despite their current financial crisis, offer a viable development model that other developing and transition countries might seek judiciously to replicate (Stiglitz, 1998). As is well known, some of the policies that are to be discouraged and subjected to tight surveillance by the WTO are credited by others for the phenomenal economic transformation of East Asia over the last 30 years.

In our view, significant further trade liberalization is likely to be beneficial for Africa's long-term development only if certain conditions are met. First and foremost, it must be part of a carefully sequenced and balanced programme for the sustained expansion of exports, through new investment, and for development more generally. Exchange rate policy must be particularly closely linked to efforts at trade liberalization. Our review of trade policy reform experiences suggests that the absence or weakness of explicit export promotion policies in Africa has a lot to do with the lack of sustainability and credibility of these reforms. The Bank could play a much more important supporting role in the design of better policy interventions to help African countries to realize the promise of improved access to developed countries' markets.

Second, for such an appropriately sequenced and balanced approach to export promotion, liberalization and development to be sustainable, it must be fully developed, and broadly understood and supported at the national level. With increasing democratization and public sector transparency in Africa, governments must be more accountable to parliaments, electorates and local pressure groups (including powerful private foreign investors). The days in which African governments negotiated their policy reforms primarily with the IMF, the World Bank and key bilateral donors, rather than within their own political systems, are rapidly coming to an end. Three further issues are important to raise in this connection.

First, to ensure that trade policy is anchored to a viable and consistent development strategy, the World Bank should design its supports so as pragmatically to assist African countries to retain and effectively use relevant (and WTO-permissible) development policy instruments, rather than crudely pushing, on the basis of theoretical principles, ideology or majority shareholder interests, for their dismantling. In particular, given the important provision under the WTO's Agreement on Subsidies and Countervailing Measures for least developed countries (or those with per capita GDP less than $1,000), which allows these countries to subsidize exports, the Bank should, where appropriate, explicitly incorporate subsidy-based export promotion strategies in future trade reforms prescribed for these countries in Africa. Generally, it should assist African members of the WTO to take full advantage of their rights therein and to defend themselves against the assaults of more powerful members. For example, the WTO could help introduce some discipline and transparency to the likely increasing role of sanitary standards as a rationale for banning or restricting exports from developing countries imposed by major Northern trading partners, as in the case of fish products exported from East Africa (e.g., Muga and Mwega, 1998).

Second, high priority should be assigned within Africa to regional approaches to trade policy, including exchanges of information and experience, liberalization initiatives (including WTO negotiations), and integration. Non-discriminatory and universal trade liberalization may, in some circumstances, greatly benefit regional trade – even disproportionately so – but it may be politically difficult to move as far as one might like with it, and it could therefore be a long time coming. Discrimination in favour of only some Northern trading partners risks retaliation by others and is politically even less appealing. Given the problems with the sustainability and credibility of unilateral (non-discriminatory) trade liberalization in Africa, and the great promise that joint bargaining and reciprocal multilateral trade liberalization offer, the Bank should rethink its approaches in this area so as to encourage regional approaches to trade policy, including liberalization, perhaps via ex post conditional lending. Despite periodic rhetorical support for regional integration in Africa, the Bank has so far done relatively little to foster it (Kapur et al., 1997: 762–4).

Third, to mitigate the possible adverse fiscal implications of trade liberalization, both IMF and World Bank interventions could be more consciously and carefully designed to enhance the fiscal positions of liberalizing African countries, in step with the progress of other reforms. Revenue-neutrality should be the minimum fiscal target in adjustment programmes.

The new capital account policies: The IMF, the WTO (and the World Bank)

The IMF has been the main player in the area of exchange rate and capital account policies. Despite the interest of the World Bank in these policies from the perspectives of their effect on, or their links to, trade performance and the health of the financial and banking sectors, the World Bank, at least at a formal level, has typically played only a supporting role. With the expected ratification of the Agreement on Financial Services, the WTO will become another major potential player in capital account policies, although its liberal orientations are broadly consistent with those of the IMF.

IMF approaches to exchange rate policy have always emphasized the anti-inflationary anchoring role of the nominal exchange rate to a greater degree than has been the norm in the more development-oriented World Bank. Now there is risk of new, and potentially deleterious, influences on exchange rate policy emanating from the IMF.

The IMF Board is currently considering a proposed amendment to its articles to mandate it to promote capital account liberalization in addition to the current account liberalization it already supports. More controversially, it is also discussing expanding its jurisdiction to transactions in the capital account, which, if done, will raise problems of overlap with the WTO (and an MAI) (Polak, 1998). At a minimum, the IMF will have to cooperate closely with the WTO on international banking, insurance and financial market issues, particularly in times of crisis (Cornford and Bradford, 1998). How the potential jurisdictional overlaps are resolved must await specific case experiences. Like the Bank, however, the IMF may be able to augment its competencies by collaborating with the WTO; again, one can hope that the more reciprocal and participatory WTO processes (in this case in the Financial Services Agreement) may be combined effectively with the research and operational competencies of the IMF.

The proposed new IMF mandate in the capital account, if not handled judiciously (and the record of the IFIs in the trade account is not entirely encouraging) has the potential to be harmful to Africa's development. As we argued earlier, reforming African countries risk losing, under IMF pressure, the option of engineering the sequencing and extent of capital account liberalization so as to be consistent with the maintenance of a stable and broadly appropriate real exchange rate, the development of local financial markets, institutional and regulatory capacities, etc. If pushed to full currency convertibility, as some already have been, they could easily fall prey to destabilizing financial crises and real over-valuation episodes, even when they are still at a very early stage of their development process. Clearly, the potential adverse implications of the new capital account policies for sensible real exchange rate policies and the health of financial institutions could have grave consequences for Africa's development prospects. In our view, whatever the eventual IMF mandate, it will be for the World Bank to espouse balanced and development-oriented approaches to the capital account in the African context. It may be time for the Bank to take more independent positions from those of the IMF on such key matters of development strategy as exchange rate policy and capital account regimes.

The harsh realities

Cooperation/coordination among the three multilateral institutions (the WTO, IMF and World Bank) and reforms of some of their approaches and conditions, as proposed above, could be helpful to African development. But are they likely? And would they be enough?

In their relationships with these (and other external) institutions, developing countries have traditionally been concerned:

- To preserve maximum freedom for domestic policy – against the pressures of powerful external actors who seek to advance their own political, economic or ideological agendas (or, in some instances, what they genuinely believe to be morally or economically "correct" policies).
- To gain explicit recognition, reflected in the existence of ODA, and "special and differential treatment" at the international level for their different, and disadvantageous, initial conditions.

In recent years, the latter concern has been increasingly disregarded as aid flows decline, "special and differential treatment" erodes, and "single undertakings" are initiated. The new world of the "level playing field" is obviously one in which the potential advantages of the economically and politically powerful, now freer to threaten and bully the weak without rules that constrain them to recognize some of their disadvantageous conditions, are enhanced. For the weak, some rules are likely to be better than no rules; but some rules/systems – particularly those that offer fair and "unequal" treatment to "unequals" and/or otherwise reflect the concerns of the weak – are better than others. The recent trends have not been favourable to the developing countries. These issues, as they relate to the WTO, are addressed by Oyejide (1997b).

In this changing context, it is not surprising that there is concern in many developing countries over the increasing exercise of external power and influence over domestic economic and other policies – what many see as a major "downside" of globalization. As noted above, some analysts (though rarely those working within developing countries) welcome, indeed actively seek to engineer, increases in the power of external "agencies of restraint" in the belief that developing countries cannot otherwise make "credible" policy commitments. The latter group typically seeks to *tighten* external discipline over developing countries' policies rather than to loosen it (albeit via ostensibly "voluntary" agreements by African governments to these ends). Such advocates are unlikely to be very sympathetic to the concerns raised in this part of our paper – over inappropriate issue linkages, undesirable cross-conditionality and undue exercise of policy leverage by external institutions.

The issue linkage problem

The problem raised for developing countries by "issue linkage" is the undesired extension of conditions and disciplines to spheres beyond those within which voluntary commitments are totally acceptable, and without which the gains from the "core" agreements cannot be realized. A prime recent example of this phenomenon was the negotiation of the General Agreement on Trade in Services, and disciplines over Trade-Related Aspects of Intellectual Property Rights (TRIPS) and Trade-Related Investment Measures (TRIMS), none of which were on the developing countries' agenda of "unfinished business" during the Uruguay Round of GATT negotiations, and which were "offered" to developing countries in the "single undertaking" on a "take it or leave it" basis. (A "positive spin" can be put on this by the frequently heard observation that such extensions of coverage make it easier to distribute gains to all – even the richest and least observant of the existing rules! – and thus to achieve some kind of agreement.)

The most obvious and important issue linkage is that between the provision of finance and domestic policies in the recipient country – aid and IFI loan conditionality. As seen above, increasing concern has been expressed about the prospective extension of conditionality to developing countries on policies relating to the capital account of the balance of payments (via a proposed amendment to the Articles of Agreement of the IMF), foreign direct investment (via the MAI and/or WTO), "governance" (via the World Bank), and on and on. There are also now three multilateral agreements on non-trade matters that authorize trade sanctions (typically non-MFN treatment) against non-cooperators – the Montreal Protocol (on CFCs), the Basle Convention (on hazardous waste) and CITES, the convention on trade in endangered species. Efforts to link trading rights to issues of labour rights and the environment raise major further potential problems for developing country exporters.

In some instances, where developing countries have potential power, they might be able to "link issues" in reverse, e.g., by relaxing their greenhouse gas controls in retaliation for bad treatment of their trade; but the weakest invariably wind up as the biggest losers from such "tit for tat" exchanges with the strong.

Cross-conditionality

There are basically two kinds of problems (for developing countries) raised in traditional discussion of cross-conditionality in the provision of finance (e.g., Commonwealth Secretariat, 1986; Junguito, 1996):

- Inconsistency of the various conditions, e.g., when the World Bank (and now the WTO) presses for tariff reductions at the same time that the IMF presses for preserving current duties so as to protect government revenues; or when the World Bank adopts a longer-term approach to exchange rate policy and structural reform than the IMF, with its emphasis on immediate stabilization.
- The "ganging up" phenomenon – the increase in the strength of external pressure via the presentation of a collective front vis-a-vis the country upon which various conditions are imposed.

The first problem has at times been an important source of confusion and difficulty, but is inherently little more than a (usually temporary) nuisance. Indeed, public disagreement and debate between IMF and Bank analysts – as in the case of the recent East Asian crisis – is likely to be socially beneficial. Certainly it is far preferable to the "back-room" dispensation of contradictory advice and conditions, and the surreptitious competition for influence that accompanies it, that has sometimes characterized Fund/Bank relationships with borrowers elsewhere.

In the African context, in which bilateral aid donors and UN agencies are also major sources of external finance, the potential for mutual inconsistency of advice and conditions is multiplied. Some European donors have not always bothered to conceal their distaste for IMF/Bank conditionality. In this context, problems often arise at a more micro level – in the prioritization of aid-financed projects, many of which are trade-related – as well as in macro issues of stabilization and development policy. Despite much attractive rhetoric about the need for African leadership (and ownership) and donor coordination, and the numerous meetings of consultative groups, round tables, global coalitions, donors and the like, the reality of ill-coordinated, but externally-driven programmemes, remains (Helleiner, 1998a).

The second cross-conditionality problem raises larger problems – the problems of achieving genuine local ownership, the problems of the weak in a world of the strong. Concentrated external pressure for reform can, in many circumstances, be socially useful – when it assists in overcoming *egregious* policy errors. But, beyond such basics as the need to overcome severe macroeconomic mismanagement, knowledge of what development policies are likely to be "best" for individual (national) economic, social and political circumstances is always a little uncertain, let alone the speed and sequencing of their introduction. Powerful external actors – often sources of finance, rule-makers and police, all rolled into one – attempt to constrain African policy makers. And they do so most effectively when they act together in their collective interest. In the 1980s and 1990s African governments were subjected to a unique degree of external bullying. "The donor community and the Bank ... applied to sub-Saharan Africa a different standard tha[t] would have been unacceptable elsewhere. ... But then Africa was on its knees and dependent. ..." (Kapur et al., 1997: 801). This is not to suggest that external pressures were always effective; they frequently were not, and this usually led either to further external pressure or to a donor search for new (often non-government) allies with which to work.

External leverage is obviously strongest when there is maximum "ganging up" on the part of potential external sources of influence – involving both full agreement on the conditions and full participation. Aid recipients have therefore sometimes sought to diversify their aid sources (even in the post Cold War period) so as to increase their options; this has usually meant significantly increased transaction costs and has not always fulfilled the objectives. Overlapping jurisdictions (as between the IMF and the Bank, or the IMF and the WTO) are sometimes useful to developing countries. Whereas they may cause inefficiencies and confusion, they may also increase the prospect of a weak developing country playing one institution off against another in the interest of its own policy flexibility and "ownership". There is great risk, however, that external financing – from the IMF, the World Bank or aid donors – will in future be conditioned, explicitly or implicitly, on total compliance with the provisions of the WTO and MAI, in addition to other matters.

African "ownership", and hence sustainable development, would be furthered if, beyond certain macroeconomic basics, the aid donors and *all* of the multilateral institutions (IMF, World Bank and WTO) "backed off" and gave African governments more policy "room". These so-called external "agencies of restraint" themselves need to be restrained. Genuinely locally-owned policies, warts and all, are more likely eventually to lead to sustainable African development than efforts to enforce external visions of policy perfection. Domestic policy debate is more likely to be productive than external policy dialogue (particularly when the latter so easily degenerates into a monologue of the powerful).

6. Conclusions

The new trade and financial regimes for the increasingly "globalized" world economy fall far short of what is truly required for effective global economic governance. The WTO, IMF and World Bank are still fairly insignificant actors in the overall scheme of things. Such power and influence as they possess are likely to be relatively more important to the weaker members of the international community of nations than to the strong. Certainly the practices and rules of these multilateral institutions can matter for African development.

Of course, development depends primarily upon events within the African countries themselves; and African governments retain some room for manoeuvre. Development policies pursued by African governments may nonetheless be significantly influenced or constrained by the activities of the WTO, IMF and World Bank. This paper has offered some suggestions for improving African development prospects through improved functioning of these institutions.

We have emphasized that domestic incentive structures are fundamentally important to the nature of the evolution and development of particular national economies and, more particularly, to sustained export expansion. When incentives are inappropriate or unstable or both, development prospects are invariably seriously weakened. By far the most important element in the incentive structure is an appropriate and stable real exchange rate. To the extent that trade policies matter, the rights of poor countries to use export subsidies seem more likely to be important, and subject to international controversy, than the import liberalization issues that most trade analysts emphasize. In short, to the extent that international regimes and advice matter to the evolution of domestic incentive structures, the IMF and the World Bank, with their macroeconomic policy advice and conditionality, are likely to matter far more to Africa than the WTO.

We distinguish between the potential roles of the IMF and the World

Bank in support of Africa's development. It is important to note that the exchange rate policy component of the "Washington Consensus" – which reflects the IMF intellectual and operational position – has never been explicitly linked to a long-term strategy of export expansion through real-exchange rate competitiveness. Thus we argue that the World Bank, rather than the IMF, should take the lead role in Africa in the future, given that it is more likely to be concerned about longer-term development, especially export-oriented growth. We also argue that the Bank may not be effective in fullfiling this role without systemetically taking positions independent from those of the IMF on such key matters of development strategy as exchange rate policy and capital account regimes.

It is obviously not enough simply to have broadly appropriate and stable incentives; there must also be capacity to respond to them – in the form of skills, infrastructure, institutions and a reasonable investment rate. As far as these other requisites for export expansion and development are concerned, it will be aid donors, the World Bank and transnational corporations that matter to Africa, much more than the WTO. The WTO's principal contribution to Africa's development prospects is likely to be its achievement of a greater degree of market access for African (as well as all other) exports abroad rather than any contribution it may make to African trade policy.

We have argued that in any case, WTO "disciplines" should be flexibly applied to the low-income African countries to permit them to construct their own pragmatic development programmes, as others have done before them, and to build the capacity for sustained and competitive export performance and development. Stronger WTO members should refrain from making unreasonable demands on the weakest ones. The WTO system is still sufficiently weak (and flexible) that, provided its more powerful members show reasonable restraint, African governments probably have little to fear from an overeager WTO secretariat. On the historical record, they may have more reason for concern about premature and ideologically-driven pressures toward trade and capital account liberalization from the international financial institutions than from the WTO. Aggressive application of IMF and World Bank conditionality to "enforce" WTO or IMF (or eventually MAI) disciplines upon developing countries is a real potential hazard in the emerging world trade and financial regime, and it will have to be resisted.

Notes

1 Even now, the IMF often shows itself ambivalent about its new role and has difficulty explaining it. In his press conference after the 1996 annual meetings, for instance, the Managing Director stated: "What we are doing is not at all development financing. But what we are doing for developing countries is the job for which we were created- – to provide our members with the necessary resources to face temporary payments crises *or deeply-rooted structural problems* [our italics] without resorting to measures destructive of national or international prosperity in the context of strong, solid, credible adjustment and reform programmes" (IMF Survey, 14 October 1996: 324.) Its trade liberalization objectives and experiences are analysed in a recent staff survey (IMF, 1998).

2 According to a recent World Bank policy review of activities, the IBRD was lending only at 55% of its capacity prior to the expansion of its lending in response to the crisis in East Asia ("Strategic Compact", 13 March 1997).

3 This could build on the currently existing informal and formal arrangments between each of the World Bank and the IMF with the WTO (see World Trade Organization, 1996).

4 This discussion on the role of trade and exchange rate policy under an EP strategy of development can be schematized in terms of a simple "stages of development" real exchange rate model (adopted from Williamson, 1997a). This is presented in the Annex.

5 The few exceptions are the relatively liberal trade regimes within the Southern African Customs Union (SACU) and short-lived episodes of liberalization following positive external shocks (Oyejide, 1997).

6 For example, Elbadawi (1996) suggests that one form of intervention could involve substantial external debt relief – as a strong signal from the international development community in support of reforms. On the other hand, again Collier (1996) recommends several domestic and external "agencies of restraint" for resolving this coordination problem. According to Collier, reforming African governments could choose to build credible domestic, or commit to external agencies of restraint as "lock-in" mechanisms, and therefore "shorten the time they have to live down their history" of policy reversals and political instability.

7 Collier and Pattillo (1997) estimate that between 1970 and 1992 about 70% of African private wealth came to be held outside the sub-Continent. Also according to estimates of Collier and Gunning (1997), the ratio of capital flight to wealth during this period was 0.37 – compared with 0.29 for the Middle East, 0.17 for Latin America, 0.04 for South Asia and 0.03 for East Asia. This contrasts sharply with the average capital per worker in Africa, at only $1,560, compared with other regions ($10,844 for the Middle East, $9,157 for South Asia, $13,018 for East Asia).

8 At the least, policies must be tailored to the specifics of local conditions, as shown in a comparison of recent Ugandan and Zambian policy reforms. Exchange controls were previously so ineffective in Uganda that their complete liberalization probably had very little practical effect. Where, however, they were still to some degree binding upon would-be capital exporters, as in Zambia in 1992–1993, liberalization permitted significant substitution out of the local currency and thus losses in a seigniorage for an already fiscally stressed Zambian government (Adam, 1995). In many African countries, the

legalization of *bureaux de change* and of private foreign currency deposits in commercial banks has already gone some way towards de facto capital account liberalization.

9 In a recent article revisiting his earlier and widely quoted paper on the "Washington Consensus", Williamson (1997b) notes that the exchange rate policy component of the Consensus – which reflects the IMF intellectual and operational position – has never been explicity linked to a long-term strategy of export expansion through real exchange rate competitiveness.

10 Recently, in the context of a wider debate surrounding the current East Asian financial crisis, the Chief Economist of the World Bank strongly and publicly criticized IMF strategy for stabilization and restructuring financial and banking institutions in the region.

11 An extreme example of where this can lead is provided by the exclusions, under US law, from the list of beneficiaries of its general system of preferences (GSP) scheme, which have included: Communist countries, members of commodity cartels, countries offering preferences to other industrial countries, countries that have nationalized US assets without adequate compensation, countries not cooperating sufficiently in the control of illegal trade in drugs, and still others *at the discretion of the President!*

References

Adam, C. 1995. "Fiscal adjustment, financial liberalization, and the dynamics of inflation: Some evidence from Zambia". *World Development*, vol. 23, no. 5 (May): 735–50.

Asea, P. and C. Reinhart. 1995. "Real interest differentials and the real exchange rate: Evidence from four African countries". Paper presented at the African Economic Research Consortium biannual research workshop, May 1995.

Balassa, B. 1964. "The purchasing power parity doctrine: A reappraisal". *Journal of Political Economy*, 72.

Blackhurst, R. 1998. "The capacity of the WTO to fulfil its mandate". In A. Krueger, ed., *The WTO as an International Organization*. Chicago: University of Chicago Press.

Collier, P. 1991. "Africa's external economic relations: 1960–90". *African Affairs*.

Collier, P. 1996. "The role of the state in economic development: Cross-regional experiences". In I. Elbadawi and K. Schmidt-Hebbel, eds., *Cross-Regional Reform and Development Experiences*, Special Edition of *Journal of African Economies* (1998).

Collier, P. 1997. "Globalization: Implications for Africa". Paper presented at the AERC/IMF Seminar on Trade Reforms and Regional Integration in Africa, Washington, D.C., 1–3 December 1997.

Collier, P. and J.W. Gunning. 1993. "Linkages between trade policy and regional integration". Paper presented at an AERC conference on Trade Liberalization and Regional Integration in sub-Saharan Africa, Nairobi, December.

Collier, P. and J.W. Gunning. 1997. "Explaining African economic performance". CSAE Discussion Paper, University of Oxford.

Collier, P. and C. Pattillo, eds. 1997. *Investment and Risk in Africa*. London: Macmillan Publishing Company.

Commonwealth Secretariat. 1986. "Cooperation without conditionality: An issue in international lending". London.

Cornford, A. and J. Bradford. 1998. "The WTO Agreement on Financial Services: Problems of financial globalization in practice". Mimeo. G-24 paper, UNCTAD.

Correa, C.M. 1998. "Key issues for developing countries in a possible Multilateral Agreement on Investment". Mimeo. G-24 paper, UNCTAD.

Culpeper, R. and C. Pestieau, eds., 1996. *Development and Global Governance*. Ottawa: International Development Research Centre/North-South Institute.

Elbadawi, I. 1996. "Consolidating macroeconomic stabilization and restoring growth in sub-Saharan Africa". In B. Ndulu, N. van de Walle and contributors, *Agenda for Africa's Economic Renewal*. New Brunswick: Overseas Development Council, Transaction Publishers.

Elbadawi, I. 1998. "Exchange rate policy and non-traditional export performance in developing counties". Paper prepared for WIDER project on Growth, External Sector and the Role of Non-Traditional Exports in Sub-Saharan Africa.

Feinberg, R. 1988. "The changing relationship between the World Bank and the International Monetary Fund". *International Organization*, vol. 2, no. 3 (Summer).

Ferrer, A. 1997. "Development and underdevelopment in a globalized world: Latin American dilemmas". In L. Emmerij, ed., *Economic and Social Development into the XXI Century*. Washington D.C.: Inter-American Development Bank and Johns Hopkins University Press.

Ganesan, A.V. 1998. "Strategic options available to developing countries with regard to a Multilateral Agreement on Investment". Mimeo G-24 paper, UNCTAD.

Helleiner, G.K., ed. 1994. *Trade Policy and Industrialization in Turbulent Times*. London and New York: Routledge.

Helleiner, G.K. 1995. "Trade, trade policy and industrialization reconsidered". *World Development Studies*, 6, UNU/WIDER, Helsinki.

Helleiner, G.K. 1997. "Capital account regimes and the developing countries". G-24 paper, in *International Monetary and Financial Issues for the 1990s*, Vol. VIII (UNCTAD).

Helleiner, G.K. 1998a. "External conditionality, local ownership and development". Mimeo, and forthcoming in J. Freedman, ed., *Transforming Development*, University of Toronto Press.

Helleiner, G.K., ed. 1998b. *Capital Account Regimes and the Developing Countries*. London: Macmillan.

Helleiner, G.K. 1999. "Africa in the global economy". In Dharam Ghai, ed., *Renewing Social and Economic Progress in Africa: Essays in honour of Philip Ndegwa*. London: Macmillan.

Henderson, D. 1998. "International agencies and cross-border liberalization: The WTO in context". In A. Krueger, ed., *The WTO as an International Organization*. Chicago: University of Chicago Press.

International Monetary Fund (Robert Sharer et al.) 1998. *Trade Liberalization in IMF-Supported Programmes*, Washington, D.C.

Jackson, J. 1995. (Quoted from Henderson, 1998).

Junguito, R. 1996. "IMF – World Bank policy advice: The coordination/cross-conditionality question". In G.K. Helleiner, ed., *The International Monetary and Financial System, Developing Country Perspectives*. London and New York: Macmillan.

Kapur, D., J. Lewis and R. Webb. 1997. *The World Bank, the First Half-Century*, vol. 1, *History*. Washington, D.C.: The Brookings Institution.

Kasekende, L. and M. Martin. 1995. "Macroeconomic policy research issues: The sequencing, consistency and credibility of structural adjustment in Africa". AERC Senior Policy Seminar. African Economic Research Consortium, Nairobi, March.

Lall, S. 1996. *Learning from the Asian Tigers: Studies in Technology and Industrial Policy*. London: Macmillan.

LeFort, G. and C. Budnevich. 1997. "Capital account regulations and macroeconomic policy: Two Latin American experiences". *International Monetary and Financial Issues for the 1990s*, vol. VIII, United Nations, New York and Geneva; and In G. Helleiner, ed., 1998. *Capital Account Regimes and the Developing Countries*. London: Macmillan.

Muga, K. and F. Mwega. 1998. "Africa and the world trading system: The case of Kenya". Paper presented at the second research workshop of the AERC collaborative project on Africa and the World Trading System. Mombasa, 26–29 April 1998.

Nash, J. 1992. "An overview of trade policy reform, with implications for sub-Saharan Africa". In J.M. Fountain, ed., *Foreign Trade Reforms and Development Strategy*. London and New York: Routledge.

Nogues, J. 1998. "Comment: The linkages of the World Bank with the GATT/WTO". In A. Krueger, ed., *The WTO as an International Organization*. Chicago: University of Chicago Press.

Oyejide, T.A. 1997a. "Trade policy and regional integration in sub-Saharan Africa". Paper presented at the AERC/IMF Seminar on Trade Reforms and Regional Integration in Africa. Washington, D.C., 1–3 December.

Oyejide, T.A. 1997b. "Cost and benefits of 'special and differential' treatment of developing countries in GATT/WTO: An African perspective". Paper presented at the first research workshop of AERC collaborative project on Africa and the World Trading System. Accra, October 1997.

Polak, J. 1994. "The World Bank and the IMF: A changing relationship", *Brookings Occasional Paper*. Washington, D.C.: Brookings Institution.

Polak, J. 1998. "The articles of agreement of the IMF and the liberalization of capital movements". Mimeo G-24 and IMF papers.

Ricupero, R. 1997. Statement by Secretary-General to Trade and Development Board. UNCTAD, Geneva, October 13.

Rodrik, D. 1994. "Getting interventions right: How South Korea and Taiwan grew rich". NBER Working Paper Series, No. 4964, December.

Rodrik, D. 1997. "Trade policy and economic performance in sub-Saharan Africa". Paper prepared for the Swedish Ministry for Foreign Affairs, November.

Sachs, J. and S. Radelet. 1998. "The East Asian financial crisis: Diagnosis, remedies, prospects". Paper prepared for Brookings Panel, 26. March.

Samuelson, P. 1964. "Theoretical notes on trade problems". *Review of Economics and Statistics*, 46 (May).

Soludo, C. 1997. "Africa: Industrialization strategy in the context of globalization". Paper presented at the AERC/IMF Seminar on Trade Reforms and Regional Integration in Africa. Washington, D.C., 1–3 December.

Stiglitz, J. 1998. "More instruments and broader goals: Moving toward the post-Washington Consensus". The 1998 WIDER Annual Lecture, Helsinki, Finland.

UNCTAD. 1996. "East Asian development: Lessons for a new global environment", UNCTAD Secretariat Report to the Conference on East Asian Development: Lessons for a New Global Environment. Kuala Lampur, Malaysia, 29 Feb–1 March.

UNCTAD. 1997. *Trade and Development Report*. Geneva.

UNDP. 1997. *Human Development Report*.

Vines, D. 1998. "The WTO in relation to the Fund and the Bank: Competencies, agendas, and linkages". In A. Krueger, ed., *The WTO as an International Organization*. Chicago: University of Chicago Press.

Williamson, J. 1997a. "Exchange rate policy and development strategy". In Elbadawi and Soto, eds., *Foreign Exchange Markets and Exchange Rate Policies in Sub-Saharan Africa, Journal of African Economies*, Supplement to vol. 6, no. 3: 17–36.

Williamson, J. 1997b. "The Washington Consensus revisited". In Louis Emmerij, ed., *Economic and Social Development in the XXI Century*. Washington, D.C.: The Inter-American Development Bank/Johns Hopkins University Press.

World Trade Organization. 1996. *WTO Agreements with the Fund and the Bank*. Document WT/L/195. Geneva: WTO.

Chapter ten

Policy Commitment Arrangements for Africa: Implications for Aid, Trade and Investment Flows

by Paul Collier, Centre for the Study of African Economies, University of Oxford and Jan Willem Gunning, Free University, Amsterdam

1. Introduction

Most African governments have weak credibility. They have trouble living down the past and hence continue to suffer from their own reputations (in countries where economic reform has not been accompanied by political change) or by the lingering reputation of their predecessors. Although this credibility problem is currently more severe in Africa than in other regions, it is far from a uniquely African problem. Currently, several countries of the former USSR have a similar problem. In the early postwar era, most West European governments faced credibility problems at least as daunting. They overcame these problems by a combination of performance and commitment arrangements. Clearly, the most important means by which a government can build reputation is through its performance. The role of commitment arrangements is primarily to accelerate the building of reputation beyond that which would occur purely through good performance.

In the limiting case a government that is resolved to maintain good performance simply uses commitment mechanisms as a signalling device.

That is, the commitment mechanism merely signals to private agents that the government has resolve, rather than in any way changing government behaviour. If the signal is effective the commitment mechanism may be very useful in accelerating the building of reputation and hence in raising investment. However, a government might wish to use a commitment mechanism not only as a signal but as a discipline that changes its own behaviour. For example, a government might resolve to avoid large budget deficits, but nevertheless find that the promulgation of a cash budget procedure provides a commitment mechanism without which it is unable to implement its resolve. In general, commitment mechanisms have both these features: they are signals to private agents about government intentions, and they are also specific procedures for converting good intentions into realized policies. In turn, a mechanism that manifestly converts intentions into realized policies will enhance credibility with private agents. The cash budget not only signals to private agents that the government is resolved to avoid large fiscal deficits, it reassures them that a viable means has been put in place for achieving this resolve.

This paper focuses on the commitment mechanisms a government can use to build credibility in trade and investment policies. We refer to commitment mechanisms as "agencies of restraint". We classify such agencies according to their domicile and the source of their power. Their domicile can be purely domestic, purely external or a hybrid. For example, a national central bank is a purely domestic agency, donor conditionality is purely external, and regional agreements are partly domestic and partly external. Agencies of restraint can derive their power through being based on penalties, through the devolution of authority or through some combination. For example, by establishing an independent central bank a government is able to restrain itself from interfering with the setting of interest rates. It achieves this through authority-shedding. However, an independent central bank thereby also acquires a role as a restraint over the fiscal policy of the government. If the government chooses to run a large fiscal deficit the central bank can raise interest rates. In turn this inflicts political costs on the government since electors dislike the increase in interest rates. Hence, an independent central bank is both a restraint upon monetary policy, based upon authority-shedding, and a restraint upon fiscal policy, based upon penalties.

We begin, in Section 2, with commitment mechanisms in the area of investment. Investor fears are partly specific to property rights over their investment, and partly much more wide-ranging with respect to the management of the economy. Investment will be deterred both if investors fear that their assets will be confiscated and if they fear that the economy will collapse into hyperinflation and a crash in the exchange rate. Between these two extremes investors are also concerned about the extent to which changes in trade policy will alter the relative prices they face. Section 3 focuses explicitly on commitment mechanisms in trade policy.

2. Investment and Capital Flows

Africa was the first continent to integrate into the global capital market with some 70% of African private wealth shifted outside the continent between 1970 and 1990. However, it has been the last continent to attract an inward flow of investment. Recently, this has begun to change: over the period 1989–94 net investment from the Organization for Economic Cooperation and Development (OECD) economies was $8 billion, a fourfold increase over the period 1983–88. To date, however, this investment has been inward looking and confined to a small section of the world's companies that happen to have an informational advantage about Africa.

Evidence on the inward-looking nature of foreign investment to Africa comes from a survey conducted of foreign investors to five East African countries conducted in 1994. It found that virtually none had considered a location outside East Africa for their project. Presented the other way round, this shows that East Africa is not on the shortlist for internationally footloose investment projects. It was considered only for those projects that could not be located elsewhere, presumably either because of natural resources, or because the investment was intended to serve the local market. As long as this inward orientation continues, foreign investment cannot power African growth: it will be growth dependent, rather than growth generating.

Evidence on the informational segmentation of corporate investment in Africa comes from its geographic composition. Over 60% of OECD investment in Africa during 1989–94 came from just two medium-sized OECD economies, Britain and France. That investment in Africa was so skewed towards the two former main colonial powers suggests that other potential investors were deterred by a lack of knowledge. Investment in Africa appears to have been only for the cognoscenti: those firms that had long-established links with Africa, overwhelmingly British or French, were in a position to detect the improved investment climate and respond to it. Other foreign firms did not invest because of a lack of knowledge.

In these two senses Africa has yet to globalize. It is not attracting investment from a global pool of investors, and it is not attracting investment that is globally, rather than domestically oriented. The same 1994 survey found that the single most important impediment to foreign investment was the fear of policy reversal. Investors doubted that reforms would be maintained. This section discusses the nature of investor fears and how African governments can use commitment strategies to allay them.

Investor fears

If a potential investment is not profitable at current prices then it is unlikely to take place. This paper is concerned not with the policies necessary to make an investment currently profitable, but with the policies necessary to induce investment for a project that is profitable at current prices. Supposing an investment to be currently profitable, investors must still be concerned about its prospects. We can distinguish between general concerns about the performance of the economy, and specific concerns about the rights of the investor. The former are straightforward: investors fear macroeconomic instability arising from unsustainable fiscal or external deficits. The latter are more complex and can be divided into concerns about property rights, about costs and about markets.

PROPERTY RIGHTS

The investor purchases an asset that generates a stream of profits. The property rights over this asset can be attacked either directly, or via the stream of profits. Vulnerability to confiscation is the most obvious, though probably not the most important of the fears of foreign investors; at times various African governments have nationalized foreign assets, with or without compensation. Property rights can also be undermined without confiscation, for example, simply by raising taxes.

The asset will normally have greater value to the company owning it than to prospective purchasers. Hence, the company will lose not only if the asset is confiscated, but if it is forced to sell. For example, if the government withdraws permission for the company to operate, then the company will incur a loss relative to its own valuation in selling the asset. The government of Kenya recently withdrew from DHL its right to operate within Kenya and this will have imposed costs on DHL even though it is free to sell its assets and repatriate the proceeds. Property rights are thus vulnerable to arbitrary changes in competition policy.

The most obvious area of investor concern is over rights of repatriation of profits. The government can restrict such rights either by overt taxation of remitted profits or by using a multiple exchange rate, or by preventing repatriation and limiting the range of domestic financial assets in which they can be held.

In attempting to guarantee property rights to a foreign investor the government faces a time inconsistency problem. That is, once the investor has made an irreversible investment the government has an incentive to break any commitment to the rights of the investor. While the relations between any single investor and the government have this structure, the problem may be overcome if investors see themselves as a group subject to equal treatment and if there is a flow of new investment. The flow of new investors then constitutes to existing investors, then it will also discourage potential investors. The problem of time inconsistency arises either if investors do not believe that the government will treat investors equally, or if the benefits from the flow of future investment are outweighed by the benefits of consication of past investments.

The last days of the Soviet Union provide a good example of the credibility problem and how it is affected by discrimination. Gorbachev recognized that the Soviet Union had a credibility problem that was inducing investors to hold off. However, he announced to an audience of potential investors:

> Those [companies] who are with us now have good prospects of participating in our great country.. [whereas those who wait] will remain observers for years to come – *we will see to it.*
>
> (*International Herald Tribute,* 5 June 1990,
> quoted in Williamson, 1994: 187).

His solution was thus to threaten discriminatory action on the part of the

Soviet government. Yet the threat of discriminatory action may paradoxically have worsened the credibility problem. His statement in effect conceded that it was perfectly possible within the Soviet system for the government to behave in a discriminatory fashion: Gorbachev's promise was that early investors would be treated more favourably than later investors. However, if the Soviet Union was a rational agent and free to discriminate, it would end up not only breaking this promise, but reversing it: when the time came, late investors would be treated more favourably than existing investors because the latter were already captive. This, in effect, was the strategy adopted by the Mugabe government during the 1990s: the rules on the repatriation of profits were much more generous for new investors than for existing investors. Hence, there is an interaction between the time consistency problem and discriminatory behaviour.

A second factor in the time consistency problem is the rate of growth. A fast growing economy has a lower risk of confiscation than a slow growing economy because there is more investment to be deterred. The most severe problems arise in slow growing economies in which there are potentially large investments that have a high risk of failure, offset by a chance of high profitability; the main example of such investments is mining prospecting. A prospecting company depends on recouping its costs of mainly failed searches by strikes that are then highly profitable. A government in a slow growing economy may have a huge incentive to confiscate a mining discovery because it is more profitable than the damage done to future investment. Knowing this, firms will not invest in prospecting and so the government is stuck with a time consistency problem.

To summarize, property rights are less credible where the government can be discriminatory in its treatment of investors without hindrance from the law, where the rate of growth is low, and where there are high risk, lumpy investments. Thus, the government of Hong Kong, with a rising stream of small manufacturing investments and a robust legal system, faces less of a time consistency problem than, say, the government of Niger.

COSTS

A potential investor may also be deterred from a currently profitable investment by fears over rising costs. The most likely areas of concern are taxes, prices and controls. Taxation is among the leading concerns of investors in Africa. It is not that current tax rates are particularly high, but rather that their imposition is in practice often arbitrary. There are also so many temporary tax exceptions for new investors that the tax burden for long-standing investors is necessarily fairly high. The tax system thus discourages long-term investment. The one component of the tax system that is much higher in Africa than elsewhere is taxes on trade. Import duties on inputs are common, and in some countries there are also export taxes. For example, Malawi recently imposed export taxes on tobacco. Among price concerns, exchange rates and interest rates probably predominate. Real exchange rates have been highly volatile in Africa, so that an activity will switch between profitability and unprofitability. Several countries have also had a history of real and nominal interest rate shocks. The control regimes previously common in Africa imposed both costs of rationing and costs of corruption. A common complaint among businesses accords with the model of Schleiffer and Vishny: because corruption is not centralized into a "one-stop-shop", there are too many people able to stop a project for it to be viable to buy them off. This is a consequence of decentralized regulation: local governments, ministries and licensing authorities all have powers of obstruction. Such decentralized power is not in itself undesirable, and is indeed common in Western societies. However, in Africa it is less restrained by transparency and civil society. Investors fear decentralized, and therefore uncoordinated, arbitrary power.

MARKETS

Markets are heavily influenced by trade policy. Domestic markets are most obviously affected. The partial, but nevertheless large, trade liberalizations of the past decade in much of Africa have radically altered markets, exposing formerly monopolistic firms to competition. For example in Zimbabwe in the early stages of trade liberalization, only 7% of manufacturing firms regarded competition as a problem; after two years of liberalization this had risen to 36%. Conversely, the ability of firms to lobby for increased protection creates a risk for investors who use inputs that might be so protected: high cost (and possibly low quality) inputs would threaten profits. We defer consideration of these market concerns until Section 3.

Commitment strategies for macroeconomic stability

We first consider the use of commitment mechanisms to allay investor fears of macroeconomic instability. We start with two purely domestic agencies of restraint, an independent central bank and a cash budget. We then introduce two external agencies, capital account convertibility and donor conditionality, and finally the hybrid of regional convergence criteria.

INDEPENDENT CENTRAL BANK

Granting independence to the central bank is the classic way in which the government can restrain itself. The perceived effectiveness of the Bundesbank, the Federal Reserve and the Reserve Bank of New Zealand has induced a widespread move towards the institution. In 1997 the British government gave the Bank of England independence over monetary policy and the planned European Monetary Institution will extend independence to most of Europe. Many African governments have adopted legislation that devolves power onto central banks and protects the governor from dismissal. However, the evidence on the effectiveness of central bank independence in developing countries is not encouraging. Cukierman et al. (1992) found no relationship between their degree of legal independence and the rate of inflation. Rather, it was the tenure of the governor that was important, suggesting that power relationships remained personalized rather than being embedded in the legal framework. The recent shift to democracy in Africa is likely to change this, making central bank independence a reality rather than a legal fiction. However, it will take time for legally independent central banks to establish their own credibility with private agents. In the short term central banks face the same credibility problem as the government and so are not an important means for credibility enhancement. It is also likely that the penalty inflicted on the government when the central bank raises interest rates is less politically costly in Africa than in developed economies. Interest rates inflict political costs in developed countries mainly because a substantial proportion of the electorate have mortgages and blame the government if rates rise.

While a central bank may have only limited effectiveness in retaining the fiscal deficit, it may have a more important function in restraining the external deficit. For example, the Central Bank of Chile is required to limit the external deficit to below 4% of GDP, the maximum amount judged to be sustainable. Such management of external deficits may be of considerable importance in reassuring investors and so avoiding currency crises.

A final area of central bank restraint, of evident importance in view of the East Asian crisis, is on the commercial banking system. In some countries this function is hived off into an independent agency responsible for banking supervision. The advantage of such a separation of functions is that the resulting agency has a clear and limited responsibility for the probity of the banking system.

CASH BUDGET

To date the most effective domestic agency of restraint upon governments has been the cash budget. The power of this rule derives from its simplicity and its conversion of what is intrinsically a continuum into a specific quantitative target, namely a zero deficit. The principle that spending should not exceed income is readily defensible in cabinet, even though as an economic proposition it is not in fact correct. The economically correct proposition, that a deficit should not over the course of a business cycle exceed the level consistent with sustainable debt accumulation, does not produce a precise target. As a result, it does not provide a defense in cabinet against incremental spending requests.

While cash budgets have proved effective in the short term, given their lack of economic rationale it seems unlikely that they can persist as long-term restraints. They therefore gradually need to be replaced by more sustainable restraints, conceivably by independent central banks.

CAPITAL ACCOUNT CONVERTIBILITY

Capital account convertibility provides a restraint upon the government because unsustainable policies are punished by capital flight. The experiences of Britain in 1992, of Mexico in 1994 and of East Asia in 1997 demonstrate the power of this mechanism to inflict punishment. However, the very fact of these currency crises also demonstrates that governments have sometimes failed to take the threat sufficiently seriously. A few African governments have recently adopted full convertibility. Since capital controls have been ineffective, the adoption of convertibility is usually unlikely to produce transitional capital flight, although this occurred in Zambia where the adoption of convertibility preceded fiscal stabilization. Rather, the expectation would be that convertibility would lead to an initial increased inflow of capital. The potential withdrawal of this capital would then constitute the penalty-based restraint mechanism. In several economies private capital inflows have become bunched into euphoric surges that have appreciated the exchange rate and financed consumption booms.

There is clearly a need for macroeconomic management to prevent such unsustainable behaviour. One possibility is for the taxation of short-term capital flows as done in Chile. However, this carries a high cost. It signals to potential investors that the government reserves the right to tax them, and reduces the liquidity of their investment, thereby confirming investors' fears about African governments. Further, it is likely to be ineffective in practice because investors can find many illegal routes for removing capital. Potentially, any commitment to capital account convertibility could be lodged either with an extension of the remit of the International Monetary Fund, or with the World Trade Organization (WTO) role in trade in financial services.

DONOR CONDITIONALITY

Donor conditionality has been used extensively as a macroeconomic policy restraint mechanism. Governments reach agreement with the IMF on monetary targets, which are then monitored. Breaches of the targets in principle attract aid penalties both directly through IMF enhanced structural adjustment facility (ESAF) financing and indirectly through cross-conditionality between IMF programmes and the aid programmes of other donors. In practice, donor conditionality – has been quite ineffective as a means of enhancing credibility despite being the major recipient of such conditionality, Africa is rated as the riskiest continent for investment. One reason for this is that fully three-quarters of IMF ESAF programmes have missed their targets sufficiently badly for the programme to be canceled or interrupted. As a result of this history, donor conditionality now faces its own credibility problem as a restraint.

REGIONAL CONVERGENCE CRITERIA

A hybrid agency of restraint that has yet to be used in Africa is regional agreements on "convergence criteria". Such criteria have recently proved highly effective in Europe. European governments agreed on targets for fiscal deficits (3% of GDP) and for government debt (60% of GDP). As with cash budgets, there is no particular economic rationale for these precise numbers, but their promulgation has a powerful political effect for two reasons. First, the quantitative target converts something that is intrinsically a continuum into something precise. This changes the politics of incremental public expenditure. While the cost of deficits is viewed as a continuum (which is correct in terms of economics), no single proposal for additional spending can be vetoed on the grounds of the clear and unacceptable cost of an increased deficit. By contrast, once there is a quantitative target, the political costs of incremental expenditure cease to rise as a continuum but become discrete: any proposal that would push the deficit over the target incurs high political costs and so can be rejected. Second, the power of the convergence criteria rests on the fact that governments that are accepted as peers have reached agreement on them and that many of these governments will meet them. Failure to achieve the target thus signals to the domestic electorate that its government has failed on its own terms. The European agreement on convergence criteria will eventually include fiscal penalties, but these are probably incidental to effectiveness. To date there have been no fiscal penalties, yet the criteria have already radically changed fiscal behaviour as governments take painful fiscal decisions in order to achieve the targets. This demonstrates that it is the existing political penalties rather than the prospective fiscal penalties that give the institution its power.

There is scope for African governments to use their regional groupings, and indeed their continental groupings (Economic Commission for Africa, African Development Bank, Organization of African Unity) to determine convergence criteria. The fiscal and debt targets need not be the same as the European criteria, nor indeed need the coverage of an agreement include or be confined to fiscal deficits and debt. However, the principle should be that African governments would themselves agree on what constituted unacceptably bad economic policies. By delineating such policies and agreeing to avoid them, governments would build political penalties against their adoption that would reduce the perceived risk to investors. This process has dramatically reduced interest rates across Europe in the past year and it can have a similar effect on investor confidence in Africa.

Commitment strategies for investor rights

We now move from general fears about the macroeconomy to specific fears about investor rights. We consider four agencies of restraint: parliament, public insurance arrangements, credit syndication and investment charters.

PARLIAMENT

One of the concerns of investors is that they should not be disadvantaged by the more favourable treatment of subsequent investors. This is a major problem with any discretionary tax incentive system. The only concession that provides safety for an incoming investor is total tax exception, because anything less than this may be trumped by a future competitor. The governments of Ghana and Kenya have attempted to enhance the credibility of fair tax treatment by removing the ministerial right to offer tax exceptions. All tax concessions must be approved by parliament.

PUBLIC INSURANCE AGENCIES

The most direct way to cope with risks is to insure against them. However, the political and policy risks that concern investors in Africa are only to a very limited extent covered by commercial insurers. Instead, several OECD governments have created public insurance schemes for investment and exports from their countries, notably Overseas Private Investment Corporation (OPIC) in the USA and ECGD in Britain. More recently, the World Bank has created its own insurance arm, MIGA (the Multilateral Investment Guarantee Agency), building on the example of the Inter-Arab Investment Guarantee Corporation. Although ostensibly insurance arrangements, these agencies are in fact better thought of as commitment mechanisms that can be used by the host government. That is, they are agencies of restraint.

The public insurance schemes act as agencies of restraint because the government of the country receiving the investment is a party to a legal agreement that commits it to compensate the insurance company for any pay-outs. For example, OPIC recovers from host governments 80% of the money it pays out to firms on claims. OPIC thus acts as an intermediary more than an insurer. Its function as an intermediary is nevertheless valuable. Firms gain comfort from the fact that their claim will be assessed impartially and payment will not be delayed. Thus, however suspect is the legal system in the host country, or however impecunious the government, if the firm has a legitimate case it will receive swift compensation. The shifting of the task of recovering compensation from the firm to the insurance agency also increases the chances that the government will indeed pay the compensation. This works in two ways: investor coordination and cross-conditionalities.

Whereas a single firm is likely only to be in dispute once with a host government that, say, arbitrarily confiscates its assets, the insurer and the government are in a long-term relationship. If the government fails to adhere to its agreement with the insurer the insurer can refuse further business in the country. This acts as a substitute for direct coordination among future private investors. Clearly, such coordination would be impossible because most firms that will become future investors do not know that they will do so. Private firms cannot, therefore, make credible threats of investment strikes in response to government behaviour. The threat of withdrawal of insurance for future investors thus acts as an indirect coordination mechanism. Were the risks instead covered by a private competitive insurance market the insurance companies would not be able to achieve the same degree of investor coordination unless they themselves acted collectively. However, collective action among competitors encounters problems of free-riding. With political risk insurance effectively supplied only by MIGA and a few national agencies such as OPIC and ECGD, the scope for collusion is much greater.

Although this coordination of investors weakens the power of the host government, it is something that it can find valuable. The government faces a problem brought about by the lack of credibility of its own assurances to individual investors, since ex post of investor commitment, the government is in such a strong position. The main consequence of this is not that the government is able to benefit from exploiting naive foreign investors, but that it forfeits the potential benefits of investment as street-wise investors go elsewhere. Investor coordination can thus be in the interests of the host government. An analogy is the way the French government of the eighteenth century rebuilt its reputation with potential creditors after a history of bond defaults. The government itself initiated bondholder coordination by creating an officially recognized association with which it dealt. With bondholder collective action facilitated (thereby increasing bondholder power vis-a-vis the government), French government bonds became less risky and so the government was able to raise more finance.

While the public insurance agencies work in part by indirect investor coordination, their main power probably comes from cross-conditionality. Behind OPIC stands the American government with its multiple powers of enforcement, including financial flows both from the US Agency for International Development (USAID) and through diplomatic channels. Behind MIGA stands the World Bank. Cross-conditionality between insurance claims and these other relationships does not have to be explicit to be effective.

The combined effect of investor coordination and cross-conditionality is that the public insurance agencies function as effective agencies of restraint. Because they recover around 80% of claims their premiums are correspondingly much lower than the underlying nature of the risks involved and so are much lower than would be charged by a competitive private insurance market.

The public insurance agencies have three disadvantages from an African perspective. First, they do not provide cover for domestic firms. Second, they are highly selective in the business they accept. Third, partly because of highly conservative capital requirements for its guarantees, MIGA is reaching the limits of its capital.

The restriction of coverage to foreign firms clearly places domestic firms at a disadvantage. In the limit this would give rise to a situation in which African wealth was held in the OECD economies, while the African capital stock was owned by OECD-based firms. Nevertheless, African firms are able to benefit indirectly from the public insurance agencies in two ways. First, they commonly seek joint enterprises with foreign firms. Association with a foreign firm increases the security of the domestic firm vis-a-vis its own government. Second, the presence of foreign firms that have protection from government abuse of power provides some defense for domestic firms. The standards the government must adopt towards foreign firms may spill over towards its treatment of domestic firms. More interestingly, foreign firms may regard the way in which the government treats its domestic firms as a signal of its true intentions towards the business sector as a whole, and thus as a guide to their own long-term security. As a result, the government may feel constrained in its behaviour towards its captive domestic firms by the response of non-captive foreign investment. Despite these indirect benefits, if public insurance were the main agency of restraint in Africa it would clearly disadvantage domestic firms. Although this pro-foreign bias is not Africa-specific, since risk is much more important for investors in Africa than in other continents, its effect in Africa will be disproportionately great.

The public insurance agencies have been accused of "cherry picking", in effect, restricting their cover to the lowest risk propositions. One reason for this may be that their capital base does not permit them to expand their business very rapidly. The present practice is for an investment guarantee to require capital backing to the full extent of the guarantee. This highly conservative practice has led to MIGA rapidly reaching the limit of its capital base.

The combination of restriction to foreign companies and selectivity among them leaves much of the potential African investment uncovered by political risk insurance. Hence, it remains important to reduce the risks facing investors through the use of other agencies of restraint.

CREDIT SYNDICATION

Credit syndication provides a further opportunity for a restraint mechanism. It relies for its effectiveness on the same two processes used by the public insurance agencies: investor coordination and cross-conditionality. For example, when large mining houses make investments in high-risk locations they typically build syndicates of as many as 60 banks from different countries. The rationale for this is not that the mining companies need the finance, since they are often among the largest financial entities in the world. Rather, by involving the banks of many OECD countries in their investment, they seek to maximize the international damage that would be done to the host government in the event of default. First, the large network of banks provides a degree of indirect coordination among the unknown population of prospective investors. Second, there is an element of cross-conditionality both because the banks that are party to the default are less likely to lend to the government, and because they are liable to lobby their own host governments for redress. Syndication functions to orchestrate the response to a default, thereby increasing the penalties and so reducing the underlying risk. Thus, while ostensibly a *risk-sharing* mechanism, it is better regarded as a risk-reducing mechanism.

INVESTMENT CHARTERS

Recently, African governments have started to promulgate investment codes. Warner (1996) proposes the essential elements any such charter should contain: basic obligations, specific obligations and a dispute resolution mechanism. The basic obligations are of transparency, the right of establishment and the right to equal treatment. The specific obligations are the adoption of international standards with respect to compensation for expropriation; the avoidance of double taxation; prohibitions of corrupt practices; and a commitment to principles of competition, including the prohibition of cartels. There should be a binding settlement mechanism for disputes between investors and states, a model being that set out in the North American Free Trade Agreement (NAFTA) treaty. At present African investment charters do not usually meet these requirements. Several national charters have recently been issued by investment authorities, but they tend not to have independent dispute resolution mechanisms, leaving the power of interpretation with either the government itself or with national courts. There have been some investment charters at the regional level. For example, both the Economic Community of West African States (ECOWAS) and the Preferential Trade Area (PTA) include investment codes. However, these are very general and the basis for their enforcement is unclear. An alternative advocated by Warner is for African governments to sign up to multilateral investment charters. There are currently schemes for an Asia-Pacific investment code and an OECD-sponsored multilateral agreement on investment that might be lodged with the WTO. Warner suggests that African governments would gain more credibility by signing up to one of these charters than from producing one that was Africa-specific.

3. Trade Policy

We now turn from investment policy to trade policy. The need for policy commitment arrangements is particularly acute in the case of trade policy. While there have been extensive trade reforms in Africa, trade policy in most countries is still extremely restrictive. On one measure of trade policy Africa was not only classified as the region with the most restrictive trade policies, but also the distance (on this measure) between Africa and next most restrictive region, the Middle East, was less than the distance between that region and East Asia, the most open region (Dollar, 1992). The growing literature on growth regressions is unanimous in identifying trade policy as a major reason for Africa's disappointing growth performance. While the consensus on the harmfulness of African trade restrictions is growing and many countries have embarked on trade liberalization, typically in the context of structural adjustment programmes, the results have been mixed.

The main problem to date has been that progress on trade reform has often not been sustained. One of the most striking facts about African trade liberalizations is that in many cases they are reversed, either partially or wholly. Oyejide et al. (1997) document this for a sample of ten countries, seven of which experienced at least one major trade policy reversal. Trade policy reversals have undermined the confidence of private investors. As a result, the question of how governments can credibly commit themselves to trade reform has become a key policy issue.

A government with a weak reputation obviously cannot rely on self-restraint. Its policies will be seen as credible only if other institutions, internal or external agencies of restraint, effectively limit its room for manoeuvre. We consider in turn domestic commitment arrangements and four forms of external agencies of restraint: donor conditionality, North-South reciprocity, regional cooperation and the WTO. There exists a substantial literature on the effects of some of these arrangements, e.g., on the welfare effects of regional trading blocs. In this paper we focus on the effectiveness of these arrangements in locking in trade reform and hence in achieving credibility. The concern with credibility is a corollary of the evidence that uncertainty about government policies, including trade policies, is a major deterrent to private investment.

Domestic agencies of restraint

The literature on agencies of restraint on trade policy in Africa is (with the exceptions of a few passing remarks) exclusively concerned with external agencies: donors, regional groupings or multilateral institutions such as the WTO. Domestic agencies of restraint on trade policy are, of course, conceivable but have so far received little attention. By contrast, in the field of monetary policy there has been a lively discussion of the merits of independent central banks. The difference is instructive. Unlike monetary policy, trade policy is ideal for conferring benefits to particular interest groups, making it an ideal target for lobbying activity. This places demands on domestic agencies of restraint that as yet are difficult to meet. There are few countries in which the legislative and judicial branches are sufficiently independent to offer the scope for effective restraint on the executive. In particular there seems to be little scope for an effective appeal to the courts against discretionary trade policy changes in response to lobbying or bribery (see Widner, 1997). Since constitutional and judiciary reform is likely to be slow, proposals for policy commitment arrangements have focused on external agencies.

DONOR CONDITIONALITY

Donor conditionality is a possible, but far from obvious choice as an instrument for achieving credibility in trade policy. Indeed, many authors have argued that in this role conditionality can be counterproductive: the limited credibility of many African trade liberalizations may well be a consequence of donor involvement (e.g., Rodrik, 1989; Collier and Gunning, 1992; Gunning, 1994). However, the ineffectiveness of conditionality in achieving credibility is not inevitable; the effect of conditionality on credibility very much depends on the donor's objectives.

Both the bilateral donor agencies and the various multilateral aid institutions pursue multiple objectives when they attach conditions to aid. In the case of aid to Africa one of the most prominent objectives of conditionality at present is that of *inducement.* The donor uses the offer of aid to induce the recipient government to change its policies. In structural adjustment programmes this has in fact become the essence of aid; the aim of adjustment lending is to induce the government to adopt policy changes it would not have been willing to implement without the offer of aid. Indeed, structural adjustment is often analysed as a principal-agent problem with the donor (the principal) having an agenda different from that of the recipient government (the agent). The resentment generated in Africa by many adjustment programmes is a measure of the extent of divergence in objectives between the government and the donor.

Inevitably, in this case, the relationship between the donor and the recipient government is not fully consensual. Clearly, if the two sides fully agreed on the desirability of policy reforms then there would be no need for inducement. An implication is that when conditionality is used for inducement then the reforms may well be reversed subsequently: the government has an incentive to maintain the reforms only as long as this is needed to obtain the aid. Sustained reform then is *time inconsistent.* Since aid is temporary the government will have an incentive to reverse policies once the inducement is removed. Private agents who know the government's preferences will be able to infer this time inconsistency problem and will therefore consider sustained reform incredible.

By its very nature conditionality aiming at inducement is incompatible with ownership. Obviously, if the government fully owned the programme it would require no inducement.

This problem of ownership does not arise if the donor acts as an agency of restraint, in fact offering the recipient government a mechanism for "lock-in" of its policies. Such a mechanism must be based on a (credible) threat, the threat that the donor will "punish" policy reversal with reduction or cessation of aid. The essence of lock-in is that the recipient government *chooses* to reduce its own room for manoeuvre, submitting voluntarily to this form of restraint.

This aspect of voluntarism is important. There have been numerous instances of donors "punishing" African governments for policy reversals by stopping aid temporarily. However, in these instances cutting off aid was not the action of a restraint agency; punishment was a unilateral action of the donor rather than the outcome of an agreed procedure, requested by a government as a means of binding itself. When the objective of conditionality is restraint rather than inducement then what the donor tries to overcome is not the unwillingness of the government to adopt or maintain desirable policies, but rather its possible inability to do so.

If the penalty is sufficiently heavy then this will achieve lock-in and thereby credibility. Pressure on the government (or one of its successors) by interest groups to reverse trade reform can be resisted effectively if the government can credibly point out that reversal would carry unacceptably heavy penalties. The aid package agreed by the donor and the recipient would then be conditional on trade reform being maintained. Such a use of conditionality for restraint would be novel.

Aid has been remarkably unsuccessful in achieving policy change in Africa. Redesigning aid to make it function as an agency of restraint may well improve its effectiveness. Indeed, such a redesign may be attractive for donors who have become disillusioned by the perceived lack of success of traditional forms of aid. However, there are several necessary conditions for credible lock-in through aid.

First, as noted, the arrangement must be voluntary. This is best achieved by relying on self-selection. An African government perceiving a need for an external agency of restraint would take the initiative to request donors to make aid conditional on maintaining policies. Second, the imposition of the penalty (the reduction or cessation of aid) must be semi-automatic. This requires a very clear specification of the circumstances in which policy reversal is deemed to have occurred. For the mechanism to be credible there should, for example, be no room for debate about whether a particular set of trade policy changes (tariff increases or the reintroduction of quantitative restrictions call for imposition of the penalty.) Third, the mechanism can be effective only if the penalty is obviously unacceptable. This suggests that there is little scope for individual donors (with the possible exception of the World Bank or the European Union) to act as agencies of restraint. The threat that a minor donor will cut off aid may well be credible, but it will obviously not be effective. A possible solution would involve a recipient government asking its consultative group to commit itself collectively to cutting off aid in case of policy reversal. However, achieving the required degree of donor coordination may well be problematic.

It is conceivable that using conditionality for restraint would conflict with performance-based lending, which is a system where aid is conditional (ex post) on outcomes (for example, economic growth) over a period of a number of years (unlike the "short-leash" lending currently practised, which is based on high-frequency monitoring). A conflict could indeed arise if aid were conditional both on outcomes over a particular period and on the maintaining of trade liberalization throughout. For in that case a trade policy reversal would trigger an aid cut-off, irrespective of changes in outcomes. While this may be seen as a drawback, this possibility seems rather academic: if the policy measures and performance indicators are chosen sensibly, then a trade policy reversal sufficiently serious to trigger the agreed penalty will also show up (eventually) as a deterioration of the performance indicators.

While conditionality aimed at restraint avoids the problem of lack of ownership, it may suffer from two other problems that currently characterize aid to Africa: that of incommensurate penalties and that of defensive lending. The problem of incommensurate penalties arises because the larger the penalty, the more the recipient government will want to avoid it. However, at the same time the larger the penalty (relative to the infraction that triggers its imposition) the more reluctant the donor may become to impose it, feeling that the damage inflicted (e.g., a macroeconomic crisis as a result of an aid cut-off) is incommensurate with the reversal of trade reform.

This raises the issue of the credibility of the donor rather than that of the recipient. There clearly is no iron-clad solution to this problem. The objection does highlight the importance of basing enforcement on rules rather than discretion. This may be facilitated by relying on multilateral enforcement, as in the consultative group scheme suggested above. The temptation to revert to discretion is likely to be much greater in a bilateral donor-client relationship than in a multilateral framework.

The problem of defensive lending arises if the imposition of the penalty would lead to a default of the recipient government on debt service to the donor. The donor might then have an incentive to avoid imposing the penalty so that the threat to do so would not be credible. As in the previous case the problem might be mitigated by relying on multilateral rules. However, negotiating a multilateral agreement might be quite difficult (as in the case of debt relief) since donors differ in their vulnerability to a default. To take an extreme example, aid from the European Union is entirely in the form of grants but World Bank aid is in the form of loans (or International Development Association "credits").

These practical difficulties in using conditionality to help a government to restrain itself are formidable. The case of the aid provided by the EU seems the most promising, for several reasons. First, the menu approach advocated in the European Commission's Green Paper on the future of the Lomé treaty can accommodate self-selection quite naturally. Second, the European Union is a major donor in most of Africa, so that it will usually be in a position to impose sufficiently severe penalties. Further, as noted, the issue of defensive lending does not arise.

This leaves the inherent problem of incommensurability. The greater the penalty the more effective it will be if credible, but also the lower the donor's credibility. It seems doubtful whether a donor such as the EU will (even at the request of the "victim") be willing to impose punitive damages. Clearly, if the EU is not fully credible in its commitment to cutting off aid in case of policy reversal then it fails as an agency of restraint.

NORTH–SOUTH RECIPROCITY

Under donor conditionality the penalty on trade policy reversal is the loss of aid. Alternatively, the penalty can be the loss of export markets. In principle this could be achieved within an African regional grouping, a case we will consider below. However, the potential for intra-African trade (other than that involving South Africa) is still quite limited. Hence such regional groups as yet cannot impose sufficiently severe penalties.

By contrast, loss of (preferential) access to a developed country market might impose severe damages. This is the basis for a proposal in a series of papers to use North–South reciprocity to achieve lock-in of African trade reform, very much on the model of NAFTA. The European Commission's White Paper on the future of the Lome treaty takes North-South reciprocity as its preferred option in negotiating with Africa–Caribbean–Pacific (ACP) countries on their future relation with the EU.

Under this proposal an African country (or, alternatively, a group of countries) would liberalize its trade policy, gaining preferential access to the market of the European Union in return. It would achieve lock-in by agreeing beforehand that if it reversed its trade reform it would thereby automatically lose the preferential access to the EU market.

The asymmetry in a North-South arrangement makes it likely that such an arrangement would be self-enforcing. Revoking the valuable access to the European Union is a credible threat precisely because the EU has relatively little to lose and is therefore less likely to be tempted not to impose the penalty.

It is noteworthy that such a combination of asymmetry and valuable access characterized both NAFTA (which the Salinas administration saw as an effective lock-in mechanism) and the Europe agreements (which offered Eastern European countries preferential access to the EU and the prospect of full EU membership).

Obviously, the proposed mechanism can be effective only if what is at stake for the African government, the preferential access to the European market, is valuable. Since European tariffs are already quite low, there does not remain much scope for valuable tariff preferences. The main area in which Europe retains significant trade restrictions on African imports is that of agricultural products. However, the history of the negotiations between the EU and South Africa on a free trade area suggests that the EU is quite unwilling to grant significant concessions for agricultural products.

What would be quite valuable for African exporters, however, is protection from anti-dumping actions by the EU. There is wide scope for the use of such actions under WTO. Indeed, this was the price demanded by some developed countries, including the United States, for making a successful completion of the Uruguay Round possible. Where exporting involves significant set-up costs, the threat of anti-dumping actions can be a powerful deterrent to a would-be exporter. EU member countries have of course agreed not to bring anti-dumping actions against each other. Similarly, in a trade accord between the EU and Iceland the EU has recently agreed to refrain from anti-dumping against Iceland. This is the model that could be adopted to assist in locking-in African trade reform. An African country (or group of countries) electing to use the EU as external agency of restraint would be offered protection from anti-dumping, conditional on its maintaining its liberal trade policy.

An obvious objection is that such a proposal would give a new lease of life to preferential trade policy arrangements (e.g., Wang and Winters, 1997). There are two counters to this. First, as we discuss below, the multilateral alternative simply does not exist: the ties that bind an African government under WTO rules are much too loose to make its trade policy credible. Second, such an arrangement could and should be as explicitly designed as temporary, creating a window in which reforming governments can achieve credibility.

The need for this is illustrated by the evidence on risk ratings (discussed in Collier and Gunning, 1997). This suggests that there is an African dummy in the sense that the risk ratings of African countries are significantly and substantially worse than can be explained in terms of observable indicators such as GDP growth and debt ratios. There is also evidence that when policies are improved risk ratings are adjusted, but only extremely slowly. Uganda, long considered as a star performer, achieved an Institutional Investor risk rating of 20 (still quite poor) only in September 1997.

This suggests that even without policy reversals it is extremely difficult for a government to achieve credibility and to attract foreign direct investment. North-South reciprocity can then be seen as a much-needed boost in credibility, enabling a reforming government to build up a reputation much more quickly than would otherwise be possible.

Another objection, also voiced by Wang and Winters, is that preferences are typically granted for short periods and unilaterally. What is so granted can be so withdrawn: preferential treatment is unreliable and therefore fails as a lock-in device. This is an important consideration. However, it does not apply to the specific form we have proposed, namely, reciprocal concessions enshrined in a five-year treaty with the EU.

REGIONAL TRADE BLOCS

A regional trade bloc, operating as a free trade area or as a common market, can also function as an agency of restraint, based on reciprocal preferential market access. Indeed, this is the form that many developed countries have used to achieve lock-in of liberal trade policies. The European common market, for example, is based on a system of (implicit) reciprocal threats: a member country introducing trade restriction would immediately face retaliation. African regional groups can adopt the same system where breach of the rules by any member would lead to expulsion from the group and hence to loss of preferential access to the markets of the other member countries. However, as we have already noted above, this penalty would be unlikely to be sufficiently severe to deter policy reversal since in Africa intra-regional trade is as yet very modest (Foroutan, 1993; Oyejide et al., 1999).

This is not to say that regional integration in Africa cannot contribute effectively to enhanced credibility of trade policy, but rather that this will take time. The present acute need for a *rapid* improvement in credibility can in our view not be met in this way.

WTO

The WTO offers two alternative ways of achieving lock-in. First, the WTO is in fact set up as an external agency of restraint: a member country binds itself by accepting the GATT/WTO provisions. This is the aspect of the WTO that is usually emphasized in discussion of Africa's role in the world economy. Unfortunately, a major limitation of the WTO is that it does not restrain trade policy very much. Notably, foreign exchange rationing, until recently the preferred trade policy instrument of many African governments, is in fact legal under WTO rules. Hence the WTO is of limited use to a reforming African government wishing to bind itself. Similarly, the WTO offers little defense against developed countries' protectionism. We have already noted above that there is wide scope for anti-dumping actions under WTO. However, there are some precedents for extending policy binding to non-tariff concerns.

What the WTO does offer is dispute settlement procedures. Since the Uruguay Round these have become faster and (while still extremely expensive in terms of legal costs) more accessible for developing countries. There is evidence that use of these procedures by these countries is increasing rapidly (Keyzer and Merbis, 1997).

The second way in which lock-in can be achieved through the WTO is through the traditional GATT process of reciprocal concessions. Usually it is implicitly assumed that this route offers little to Africa. Wang and Winters (1997) have recently shown that this view is mistaken. African countries have negotiating rights (entitling them to initiate negotiations) on a substantial part of their exports to the EU. Under the GATT "request and offer system" country A can request country B to reduce a tariff on one of A's exports (in return, of course, for a reciprocal concession on a tariff imposed by A on one of B's exports) only if A is the principal supplier of that good to country B. This system would seem very much to favour large countries: they would have the right to initiate negotiations even for goods that in relative terms were unimportant to them, accounting for a small proportion of their total exports.

Wang and Winters (1997, Table 3) have investigated whether this in fact dooms African exporters to passivity in future trade negotiations. Interestingly, they find that many African countries are principal suppliers of at least some goods and, more importantly, that these goods account for a substantial part of their exports. These goods are therefore relatively important to the exporter. However, rather surprisingly, where African countries are the principal supplier they often account for a large part of European imports. This suggests that African exporters may have considerable leverage. In some of these cases substantial tariffs still remain. Hence there are unsuspected and unexploited opportunities for Africa in future negotiations.

"By offering suitable reciprocal concessions they should be able to achieve significant liberalizations in these areas" (Wang and Winters, 1997: 3). Eventually this could lead to lock-in as an exporters lobby for maintained liberalization would develop. This is likely to be a slow process, however.

WTO participation therefore involves two serious limitations. First, the discipline it imposes is still quite weak. Second, the negotiating process at the heart of the WTO cannot offer African countries the rapid improvement in credibility that at present they urgently need.

4. Conclusion

Africa currently faces a credibility problem that is deterring investment. This is particularly severe in the areas of macroeconomic policy, investor rights and trade policies. If an African government maintains good polices in these three areas it will, over time, overcome the credibility problem. The question we have posed in this paper is whether this process can be accelerated by the use of commitment mechanisms. We have reviewed a variety of agencies of restraint. Many of these are potentially useful for Africa. There is particular scope for hybrid agencies that involve cooperation between African governments, sometimes in conjunction with OECD governments. There is scope for the gradual evolution of purely domestic agencies from the present heavy reliance upon cash budgets to reliance upon independent central banks. There is also scope for greater use of instant restraints, notably capital account convertibility.

In the field of trade policy we have suggested that some possible agencies of restraint can be effective only after a long delay. This would apply to domestic agencies of restraint that require constitutional changes and reform of the courts. It would also apply to reliance on reciprocal concessions within the WTO. Africa has made little use of the WTO. Active membership would offer the form of restraint that has proved most effective in restraining the trade policies of developed countries. We have stressed that African countries not only have much to gain from the WTO negotiating process but actually have substantial leverage. While this route must be followed it does not offer the quick improvement in credibility that African countries now most need.

Donor conditionality has often made trade reform time inconsistent. It has thereby undermined credibility. Donors could make a useful contribution by abandoning the current counterproductive form of conditionality.

We have suggested that conditionality can strengthen credibility if it is aimed at restraint rather than inducement. The European Union is in a position to function in this positive role, as an external agency of restraint for African countries that would self-select participation in such a system. In this case aid would be conditional on sustained trade reform. We have expressed some doubts about the credibility of the EU cutting off aid in the case of trade policy reversal.

North–South reciprocity would involve reciprocal preferential access between Europe and an African country or regional bloc. We have suggested that preferential access of Africa to the European market might take the form of a temporary safeguard against anti-dumping actions. While this is not a mechanism for achieving long-run lock-in, it is at present the most promising option for a quick improvement in trade policy credibility. The evidence on risk ratings indicated that such a quick improvement is highly desirable.

Agencies of restraint may collectively be effective in accelerating the improvement in risk assessments, and so raise investment rates. However, two important questions remain unresolved. The first is which agencies are most effective in which environments. Some agencies, such as cash budgets, are probably effective initially but are not sustainable. Others, such as independent central banks, may gradually accumulate effectiveness. The second question concerns the trade-off between rules and discretion. Rules inflict some costs on the economy because they limit the ability of the government to respond to unanticipated circumstances. Further, it may be that the only rules that are sufficiently simple to be politically feasible are unable to accommodate shocks and so inflict high real costs to shock-prone economies. A classic unresolved trade-off of this type is between fixed and flexible exchange rates. The current trend in policy outside Africa, however, is to shift more policy choices from discretion to regulation, often in the context of their internationalization. African governments may find that if they choose not to participate in this trend they will further marginalize their economies.

Notes

1 We see Wang and Winters (1997) for a survey of the evidence for Africa on the detrimental effects of trade restrictions. Collier and Gunning (1997) give a survey of

growth regressions estimates and discuss the various trade policy measures used in that literature.

2 We have argued elsewhere (Collier et al., 1997a) that inducement conflicts with each of the other four possible objectives of conditionality: with paternalism, selectivity, restraint and signaling. While the use of conditionality for inducement has generally been ineffective, it has an opportunity cost in terms of these other objectives.

3 One indication that private agents attach low credibility to conditionality as currently practised is the finding of Rodrik (1996) that agreements with the IMF *reduce* private capital flows.

4 It may be noted that in the case of inducement, aid is used by the principal (the donor) to ensure that a policy is *adopted* by the agent (the recipient government), while in the case of restraint the objective is that an existing policy is *maintained*. However, it would be wrong to see restraint as negative inducement. The essential difference is that the relationship between the two parties is fully consensual in the latter case, but not in the former.

5 Since here we consider donor conditionality the penalty would be the loss of aid. Another possibility would be the loss of access to the donor's market. This case we consider below.

6 Such redesign of conditionality has been proposed as a possible option on a "menu" of a future Lomé treaty. The idea is that aid from the European Union to the ACP countries would not necessarily take this form, but that countries that wanted to use the EU as an agency of restraint could choose this option from the menu. Hence restraint would be entirely based on self-selection. See, e.g. Collier et al., (1997).

7 For a detailed discussion of performance-based lending, see Collier et al. (1997a).

8 For example, Fine and Yeo (1994), Collier and Gunning (1995a/b), Collier et al. (1997).

9 This is an important difference with the use of conditionality as a restraint mechanism. In that case the "North" (i.e., the donor) may indeed be tempted not to impose the penalty because he does have much at stake: the debt service on pervious loans. As noted above, this may lead to defensive lending.

10 Indeed, as Wang and Winters (1997: 24) point out" Africa faces lower bound tariffs on average than other developing countries – i.e., its exports are concentrated, on average, on low-tariff products – and the differences are all significant.

11 Such protection would be politically feasible only if offered for a limited period. We have suggested elsewhere (Collier et al., 1997) that this type of North–South reciprocity might be one of the options in a future Lomé treaty. The anti-dumping protection would then be automatically limited to the period of the treaty, probably five years.

References

Baldwin, R.E. 1997. "The causes of regionalism". CEPR Discussion Paper No. 1599, March.

Collier, P., D. Greenaway and J.W. Gunning. 1997. "Evaluating trade liberalization: A methodological framework". In A. Oyejide, I. Elbadawi and P. Collier, eds., *Regional Integration and Trade Liberalization in Sub-Saharan*

Africa. Volume 1: Framework, Issues and Methodological Perspectives. Basingstoke and London: Macmillan.

Collier, P., P. Guillaumont, S. Guillaumont and J.W. Gunning. 1997. The future of Lomé: Europe's role in African growth". *The World Economy,* vol. 20: 285–05.

Collier, P., P. Guillaumont, S. Guillaumont and J.W. Gunning. 1997a. Redesigning conditionality". Forthcoming in *World Development.*

Collier, P. and J.W. Gunning. 1992 "Aid and exchange rate adjustment in African trade liberalizations". *Economic Journal,* vol. 102: 925–39.

Collier, P. and J.W. Gunning. 1995. "Trade policy and regional integration: Implications for the relations between Europe and Africa". *The World Economy,* vol. 18: 387–410.

Collier, P. and J.W. Gunning. 1995a. "Restraint, cooperation and conditionality in African trade policy". Paper presented at the XIth World Congress of the International Economic Association, Tunis.

Collier, P. and J.W. Gunning, 1997. "Explaining African economic performance". CSAE Discussion Paper.

Dollar. 1992. "Outward-oriented developing economies really do grow more rapidly: Evidence from 95 LDCS 1976–86". *Economic Development and Cultural Change,* vol. 40: 523–44.

Fine, J. and S. Yeo. 1994. "Regional integration in sub-Saharan Africa: Dead end or a fresh start?" Mimeo. AERC.

Foroutan, F. 1993. "Regional integration in sub-Saharan Africa: Past experience and future prospects". In J. de Melo and A. Panagariya, eds., *New Dimensions in Regional Integration.* Cambridge: Cambridge University Press, for the CEPR.

Gunning, J.W. 1994. "Trade reform in Africa: The role of donors". In J.W. Gunning, H. Kox, W. Tims and Y. de Wit, eds., *Trade, Aid and Development: Essay in Honour of Hans Linnemann.* Basingstoke and London: Macmillan.

Kezyer, M. and M. Merbis. 1997. "GATT/WTO: the record since the Marrakesh 1994 agreement". Forthcoming in *De Economist.*

Oyejide, A., B. Ndulu and J.W. Gunning. 1999. "Regional integration and trade liberalization: Evidence from country case studies. Introduction and Overview". In A. Oyejide, B. Ndulu and J.W. Gunning, eds., *Regional Integration and Trade Integration and trade Liberalization in sub-Saha-*

ran Africa. Volume 2: Country Case Studies. Basingstoke and London: Macmillan.

Oyejide, A., I. Elbadawi and S. Yeo., eds. 1999. *Regional Integration and Trade Liberalization in sub-Saharan Africa. Volume 3: Regional Case Study.* Basingstoke and London: Macmillan.

Rodrik, D. 1989. "Credibility of trade reform: A policymaker's guide. *The World Economy,* vol. 12: 1–16.

Rodrik, D. 1996. Why is there multilateral lending?" In M. Bruno and B. Pleskovitc, eds., *Annual World Conference on Development Economics 1995.* Supplement to the *World Bank Economic Review.*

Wang, Z.K. and L.A. Winters. 1997. "Africa and the global economy". AERC Plenary paper, Nairobi, May; *Journal of African Economies,* AERC *Supplement,* vol. 7, sup. 1, June 1998: 37–69.

Widner, J. 1997. "The courts as restraints". Forthcoming in P. Collier and C. Pattillo, eds., *Risk and Agencies of Restraint: Reducing the Risk of African Investment.* London: Macmillan.

Chapter eleven

Capacity Building Implications of Enhanced African Participation in Global Trade Rules-Making and Arrangements

by John F.E. Ohiorhenuan, United Nations Development Programme, New York

Acknowledgements

The assistance of Bamidele Thomas and Lily Ohiorhenuan in writing this paper is gratefully acknowledged. I also acknowledge the comments of Minh Pham, Lynn Mytelka, Walter Kennes, Cecil Taffe, Charles Gore and participants at the AERC Accra workshop on an earlier draft. The views expressed here are mine alone and do not reflect the views of the United Nations Development Programme.

1. Introduction

The General Agreement on Tariffs and Trade (GATT) was created in 1947 in the expectation that it would soon be incorporated into a proposed International Trade Organization (ITO) that would regulate key aspects of international trade. However, when several countries failed to ratify the ITO charter, the organization did not come into existence. But the idea of creating a more open multilateral trading system remained and GATT assumed the role of bringing countries together in a series of negotiations towards greater liberalization of world trade[1].

Over 50 years, eight "rounds" of talks were conducted under the auspices of GATT. The final round was the Uruguay Round, launched in 1986 in Punta del Este, Uruguay (hence the name), and formally concluded in April 1994 in Marakesh, Morocco. The Uruguay Round marked a watershed in international trade relations, consolidating multilateral agreements relating to trade in goods, bringing trade in services under international discipline for the first time, adopting an agreement relating to intellectual property rights, securing further liberalization of trade in general, and establishing the World Trade Organization (WTO). Under this new trade regime, countries acceding to WTO membership are expected to adopt national legislation and regulations to implement the three major agreements (on goods, services and intellectual property rights). They are also committed to continuing negotiations for further trade liberalization under the aegis of the WTO.

This paper is concerned with the capacity building implications of the new trade regime for African countries. Specifically, it seeks to determine the human and institutional capacities that would enhance the effectiveness of participation by African countries in global trade rules-making and the capacities that would permit these countries to take better advantage of the opportunities offered under the new global trade regime.

The first part of the paper reviews the process and content of the Uruguay Round, highlighting the factors that may have constrained full and effective African participation. The second part examines the capacity building implications of the rights and obligations of African countries under the expanded multilateral rules and disciplines of the WTO. An attempt is also made to provide a heuristic tool for determining capacity building requirements more systematically in the context of the long-term adjustment imperatives of the new trade regime.

2. Africa and the Uruguay Round

Antecedents to the Uruguay Round

The early rounds of multilateral trade negotiations tended to focus on tariff reductions for specific products. This product-by-product approach to negotiation in these rounds inevitably resulted in limited reduction in tariffs in the early days. In the five separate rounds held between 1947 and 1962,[2] overall tariff was reduced by only 35%. However, the Kennedy

Round (1962–67) and the Tokyo Round (1973–79) significantly broadened the agenda for trade liberalization and introduced further substantial tariff reductions. As a result, average tariffs were down from 40% at the end of the 1940s to about 5% in 1991 (Konate, 1994).

The Tokyo Round negotiations also focused for the first time on reductions in non-tariff barriers (NTBS). A code of conduct was prescribed for signatories in order to reduce the restrictive and unpredictable effect of non-tariff barriers. These codes included an agreement on government procurement, uniformity in the application of duties in countervailing and anti-dumping cases, as well as standards drawn on customs valuation and import licensing practices. Furthermore, a general system of preferences (GSP) was established to accord selected exports of developing countries preferential treatment in developed country markets.

Despite these considerable achievements, several critical issues remained unaddressed. First, protectionism had increased in many industrial countries mostly through a proliferation of various forms of NTBS, such as the Multi-Fibre Agreement and voluntary export restraints. Second, previous rounds had failed to address some critical issues of protectionism, especially regarding trade in agriculture and services. Services in particular had increasingly become a major item of international trade, particularly among developed economies, but had been completely excluded in all prior GATT negotiations. In the case of agriculture, major developed economies had traditionally provided a high level of subsidy and, projecting the sector as "sensitive", had essentially kept it off the negotiation agenda. By the 1980s, however, it had become necessary to address this issue in order to preempt the growing danger of a large-scale agricultural trade war in the global economy.

Third, the dispute settlement mechanism had proved to be largely ineffective, since parties to trade disputes could ultimately block any settlement recommendations reached. Also, even at the initial procedural stages, the requirement of consensus in order to advance from one stage to another inevitably resulted in sluggish dispute settlement proceedings. To address some of these outstanding problems, the Uruguay Round of multilateral trade negotiations was launched in September 1986. At its conclusion in April 1994, it had achieved many of its initial objectives and made significant inroads in other areas as well.

Main results of the Uruguay Round

The results of the Uruguay Round in strengthening the legal and institutional framework for international trade may be summarized under five broad headings:

- General Agreement on Tariffs and Trade (GATT 1994) and associated agreements regarding trade in goods.
- General Agreement on Trade in Services (GATS).
- Agreement on Trade-Related Aspects of Intellectual Property Rights (TRIPS).
- Plurilateral agreements on civil aircraft, government procurement, dairy agriculture and bovine meat.
- Marrakesh agreement establishing the World Trade Organization (WTO).

The first three agreements have been collectively referred to as the "multilateral agreements" and members of the newly-created WTO are obliged to enact them within their national legislations and implement them as stipulated. These agreements together with the related "understandings and decisions"[3] form the core of the multilateral trading system. The plurilateral agreements were negotiated on a voluntary basis within GATT and apply only to those members of the WTO who choose to accede to them.

The establishment of the WTO is perhaps the single most critical outcome of the Uruguay Round. With its entry into force on 1 January 1995, it took on all prior agreements and arrangements reached under GATT – without exception. In what is known as the Single Undertaking Rule, all member countries are committed to abiding by the terms of the multilateral agreements. Furthermore, the conference or round-based mode of trade negotiations was replaced by a permanent membership-based forum for continuous negotiation on multilateral trade issues.

The entire framework of GATT, which was strengthened considerably in the Uruguay Round, is based on four basic rules (ITC/UNCTAD/WTO and Commonwealth Secretariat, 1995). First, the principle of protection through tariffs prohibits the use of quantitative restrictions except in a limited number of situations. Second, under the principle of reduction and "binding" of tariffs, countries are expected to reduce and possibly eliminate tariffs, and to commit to binding the tariff against further increases. Furthermore, countries are urged to eliminate NTBS, converting these, where necessary, to tariffs (so-called tariffication).[4] The tariff equivalent of non-tariff measures was calculated on the basis of the average world market price for the product subject to non-tariff measures and its guaranteed price in the importing countries. Tariff rates resulting from tariffication as well as tariffs applicable to other products have been bound against further increase. Third, the non-discrimination rule enjoins countries to extend to all other countries equal treatment in the application of trading rules (most-favoured-nation [MFN] treatment).[5] Fourth, the national treatment rule prohibits countries from treating imports less favourably than equivalent domestically produced goods. Thus, for example, higher sales taxes or other levies cannot be charged on imports.

One of the more significant achievements regarding trade in goods was the agreement relating to agriculture. Prior to the Uruguay Round, agriculture was one of the more heavily protected areas of trade, with average levels of protection[6] reaching almost 80 in developed countries in 1986 (Ingco, 1995). More than most other areas of trade, protection of agricultural goods was significantly broader and more varied, with restrictions being applied both at the border through tariff and non-tariff measures and through the internal use of export subsidies and price guarantees. With the agreement on agriculture concluded in the Uruguay Round, all participating countries now have scheduled commitments in quantitative terms that define what they can and cannot do in the areas of market access, domestic support and export subsidies. Table 11.1 presents an overview of the main agreements in each area.[7]

Regarding market access, all border NTBS are to be "tariffied". Tariffs on agricultural products will be reduced on average by 36% in the case of developed countries and 24% in the case of developing countries, with minimum reduction in each tariff line of 15% and 10%, respectively. Developed countries are to achieve the tariff reductions over a period of six years, while developing countries have ten years to do so.

As many of the duties resulting from tariffication will be at levels that would effectively ban imports, it was also agreed to provide quantitative guarantees of minimum market access. Tariff quotas were established in cases where imports constitute less than 3% of domestic consumption, with

Table 11.1: Liberalization commitments in agriculture

	Market access		Domestic subsidies	Export subsidies	
	Prices	Quantities		Oulays	Quantities
Developed reduction countries	Tariffication and tariff reductions of 36% over 6 yrs	Tariff quotas for 3% of domestic consumption, rising to 8% after 5 yrs	20% reduction in aggregate in 6 yrs	34% reduction in 6 yrs	21% in 6 yrs
Developing reduction countries	Tariffication and tariff reductions of 24% over 10 yrs	None	13.3% reduction in 10 yrs	24% reduction in 10 yrs	14% in 10 yrs
Least developed countries	None	None	None	None	None

Source: Agosin et al. (1995, Table 2).

this access rising to 8% after five years. Special safeguards against import surges or persistent import price declines were also agreed for tariffied products.

With regard to domestic subsidies, the agreement excluded from reduction commitments domestic assistance measures that have minimal impact on trade (the "green box" measures). These measures include government assistance for research, pest or disease control, infrastructure, and food security, as well as direct payments in the framework of environmental or regional assistance programmes. All other domestic support measures were included in the so-called -"aggregate measures of support" and are to be reduced by 20% over six years for developed countries and 13.3% for developing countries over ten years.

In the case of export subsidies, developed countries are to reduce the budget for such subsidies by 36% over six years from the average level prevailing in 1986–90. Subsidized quantities are also to be reduced by 21%

Table 11.2: Tariff reductions on industrial products by developed countries*

Origin of imports	Weighted average tariff (%)		
	Pre-UR	Post-UR	% reduction
Developed	6.3	3.9	38
Developing (exc LLDCs)	6.8	4.3	37
Least developed countries	6.8	5.1	25

* All industrial products, exluding petroleum.

Source: Rodrick (1995, Table 2).

over the same period. For developing countries, the subsidy reduction requirements are two-thirds of the developed country requirements and are to be implemented over ten years.

Unlike agriculture, industrial products had been subject to continual tariff liberalization in the seven previous rounds held under GATT. As a result, tariffs on many industrial product categories were much lower than in other areas of trade at the onset of the round. While the Uruguay Round has followed in the footsteps of previous rounds in further reducing tariffs and extending binding commitments on industrial goods, the major contribution and emphasis of the round has been on liberalizing non-tariff restrictions to trade in the sector. Of particular significance are the commitments made in the areas of quotas on textiles and clothing, and general subsidies on industrial products.

The Uruguay Round reduced average tariffs on industrial products in developed countries from to 6.3% to 3.9% (see Table 11.2). However, tariffs remained somewhat higher on imports from developing countries owing to the generally higher tariffs on textiles, clothing, and fish and fish products. For industrial imports from developing countries and LDCs, the Uruguay Round reduced tariffs from 6.8% to 4.3% and 5.1%, respectively (see Table 11.2).

More significant, perhaps, than the tariff reductions are the increases in the extent of bindings. Prior to the Uruguay Round, developing countries had on average 22% of their industrial tariff lines bound, and only 14% of their industrial imports came in under bound rates. These ratios have now increased to 72% and 59%, respectively. For developed countries the propor-

Table 11.3: Pre and post Uruguay Round tariff bindings for industrial products*

	Import value ($ billion)	% of tariff lines bound		Percentage of imports under bound rates	
Country groups		Pre-UR	Post-UR	Pre-UR	Post-UR
Developed countries	737.2	78	99	94	99
Developing countries	36.2	22	72	14	59
Countries in transition	34.7	73	98	74	96

* Excluding fuels

Source: Rodrick (1995, Table 4).

tions of tariff lines bound and of import under bound rates was raised to 99% from 78% and 94%, respectively (see Table 11.3).

Duty-free access for industrial imports to both developed and developing countries also increased considerably. Once the Uruguay Round concessions are implemented, duty-free access by developing countries will increase from 12% to 37% of the value of imports into the United States, from 24% to 36% of imports into European Union, and from 25% to 48% of imports into Japan (UNCTAD, 1994: 34). The degree of tariff escalation has also decreased as a result of significant tariff cuts at all processing stages.

The Uruguay Round also provided for the phase-out of the Multi-Fibre Agreements (MFA) by 1 January 2005. This arrangement had been used by developed countries to protect their textile sectors by imposing quotas on imports from developing countries. Under the Agreement on Textiles and Clothing, MFA restrictions will be phased out in four stages, eventually to be subject to rules governing industrial products.

Two agreements regarding the use of non-tariff measures are particularly significant. The Agreement on Subsidies and Countervailing Measures has, for the first time, extended the prohibition on the use of subsidies to developing countries, which have been given a transitional period of eight years to modify their existing subsidy regime.[8] In the Agreement on Safeguards, the application of such measures as voluntary export restraints (VER) has been prohibited and anti-dumping rules have been further clarified. The safeguard agreement elicited a commitment to eliminate all

VERS except one, within four years.[9] The anti-dumping clarifications help to determine more clearly when a product is being "dumped" and the necessary procedures to be followed by importing/exporting countries to pursue retaliatory or remedial action (i.e., restriction through tariffs, anti-dumping or countervailing duties).

The General Agreement on Trade in Services (GATS) was predicated on the fact that trade in services, unlike commodities, requires proximity between suppliers and consumers. Accordingly, the Uruguay Round's approach was to focus on regulatory barriers. The agreement defines trade in service sectors, under the following four categories: (1) consumption abroad of services; (2) cross-border supply of services; (3) movement of labour; and (4) establishment of commercial presence in conjunction with the provision of services. The agreement extends to services the general GATT principles and obligations to which all WTO member countries are expected to adhere. Key provisions include the following:

- *Extending MFN treatment to trade in services:* All countries are required to extend commitments made in services to all WTO member countries, with some exceptions provided in the case of regional agreements.
- *Promoting transparency in regulations governing services:* In order to facilitate greater transparency in trade of services, countries are required to establish one or more enquiry points from which other members can obtain information on national regulations in service areas of interest. Developed countries specifically are urged to establish contact points from which service exporters from least developed countries can obtain information on regulations more easily than through the general enquiry points.
- *Rules governing monopolies and exclusive services as well as other business practices restraining competition:* Members are discouraged from exercising monopoly power or using other means of restraining competition in a manner inconsistent with general obligations and specific sectoral commitments.
- *Increasing the participation of exporters from developing countries in the trade of services:* This provision calls on countries to provide greater access for developing country exporters of services

> through such means as the improvement of access to distribution channels and information networks. It also accepts the use of relatively higher protection in developing countries' service sectors as a means of strengthening domestic service capacities.

In addition to these general obligations, individual countries submitted schedules listing specific commitments to liberalization in selected service sectors or subsectors. But perhaps the most significant dimension of GATS is that it laid the framework for initiating future negotiation on trade in services within the multilateral system.

The Agreement on Trade-Related Aspects of Intellectual Property Rights (TRIPS) establishes minimum standards of protection for each category of intellectual property rights. They incorporate and extend to all WTO members the substantive obligations of the World Intellectual Property Organization (WIPO) as well as the Berne and Paris conventions on copyright and industrial property, respectively. They also include the setting of standards on categories of IPRS lacking these (i.e., patents, industrial designs and trademarks), setting of disciplines relating to the enforcement of IPRS and providing an effective dispute settlement mechanism for resolving IPR issues.

From the time WTO became operational, developed countries were allowed one year to meet obligations, developing countries five years and least developed countries, 11 years, with the possibility of an extension. A key feature of the agreement on TRIPS is the requirement that all signatories provide effective procedures within their national laws for the protection and enforcement of IPRS for holders of these such as private enterprise.

The Dispute Settlement Understanding (DSU) incorporates major improvements in the dispute settlement mechanism. A very important change is the elimination of the requirement of consensus for the adoption of panel rulings. This cumbersome system had significantly hindered the effectiveness of the previously existing GATT mechanism since any one country opposing the decision could block rulings by dissent. A consensus will exist instead only to halt proceedings from advancing at any stage so that the potential for procedural blockage is much less reduced. Rulings, once made, are also to be reviewed by an independent body before a panel's recommendations become legally binding.

In order to hasten the process itself, shorter time limits for each stage of the procedure have also been introduced. Finally, whereas dispute settlement procedures had formerly been established under individual agreements (on trade in goods, etc.), the Uruguay Round provides for the incorporation of all these into a single body, the Dispute Settlement Body, to be administered under the auspices of the WTO. This ensures that dispute settlement will be a major component of future trade negotiations within the multilateral trading system.

The decision on trade-related investment measures (TRIMS) applies some GATT rules to recipients of foreign direct investment. Like the TRIPS agreement, it established minimum commitments in the area of trade related investment flows by prohibiting countries from using the following five basic categories of TRIMS: local content requirements, domestic manufacturing and trade balancing requirements, foreign exchange restrictions, and domestic sales requirements. Effectively, the TRIMS bar the use of basic types of quantitative restrictions often imposed on investors by recipient countries. Developed and developing countries are granted adjustment periods of one year and five years, respectively, to comply with these provisions, while least developed countries are granted a seven-year transition period.

The Trade Policy Review Mechanism (TPRM) has been given permanent status in the WTO, extending the mandate provisionally granted in 1989 following the midterm review of the negotiations held in Montreal. The main objectives of the TPRM are to contribute to improved adherence by all members to rules, disciplines and commitments made under the multilateral trade agreement, by achieving greater transparency in and understanding of the trade policies and practices of members.

The TPRM also provides for a Trade Policies Review Body (TPRB) to examine regularly the trade policies and practices of WTO members, every two years for the four major traders (European Union, USA, Japan and Canada), every four years for the next 16 leading traders, and every six years for the remaining traders. The TPRB will also carry out an annual overview of developments in the international trading environment, assisted by an annual report by the director-general, setting out major activities of the WTO and highlighting significant policy issues affecting the trading system. By placing member countries' trade under regular scrutiny, the trade policies review process induces each country to examine carefully the structure and impact that these policies have on its domestic economy.

In summary, it may be useful to identify the opportunities and challenges that Africa faces in the new trade regime:

- The reduction of MFN tariffs as the result of the Uruguay Round presents African economies with both opportunities and risks. Opportunities come in the form of lower barriers to entry into export markets. Increased exports of traditional farm produce (especially tropical) and of products extracted from natural resources may result, because of improved access to developed country markets. However, the remaining tariff escalation in agriculture and mining may still place a significant burden on the industrial upgrading efforts of developing countries that are heavily dependent on the exports of raw materials and agricultural products. Moreover, the lowering of tariffs may put competitive pressure on exports from some sectors whose access was hitherto facilitated by preferential tariffs under the GSP and the Lomé Convention. Without the price advantage facilitated by the preferences, some African countries may not be able to maintain their market shares, and hence may experience a loss of export revenue. This risk must not be overestimated, however. Experience has indicated that most preferential tariffs have not been fully utilized in the past.
- Other short-term effects are expected as a result of the reform process in agriculture and those concerning intellectual property rights. The reform process in agriculture could lead to higher prices for basic food products and therefore involve transitional cost in terms of higher import bills for low-income food-deficit African countries. In recognition of this, the Uruguay Round agreements provided for food aid plus some financial and technical assistance to improve agricultural productivity. In addition, the broader and stricter patent protection may result in higher prices for high technology and pharmaceutical products.
- In the context of global integration through the WTO, regional trade and investment integration within Africa is also likely to present both risks and opportunities. On the opportunity side, regional trade and investment integration may provide an avenue for a much needed diversification of the export base of African

countries and a market around which to create economies of scale. On the risk side, as trade implies some degree of specialization, regional integration may also require a degree of domestic restructuring and policy harmonization, which are not costless.

- The TRIMS decision represents a further loss of policy options for sub-Saharan African countries. In the shortrun, however, these countries will not have to make the adjustments entailed by the agreement since liberalization of investment policies is an integral component of their current structural adjustment programmes. Ultimately, the loss or gain to developing countries of the TRIMS decision will depend principally on whether open investment regimes will provide the economic benefits as expected.
- The Uruguay Round agreements place additional limits on the policy discretion of African countries, for example, with the new constraints on industrial policy arising from the agreement on subsidies. On the other hand, as Rodrick (1995) has observed, the WTO represents a real asset as a "commitment technology" for reformist governments to lock in policy reforms and render them irreversible. With the mix of risks and opportunities created by the new rules of the multilateral and growing regional trading systems, African countries must recognize that while the fundamental policy problem of constrained optimization has not changed, the parameters and boundary conditions have changed. Accordingly, African policy makers need more than ever to be well informed about the implications of the new trade regime and the obligations and privileges of membership in order to make the right decisions.

The likelihood of considerable adjustment pressures on developing countries, and in particular LDCS (33 out of the 48 are in Africa), was recognized at the Marrakesh Ministerial Meetings in 1994. As a result, the Uruguay Round agreements incorporated a range of measures for staggering the adjustment process in order to minimize its costs. It may be noted, however, that while compliance by the LDC members is obligatory, the provisions for technical assistance to them in mitigating adjustment costs are mainly discretionary.[10]

Constraints on African participation in the Uruguay Round

Perhaps the only two possible generalizations about African countries' participation are, first, that it was uneven, and, second, that overall the level of participation was considerably higher than in previous rounds. Of the 119 participants in the negotiations, 36 were African countries. However, considering that GATT contracting parties were automatically regarded as participants, real participation was significantly less. Indeed, according to Konate (1994), only 12 African countries[11] played an effective role by virtue of their presence in Geneva.

There is also a perception among some developing country observers (e.g., Ragahavan, 1990) that the Uruguay Round was unbalanced and weighted against the Third World both in the plethora of issues for negotiations and in the agenda. Moreover, there are indications that the negotiating process was less than fully transparent. Informal agreements on the most critical issues were reached in the "Green Room"[12] consultations. Since participation in these consultations was by invitation only, it was not difficult for the process to be scheduled in favour of the more powerful (mainly industrialized) countries.

The playing field was also uneven in another sense. While the intergovernmental negotiations were private and the documentations restricted, the delegations of the major powers incorporated all necessary expertise, including senior executives of transnational corporations as advisers. In the case of the United States, for example, Cargill, a major player in global agricultural trade, exerted a strong influence on the Uruguay Round negotiations on agriculture. According to Ritchie (1996), a senior Cargill executive takes credit for being "one of the principal architects of the US proposal". He had written the Reagan Administration's proposal and was later hired to be its chief negotiator. American Express was also involved and was influential in the GATS treaty. Certainly, for most African countries, such support was not available.

In general, effective participation of African countries in the Uruguay Round negotiations was constrained by inadequate understanding of the complexity of issues to be negotiated, including a dearth of in-depth analysis of the implications of various proposals for their national interests, and a weak institutional structure for remaining on top of developments in the negotiations. In an attempt to correct for these weaknesses African countries had sought international assistance at the beginning of the round. The evidence suggests that some modest gains were obtained but that the weaknesses were still quite deep. Some of this evidence may be found in the evaluation study of a UNDP/UNCTAD project launched in 1987 to support sub-Saharan African countries in the trade negotiations. The objectives of the project, which was developed in response to requests by several African countries, included strengthening the negotiating capacity of African countries, facilitating the identification of their trade policy interests, and helping them to pursue these interests through bilateral and multilateral negotiations.

In pursuit of these objectives, the project prepared several specialized studies, provided advisory services to Geneva-based and capitals-based negotiators, organized several seminars to inform and train policy makers on key policy issues, and provided advice in organizing national negotiation units, accessing trade data and preparing negotiation strategies. The evaluation report on the project commissioned by UNDP in 1994 found that the initial conditions were so difficult that even with the project's substantial contribution, the constraints remained severe (Noyelle, 1994).

Thirty-six major studies were prepared and widely distributed, covering issues related to agriculture, services and other "new issues". However, due to budget constraints, the studies focused more on the perspective of groups of countries rather than individual countries. In many cases, therefore, African negotiators were able to identify and propose common positions, but did not have the country-specific analytical work that would have buttressed individual county negotiating positions.

Similarly, 75 regional, subregional and inter-regional seminars were organized by the project. However, the information disseminated at these meetings focused on regional issues and was not geared to national specifications. Thus, while more than 1,000 policy makers and negotiators participated in these events, they mostly gained only a broad understanding of issues and were not equipped with the technical and strategic competencies that would have made their participation in the negotiations really effective.

There was clear recognition of the critical importance of accurate information for developing negotiation strategies. Accordingly, in the course of the project, the SMART (System for Market Analysis and Restrictions on Trade) software and data base (jointly developed by UNCTAD and the World Bank) was installed in eight African countries. While other countries knew about the system through some of the seminars, they did not have access to it. Moreover, even some of the eight countries lacked the specialized human resources to take full advantage of the system.

In terms of the institutional framework for negotiations, with typically only one negotiator, it was physically impossible for most African countries to follow developments on all negotiating fronts simultaneously. Moreover, the Geneva-based negotiators were very weakly connected to their capital-based principals. Not only was communication not very regular, but the content of the instructions tended to lack specificity, which could only have been derived from rigorous analytical studies and scenario analyses. In addition, inter-ministerial consultative mechanisms within the countries were weak or even absent.

The main weakness in the institutional framework for most countries was that the national agency overseeing the negotiations (typically, the external trade department of ministries of trade) was historically one of the weakest of all government agencies.[13] Accordingly, it not only lacked the power and capacity to coordinate consultations, it was often not even able to secure the appropriations to support investment in background work for the negotiations.

3. Capacity Building Implications of Effective Participation in the New Trade Regime

With the coming into existence of the WTO, African member countries must now address the issue of what is required for effective participation in the new global trade regime. Three major sets of requirements are indicated:

- Requirements of compliance with WTO membership.
- Requirements of effective participation in rules-based multilateral trade decision making.
- Requirements of enhancing competitiveness in international markets and in newly contestable national markets.

Capacity to comply

WTO membership implies an obligation to comply with the various agreements and understandings entered into. It also means that countries must develop the capacity to exercise their rights more actively, as well as protect and project their national interests. This is particularly important because, as with any large legal framework, actual rights and obligations will only be established through claims and counter claims until a robust body of precedents is in place. One certainty facing African countries is the difficult and challenging task of institutionalizing and upgrading their trade legislation aimed at implementing the WTO agreements and developing a regulatory framework on an economy-wide basis. In many African countries, legislation and regulations may not yet exist in areas covered by the multilateral trade obligations and, in cases where they do exist, they are usually less detailed than the multilateral agreements (whereas the national laws and regulations of the major developed countries tend to be more detailed than the multilateral agreements).

African countries have to introduce new legislation and modify existing laws and regulations, as well as adopt new tools and administrative procedures for, say, containing unfair import competition. They need to overhaul their trade regulation frameworks and bring them in line with the WTO agreements. It is also necessary to integrate the emerging trade policy framework with the rest of the legal system to ensure internal consistency, as well as avoid trade policies and practices that can be easily challenged by other WTO members. In order to pursue this objective, African countries must develop a new administrative culture and expertise. For example, the independence of the relevant judiciary organs must be ensured, and a nucleus of legal experts and economic consultants conversant with international trade law will have to evolve. A critical mass of such expertise is also imperative for African countries to be effective in resisting infringements of their rights and pursuing claims and defending themselves against claims by other countries.[14]

Institutions directly responsible for implementing obligations under individual WTO agreements would have to be strengthened, with the objective of ensuring effective compliance with obligations. For example, notifications would have to originate from the relevant department of the ministry responsible for the policy governed by the particular multilateral trade agreement (MTA), e.g., agricultural subsidies, investment measures, intellectual property rights. Some MTAs, such as on the technical barriers to trade and GATS would require contributions from a number of ministries, but these could be coordinated by the inquiry points each WTO member is required to establish. Compliance with obligations requires not only the adoption of legislation and regulations consistent with the MTAs, but also the establishment of detailed administrative practices for the daily operation of the agreements, such as in the case of the TRIPS, custom valuation agreements, the allocation of agricultural tariff quotas, etc. The institutions would have to be made directly responsible for ensuring that the benefits and advantages offered take real effect.

The capacity to meet obligations and exercise rights would suggest that among other things, the coordination function and the maintenance of effective regulatory bodies would also be a major priority. Where such coordination was carried out through ad hoc mechanisms during the Uruguay Round, governments would be advised to consider the establishment of permanent mechanisms to prepare for future initiatives. Moreover, the coordination function could extend to liaison and public relations, with the private sector and other interest groups, so as to mobilize their support, establish national consensus and obtain information, as well as to promote a wider understanding of the system of trade rights and obligations with a view to facilitating their implementation.

Capacity to negotiate

The issue of negotiation is probably the most arduous task facing Africa, for only when a country can truly negotiate on its terms in the new trade regime, can it hope to participate fully in the multilateral agreements. The member-driven, continuous dialogue nature of the WTO process places a severe strain on resource-constrained African countries. For example, with an average of 46 meetings a week in the WTO, developing countries with two to four people covering WTO and other international agencies face an impossible task.[15] The built-in work programmes for negotiations, notification and transparency requirements of the WTO, and the need to defend one's interest effectively, place a real burden on African countries, which individually have inadequate human, institutional and financial resources to meet all the new challenges. In addition to the follow-up negotiations on several Uruguay Round provisions, a number of new issues were added to the agenda at the WTO Singapore Ministerial Conference, and other issues are on the horizon, being pushed by industrial countries.

An essential part of trade negotiations is the identification of negotiating objectives, with a view to adopting a proactive as opposed to reactive stance in trade negotiation discussions. The dominant tendency has been for African countries to react to proposals or agendas drawn up by other participants in the process of negotiations. In contrast, in preparing for trade negotiations, the industrialized countries mobilize considerable resources to identify negotiating objectives, analyse the position of their trading partners and elicit national consensus (UNCTAD, 1996). Clearly defined national negotiating objectives also help forge stronger regional or subregional trade negotiating positions in multilateral trade negotiations. A more focused approach to the trade policies of African countries must be adopted, mainly at the instigation of the ministries of trade and finance.[16]

The identification of trade issues of interest to African countries would need to be accompanied by strengthening these countries' actual negotiating capacities in multilateral trade issues. The active participation of African countries in trade negotiations being a fairly new phenomenon, appropriate skills are yet to be accumulated to provide a solid backstopping to the increasingly complex and widening scope of the multilateral trade agenda. As an interim measure, crash programmes and short-term courses would provide some basic competencies. For example, the UNCTAD Train for Trade programme has been used to a great effect for training a number of people from African countries to become acquainted with international commercial diplomacy. But there is no real substitute for building domestic competencies.[17]

For African countries to be proactive in initiating agenda items based on clearly identified national and/or regional objectives, greater awareness of the potential of the rule-based multilateral trading system must be institutionalized. It is therefore important to view new attitudes and new practices as crucial elements in the development of capacity to negotiate effectively. Studies and analyses of issues considered to be strategic to effective participation in the international trading system need to be undertaken as a basis for initiating negotiating proposals in the WTO independent of the agenda initiated by others. Such studies could be commissioned to local and international policy research institutions. But translating such studies into negotiating positions and using them effectively in the actual negotiations requires the existence of a critical mass of trained analysts and negotiators in the appropriate government departments.

In essence, African countries must develop and sustain their trade administration machinery by establishing new competencies, including strengthening the capacity to cope with increasing information and data and establishing structures and processes that permit these to be used effectively by government, research institutions and the private sector.

In the long term, intensified efforts are required to incorporate trade relations and trade policy issues into universities' basic curricula in law, economics, political science, international relations, etc. Specialized training facilities could also be established such as postgraduate academies preparing trade negotiators, as well as on-the-job training through the inclusion of junior officials in trade delegations. Incentives will have to be offered for the training functions of research and academic institutions to become more focused on trade issues, while efforts should be made to consolidate and maintain an institutional history of national participation in trade negotiations. Where necessary, academic institutions in the developed countries could be associated at a fair price with African institutions to transfer the "technology" of trade policy analysis to local universities and research institutes. Until these and other efforts bear fruit, it will be critically important to determine priorities for the employment of scarce human resources.

An important factor in the capacity to negotiate would be to focus on those areas in which strong negotiating capacity from African countries would significantly enhance their trade and development prospects. There are three different areas in which WTO members could influence and advance their trade interests through negotiations in the WTO. First, through the submissions of proposals related to the provisions of existing agreements, such as proposals for further tariff cuts targeted to particular products and/or sectors; second, through the submissions of proposals in respect of the built-in agenda in existing agreements, such as the availability of patent or sui generis protection of plant varieties when this provision in the TRIPS agreement comes up for review in 1999 as stipulated in the agreement; third, through initiation of proposals on new trade-related issues for negotiations, for example, the interaction between trade and monetary matters or a multilateral framework for investment. Recognizing the heterogeneity of African countries, each country's capacity building programme must reflect its own specific circumstances.

The ministries that will be involved in these issues, mainly the ministries of finance and trade, should be given a focused role in terms of implementing the development of capacity to negotiate. In addition, the mechanism for collaboration between these two departments should be explicit and the processes for overall inter-ministerial coordination should be strengthened. Moreover, governments in several other departments need staff with greater knowledge about trade and investment. This should be addressed in part through training courses. Often, however, the development of expertise in these areas coupled with salary constraints in the public sector leads to a brain drain out of government. Thus, the incentive structures for government officials need to be examined and reformed to keep these trained functionaries in government.

Capacity to compete

While it is important to develop the capacities for compliance and negotiation, the real challenge for Africa lies in the capacity to compete. The continent faces a herculean task on the eve of globalization in overcoming supply-side impediments to competitiveness. Increasingly over the past decades, it has become clear in the literature on development and growth that while much remains to be done in the public sector domain, the real pay-off lies in strengthening capacities in the private sector.

Over the past ten years, the worldwide liberalization of trade, investment and finance, and the impetus this process has given to the globalization of information, production and markets, is creating new opportunities as well as challenges for accelerated growth and development. The favourable outlook predicted for international trade over the next five years is likely to stimulate foreign direct investment while offering greater opportunities to secure non-debt-creating long-term investment finance from abroad, as well as access to technology and high quality skills.

The main impediments African countries face in their ability to take advantage of these new global opportunities lie in deficient supply side conditions. Such constraints include: weak technological capacity; weak entrepreneurial, marketing and technical capacity; the paucity of long-term finance; high transport costs; expensive trade credit and pre-shipment finance; inadequate legal and regulatory frameworks; and, most often, the lack of a coherent strategy for export sector development. Deficiencies in the physical infrastructure, weak enabling institutions (e.g., export promotion agencies, technology extension centres, etc.), and inefficient and often corrupt customs are also major constraints in many countries.

The capacity to compete is obviously a complex policy challenge, which, moreover, must be grounded in national specificities. It is possible, however, to outline the elements of a general capacity building response.[18] The problem needs to be posed as that of strengthening the institutions and systems that must support the capacity of African operators to compete internationally. The main agenda here would be to enhance the national and regional institutions geared to providing exporters with meso-level support services such as trade promotion, trade-related financing, access to technology and intellectual property rights protection, as well as standards and quality assurance services.

The experience of fast-growing Asian and Latin American economies suggests that success in export performance can be attained in a relatively short period by establishing an appropriate mix of support mechanisms and processes. It is crucial in this respect to rationalize and strengthen the linkages among several organizations such as ministries of trade and finance as well as trade promotion, investment promotion and technology policy agencies. African countries would have to further develop the capacity to trade by ensuring appropriate human resources in these agencies and providing them with appropriate tools.

The capacity of private sector organizations, such as chambers of commerce and manufacturing associations, to design and implement trade strategies also requires considerable enhancement at national and subregional levels in Africa. It is not expected that governments would provide large-scale subsidies to private sector organizations. Rather it is the business of the private sector to look after its own interest. However, facilitating access to information and building awareness of external trade opportunities and requirements is one area where public sector support could be very effective.

In addition, the ability of African businesses to exploit international market opportunities depends largely on the availability and efficacy of support tools, particularly trade information systems, and trade-related financial instruments. A crucial aspect of this question has to be the relationship between the government and the private sector. The emergence of a new generation of export-oriented firms will depend on the capacity of African governments to develop, in close collaboration with the private sector, an overall development strategy that places trade at its centre and examines national development issues in a global context. In some cases this will focus on the expansion of current exports; in others the emphasis will be on increasing commodity and market diversification. In all cases, however, competitiveness will mean fostering a culture of innovation, particularly because of the growing knowledge-intensity of production at all stages and in every sector. Fostering innovativeness will oblige public policy to explicitly nurture interaction among private sector actors as well as ensure policy coherence in building support structures for private enterprise.

In devising these new policy packages, governments need to find new ways of working with the private sector. Too often the interface with the private sector is deficient in the policy-making process, and alternative models for consulting with the private sector need to be examined. But a few countries (such as Mozambique, Ghana and Zimbabwe) are experimenting with them. In addition, ways of including broader representation of civil society are necessary to ensure broad-based understanding of and support for the policy options eventually chosen.

Furthermore, a system of quality assurance is imperative for competitiveness in regional and global markets. For example, third-party certification of conformity with ISO9000 and ISO14000 standards is becoming a prerequisite to enter European markets. African firms are often insufficiently informed about conditions for market access, which include standards, quality restriction, packaging and labelling requirements as well as inspection procedures. Accordingly, national bureaus of standards must be strengthened as must the one pan-African quality assurance organization, ARSO.

A critical weakness in the pursuit of international competitiveness by African countries is that African producers and traders face very high costs in trade related financing. It is important for African countries to begin to establish national data bases for credit evaluation of commercial producers. Again, these systems need not (indeed should not) be located within the government bureaucracy. But some initial public investment would be called for in determining minimum institutional and data requirements. Identifying and providing initial support for establishing an appropriate national host agency may be necessary.

It is difficult to be exhaustive in identifying the capacities necessary for enhanced international competitiveness. It is clear, however, that developing these capacities requires intensive public-private collaboration. In addition to the areas already discussed, such collaboration would be required to strengthen the infrastructure for technology dissemination/adaptation and the mechanisms for copyright enforcement and trademark protection.

Determining capacity building requirements more systematically

Developing the capacity for enhanced African participation in the new trade regime is clearly a very complex problem. First, the problem has to be made country-specific, as much depends on initial conditions. Second, strengthening the capacity to trade internationally is inextricably linked to the broader question of enhancing development management. It is within this larger context that priorities for action would be determined.

To obtain a better policy grasp of the problem, it may be useful to analyse the several dimensions of the capacities that are to be installed and/or enhanced. By thus first determining the parameters of the problem, it becomes easier to break it down into smaller parts. A useful approach to this disaggregation is a capacity building requirements table (CART). Originally developed in the context of global environmental issues, CART helps to focus attention on the multi-dimensionality of capacity building (Ohiorhenuan and Wunker, 1995). CART is a matrix that cross-tabulates the primary objectives of a capacity building intervention against four critical dimensions of capacity: human resources, organizational processes, physical resources and external support. These may be elaborated as:

- *Human resources:* This includes technical, administrative, professional and management skills as well as support skills, and a general orientation to new ways of delivering a product or service.
- *Organizational process:* This refers to systems management capabilities and internal organizational procedures and processes, including the assignment of accountability. It also covers the process through which the entity deals with, and grants the public access to, its services.
- *Physical resources:* This dimension addresses the direct material aspects of capacity building, including the budgetary and finan-

cial ability of an organization to deliver on its objectives. Capacity building efforts would address not only the initial capital outlay but also the operation and maintenance requirements.
- *External support:* This involves eliciting the support and commitment of significant outside individuals and groups for the goals of an institution. Any capacity building intervention should consider the social forces that may be conducive or hostile to the long-term survival of the enterprise.

A simplified CART is shown below with six rows and four columns (see Table 11.4). Each row describes the total requirements for attaining a particular capacity building objective, while each column describes the full requirements of one resource to meet all six objectives. The six major objectives identified are:

- Development of international trade strategies, policies, and plans of action.
- Promotion of international trade research.
- Modification and adaptation of legal and regulatory frameworks for trade.
- Fostering competitiveness and innovation.
- Facilitation of dialogue and consensus building within government and among different interest groups, and with private sector organizations.
- Promoting outreach and enhancing public awareness about new global liberalization issues.

While these objectives are interlinked (for example, trade strategies and policy development can facilitate intra-governmental cooperation), the categories are sufficiently exclusive to allow for a systematic analysis of capacity building requirements. Reading down a column, each row describes for each objective the requirements under one of the four critical dimensions (e.g., human resources). Reading across a row, one obtains a robust picture of requirements under all four dimensions to attain a specific objective (e.g., trade strategy and policy). In other words, the summation across any one row represents the total requirements for one primary objective.[19]

Table 11.4: A simplified CART

Objectives	Dimensions of capacity			
	Human resources	Organization process	Physical resources	External support
International trade strategy & policy				
Trade, economic and socioeconomic research				
Legal framework				
Fostering innovation				
Consensus building				
Public outreach				

In developing a capacity building initiative, the main stakeholders would work together to identify all the possible organizations and entities that could be targets for strengthening in order to attain specified immediate goals. From the list of all possible targets, the vital ones would be highlighted and their needs under each dimension of capacity building would be assessed. The nature of CART is such that it would force the policy maker to be as specific as possible in determining the tasks to be performed and the objectives to be attained. It is beyond the scope of this paper to produce an actual CART, as this would require detailed assessment of a particular country situation. However, Table 11.5 illustrates the kind of questions that must be answered in relation to the one objective of strengthening trade policy capacity.

4. Conclusion

The main objective of this paper has been to analyse the human and institutional capacities that would enhance the effective participation of African countries in world trade. Specifically, the paper sought to determine the human and institutional capacities that would enhance the effectiveness of participation by African countries, in global trade rules-making and the capacities that would permit them to take better advantage of the opportunities offered under the new global trade regime. The paper briefly reviewed the antecedents to the Uruguay Round and summarized the main results

Table 11.5: Illustration of the capacity requirements for one major objective

Objectives	Dimensions of capacity			
	Human resources	Organization Process	Physical resources	External support
Strengthen capacity for trade strategy & policy formulation – trade ministry	Critical mass of trade policy analysts, information managers, & macroeconomists	Organization & methods in trade ministry, systems of reward & incentives	Budget appropriations for staff payments, studies, information system hardware & software	Links with central bank, ministry of finance, chambers of commerce

of the round itself. It would appear that the new trade regime offers both challenges and opportunities for African countries.

The paper focused on the participation of African countries in the Uruguay Round and on the effectiveness of this participation. While African countries were more involved in the last negotiations than in earlier rounds, there is a perception that had certain capacities been in place they would have done much better. The main conclusion emerging from this paper is that African countries need to focus on the issues of capacity building, at both the national and subregional levels, and adopt a more dynamic approach that would involve the collaboration of the private sector, as well as take into account the many dimensions of capacity when designing and implementing trade policy.

The following recommendations may be highlighted for building capacity in the new global trade regime. The imperative to fully understand the contents, implications, benefits and constraints of the WTO indicates an urgent need for information in Africa about the new trade regime. The information campaign must involve government officials, private sector organizations such as the chambers of commerce and manufacturers associations, and academic institutions and civil society organizations.

The requirements of compliance indicate the need to develop a critical mass of specialized skills over the medium term. In the short term, existing competencies must be used more efficiently, departmental responsibilities must be more clearly defined and inter-ministerial coordination must be enhanced. The possibility of sharing expertise and experience among African countries should be fully explored and the support of African regional institutions should be elicited. Furthermore, African countries should actively exploit the technical assistance possibilities offered in the Final Act of the Uruguay Rounds.

Developing the capacity to participate effectively requires that African countries strengthen their representation in Geneva and raise the level of coordination between the Geneva missions and their capitals. Countries should also explore mutually advantageous divisions of labour, not only with other African representations but also with other developing country missions. In addition, there is some room for a common institutional support machinery to focus on the critical issues of common concern to African countries. But this should not be regarded as a substitute for the clear identification by countries of their own specific objectives.

The long-term pay-off for African members of the WTO lies in taking maximum advantage of the new opportunities offered by the new trade regime by aggressively nurturing the competitiveness of the private sector. This requires serious efforts to establish an enabling environment, streamline and simplify administrative procedures, reduce operating costs, and institute a broad range of trade facilitation instruments. In addition, it is important to foster an innovation culture, paying particular attention to intersectoral and inter-enterprise linkages. African firms, with the full support of public policy, need to undergo a more or less radical restructuring and an enhancement of their financial, technological and managerial capacities. The strengthening of social dialogue and of public–private partnerships should be pursued as a means of deepening social capital.

It must be stressed that capacity development for trade cannot be wholly separated from the larger question of reconfiguring the institutional framework for public policy. The CART methodology presented in this paper is meant to highlight the imperative of defining objectives explicitly and analysing the full ramifications of pursuing these objectives. In defining objectives for enhanced participation in a globalization regime, it is important to keep in view other aspects of economic and social policy. Moreover, the problem of capacity is as much one of additional competencies as it is of better utilization. African countries must, therefore, focus simultaneously on human resource development and improvements in structures, processes, mechanisms and incentives.

Finally, African countries need to view the Uruguay Round agreements and the new multilateral trade framework as a challenge rather than as a threat. Only with such a positive stance will they truly be able to participate as full members of the emerging global order.

Notes

1 China and the former Soviet Union were the main abstainers from these talks.

2 Geneva, 1947; Annecy, 1949; Torquay, 1951; Geneva, 1956; Geneva (or "Dillon"), 1960–1962.

3 Perhaps the three most critical "understandings" are those regarding rules and procedures governing the settlement of disputes, trade-related investment measures (TRIMS) and the trade policy review mechanism (TPRM).

4 Exceptions are recognized for countries experiencing severe balance of payments difficulties where imposing trade barriers may be necessary as an emergency measure.

5 Exceptions are provided in the case of regional trading arrangements as well as for the special and differential treatment of less developed countries such as is contained in the general system of preferences (GSP).

6 Calculated as the gap between domestic and world prices of agricultural products in OECD countries.

7 The next four paragraphs rely heavily on Agosin et al. (1995).

8 It has been observed that the agreement on subsidies explicitly forbids the use of the kind of incentives that were the hallmark of industrial policy of Korea and Taiwan: subsidies contingent on export performance.

9 The exception was to accommodate the European Union's wish to continue to restrict Japanese auto imports.

10 The level of commitment to assist developing countries in meeting the institutional and administrative requirements for WTO membership varies from "sympathetic consideration" to "best endeavours", "second level obligations" or "facilitation". Only in a few instances are these firm commitments in terms of "full obligations" or "increased assistance". Regarding dispute settlement there was a commitment to "a" legal expert from WTO. On customs valuation, countries have "the right to request, and obtain, technical assistance from developed countries" (see Weston, 1995).

11 Morocco, Tunisia, Egypt, Côte d'Ivoire, Senegal, Nigeria, Ghana, Cameroon, Madagascar, Kenya, Tanzania, Zimbabwe.

12 So named after the colour of the wall decor of the GATT Director-General's conference room in Geneva.

13 In some countries, such as Nigeria, it was the Ministry of Foreign Affairs that was responsible for the negotiations, and the involvement of the Ministry of Trade was negligible. In essence, therefore, not only was Nigeria's participation driven by foreign policy rather than economic considerations, the lead agency had only limited substantive collaboration with the major domestic ministries.

14 Given the mass of information and the highly specialized legal skills required to fully understand the implications of the new global trade regime, a logical course of action for African countries would be to pool resources for building such a core of expertise.

15 As of April 1997, the WTO had 131 members. Of these 131 members, 97 had one or more full-time representatives resident in Geneva, but in many instances they also have to cover other international organizations headquartered in Geneva (UNCTAD, ILO, WHO, WIPO and so forth). The remaining 34 governments are represented either by staff at embassies elsewhere in Europe or staff in the national capital. Many of these countries are small in terms of population. Eight of the members without a resident representative in Geneva are Chad, Guinea, Rwanda, Niger, Malawi, Burkina Faso, Mali and Mozambique (Blackhurst, 1997). Blackhurst also posits, with some justification, that those delegations in Geneva that are small are also likely to have limited back-up support from their capitals. Certainly, there is no reason to believe that coordination among the several government departments with a role in trade matters – trade, finance, health and safety standards, agriculture, customs, banking, insurance, patents and trademarks, competition laws, telecommunications – has improved dramatically in the last five years. This current situation provides the baseline for analysing the capacity requirements of effective participation.

16 The WTO and UNCTAD are providing some support for developing countries in the form of specialized (e.g., anti-dumping issues) or general (e.g., Uruguay Round results) seminars, workshops, briefings, technical missions and trade policy courses. However, both institutions are resource constrained and their mandates, especially WTO's, limit the extent to which they can serve particular national interests. A high level meeting on least developed countries, convened in Geneva in October 1997, attempted to coordinate the technical assistance support of six major agencies – IMF, ITC, UNCTAD, UNDP, World Bank and WTO. Twelve countries presented their needs for support on trade matters and the agencies indicated how they were responding to these needs. However, the needs assessment tool prepared jointly by the agencies was rather simplistic and the outcome was hardly more than a shopping list. Moreover, the agencies' responses did not constitute a coordinated package. Following that meeting, UNDP's Africa Bureau is considering sponsoring country-led trade-related round tables to formulate coherent programmes and elicit coordinated technical assistance.

17 Given the high cost of servicing a trade negotiating team in Geneva, the small size of the existing missions and the complexity of the negotiating agenda, not to mention the multiplicity of the negotiating bodies, it is necessary, until capacity is acquired, to maximize the use of those few who are present. This is only practicable when clear issues of common interest to a group of countries can be identified. A jointly owned institutional support machinery could assist in coordinating such interests. But the fact would remain that even where this is feasible, a common position can only be forged from clearly articulated country interests (UNCTAD, 1997).

18 This outline is based in part on UNDP (1996).

19 The approach here inverts the more traditional approach to capacity building of taking particular institutions as the starting point. From our earlier discussions we know that a large number of public and private organizations must be involved in trade matters. By starting with the question: Capacity building for what? a somewhat more coherent

approach emerges of looking at each possible player in relation to the priority objectives.

References

Agosin, M., G. Crespi, D. Tussie, D. Rodrick and D. Weston. 1995. "The Uruguay Round: Unraveling the implications for the least developed and low-income countries". In UNCTAD *International Monetary and Financial Issues for the 1990s*, vol. VI, UNCTAD/GID/G24/6. New York and Geneva: United Nations.

Bhagwati, J. 1996. *Global age from a sceptical South to a fearful North*. Seventh Raul Prebisch Lecture, given at UNCTAD IX, Midrand, 29 April.

Blackhurst, R. 1997. "The capacity of the WTO to fulfill its mandate". In A. Krueger, ed., *The WTO as an International Organization*. Chicago: University of Chicago Press.

Collier, P. and W. Gunning. 1995 "Trade policy and regional integration: Implications for the relations between Europe and Africa". *The World Economy*, vol. 18, no. 3 (May): 387–410, May.

Business Guide to the Uruguay Round, International Trade Center UNCTAD/WTO and Commonwealth Secretariat, Geneva, 1995.

Erjavec, M. 1995. "Africa and the Uruguay Round: Ghana". Country Analysis prepared for the Canadian International Development Agency. Ottawa, December.

Fletcher's Page on Trade: www.tufts.edu/departments/fletcher/multi/trade.html

Grimwade, N. 1996. *International Trade Policy: A Contemporary Analysis*. London and New York: Routledge.

Hamilton, C., ed. 1990. "Textiles Trade and the Developing Countries: Eliminating the Multi-Fibre Arrangement in the 1990s". Washington, D.C.: World Bank

Harmsen, R. and A. Subramanian. 1994. "Economic Implications of the Uruguay Round". *In International Trade Policies: The Uruguay Round and Beyond*, VII. Washington, D.C.: IMF.

Ingco, M.D. 1995. "Agricultural trade liberalization and the Uruguay Round: One step forward, one step back?" Policy Research Working Paper 1500. World Bank, August.

International Trade Center: www.unicc.org/itc/Welcome.html

Kirkpatrick, C. and J. Weiss. 1995. "Trade diversification in sub-Saharan Africa and in the African least developed countries: Efforts, constraints and results", Geneva: UNCTAD.

Kirmani, N. and N. Calika. 1994. "International Trade Policies: The Uruguay Round and Beyond". Washington, D.C.: World Bank 1995.

Konate, T.M. 1994. "The implications of the Uruguay Round for Africa". Policy Management Brief No. 1. Maastricht: ECDPM, June.

Levy, B. 1993. "An institutional analysis of the design and sequence of trade and investment policy reform". *World Bank Economic Review*, vol. 7, no. 2: 247–262.

Noyelle, T. 1994. "An evaluation of UNCTAD/UNDP Project RAF/87/157: Support to Africa in the Uruguay Round of multilateral trade negotiations and to the external sector of african countries". Report submitted to UNDP, Regional Bureau for Africa. October.

Ohiorhenuan, J.F.E. and S.M. Wunker. 1995. "Capacity building requirements for global environmental protection". Global Environmental Facility, Working Paper No. World Bank, June.

Raghavan, C. 1990. *Recolonization: GATT, Uruguay Round and the Third World.* Penang and London: Third World Network/Zed Books.

Rausser, G. 1995. *GATT Negotiations and the Political Economy of Policy Reform*. Oxford: Oxford University Press.

Ritchie, M. 1996. "Control of trade by multinationals: Impact of the Uruguay Round of GATT on sustainable food security". *Journal of the Society for International Development*, vol. 4 (December): 40–45.

Rodrik, D. 1995. "Developing countries after the Uruguay Round". In UNCTAD, *International and Monetary Issues for the 1990s*, volume VI. New York: United Nations.

Sazanami, Y. 1995. "Post-Uruguay Round issues and the World Trade Organization". *Japan Review of International Affairs*,vol 9, no.2 (March): 125–136.

Tangermann, S. 1995. "Implementation of the Uruguay Round Agreement on Agriculture by major developing countries" (UNCTAD/ITD/16).

UNCTAD. 1994. "A preliminary analysis of the results of the Uruguay Round and their effects on the trading prospects of developing countries". United Nations document: Report /TD/B/WG.4/13, June. Geneva.

UNCTAD. 1995(a). "An analysis of trading opportunities resulting from the

Uruguay Round in selected sectors: Agriculture, textiles and clothing, and other industrial products". Report /TD/B/WG.8/2, UNCTAD Secretariat, July.

UNCTAD. 1995(b). "Some perspectives on agricultural protectionism, diversification and economic growth". Report /COM/68, UNCTAD Secretariat, July.

UNCTAD. 1996. "Strengthening the participation of developing countries in world trade and the multilateral trading system." UNCTAD Secretariat (TD/375), May.

UNCTAD. 1997. "The Uruguay Round and its follow-up: Building a positive agenda for development". United Nations Publication E.97. II.D.14. Geneva: United Nations.

UNCTAD. 1997. "Identification of multilateral trade isues of interest to Africa". Discussion paper prepared for UNDP-sponsored brainstorming meeting of African trade Experts. OAU/AEC Headquarters, 14–15 April, Addis Ababa.

UNDP, Regional Bureau for Africa. 1987. Project RAF/87/157. "Support to Africa in the Uruguay Round of multilateral trade negotiations and to the external sector of African countries". New York: UNDP.

UNDP, Regional Bureau for Africa. 1996. "Capacity building for trade and development in sub-Saharan Africa". Project RAF/96/001. New York: UNDP.

World Bank. 1996. *Global Economic Prospects and the Developing Countries.* Washington, D.C.: The World Bank.

World Bank. 1995. *Global Economic Prospects and the Developing Countries.* Washington, D.C.: The World Bank.

WTO. 1995. "Market access for goods: A Uruguay Round summary for developing country exporters", International Trade Forum.

Yeats, A.J. 1994. "What are OECD trade preferences worth to sub-Saharan Africa?" Policy Research Working Paper 1254, World Bank International Trade Division, February.

Index

D

E

U

V

W

Z